The Structures of History

CHRISTOPHER LLOYD

BLACKWELL
Oxford UK & Cambridge USA

Copyright © Christopher Lloyd 1993

First published 1993

Blackwell Publishers
108 Cowley Road
Oxford OX4 1JF
UK

238 Main Street, Suite 501
Cambridge, Massachusetts 02142
USA

British Library Cataloguing in Publication Data

A CIP catalogue record for this book is available from the British Library.

Library of Congress Cataloging-in-Publication Data

Lloyd, Christopher, 1950–
    The structures of history / Christopher Lloyd.
        p.   cm. — (Studies in social discontinuity)
    Includes bibliographical references and index.
    ISBN 0–631–18464–3 (alk. paper). — ISBN 0–631–18465–1(pbk. : alk. paper)
    1. History—Philosophy.   I. Title.   II. Series.
D16.9.L613   1993
901—dc20   92–32022
                                                                          CIP

Typeset in 10 on 11$^{1}/_{2}$ pt Ehrhardt
by Graphicraft Typesetters Ltd., Hong Kong
Printed in Great Britain by TJ Press Ltd., Padstow, Cornwall

This book is printed on acid-free paper

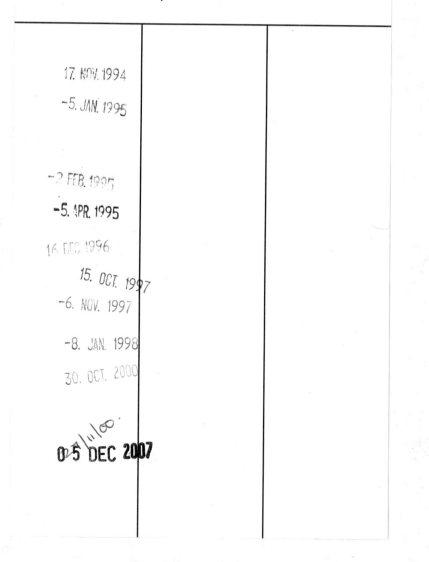

Studies in Social Discontinuity

General Editor: Charles Tilly, The New School for Social Research

Studies in Social Discontinuity began in 1972 under the imprint of Academic Press. In its first fifteen years 53 titles were published in the series, including important volumes in the areas of historical sociology, political economy and social history.

Revived in 1989 by Blackwell Publishers, the series will continue to include volumes emphasizing social changes and non-Western historical experience, as well as translations of major works.

Published:

The Perilous Frontier
Nomadic Empires and China
Thomas J. Barfield

Regents and Rebels
The Revolutionary World of an Eighteenth-Century Dutch City
Wayne Ph. te Brake

The Word and the Sword
How Techniques of Information and Violence Have Shaped Our World
Leonard M. Dudley

Coffee, Contention, and Change
in the Making of Modern Brazil
Mauricio Font

Nascent Proletarians
Class Formation in Post-Revolutionary France
Michael P. Hanagan

The Structures of History
Christopher Lloyd

Social Evolutionism
A Critical History
Stephen K. Sanderson

Coercion, Capital, and European States
AD 990–1990
Charles Tilly

Anti-Semitism in France
A Political History from Léon Blum to the Present
Pierre Birnbaum

In preparation:

Forget the Family
David Levine

Contents

Figures

Tables

Series Editor's Preface

Studies in Social Discontinuity present historically grounded analyses of important social transformations, ruptures, conflicts, and contradictions. Although we
at Blackwell interpret that mission broadly, leave room for many points of
view, and absolve authors of any responsibility for proselytization on behalf of
our intellectual programme, the series as a whole demonstrates the relevance
of well-crafted historical work for the understanding of contemporary social
structures and processes. Books in the series pursue one or more of four
varieties of historical analysis: (i) using evidence from past times and places
systematically to identify regularities in processes and structures that transcend
those particular times and places; (ii) reconstructing critical episodes in the past
for the light they shed on important eras, peoples, or social phenomena; (iii)
tracing the origins or previous phases of significant social processes that
continue into our own time; (iv) examining the ways that social action at a
given point in time lays down residues that limit the possibilities of subsequent
social action.

The fourth theme is at once the least familiar and the most general. Social
analysts have trouble seeing that history matters precisely because social interaction takes place in well-defined times and places, and occurs within constraints offered by those times and places, producing social relations and
artefacts that are themselves located in space-time and whose existence and
distribution constrain subsequent social interaction. The construction of a city
in a given place and time affects urban growth in adjacent areas and subsequent
times. Where and when industrialization occurs affects how it occurs. Initial
visions of victory announce a war's likely outcomes. A person's successive
migrations have cumulative effects on his or her subsequent mobility through
such simple matters as the presence or absence of information about new
opportunities in different places and the presence or absence of social ties to
possible destinations. A population's previous experience with wars, baby booms,
and migrations haunts it in the form of bulging or empty cohorts and unequal
numbers of the sexes. All these are profoundly historical matters, even when

they occur in the present; time and place are of their essence. They form the essential subject matter of Studies in Social Discontinuity.

Edward Shorter, Stanley Holwitz, and I plotted the Studies in Social Discontinuity in 1970–1: the first book, William Christian's *Person and God in a Spanish Valley*, appeared in 1972. Over the years, Academic Press published more than fifty titles in the series. But during the early 1980s publication slowed, then ceased. In 1988 Blackwell agreed to revive the Studies under my editorship. *The Structures of History* appears as the tenth book of the renewed series.

Christopher Lloyd distinguishes between the history of events and social structural history, the latter concerning the 'systems of social rules, roles, relations, and symbols in which events, actions, and thought occur and lives are lived'. Most books in this series transgress Lloyd's boundary by dealing with events in the light of ideas about structures. Lloyd's book offers instead a sustained reflection on the nature of both historical genres, especially the history of social structures. In a time when half-articulated scepticisms, idealisms, and relativisms are popping up like dandelions in a summer lawn, Lloyd makes a strong case for the possibility and desirability of cumulative, reliable knowledge of social affairs. He has not written a tract against postmodernism, although he makes clear his disputes with recent arguments in that vein. Rather than waste time on polemics, anathemas, and the parading of bad examples, he proceeds briskly to the business at hand: searching for the intellectual conditions that will support a 'unified and transformative science of society'. He finds them in a combination of realism, structurism, and history.

Christopher Lloyd delineates these doctrines and their intersections with exemplary care. In advocating realism, he argues against the cascade of idealisms and scepticisms that have inundated recent general debates about social science and history. In advocating what he calls structurism, he breaks with both the methodological individualism and the holism which social analysts have commonly thought to be their only alternatives. In advocating history, he strides in a direction that much of social science (even some of economics, that most ahistorical of social sciences) has recently been taking. But even there he makes a distinctive contribution, constructing a critique of historical materialism that invites us not to reject its entire project and epistemology, but to pursue its problems more effectively.

There Lloyd is at his best: determined, unruffled, lucid, patient, and sure-handed as he presents controversial views. We have been waiting for a voice like his.

Charles Tilly
New School for Social Research
New York
January 1993

Acknowledgements

The final draft typescript has been read by A. W. Coats, Bruce Caldwell, Dennis Smith and Charles Tilly. Malcolm Falkus also read most of an earlier draft. I thank them for their very valuable comments, not all of which I have felt able to incorporate into the text. Of course they bear no responsibility for the final product. Anonymous referees made very helpful comments on earlier versions of chapters 4 and 6. I express my thanks for this assistance.

Earlier versions of some chapters, much amended and reconstructed here, have appeared in several journals: in *History and Theory* (copyright Wesleyan University Press) 'Realism and Structurism in Historical Theory', XXVIII, 1989, pp. 296–325, and 'The Methodologies of Social History: A Critical Survey and Defense of Structurism', XXX, 1991, pp. 180–219; and in *Theory and Society* 'Realism, Structurism, and History: Foundations for a Transformative Science of Society', 18, 1989, pp. 451–94 (reprinted by permission of Kluwer Academic Publishers). I thank these journals for permission to reproduce passages from these articles.

The quotation on pp. xvi–xvii from Dudley Shapere, 'Method in the Philosophy of Science and Epistemology: How to Inquire about Inquiry and Knowledge' is reproduced from N. J. Nersessian (ed.), *The Process of Science*, Martinus Nijhoff, Dordrecht, 1987 (reprinted by permission of Kluwer Academic Publishers). I thank the publisher for permission to reprint this material here.

An Internal Research Grant from the University of New England has provided assistance with my research expenses since 1986, including travel to other libraries in Australia to gather material. From 1990 an Australian Research Council grant enabled me to visit libraries and bookshops in Britain and the United States. Both sources of funding were valuable in enabling me to have access to resources not available at the University of New England and I place on record my gratitude.

The staff members of the Dixson Library at the University of New England have been courteously and efficiently helpful to me over many years. In particular, the members of the loans and interlibrary loans sections have tolerated my many requests with constant good humour and diligence. I thank them very much.

My strongest thanks go, firstly, to Linley Lloyd for her invaluable editorial help, intellectual companionship, constant good humour, and love. The book could not have been written without her assistance. Secondly, I thank our children Tamsin, Kieran, and Aneyrin for their enthusiasm for life and learning, their love, and their patience.

C. L.
Armidale
April 1992

Shapere on the Significance of Science

'To those attempting to understand the knowledge-seeking and knowledge-acquiring enterprise – to understand how we should go about trying to get knowledge, and what it is that we have if we get it – one of the major lessons of science in the twentieth century is this:

> The results of scientific investigation could not have been anticipated by common sense, by the suggestions of everyday experience, or by pure reason.

I will call this the *Principle of Rejection of Anticipation of Nature* ...
The full significance of the principle is a product of scientific enquiry, and especially of the results of that enquiry in this century; it is not an *a priori* stricture, laid down, for example, by the nature of enquiry or scientific method itself ... The evidence in its favor is indeed overwhelming; even a brief survey of just some of the more familiar such evidence can only lead to its acceptance ... Nor is such evidence limited to the physical sciences. Who could have anticipated the complexity of the processes of life – of heredity and development, or of the nervous and immune systems? ...

But if so many of our contemporary scientific beliefs could not have been anticipated by common sense, the suggestions of everyday experience, or pure reason, then how *have* we managed to think of them and come to adopt them? ... That understanding is gained through a second great lesson of modern science, one which furnishes profound insight into not only the knowledge-seeking but also the knowledge-acquiring aspect of the scientific enterprise.

This positive lesson of modern science stems from the fact that the sorts of considerations that have led us to alter our beliefs about nature, at least when those considerations are ones we call 'rational' or 'based on evidence', have themselves been scientific ones. For twentieth-century science, even more than its predecessors, has shown the possibility of formulating our beliefs in ways that make it possible to subject them to scientific scrutiny, and thereby to see how we might modify or reject and replace them if necessary . . . It is thus through this incorporation of beliefs into the scientific process that it has become possible to modify or reject so many beliefs which had previously seemed unassailable, and to arrive at so many beliefs of modern science which could not otherwise have been anticipated – and . . . to have done these things for good reasons. This record of achievement provides the second major lesson of modern science, a lesson which can be formulated as a principle:

> Every aspect of our beliefs ought, wherever possible, to be formulated, and to be brought into relation to well-founded beliefs, in such a way that it will be possible to test that aspect.

In short, this second lesson of modern science tells us to internalize all aspects of our beliefs into the scientific process. For that reason, I will call it the *Principle of Scientific Internalization*, or, more briefly, the *Principle of Internalization*. It is a *normative* principle; and its value, its necessity, as a policy, a guiding principle, of science is something that has itself been learned through the scientific process, through a record of achievement that led to its adoption.

In connection with the two lessons or principles, it is important to realise that radical changes in the fabric of science have not been restricted to alterations in our substantive beliefs about how things are. They have also extended to the methods and rules of reasoning by which we arrive at those beliefs, and the aims we have in seeking them.'

Dudley Shapere, 'Method in the Philosophy of Science and Epistemology: How to Inquire about Inquiry and Knowledge', (1987), pp. 1–2.

Introduction

I

The macro structures of economies and societies and the causal mechanisms of their formation and history are beyond common-sense understanding. Only a form of analysis and a mode of understanding that penetrates to the obscured structural relations and imperatives of economies and societies can begin to reveal and explain the real history and powers of the organizational basis of social life. This, virtually a truism, seems to have been well understood by many social scientists for two centuries. Yet, surprisingly, there are still some in the history profession who believe that no special general concepts, methods, forms of explanation, or theories, apart from those intuitively absorbed from the prevailing form of 'common sense', are required to grasp the histories of economies and societies or the reasons for human actions or the causes of events.

The social sciences are today in a state of methodological and theoretical confusion masquerading as pluralism. The analysis and writing of the history of economies and societies is now undertaken under many guises – 'old' economic history, 'new' economic history, 'old' social history, 'new' social history, historical sociology, historical political economy, ethnographic history, geographic history, and so on – employing many methodologies and theories. Nevertheless, explanations of the histories of economies and societies generally strive for objectivity and empirical adequacy. There is a widespread recognition by such historians of the possibility, as a regulator of practice if not as an achieved goal, of truthful explanation in the correspondence sense of truth, yet methodological diversity and confusion reign.

This book is about how the historical processes of structural change in economies and societies are being conceptualized and explained and about how the main concepts and forms of explanation could be improved. The starting-point is an awareness that there are major methodological and conceptual weaknesses in the explanations currently provided by many historians of economic and social structures. Empirical weaknesses in explanations will always be with us, in the sense that more information about present and past economies and societies is constantly becoming available as a result of theorization, research, and the process of social change itself. But methodologies and general concepts may be susceptible to permanent improvement as a result of analytical thought, including examinations of conceptual systems, of the logic of enquiry and reasoning employed by particular sciences, and of how some sciences have become more advanced than others. In particular, the crucial process of forming a coherent *domain of scientific enquiry* for economic and social structural history must be examined.

This examination is not overtly concerned with the empirical validity or strength of particular explanations of economic and social change. Empirical enquiry always takes place within certain methodological and theoretical frameworks. The value of these frameworks rests ultimately on their usefulness in helping us understand and explain the world, but the relationship between the empirical power of explanations and their frameworks is not a simple matter. The complexity of that relationship and the use of frameworks in enabling and disabling explanation must be explored thoroughly before the problem of empirical validity can be reconsidered. The history of science seems to indicate that the long-run value of frameworks, including general theories, is not dependent to begin with on simple empirical confirmation. As Descartes, Hume, Kant and the Enlightenment tradition taught, the question of *how* we know is prior to *what* we know.[1]

The examination may help to provide a new basis for the necessary re-integration of socio-historical enquiry. As Immanuel Wallerstein has recently argued, the time seems ripe to go 'beyond *Annales* . . . beyond multidisciplinarity, beyond (above all) the idiographic–nomothetic antinomy'. This is because he sees the historical social sciences as a single discipline. Unfortunately at the moment they are not, but they should be because, as he correctly goes on to say,

the historical social sciences can only proceed on the premise that humans live inside historical systems that are large in scale, long in time, but nonetheless have natural lives. These historical systems come into existence and eventually they go out of existence. All systems are systemic, that is, they have structures. But all systems are simultaneously historical, that is they have not only cyclical rhythms (or *conjonctures*) but secular trends, which is why their natural lives come to an eventual end. No scholarly work is useful unless it simultaneously analyzes the unchanging or repetitive and the instantly and eternally changing.

Furthermore, we must abolish the nineteenth century's holy trinity of politics, economics, and culture as the three presumably autonomous spheres of human action, with separate logics and separated processes. We must invent new language that will permit us to talk about the eternal, instantaneous, continuous movement of all social processes in and among these three supposedly distinctive arenas.[2]

II

In spite of the radical critique of knowledge by post-modernist philosophers the will to truth and the consequent search for certainty remains perhaps the most powerful motivator of intellectual endeavour. But this fundamental motivation and rationale of modern thought is under attack as rarely seen before during the era of Enlightenment and post-Enlightenment. The general systematic activity of building explanatory social theories that has gone on, through various vicissitudes, since the seventeenth century (and which started much earlier if we include medieval thinkers such as Ibn Khaldûn, and even further back if we consider Plato and Aristotle to have been thinking about these problems) is being rejected by radical neo-Nietschean critics of the epistemological enterprise. The task of explanation has to be justified anew, it seems. At bottom is the fundamental issue of how we are to live our lives – in what social arrangements, by what norms, upholding what morality? Are there universal laws or rules or structures governing the possibilities of social life? Does it indeed make sense to ask these questions or should we simply be getting on with living as best we can under the circumstances in which we find ourselves? Of course these questions have long since been asked. They are at the heart of religion and philosophy. It seems to be the fate of humans to be dissatisfied with daily life and its local conditions and to seek instead for the meanings and the causes of life, social arrangements, and the nature of the world in order to ameliorate them. Central to intellectual processes and structures is the imagining of new and better social arrangements and forms of social and personal life.

General understandings that human life takes place in ordered social structures, which constrain actions and beliefs, and attempts to conceptualize and explain the nature and effects of these structures have been developed during the past couple of centuries. However, the debates between modernist and postmodernist modes of thought over the logic, meaning, efficacy and relevance to social enquiry of scientific reasoning have reached new levels of intensity in recent years within Western culture. The internal collapse of Eastern European Communism has hastened and been hastened by disenchantment with (perverted) forms of modernism. Marxism at its best is modernist and enlightened and was used as the (distorted) ideological and rhetorical legitimation of so-called 'modernization' in Eastern Europe and elsewhere on the supposed grounds of its scientificity. Similarly, in the Western capitalist world other forms of 'scientific' reasoning have been attacked lately. Everywhere now there are rejections of the modernist project of constructing a universal, rational, scientific basis for natural, social, and historical knowledge and for political action, which Marx and Engels, among many others, did so much to advance.

The extended articulation and defence of scientific history in this book tries to design and situate its fortifications so as to deflect the attacks of advocates of relativism, post-modernism, pragmatism, and 'common-sense' historiography. The fortifications are built on a prominent outcrop of the territory of analytical philosophy of science, and are constructed out of materials gathered from scientific realism. To the advocates of hermeneutical relativism, post-modernism, and pragmatism, arguments for a science of history are now atavistic and naïve; and to the 'common-sense' practitioners of traditional interpretive history they are irrelevant. Attempts to conceptualize and discover the *real* hidden structures of society and the *real* processes of social structural change are unfashionable and outmoded to all these opponents. But I persist in holding that the structural histories of economies and societies, like the histories of the earth and the biosphere, proceed largely independently of beliefs, concepts, theories, ideologies, and philosophies about them. The emphasis should not be on the autonomy of discourse and language nor on the autonomy of the phenomena of the social world but on *discovering* the relative autonomy of the structuring and transforming social processes of societal evolution. Theorists and philosophers only try to conceptualize the world or merely interpret each other's imaginative theoretical creations; the point is to *explain* the origins and nature of the real structures of the world and their transformations.

Economic and social historians (or structural historians, as I shall usually call them) have been labouring at this knowledge-constructing task for two and a half centuries. In what ways do they go about their task, what success can they hope for, and how successful have they been? These are largely methodological and philosophical questions, but ones that can satisfactorily be answered only by a careful analysis of the presuppositions, practices and results of such historians, an analysis that should employ some of the conceptual and analytical tools of the philosophy of explanation. Such an analysis does not imply that philosophy is the arbiter of practice and truth, only that it has a powerful set of tools to help with the job. An alternative view, that practice must be its own evaluator, secretes an a priori epistemological conception behind a supposedly pragmatic and humanistic exterior. The problem with hidden epistemologies is that they can mislead practitioners into believing that 'common sense' (for which we should read 'the currently prevailing idea of naïve empiricism') or personal empathic insight or rhetorical persuasiveness are the only possible arbiters of interpretation and explanation. In that case the rational idea of 'truth' is rejected in favour of pre-rational or irrational 'understanding', which cannot be shared widely. The rejection by many historians of any attempt by philosophers and methodologists to criticize their practices and arguments from some external methodological and historical point of view must arouse suspicion that they do not wish to be confronted with the logical and explanatory implications of their own assumptions and presuppositions, and hence do not wish to have the strength of their own arguments and conclusions tested at all. The persuasiveness of explanations *is* at issue, the question being of *how* explanations persuade.

III

Economic and social structures are mysterious formations – at once intangible, invisible, even somewhat incomprehensible, yet powerful and in many cases vast and very long-lived. Their very existence, let alone their nature and historical character, was long obscure to rational, systematic enquiry. Gradually in seventeenth-century Europe and more so in the following century, thinkers began to construct concepts about economic and social structures, or about what they first called 'political economy' or 'civil society', and about how such structures have evolved through human history. For most political economists and sociologists of the eighteenth and nineteenth centuries there was no distinction between the study of societies and the study of their evolution – that is, no historical/present methodological distinction. However, with the gradual development of social studies in the eighteenth and nineteenth centuries there began the processes of separating social enquiries from those into political and military events and the activities of powerful individuals and elites, and of separating present-oriented enquiries from historical ones. The society/politics/history (or economy/politics/history) intellectual distinctions have been apparent in one form or another in European thought since the mid-eighteenth century. They have been attacked and defended down the centuries. For much of the twentieth century history and sociology have staked out opposing territories on the spurious past/present dichotomy. But in recent decades there has been a strong move on a broad front by many historians and sociologists finally to do away with these distinctions and replace them with interdisciplinary history, or social history, or historical sociology, or historical political economy, or historical economics. The original concern of sociology and political economy with large-scale, long-run social change has been re-emphasized. The advocates of all these, sometimes syncretic, unions usually believe correctly that there is no ontological or methodological basis for the old society/history distinction. However, I shall argue that these necessary (but sometimes over-simplified) attempts at unification often miss the real, defensible basis of empirical/theoretical and event/structure divisions. But these divisions, which are rational on heuristic grounds, must be seen as existing within a wider, unified field of socio-historical concepts and methodologies, because events (including actions) and structures can and must be explained at once separately on one level but together on another, deeper level. The need for and resolution of separation within a layered methodological unity will become clear as we proceed.

The writing of economic and social history is viewed herein as part and parcel of the social studies rather than as part of some *sui generis* historical discipline. There seems no longer any use in seeking to make a contribution to debates over the supposedly peculiar nature of historical knowledge or the place of narrative versus analytical reasoning in historical understanding. That there should be no fundamental distinctions between historically oriented and present-oriented enquiries into economies and societies and between narrative and analytical reasoning are basic assumptions. All economies and societies are historical in two senses – real and changing – whether they exist now or have ceased to exist. Therefore, all enquiry in the social studies should be historically oriented. This means that all eras and processes require a historical consciousness for their understanding. The old, and apparently fading, institutional and methodological distinctions between history and the social studies reflect philosophical, emotional, and psychological predispositions rather than ontological or epistemological necessities.

<h2 style="text-align:center">IV</h2>

A central contention herein will be that the institutionalized 'disciplines' of economic history, social history, historical political economy, and historical sociology should be considered together as one domain of enquiry – the domain of social structural history. This is because they all deal, or should deal if they are true to their self-designations, with the problem of the history of social structures and not with the history of events and actions, even if those events and actions are supposed to be peculiarly economic or social. The basic operational distinction within the social sciences should be between the study of events and the study of structures. And structures include political systems, mentalities, and cultures as much as economic and social systems. The defence of an event/structure distinction and a merger of economics and sociology will require an argument about the common nature of economic and social structures and how they relate to events. This argument is crucial because concepts of structure tend to license various approaches to explaining its history. The various 'disciplines' just mentioned all adopt similar but different concepts of their object.

I shall argue that social structures (including economies) are neither patterns of events, actions, and behaviour nor reducible to social phenomena, but have a form of structural existence that is at once relatively autonomous but not separate from the totality of phenomena that occur within them. Nor are structures holistic or completely autonomous. This is not a novel argument but apparently it still needs defending because it is not sufficiently widely or well understood.[3] I have argued elsewhere and do so again below[4] that if social history is to be a distinctive field of enquiry it must be about the history of social structures and requires a methodology relatively distinct from the history of events. But some readers apparently have not grasped this essential point and so believe that all self-styled social-history writing is included within the category 'social structural history'. Much of what is designated as social-history writing is in fact about events rather than structures, and so does not require a methodology any different from that for explaining any kind of event. In that case 'social history' does not refer to a distinct kind of discourse or domain, so it does not even require a separate label. That it has a separate label says more about the intent of the practitioners and labellers than about their methodology. It also indicates that the methodological self-understanding of practitioners of a discipline is not necessarily a reliable guide to their real foundations, practices, and results.

Herein I examine the underlying individualist and holist methodologies (which are often only unexamined assumptions) for approaching the explanation of the history of economic and social structures. I argue that there exists a third alternative to individualism and holism, which I call 'methodological structurism'. Like the other two, this third methodology is interconnected with a concept of structure and a concept of structural change. But, unlike the other methodologies, it has not been well articulated or extensively defended.[5] Methodological structurism, I shall argue, now exists quite widely as an unexamined assumption within the explanations of many historians. I shall try to articulate it and show why it is the most appropriate methodology for approaching the explanation of structural history.

Structurism can also be understood in a wider sense as an approach to social explanation that has methodological, sociological, and historical dimensions, all of which logically and conceptually reinforce each other. This reinforcement is a crucial component in making possible the scientific explanation of structural history.

V

Most historians, many sociologists and economists, and many philosophers reject the notion of a 'scientific approach' to society and its history, while a few embrace it enthusiastically. The embracers, such as the cliometric historians, have sometimes equated 'science' with quantification, but this idea is now well understood as seriously defective, as I shall show in chapter 4. That there are large and sometimes mutually incomprehensible differences between approaches to explanations in the socio-historical disciplines is of course well-known. In chapter 2 I will survey the range of approaches to show the extent and variety of differences. Many historians have been happy with methodological pluralism, fuzziness, and idiosyncrasy, even seeing them as virtues, because they believe not only that human thought and the social arrangements that it is about are free and unconstrained in their development by objective structures, but also that repugnant 'scientistic' explanations lead to narrow 'technocratic' considerations about social 'engineering'. There have long been defences (including the currently popular post-modernist and pragmatist theories and the traditional 'common-sense' interpretism) of a humanistic form of enquiry into social life that is akin to artistic or literary interpretation and must not be forced into preconceived objectivist channels. For many such

writers, social life is a multi-faceted 'text' that must and can only be reinter-
preted constantly from within particular discourses. For them there is no such
thing as objective social structure but only fluid social life. Social life can be
apprehended and understood from many points of view rather than objectively
explained. Related to this argument but also more widely adopted is the view
that social and political concepts and explanations are 'essentially contestable'
because of the multi-faceted, dynamic, and supposed phenomenologically
constituted character of society and social relations. On the other hand, there
are also strong traditions of self-styled 'scientific' enquiry, including neo-
classical economics and its cliometric offshoot, and Marxism, which, while not
necessarily seeing economic and social explanation as methodologically akin to
physical science, attempt to make truthful explanations (employing general concepts and theories, factual evidence, and logical inferences) of supposed objectively existing social structures, events, and processes.

It is not necessary to choose between being a partisan supporter of either
hermeneutical understanding or scientific absolutism. The poles of possibility
in social epistemology are neither so simply delineated nor determining of
actual methodologies. The employment of hermeneutical interpretation and
essentially contestable concepts; understanding society as at least in part
phenomenologically constituted; making progress in explanations; and producing scientific results are all compatible with each other, providing we understand
the roles each should play in a piece of social research. Indeed, we should see
them all as essential parts of social explanation. But in discussing the question
of science, explanations that are developed in physics, chemistry, and biology
are neither good nor bad models for social explanation. While discussions of
the question of scientific versus non-scientific knowledge are not irrelevant, it
is a question, rather, of defining what is meant by 'social science' here in terms
of possibilities and actual practices and showing its power as a description to
delineate the strengths of various explanations. The sciences do share certain
fundamental characteristics that set them apart from other forms of discourse.
The post-structuralist, post-modernist, post-Enlightenment modes of discourse
that attempt to put aside questions of objectivity, truth, and progress of discovery would see this kind of reasoning as irrelevant. But relativism, however
cleverly and attractively packaged, is still relativism and so suffers from its
inherent defect of tending toward nihilism or at least an avoidance of practical,
real-world issues and problems.

Several arguments for a science of history, ranging from positivism to
structuralism to realism, have been made by adherents of the Marxist tradition.
This tradition has been fruitful in terms of methodology and theory, but its
limitations are now very apparent and have to be transcended if a better conception of science and more adequate explanations are to be achieved. I will
develop a concept of the domain of the science of social structural history that
tries to do justice to both the objectivity and the subjectivity of social structures and their history and tries to show why a scientific methodology is

different from and preferable to a non-scientific one. I will try to show how the concept of 'domain' is very valuable as a means of theoretically constituting objects for enquiry, as well as incorporating and doing justice to the history of science and its accumulation of knowledge.

It is now widely understood that the logical structure of explanations of physical and biological nature is not well reconstructed by empiricist and positivist philosophy. The reasons why empiricism and positivism are completely inappropriate descriptions of social and historical science will be defended by articulating the close relationship between structurism and the anti-positivist realist tradition in the philosophy of explanation. Given the widespread attacks on empiricism and positivism of recent decades, another critique of these epistemologies should not be necessary but unfortunately empiricism and positivism are still associated in the minds of many historians and economists with the idea of scientific history. Moving toward a framework for a science of social structural history constructed partly on the basis of a realist philosophy of explanation is one of the fundamental goals of this methodological discussion.

In the end I hope to have established the following theses:

1 There can be formulated a scientific domain of social structural history.
2 Structurism is the most appropriate basic methodology for the domain of structural history explanation.
3 Structurist methodology and structurist theory are mutually reinforcing.
4 Structurism and realism are the proper foundations for a science of structural history.
5 Structural history should be part of a methodologically unified socio-historical science.

In order to try to establish these theses the book has the following structure:

1 Chapter 1 outlines the history of structural history writing; discusses the basic concepts of a science of society and of a scientific domain; discusses the importance of sociological realism; and outlines the compositional and evolutionary problems of the putative domain of structural history.
2 Chapter 2 critically surveys the existing approaches to economic and social history and argues that the realist–relational approach is based on the methodology of structurism.
3 Chapter 3 contains a detailed analysis of methodological structurism in abstract and as the deep foundation of the work of certain prominent historians, most notably Clifford Geertz and Emmanuel Le Roy Ladurie, who are discussed in detail.
4 Chapter 4 contains a detailed defence of the proposition that structurism and realism are the proper foundations for the scientific domain of structural history.

5 Chapter 5 examines the relationship between historical materialist theory and structurism and argues that structurism denies the possibility of an ahistorical general theory of history such as historical materialism.
6 Chapter 6 explores the normative implications for practical action of establishing a science of structural history on realist and structurist grounds.

1

Explaining the History of Economic and Social Structures

The fundamental problem addressed here is how to improve explanations of the history of economic and social structures. To begin with, this task must involve examining the serious philosophical and methodological disagreements that exist between practitioners and exploring how to develop a rational consensus on how the field or discipline should proceed. This opening chapter is concerned with outlining the general problems of methodologies of social structural history and how we might move towards a resolution of these problems. Many issues are raised here but few are dealt with comprehensively, as the following chapters study particular issues in greater detail. This chapter opens up the problems and tries to set them in their overall context and relationships with each other.

EARLY APPROACHES TO THE WRITING OF ECONOMIC AND SOCIAL HISTORY

The writing of the history of economies and societies in the West was a product of the eighteenth-century Enlightenment and particularly of the coming into European consciousness of the differences between the social organizations and material wealth of European states and those of the peoples of the Americas, Africa, and Asia. Giambattista Vico's *New Science* of 1725[1] can be seen as indeed new in Western thought, for he wanted to theorize, describe, and explain the history of whole peoples and their forms of social organization. But even his radical work had some roots in the previous century's empiricist philosophies of Hobbes and Locke, and the Enlightenment desire to see humankind as the measure of all things. The comments by Hobbes and Locke about the material attainments of 'primitive' peoples were also influential on later writers, notably Smith and Turgot.[2]

However, there was at least one very important non-Western predecessor of these writers – the fourteenth-century Maghrebian Ibn Khaldûn, whose fundamentally important work of structural history, *The Muquddimah*, was lost to Western thought until the nineteenth century and has been fully appreciated only since the 1960s. It is now clear that this great work on the foundations of Islamic civilization and society provides the first known attempt to write a theoretical and empirical work of structural history.[3]

Systematic ideas about the economy as a partially separate realm of action were emerging in Britain and France by the early seventeenth century. These ideas usually centred on the role of commerce in promoting the wealth of the state. And it was consideration of the importance of commerce *vis-à-vis* agriculture and the rise of manufacturing, combined with the idea of social and economic differences among peoples, that led to the development of the first systematic economic histories and historical sociologies in the mid-eighteenth century. In other words, it was the beginning of rapid economic development and the possibility of individual economic and political freedom that helped prompt the emergence in Britain and France of thought about economic and social change. As Karl Marx was later to comment, because in earlier forms of society there was no possibility of development of the individual or society there was therefore no enquiry into the causes of wealth.[4] The central contributor to the first general body of enquiry into the history of the causes of wealth (i.e., into what we would now call economic development) was Adam Smith, whose pioneering work began in the early 1750s. Other members of the so-called Scottish historical school, notably John Millar and Adam Ferguson, also contributed to the development of an embryonic historical materialist account of economic and social structural change based on a theory of four stages of economic history.[5]

Remarkably, at about the same time or even a little before the Scottish approach was being developed there were parallel developments in France, especially by A. R. J. Turgot. He had been influenced by Montesquieu's book on *The Spirit of the Laws* (1748). Although Montesquieu had not himself presented a structural history, he was concerned to trace what we would now call the socio-political origins of legal systems. Turgot developed a theory of the stages of economic development that was similar to that of the Scots.[6]

The emergence of these forms of historical political economy and historical sociology in Britain and France in the second half of the eighteenth century, against the background of comparatively rapid economic and social change in certain regions, had no counterpart in Germany. Instead it was the idea of universal history that dominated this country.[7] This idealistic and rationalistic genre was increasingly practised throughout Europe from the early eighteenth century and it attempted to tell the general story of whole idealized peoples, empires, and states (rather than the structures of economies and societies and individual economic initiatives) from ancient to modern times. Kant and Hegel made notable contributions and this stream of work culminated in Germany in the writings of von Ranke. He was a precursor of the modern academic general history that became fully institutionalized in Anglophone universities in the late nineteenth and early twentieth centuries.[8]

Smith forms a link between the eighteenth-century Scottish historical and totalizing approach to economy and society and the later abstract, individualist, and ahistorical approach of utilitarian classical economics. The economy became increasingly abstracted from the social totality and from its own past as, under the growing aura of physics, the 'science of economics' was developed, especially in Britain and Austria, by Ricardo and the Mills.[9] By the late nineteenth century the marginalism of Menger, Jevons, Walras, and Marshall had completed the process of abstraction, deductivism, and ahistoricalism. Henceforth mainstream theoretical economics was divorced from history, sociology, and politics and was later based explicitly on logical empiricist (nomological, deductive, and reductionist) epistemological notions. But from the 1950s a school of 'new' economic historians developed in America, employing neo-classical theory to engage in retrospective (present-oriented) 'historical', quantitative, economic analysis in opposition to the more orthodox, inductive, 'old', economic history of that time.

Meanwhile, in early nineteenth-century France Saint-Simon and Comte made sweeping attempts to found a new all-encompassing philosophical approach to society and its history. Their aims were, in a fashion somewhat similar to each other, to combine their positivist philosophical notions with the powers of natural scientific thought and the new industrial class to found a new world order ruled by social laws of development they thought they had discovered. Comte was especially concerned to enunciate the supposed developmental laws of social organic evolution. 'Positivism' and 'sociology' (two of his coinages) were combined to produce the first thorough-going version of historical sociology. It was based on an a priori holistic concept of society – a society supposedly driven through stages by evolutionary 'laws' that could be discovered by a 'scientific' method of observation – rather than on an empirically developed model or theory of social structure. Comte did not undertake empirical enquiry in the more modern sense of the term, but he did influence strongly the subsequent tenor of much of European social thought.[10]

The German historical school of economists, who began their work in the 1840s, were influenced by the positivist search for laws of historical evolution. German historical economics was a school of thought which developed parallel to and in opposition to the growing ahistorical, rationalist, and abstract character of English and later Austrian economics. This was the first real school of socio-economic ideas since the Scots a century earlier and it presaged a pervasive development in modern social thought – a coherent school of ideas based on certain foundational meta-concepts and epistemological commitments, as well as institutionalized personal loyalties and obligations. Since the mid-nineteenth century there have been many others.

The phenomenon of schools owes more to external (socio-cultural) than to internal (logical and conceptual) influences on the development of proto-sciences and other academic fields. As Pierre Bourdieu has argued,[11] fields of enquiry are spaces in which there is a struggle for recognition by peers. When sciences are immature, this often takes the form of conflicts between social groups, in each of which there are leaders and followers. Nevertheless, it is still possible for there to be progress in the field itself in terms of its contribution to knowledge. The history of the natural sciences in the nineteenth century would seem to bear this out, for they too were characterized by schools from which emerged inter-school consensuses, unified domains, scientific progress, and the corresponding decline in the strength and pervasiveness of schools in the later twentieth century.

Like many schools, the German economists had an ideological as well as a theoretical foundation.[12] They were interested, as the earlier mercantilists had been, in promoting the health of the whole nation. This involved studying empirically the peculiar history, character, and circumstances of each nation, but within a general theory of stages. Writers such as Roscher, Knies, and Hildebrand in the 1840s, and later Bücher and Schmoller,[13] proposed evolutionary stage theories of economic development reminiscent of that of the Scots almost a century earlier. The German historical economists had a powerful influence on German nationalism, economic and social policy, and social thought generally, through the Verein für Social Politik. Gustav Schmoller, one of the members of the younger school in the 1880s, sparked off the *Methodenstreit* with his attack on the deductivist and abstract character of Carl Menger's marginalist economics. Karl Marx was one of the early critics of the historical school for what he saw as their failure to understand the structure and dynamics of the capitalist mode of production;[14] and Max Weber was partly educated in their approach, conducting his early research under the auspices of the Verein, although rejecting their quasi-positivist and evolutionist methodology.[15]

In contrast with the powerful influence and official acceptance in Germany of the historical economists, Marx and Engels were for most of their lives marginalized outcasts, their work, apart from their more political pamphleteering and journalism, known only to a few fellow revolutionaries. It was not until the rise of the German Social Democratic Party from the late 1870s that their social, economic, and historical ideas came to have a wider prominence. But even then they were poorly understood. Their structural historical writings contained a more refined and sophisticated version of historical materialist theory than had hitherto been developed. They were particularly influenced by Hegel's idea of the dialectics of world history, by Adam Smith's political economy, and by historians of ancient societies such as Niebuhr and Maine, in their approach to the question of the origins and character of modern capitalism and what had preceded it. They were opposed to empiricism and holism and to evolutionary theories of historical change. They defended what we would now call a realist social ontology and epistemology.[16] The importance of this philosophical basis was that it underpinned their presentation in the mid-1840s of the first well-developed theory of social structure and its internal dynamics, and its relationship to economic, political, and legal change. There had been intimations of theories of structure earlier, as in the works of Millar,

Ferguson, Saint-Simon, and Comte, but none of the earlier writers had a well-developed account and they all lacked the empirical base of Marx and Engels. The latter expressly abandoned conjectural, speculative thought in favour of careful empirical enquiry into the real origins and history of the economic and social structure of bourgeois society.

Evolutionism and holism, rather than materialism and realism, were the dominant influences on English sociology and anthropology in the second half of the nineteenth century. The general idea of evolution – that systems and entities evolve through stages from lower to higher or from simpler to more complex – was an ancient notion, but by the early to mid-nineteenth century it was being extensively applied as if society were analogous to a holistic organism. Perhaps the most important influences on the English evolutionary sociologists – notably Spencer, Maine, and Tylor, and later Hobhouse[17] – were the positivism and organicism of Comte, the development of biological science, the geology of Lyell, and later Darwin's theory of biological evolution. But of course Darwin was himself influenced by earlier evolutionary ideas in economics and sociology, such as those of Malthus. By the early twentieth century some of these evolutionary sociologists were describing their approach as 'historical sociology'.[18]

Contemporaneously with the evolutionary historical sociology school there developed in Britain a well-integrated school of evolutionary historical economics. Like the German historical school, these writers, notably Rogers, Leslie, Toynbee, Ashley, Cunningham, Hewins, and Unwin,[19] reacted against the abstraction, individualism, and deductivism of classical and neo-classical economics and proposed instead a relativist, inductive, and historical approach to explaining political economy. They had little lasting influence on economics but brought into being the modern 'discipline' of economic history, which henceforth became institutionalized in Anglophone universities, especially in Britain and Australasia and to some extent in North America. The division that developed between economics and economic history was based on a fundamental disagreement over philosophy and methodology, an abstract versus historical split which, from the perspective of the late twentieth century, seems to have been more harmful in the long run to economics than to economic history. The weakness of economic explanation springs partly from its lack of interest in social institutions, its lack of historical specificity, and a misguided attempt by some economists to construct a positive science of society on the perceived model of physics.

It can be said with a high degree of justification that by the late nineteenth century there had developed four main philosophical or metaphysical conceptions of the nature of social structure, which had fundamental implications for approaches to its dynamics and its history. (At that time the later distinction between history and sociology had not yet become significant.) The four conceptions were individualism, holism, realism, and phenomenology. Each of these was loosely nationally located and associated with a particular epistemology, as shown in figure 1.1. The national differences can largely be traced to the influence of the local traditions of the preceding Enlightenment era. The development of structural historiography in the twentieth century until the 1950s was broadly along the lines of the three main national and linguistic traditions: Anglophone, Francophone, and Germanic. From the 1960s there began a blurring and a melding so that by the 1970s these distinct national traditions had largely disappeared.

In France Émile Durkheim was a dominant figure at the turn of the century and greatly influenced French social science for several generations. He had been influenced by Saint-Simon and Comte and developed an objectivist and functionalist account of social structure and social behaviour. Perhaps more than any other he was responsible for the institutionalization and widespread propagation of sociology as a new theoretical and empirical positive science. His principle of functionalism, an explanatory teleological claim about the relationship of actions and structure, was widely adopted in twentieth-century anthropology and sociology, for example, by Bronislaw Malinowski, A. R. Radcliffe-Brown, and Talcott Parsons.[20] Durkheim was also one of the influences on the development of structuralist anthropology by Lévi-Strauss and of the *Annales* School of structural history.

In Germany, the revival of Kantian philosophy in the late nineteenth century by Dilthey, Windelband, and Rickert was a powerful influence on developments in social explanation. Max Weber's work from 1903 onwards contains an impressive attempt to transcend the *Methodenstreit* debate between positivism, relativism, hermeneutics, and historicism, and in so doing to develop a sociology that could combine objectivity and subjectivity, scientific enquiry and hermeneutics.[21] His works of historical sociology and economic history also reveal a strong influence from Marx, although it is perhaps going too far to suggest that Weber employed historical materialism in those works. His emphasis on Western rationalism, the cultural imperatives and constraints on action, the role of entrepreneurship in economic development, and the growing bureaucratization of capitalist, modern society[22] are all themes that have reverberated and recurred in the burgeoning and spreading neo-Weberian and hermeneutical social-science literature of the twentieth century. As with all seminal thinkers, Weber's work has been interpreted and appropriated in widely varying ways. Some recent works of historical sociology influenced by his ideas, such as those by Benjamin Nelson, Ernest Gellner, Clifford Geertz, Albert Hirschman, and Charles Tilly,[23] have been among the foremost products of twentieth-century social science.

The French and German traditions of functionalism, structuralism, Marxism, and historicism all saw a central role for a grand theory that conceptualized the sweep of historical change and formed part of the framework of rationalist and idealist explanations. In contrast, in Britain and some other parts of the Anglophone world the emphasis was on supposedly theory-neutral (or theory-devoid) observation and fact-gathering. This empirical method (more

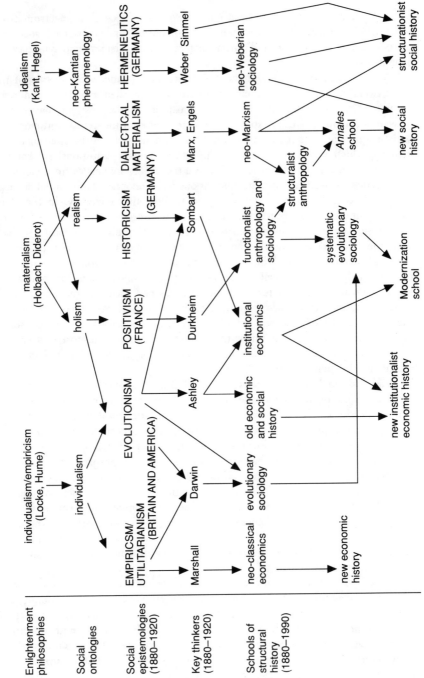

Figure 1.1 The history of structural historiography

correctly labelled 'naïve empiricist') ran across the ideological spectrum from left to right, across disciplines from macro-historical or evolutionary sociology to 'old' economic history, 'old' social history, labour history, and neo-classical economics.

The old versions of Anglophone economic, labour, and social history of the early twentieth century were closely interrelated in their empirical and non-theoretical methodology and in their opposition to the abstractions of neo-classical economics. A major split had occurred between theoretical and empirical social enquiry in Britain and some other Anglophone areas in the late nineteenth century, which was not reflected in the other linguistic traditions. In America the situation was more complicated, because there were influences from Germany and France as well as Britain. Institutionalist economics had gained a large following, as had empirical sociology and functionalist sociology. In the 1950s three significant new approaches to structural history were developed there. Cliometrics, or 'new' economic history, attempted to unite a historical approach with the latest neo-classical economic theory to explain long-run change in series of economic data. This was a form of applied economics or historical economics that was not really interested in the complexities of the past *per se* but in devising empirical tests for modern theory.[24] Second, the new institutional economic history has attempted to apply neo-classical theory to explain the long-run history of real economic systems conceived in greater socio-political complexity.[25] And third, the functionalist school has tried to employ Parsonian social theory to study the problems of industrialization and modern-ization in the postwar world.[26]

Meanwhile in France the most powerful and influential school of structural historians developed around the journal *Annales* and later at the École des Hautes Études en Sciences Sociales.[27] The *Annalistes* combined a structuralist methodology, sophisticated forms of social theory, and rigorous empirical and statistical methods to examine the long-run history of macro socio-economic structures and cycles. The major rival to the *Annales* approach in France was the revival of Marxism in the sixties, which was a worldwide phenomenon. Marxism was also a major influence in the burgeoning development of the new social history in Britain and America. The only significant form of Marxist thought in Britain in the postwar years was in history writing where the Marxist school was partly a continuation, but with an explicitly theoretical orientation, of a radical historiographical and political tradition stretching back to the seventeenth century.[28]

In the 1970s social history became an amorphous all-encompassing move-ment in Anglophone historiography, engulfing areas of cultural, economic, and political history writing. 'Social history' came to mean almost all things to all people. Under this rubric were various individualist, holist, and structurist methodologies. More recently, 'historical sociology' has also encompassed the same range of methodologies. In the next chapter I shall examine these developments. The 1980s has seen a breakdown of disciplinary boundaries so that the old history/theory division in Anglophone countries has begun to be seen as the absurdity it always was. One of the most significant results of the re-theorization of history is the development of historical anthropology or the history of mentalities and cultures. We are also now seeing the disappearance of the old schools of structural history writing derived from positivist, functionalist, Marxist, and Weberian antecedents early in this century or from the nineteenth. Various new syntheses are being proposed, most notably the 'structurationist paradigm' and the new cultural history, to be discussed in the following chapter.

TOWARDS A SCIENCE OF SOCIAL STRUCTURAL HISTORY

Many of the early writers of structural history, including Saint-Simon, Comte, Marx, Engels, Spencer, Durkheim, Sombart, and Braudel believed, and many contemporary writers, such as Fogel, Wallerstein, and Gellner believe today, that they were and are establishing or contributing to the development of a *science* of history. But understandings of what that means in the abstract and entails in practice are remarkably various and often poorly analysed. One thing seems to be constant from the long history of discussions and attempts to establish a science of society and history, and that is the long shadow cast by the sciences of nature. Whether to live within the shadow or escape into a non-scientific meadow of luxuriant relativism has seemed to be the dichotomous (and too restrictive) choice for historical explanation.

The paradigm of explanation is indeed that of the mature sciences of nature. It has long seemed clear that these sciences have great power to *explain* rather than just describe the phenomena of the natural world. In the twentieth century there have been vast strides in the success of the sciences as measured by the power of their explanatory knowledge to permit technology and engineering in natural contexts. The complexities of natural structure have been revealed as opaque to common sense yet available to systematic rational enquiry and deliberate control through intervention. Those complexities, while often unpredictable in advance of discovery and therefore surprising, have been found everywhere to contain real, structured systems of elements, powers, and relations that can be formalized mathematically.

Of course the general picture of success must be tempered with, first, the knowledge that there have been many false turnings in the evolution of the sciences; second, an admission that there remain many areas of ignorance and falsity; third, a realization that there can be no warrant for believing in an approaching denouement of scientific knowledge; and fourth, a recognition of the many unintended, sometimes disastrous consequences of physical and biological engineering.

Looking back on the advances made by science in the past couple of centuries, philosophers and historians have attempted to develop an understanding of how it has been possible for science to be so successful if, as Dudley Shapere put it in the quotation on p. xv above, 'so many of our contemporary scientific beliefs could not have been anticipated by common sense, the suggestions of everyday experience, or pure reason.' Appeals to some set of ahistorical meta-scientific rules of discovery will not answer this question because scientific knowledge has always been contingent and the rules have undergone occasional upheavals. I argue here that the reasons for scientific success lie in a combination of:

(a)   the implicit use of the idea of critical scientific realism, as recently articulated and developed by Richard Boyd, Clifford Hooker, Roy Bhaskar, Brian Ellis, Wesley Salmon,[29] and others, which argues a posteriori that discovery of the structures of nature and consequent successful intervention in nature could not have been possible without the *prior* mind-independent reality of the law-governed structures of nature. In other words, this is a transcendental argument from the obvious persistent success of science and engineering to a claim about what the world must be like in general terms for that success to have occurred;

(b)   the principle of 'scientific internalization' to which Shapere appeals;

(c)   the rational construction of an interconnecting and reflexive network of reasoning that links theories, hypotheses about causal mechanisms and causal relations, and rigorous testing of those hypotheses through the use of models, analogies, experiments, observation and other data collections;

(d)   the three foregoing factors having allowed the development of theories that more or less accurately analyse the world into its actual, natural kinds and the real causal relations that inhere in systems linking natural kinds. That is, scientific theories have made discoveries possible and earlier discoveries, using proto-theories, have made the refinement and development of theories possible. The mutually reinforcing relationship between theories and discoveries has been cemented by successful engineering in the laboratory and in nature.

These four features of science do not of course amount to a definite and unrevisable model of 'scientific method'. Our accumulated knowledge of entities, structures, and systems, which does not have to pretend to any absolute or even provisional finality or unrevisability, is the result of a complex and adaptable approach, rather than a fixed 'methodology' in the usual sense of that word, linking ontological beliefs, general theories, linguistic devices, theorizing about causes, constant testing, and revision of knowledge. (These ideas about the methodology and success of science will be discussed in greater detail in chapter 4.)

The old problem of the scientific character or otherwise of enquiries into the history of economies and societies is still a central issue for many practitioners and methodologists.[30] Unfortunately, progress towards delineating, let alone resolving the problem has been bedevilled by an inadequate conception of scientific methodology and of the actual methodology of many social structural historians. Both the proponents and opponents of scientific history have usually adopted a simplistic, empiricist, quantitative conception of science, which neither does justice to science nor allows the possibility of a truly scientific social history. No philosophical or historical student of scientific method seriously defends the conception of science advanced by the vulgar empiricist defenders of cliometrics and positivist economics. The historical, social, and psychological sciences have long been sidetracked by over-zealous scientistic but ill-informed advocates of quantification and statistical techniques (as if they were talismans) or of behaviourism, or absolute objectivism, who lack a wider and deeper framework of concepts of a truly scientific nature in which to locate their superficial empiricism. It is no wonder that traditional historians, whether they deal with politics, culture, economy, or society, have felt unattracted by the 'scientific' approaches being offered to them. Meanwhile, some historians of social structures, as well as other social scientists, have been developing genuinely scientific approaches to their explanatory tasks, usually without being very conscious of the scientificity of their methodology.

My (somewhat old-fashioned but still essential) tasks in this regard are to develop in detail the sketch of a realist account of scientific reasoning (including social science) that I have just given, to discuss reasons for its superior strength compared with other models of explanation, to argue that structural history should endeavour to become scientific, and to show how structural history enquiry can be and sometimes is scientific. In chapters 3 and 4 I shall try to show in detail how scientific realism overcomes the problems of both empiricism and relativism and in so doing supports the methodology that I call 'structurism' for structural history. Scientific social structural history, I shall argue, must weaken the claim of absolute objectivity that positivists have made while rejecting the relativist, pragmatic, and common-sense modes of reasoning that have hitherto been the main alternatives. But hermeneutical interpretation must play a role within a scientific framework. The sharp dichotomy between interpretive and scientific history was always false. The concept of truth must be retained, but in a weaker and more complex form than a simple correspondence idea.

INTERRELATIONSHIPS OF PHILOSOPHY, METHODOLOGY, AND THEORY IN SCIENTIFIC EXPLANATION

In order to see if it is possible for a science of social structural history to be developed which has at least a family resemblance to the sciences of nature we must know something of the character of scientific explanation as it exists. Essentially this means examining the relationship between metaphysics, methodology, and general theory in advanced science. Here I shall raise the main aspects of the problem that have to be considered, leaving the detail of the argument to chapter 4.

Philosophy and methodology

To explain something essentially involves giving an account of why it happened and/or why it is the way it is in terms of its supposed causal relations with other things. All explanations employ, whether deliberately or passively, general concepts and general theories, which are used to produce causal hypotheses, interpretations of evidence, and causal understandings of particular kinds of phenomena and processes. It is now well understood that these general concepts and general theories are parts of background frameworks or traditions of beliefs, ideas, knowledge, and assumptions that all explanations employ. These frameworks include philosophical and methodological assumptions, which are sets of ideas and beliefs about the entities and processes of the world and of how we can have knowledge of them.

The framework concepts and general theories that the advanced sciences employ pertain to what have been called 'domains' of knowledge by some philosophers of science, most notably by Dudley Shapere.[31] These domains, such as particle physics, polymer chemistry, plate tectonics, virology, neurophysiology, insect population dynamics, and so on, are bodies of subject-matter that have become delineated by the way in which the entities, powers, and systems of the world have been theorized and discovered to be naturally delineated and interrelated. Domains of science are the result of the history of scientific methodology, theory, and discovery over many centuries, and even at a mature stage they are in a process of constant piecemeal refinement and very occasional wholesale reordering and unification. There seems to be a strong long-run tendency to unify domains of subject-matter so that general theories become increasingly comprehensive. Indeed, it seems that part of the essential character of scientific explanation is to reduce the number of domains and theories to fewer and more comprehensive ones. This is a main reason why there are occasional revolutions in thought.

The processes of constitution and unification of domains and the role that domains play in explanation are of vital importance to philosophers and historians of explanation and should also be important to all those practitioners of a science or proto-science, such as social structural history, who wish to improve their explanations. The historical process of inchoate enquiry whereby scientific domains came to be established in a piecemeal and unpredicted fashion must be distinguished from the process of reasoning that, *ex post facto*, reconstructs the logical connections between the assumptions and abstractions of domain frameworks and the ongoing empirical research that takes place within them. The process of discovery and the constitution of domains is not the same as the logic of rational analytical reconstruction, formalization, and criticism of scientific explanation. While here I am primarily concerned with making a rational reconstruction rather than analysing the process of discovery, I am trying not to lose sight of the historical and epistemological primacy of the latter process. Sciences are not established by deductive analytical reasoning alone but by practitioners gradually discovering how the world really is and what the appropriate methodologies and general theories are for making discoveries. However, scientists can only do that within a prior proto-scientific framework of an ill-defined and perhaps somewhat incoherent sort, which provides them with some general methodological ideas and some concepts, even if these are later refined and/or abandoned in the light of the discoveries they helped to establish. Observation, understanding, and discovery never occur except within some sort of intellectual framework. The difference between scientific and non-scientific understanding is not the development of a framework out of intellectual anarchy, as Kuhn seems to think. On the contrary, science is but one among many kinds of world-view but it is vitally different from all the others in its explanatory power and ability to examine critically all other frameworks, as well as reflexively to examine itself. In this reflexive way the sciences emerged from the pre-scientific world of early modern Europe.[32] But when proto-scientific enquiry reaches a degree of refinement and explanatory power then there is a vital role for methodological analysis and criticism that is able to help sort the valuable from the valueless aspects of proto-frameworks and show sceptics that a new science is being born.

Thus analysis and criticism of proto-sciences that draw upon knowledge of the reasoning of the mature sciences only really became possible after the mature sciences had reached a certain degree of power in the nineteenth and early twentieth centuries. Nevertheless, the wish to apply 'scientific method' to all kinds of enquiry goes back to the early Enlightenment, as shown by Vico's desire to apply Bacon's prescriptions and Hume's belief that he was employing Newtonian principles to reconstruct the foundations of human understanding. The French Enlightenment of the second half of the eighteenth century witnessed many attempts to establish sciences of the mind and human nature on supposed Newtonian, mechanistic principles.[33] From the 1940s under the initial impetus of logical positivism there began an explosion of philosophy of science literature[34] analysing both mature and immature sciences. Critics of the social enquiries have appropriated arguments from philosophers of science, often piecemeal, usually with a view to making the disciplines more scientific.[35] Thus the methodological critic of the immature or proto-science could be seen as the midwife of new sciences, drawing upon the re-analysed, reconstructed, and articulated understandings of existing sciences.[36] This seems to me a basically correct strategy provided, crucially, that two important points are understood: that the sciences are not uniform (that is, that the form and methodology of each science is strongly influenced by its subject-matter) and that we have adequate accounts of the structures of reasoning of the advanced sciences. This last point is, of course, a major problem – how to develop adequate accounts of science.

Methodological enquiry into a science that has already reached maturity (assessed in terms of the coherence, completeness, theoretical fruitfulness, and explanatory power of its domain framework) has a role somewhat similar but different from that of the midwife of a new science. This role is the analysis and criticism of the reasoning of everyday theoretical and empirical enquiries – a post-natal function, as it were. Here scientific framework-building is no longer occurring except at rare times of crisis. The history of science can be read as indicating that such crises can be prompted by philosophical discussions of the nature of the entities, systems, and processes being examined and/or by methodological analyses of the reasoning of everyday enquiries. Such crises are usually resolved by unifying previously separate domains through the development of new methodologies and more encompassing general theories.

It is a central thrust of the Wittgensteinian, Neo-Nietzschean, post-structuralist, and post-modernist critiques of philosophy to reject all foundational and/or metacritical roles of philosophy and general theory. Philosophers and methodologists such as Richard Rorty, Michel Foucault, Jacques Derrida, Stanley Fish, Jean-François Lyotard, Donald McCloskey, and Richard Harvey Brown[37] have all advanced in differing idioms the general idea that the role of methodological criticism is to articulate the pragmatic, linguistic, and rhetorical devices of persuasion and the sociological, psychological, and political contexts of discourses rather than to establish meta-rules of assessment of the validity of theoretical and factual statements. Overarching meta-criticism that draws upon some supposedly 'privileged' level of presuppositions, concepts, and knowledge is held to be unsupportable because there can be no real foundation for the supposed foundation. All knowledge is constituted in and by forms of discourse or language. The role of the historian is then taken to be to analyse texts (or text analogues) for their place in discourses and for what they reveal about the internal power structures of discourses, rather than for what they might also tell us about any supposedly objective real structures of societies and history. 'Historical reality' only has meaning from a standpoint within a discourse.[38]

While relativists are right to reject untestable metaphysical and methodological assumptions, to emphasize persuasion, and to draw attention to the socially and linguistically relative contexts of texts and truth concepts, they do seem to ignore the possibility of reflexive examination of all foundational metaphysical and epistemological propositions, and hence the adoption or affirmation of certain explanatory foundations, such as those of scientific realism, only after rational enquiry and testing. Having relatively stable philosophical and methodological foundations for explanation seems to be necessary, but it does not mean that they are unrevisable or privileged. Indeed, in the mature sciences foundations have changed because of the scientific process itself. Their survival depends mainly on their long-term explanatory usefulness. Explanatory usefulness, in turn, is founded on the twin notions of discoverable order and the power of science to intervene in the order in predictable ways.

The fundamental problem with relativism is that it is unintentionally dishonest in the sense that, disclaimers notwithstanding, it does contain its own disguised assumptions or tacit commitments to 'privileged' sets of notions or concepts which are in fact not 'problematized'. For example, the deep structures of grammar, semantics, and logic are not usually questioned and the relationship that the universal structures of natural languages and natural logic have within pre-theoretical and pre-scientific forms of reasoning are not questioned. The continuous rather than disjointed relationship of pre-theoretical and pre-scientific reasoning and understanding with modern theory and science has been well established.[39] In other words, there seem to be some universals of thought, or at least the relativists have not shown otherwise.[40] If there are universal elements of human thought and language, and these are a natural outgrowth of human life and thought in their interaction with the environment, then there are limits to the kinds of social structure that can be developed and how and what it is possible to think. Those possibilities and limits are governed by the nature of the universe. Thought is parasitic upon nature in a general sense but is nevertheless very powerful in its capacity to conceptualize and construct theoretical patterns that supposedly describe and analyse the universe. Science itself has shown that the nature of the universe is the ultimate foundation and reference for thought. Imagination is not unconstrained. The relativists have lost sight of this in their excited but naïve 'discovery' of the great power of language and imagination to mould our beliefs, understandings, and relationships. But that power is not unlimited. Language cannot mould physical and biological nature. How thought and its particular theoretical and conceptual products relate to the world is the age-old epistemological issue. The idea of thought or philosophy as edification and rhetoric is attractive, but ultimately it cannot advance the human quest for improving the quality of personal and social life. That requires knowledge of the real natural and social contexts of action and consciousness, knowledge that is ultimately persuasive because it allows scientific interventions from non-scientific motives.[41]

The romantic, hermeneutical, relativist stream of meta-thought about social and human enquiries vigorously rejects the idea that they can and will become like the sciences of nature. This of course presupposes a certain conception of science as containing a fixed epistemological relation between external object and human enquirer, and a conception of human action, consciousness, and social relations which supposes that they cannot be studied in the same way as nature. However, the sciences do not have to have identical methodologies. The search for the ahistorical, correct methodology for all science has proved not only illusory but dangerous. Each science has pursued its own path towards maturity. Nevertheless, while each science has its peculiarities, each can be construed as scientific in a fundamental sense that I shall try to articulate in detail in chapter 4.

The a priori rejection of a scientific approach to social structural history can be countered at first by showing that in fact the social sciences are indeed following their various peculiar paths of progress towards domain construction. If they are to be taken seriously in their explanatory aims, insofar as they have them, then they must do so. Adequate explanation and its improvement seem to require domain coherence and appropriateness of concepts to their object. In the social sciences the highly contentious process of initial establishment of domains of knowledge and their methodologies is still going on. This is the latest stage in a process three centuries long. The construction and acceptance of social science domains has not yet reached the stage where there is a consensus on defining concepts, methodologies, and general theories.

This book is partly about how we might better constitute methodologically and theoretically the putative domain of social structural history, and about how its foundations, or framework of methodology and concepts, may be defined and strengthened. We should not consider this domain of the history of social structures to be different from one that would study such structures as if they were static or existing only in the present. Social structures are inherently historical in the dual and paradoxical senses of temporally continuous and constantly changing. Therefore the abstract sociological and economic concepts that structural history employs should have an inherently historical and dynamic reference. From this point of view, one of the major defects of modern mainstream economics is its bracketing of dynamics in favour of building abstract models, which then have to have dynamic variables somehow grafted onto them in order to study history. Model building is not itself a problem; in fact, abstractions are necessary to explanation. It is the ahistorical assumptions behind them and the static concepts of many models that must be criticized.

The view that the very historicity of society rules out scientific knowledge because such knowledge can be only of space-time invariant structures can be disposed of quickly. Because nature is ruled by universal, atemporal laws but society is not, goes the argument, there is a fundamental difference in the ontology so that the discovery of 'laws' of social structural composition and history is impossible.[42] But the counter to this is threefold. First, society is not the only historical system. The entire universe, including the planets, the geology of the earth, the biosphere, and the evolution of life-forms are all historical in the sense of having specific, changing processes. Second, science is not necessarily characterized by the aim of discovering laws. More basic characteristics are the form of rationality, the structure of reasoning, reflexivity and self-criticism, and empirical objectivity. There seems no prima facie reason why the study of the history of social structures cannot employ a form of rationality and a system of reasoning that resembles those of the sciences of nature. Third, it may turn out that the history of social structures is in fact law-governed in a way similar to the history of the geomorphology of the earth, for example, or perhaps, more plausibly, the history of a complex ecosystem. Shapere's Principle of Rejection of Anticipation of Nature (see the quotation on p. xv) should be applied to society too. The structure of society and the mechanisms of its history are not immediately available to common-sense perception and understanding. The idea that because we are 'internal' to society we can intuitively grasp its structure is no more plausible than the idea that because we are 'internal' to our own bodies or our own psyches we can intuitively understand them. Nevertheless, it seems clear from the history of the sciences that there is a chain of reasoning, with certain jumps in the sequence perhaps, that links common sense with scientific knowledge. But the natural sciences have moved a long way from common sense. Knowledge of social structural history has not moved as far yet. It seems that the problem lies partly in the inappropriate methodologies being employed by many practitioners. (See chapter 2 for a discussion of existing methodologies.)

In a work of analysis of the methodologies of particular branches or domains of sciences and other intellectual fields the first task is to ascertain how those branches, domains, and fields describe and explain what they wish to describe and explain. What is the framework of philosophical and methodological assumptions in which descriptions and explanations are made and what are the connections between framework, theories, and explanations? In fact, philosophical and methodological assumptions and concepts are both necessary to empirical enquiry and always present in one form or another. This is not to say that such assumptions are always easily recognizable or separate from empirical thought. But they always form a sometimes implicit, sometimes explicit level of general beliefs or vague ideas, which may or may not be expressed as concepts, about how the empirical discipline should proceed. They are closely tied to empirical enquiry, but it is possible to separate them analytically. Separation and clarification of frameworks is the first task of analytical philosophical enquiry, upon which the second task depends.

The second task is to develop criticisms of the coherence, strength, adequacy, and plausibility of the methodologies and explanations, with a view to offering constructive assistance to the ongoing process of empirical research. Not all the empirical researchers in a putative domain are at the same methodological level or employing the same methodology. Rational philosophical and methodological enquiry, then, is (or should be) the ally of empirical enquiry, especially in immature sciences.

In its heyday in the 1960s analytical philosophy of history was not much concerned with criticism but just with trying to analyse the writing of history. The task was seen as a more or less passive examination and articulation of the existing explanatory assumptions and practices of historians, the counterpart to analytical philosophy of science. Many of these philosophers were concerned to show that historical knowledge is a distinctive and viable form of knowing, with its own logic, standards, and rationale.[43] Since then this attitude has been eroded for several reasons. One is a growing realization by many historians that they must become interdisciplinary and combine with the social and psychological sciences in various ways in order to construct explanations. Another is the crisis that developed in the 1960s in the philosophy of science, prompting much uncertainty about the nature of scientific and other forms of knowledge. Historians have to some extent been affected by these debates. However, the idea that explicit philosophical and methodological criticism can be of assistance to empirical research is still not popular among historians. Such criticism is much more popular these days among sociologists and is probably gaining popularity from a low level among economists. One of the determinants of the resort to methodological criticism is the degree of internal coherence of empirical disciplines, such as economics or history, in terms of shared beliefs about rationale, goals, and procedures. When this coherence is not present – sometimes because of perceived failures in explanation or the creation of new approaches – then the resort to philosophy and methodology for assistance becomes more acceptable. That is, questions about the methodological and philosophical assumptions of the discipline are raised by empirical practitioners because of perceived problems of empirical explanation. This is the main reason why there have been debates such as those between Lawrence Stone, Eric Hobsbawm, and Philip Abrams in *Past and Present* in 1979–80, and many other recent contributions to methodological discussions about economic and social history and historical sociology.[44]

The nature of theory

The separation of philosophical and methodological questions about explanation from substantive theoretical ones is important. The failure to do so is common and misleading. Lawrence Stone's *Past and Present* article of 1979 shows that he did not grasp the difference between 'structuralism', which is part of a methodology, and 'historical materialism', which is a theory of structural change. Problems of constructing particular theories and applying them arise *within* fields of enquiry, which have a distinct and relatively coherent philosophical and methodological framework that delineates a distinct subject-matter. Frameworks contain metaphysical beliefs (often well founded), general concepts about the nature of the objects of enquiry within the domain, general methodological principles, and a collection of linguistic explanatory tools, such as metaphors, analogies, similes, and source models. Scientific theories employ these beliefs, principles, tools, and models to construct putative causal explanations of types of phenomena and processes so that particular phenomena and processes can be explained.[45] However, this is only one of several understandings of theory prevalent in the social and human studies.

A second understanding sees theory as the process of concept formation through which phenomena and processes are brought into taxonomic and explanatory classifications and other linguistic devices such as analogies and metaphors. A third and related understanding sees theory as model-building, whereby ideal types, analogous descriptions, and sets of mathematical equations are devised for manipulating data and solving problems of interrelationships between sets of observations. These two understandings can be seen as subsidiary to the first idea of scientific theory mentioned in the previous paragraph, provided theory is seen in a realist rather than an instrumentalist sense.[46] In the classical period of social science in the late nineteenth and early twentieth centuries the task of social theory was seen as providing explanations of social relations, partly with a view to forming a basis for political action.

A fourth and quite different understanding of social theory has seen it as, in effect, imaginative, linguistic, rhetorical constructions of possible entities, episodes, or scenarios which are sometimes supposed to cast light upon a shadowy true reality that is never defined or directly studied. One form of this idea considers society to be a text that requires interpretation from some point of view, but there is no one truthful interpretation. The difference between such a hermeneutical and phenomenological theory and imaginative artistic productions seems minimal, as indeed some defenders of this approach have recognized.[47]

Some practitioners of so-called 'social theory' who engage solely in textual criticism produce what Pierre Bourdieu has called 'theoretical theory' and contrasted with 'scientific theory'. The latter, he said,

takes shape for and by empirical work and gains less by theoretical polemics than by confrontation with new objects. Consequently, to truly side with science means making a choice, a rather ascetic one, to devote more time and effort to the exercise of theoretical findings by applying them to new research projects rather than preparing them somehow for sale by dressing them in the trappings of a meta-discourse – destined less to verifying the thought than to publicizing its importance and value or to making its benefits immediately apparent by circulating it in the innumerable events that the jet age and the age of conferences provide for the narcissistic researcher . . .

To treat theory as a *modus operandi* which directs and organizes practically scientific practice, means obviously that one has given up the somewhat fetishistic accommodativeness that 'theoreticians' usually establish with it.[48]

Unfortunately, too much so-called 'social theory' is of this narcissistic kind, tracing the genealogy of concepts and elaborating their internal coherence but having no empirical reference except to other texts within the 'discourse'.

Some other forms of 'grand theory' (such as Marx's materialist theory of praxis and structural change, Durkheim's functionalist theory of religion, Parsons's functionalist theory of social evolution, Rostow's stages theory of economic growth, Olson's rationalist economic theory of the rise and decline of nations, Bendix's historical sociology of nation building, Elias's theory of social figurations, Touraine's sociology of action, and Mann's theory of social and state power)[49] are constructions of very general concepts and theories supposed to apply to all or many social structures and situations. But sometimes they are so general that it is not at all clear how they are supposed to explain particular cases. In fact, some of these theories are rightly seen as being rather models or concepts that are part of an explanatory framework, having very little empirical content or reference. Insofar as they are empirically referred and exemplified, as are those of Marx, Olson, Bendix, Bourdieu, Elias, Touraine, and Mann, for example, we can say that they are forms of scientific (or proto-scientific) theory. Some others, such as those of Parsons, Rostow, and Giddens, are closer in conception and value to the imaginative constructions of the 'theoretical theorists' scorned by Bourdieu. Of course it can be argued that the meta-theorizing of the Parsons/Giddens kind provides fruitful and powerful methodologies, hypotheses, and concepts for other researchers to employ. As far as they do, then the theorizing is valuable.

Summarizing the distinctions I have tried to make in this section, there are:

(a) *Philosophical problems*, which concern issues about existence and explanation – i.e. very general ontological and epistemological issues that remain tacit for most of the time and are only analysed by explicitly philosophical enquiry.

(b) *Methodological problems*, which are more concrete in that they concern the delineation of domains and the actual explanatory practices and forms of reasoning of particular sciences or disciplines. Methodological issues have a more general currency than philosophical ones, particularly in times of crisis.[50]

(c) *Scientific theories*, which are concepts, models, and statements of a general kind about the structural mechanisms, powers, and causal relationships between types, kinds, and classes of entities, events, and processes within a domain. Theories are used directly to explain particular events and processes. We should distinguish general theories, which attempt to encompass all the main structures, mechanisms, relationships and phenomena in a whole domain (e.g., general relativity, quantum thermodynamics, plate tectonics, Darwinian evolution, neo-classical economic equilibrium theory, historical materialist class theory, Freudian psychoanalysis) from theories of more particular events and processes. The latter are formulated employing general theories, concepts, and linguistic devices such as analogies, similes, and models, but they are evaluated by bringing them into direct confrontation with empirical evidence, a procedure that may force changes in both the theory and the organization, character, and meaning of the evidence.

Philosophies, methodologies, and general theories form the framework for formulating particular theories, research methods, and concrete explanations of a domain and are therefore somewhat remote from empirical questions. Whether the framework is explicit or largely tacit depends to some extent on the degree of advancement of the science and the degree of consensus among practitioners. Greater advancement usually means greater consensus, which usually leads to the framework remaining tacit. Methodological contention is sometimes a sign of immaturity. The evolution and survival of the framework is ultimately dependent in a general but indirect sense upon empirical explanatory adequacy and progress.

The bulk of the rest of this chapter is devoted to discussing the philosophical and methodological issues involved in explaining structural history. Employing some of the points I shall presently make and the important distinctions between philosophical, methodological, and theoretical ideas just discussed, I shall go on in chapter 2 to construct a critical survey of the existing approaches to writing social structural enquiry. Some of these approaches are based upon a distinct set of philosophical assumptions and methodological concepts, but others such as Marxism, behaviourism, functionalism, and neo-classicism are in fact just general theories and so do not or should not have the status of genuinely separate approaches. The philosophical and methodological foundations of approaches have to be articulated before their theories and explanations can be compared, therefore this book is not about theories as such, although I shall discuss aspects of the theory of historical materialism in chapter 5 because it has often been considered to provide a scientific approach to structural history. In chapter 3 I shall examine in more detail the work of some examples of a structurist approach to structural history, because I want to argue for its superiority.

THE CONCEPT OF SCIENTIFIC DOMAIN

In coming now to examine the methodological problems of contemporary structural historiography the problem of the framework of explanation must first be considered. This is because the structure of explanation is not confined to a supposedly fundamental logic of enquiry or a fundamental distinction between theory and observation, as many philosophers of explanation, including the logical empiricists from the 1930s to the 1950s, long believed. A simplistic version of this belief was very influential in economics and parts of economic history, sociology, and psychology, so that some practitioners were led to believe that only a nomological, deductive, reductionist, and abstract model of explanation was permissible for social enquiries that wished to be scientific and therefore genuinely explanatory.[51] The logical empiricists concentrated on articulating what they saw as the universal logic of discovery and/or confirmation in science. They held that science should have no metaphysical presuppositions, but there was a debate among them about the instrumental versus realist reference of theories of unobservables. Science, on the supposed model of physics, was thought to be quintessentially logical, objective, reductionist, and separate from other existing forms of so-called 'explanation', especially from the relativist and holist hermeneutics thought to be the method of humanistic enquiry. But starting with Weber early in the century, then Mannheim and Adorno in the thirties, Collingwood in the forties, Popper, Scriven, Hanson, Feyerabend, Quine, and especially Kuhn in the late fifties and early sixties, there has been ever since a welter of discussion about the intellectual, psychological, institutional, and sociological organization and interestedness of science and other forms of explanation. The rationality, logic, objectivity, coherence, validity, and separateness of the sciences have all been thrown into doubt by various relativist and realist arguments.

Perhaps the greatest advance in understanding the nature of explanation made in the post-positivist and post-Kuhnian era is the general realization that methodologies, theories, and explanations are related to each other via extra-logical, historically variable constellations variously described as 'background knowledge', 'traditions', 'paradigms', 'research programmes', 'fields', or 'domains'. We can call all of these 'framework concepts'. The major problem thrown up by this realization is the question of the relationship between frameworks and the objectivity and progress of knowledge. What are the connections between frameworks, research and explanatory activity, observational evidence, and reality? Must all the sciences have a similar form of reasoning that connects all these? Do the sciences have a superiority over other forms of explanation and understanding in the ways in which their frameworks relate to evidence and reality? Why do frameworks change? Are the sciences always objectively progressive in their discoveries?

Thomas Kuhn argued that sciences normally proceed in their research projects and activities within paradigm theories that provide the presuppositions for determining what is to be investigated, how, and the validity of the results. Paradigms are replaced in 'scientific revolutions', not because objectively better ones have been developed but because the old ones are subjectively thought to be adequate no longer. Sciences are demarcated from non-sciences by the existence of consensual paradigms. The rationality of science is relative to the paradigm and so is historically specific rather than universal. Paradigms, he said, are formed and changed as much by social and psychological influences as by cognitive value.[52]

Karl Popper's rationalist and realist response to Kuhn was to defend the idea of science being a rational and incremental enquiry aimed at making real discoveries through a trial and error process of hypothetico-deductive reasoning and objective empirical testing. The scientificity of a theory was to be judged by its falsifiability, which in turn was to be judged by its empirical power. Theories could be corroborated to a lesser or greater degree, thus allowing progress, but never proved absolutely true. But the ideal of truthful discovery operates, he believes, as a powerful regulator of practice. The value orientation of science is its truth-seeking goal, a goal that it can never ultimately attain.[53]

Building upon some of Popper's ideas, Imre Lakatos developed the concept of a research programme to describe the relationship between theories in a science. The research programme is a set of, first, methodological rules, background knowledge, and basic laws, none of which is subject to testing, and, second, new hypotheses and models, which draw upon the background knowledge and are retained if empirically corroborated. Increasing degrees of corroboration of successive theories show that a programme is progressive.[54] Both Popper and Lakatos, like the logical empiricists, saw a strict separation between internal (i.e., logical) and external (i.e., sociological) dimensions of scientific activity. This is not so, according to certain sociological, post-structuralist, and pragmatist critics of science such as Michel Foucault, Pierre Bourdieu, Paul Feyerabend, Richard Rorty, Barry Barnes, and David Bloor,[55] all of whom have questioned the idea of science as objective and incrementally progressive.

Michel Foucault rejected the notion that there could be progress in epistemology and knowledge and attempted to construct an archaeological analysis of intellectual and cultural systems of ordering the world – 'discursive formations' – which are discontinuous one with another. Each discursive formation has its own deep set of rules, concepts, and governing statements that make possible the subsequent development of definitions of objects, concepts, and discoveries. Each formation has to be examined for its complex structure and not from some meta-discursive standpoint. The attempt to write the overall history of discourses should be abandoned in favour of the genealogy of each discourse's concepts and an examination of the power structures within them.[56]

Pierre Bourdieu has analysed science as consisting of a series of fields of activity, each of which has a form of interest that is part socio-political and part intellectual. A scientific field is an objective space in which there is play of opposing forces struggling for scientific rewards. Neither a strictly epistemological, logical analysis of science nor an analysis of the social conditions of practice and knowledge alone can sufficiently grasp the content and power of a field. It is the field that assigns the function of the researcher, the choices of topics, methods, and so on. The goal of the scientist, according to Bourdieu, is to achieve recognition from competitor peers. However, in pursuing this social goal the scientist can also further the progress of the science itself.[57] There is a two-way relationship between internal and external determinations of scientific progress, which is made possible by the relationship between the scientific field and what he calls the 'habitus'. The habitus is the principle of a form of subjective, implicit, practical knowledge that is unconscious and not requiring consciousness, although it masters objective necessity, thus enabling social competence. 'The field, as a structured space, tends to structure the habitus, while the habitus tends to structure the perception of the field.'[58] By seeing the 'ontological complexity' of the two the subjective/objective dichotomy in explanation is overcome, in Bourdieu's account.

As all these arguments indicate, there are fundamental questions about the rationality, interestedness, power, and validity of the scientific enterprise and its products. Moreover, there is an increasing degree of consensus around the idea that, contra Kuhn, non-scientific discourses are like sciences in being characterized by paradigms as well. The question then becomes one of distinguishing scientific paradigms or frameworks from non-scientific ones. The great divide (if it is great) between the pre-modern, pre-scientific mode of cognition and the modern scientific mode has been explored extensively by anthropologists such as Lévi-Strauss, Bourdieu, Horton, and Gellner,[59] who have much more of significance to say about frameworks of knowledge than do ahistorical philosophers.

It is of course notorious that modern social enquiries have not been able to develop consensual paradigms in spite of many attempts by thinkers from Comte onwards to do so. Is this because of the recalcitrance and complexity of the subject-matter – people and their shifting social arrangements – or because of something lacking in the scientific mode of reasoning? Perhaps it is both. Is scientific reasoning incapable of grasping a subject-matter that is humanly historical? But of course, many of the sciences of nature also deal with historical systems. It seems that the problem has been methodological. Attempts to construct a scientific framework for social analysis have usually been on the level of logic rather than socio-anthropological and practical. What makes a scientific discourse scientific is not its logic but the combination of its rationality (of structure of reasoning), orientation to the world, and practical application. The recent arguments of Dudley Shapere, including his concept of 'scientific domain', provide an important but incomplete way, for reasons I shall try to indicate, of approaching these questions about scientific explanation. His arguments, especially about domains, provide assistance in trying to improve approaches to social structural history.[60]

Like Bourdieu, Shapere's fundamental argument is that there are no universal meta-epistemological or meta-logical criteria for judging good and bad explanations (or even what counts as an explanation) that are independent of the criteria established and employed by the advanced natural sciences. If we wish to understand the epistemological and methodological principles of scientific explanation we must carefully study the history and present practices of science itself. There can be no essentialist viewpoint of Kantian or logical empiricist or any other kind that is able to interpret and explain science independently of science according to some extraneous standard. All such standards, in Shapere's view, fail to grasp the actual reasoning employed by particular sciences. Thus the nature of scientific enquiry and the status of scientific explanations are empirical questions and the sciences differ from each other. Nevertheless, empirical research into the structure of discourses has revealed that the advanced sciences do have certain distinguishing features demarcating them from other forms of enquiry because, according to Shapere, the sciences have adopted in the twentieth century two fundamental principles: 'the Principle of the Rejection of Anticipation of Nature' and 'the Principle of Scientific Internalization' (as defined in the quotations on pp. xv–xvi above). Scientists seek and acquire knowledge which cannot be anticipated in advance. They do this through a process of building on those existing beliefs or knowledge which are free from reasons for doubt, so that all the beliefs of science become part of science itself and are not external, unquestioned assumptions.

For Shapere, rationality is the central feature of science: 'to count as a reason, a claim must be relevant to the subject-matter under consideration or debate. And thus the clear delineation of a subject-matter, and of the body of other claims relevant to that subject-matter, itself constitutes the development of a science based on reasons.'[61] These two features – a clearly delineated subject-matter and a body of other claims – he calls respectively 'domains' and 'background information'. In his view the formation of these features constitutes the development of the rationality of science.

The development of science thus consists in a gradual discovery, sharpening, and organization of relevance-relations, and thus in a gradual separation of the objects of its investigations and what is directly relevant thereto from what is irrelevant to those investigations: a gradual demarcation, that is, of the scientific from the non-scientific. Indeed, to the extent that an area of human activity manifests the sorts of developments I have been describing, to that extent the area is considered paradigmatically scientific. In other words, *this* is what we have come to *call* 'scientific'. In that development, science aims at becoming, as far as possible, autonomous, self-sufficient, in its organization, description, and treatment of its subject-matter – at becoming able to delineate its domains of investigation and the background information relevant thereto, to formulate its problems, to lay out methods of approaching those problems, to determine a range of possible solutions, and to establish criteria of what to count as an acceptable solution, *all in terms solely of the domain under consideration and the other successful and doubt-free beliefs which have been found to be relevant to that domain; that is, to make its reasoning in all respects wholly self-sufficient.*[62]

Shapere emphasizes that the idea of 'reasons' that he employs is independent of the specific character of reasons. Scientific rationality – the reasons science has for holding its beliefs to be good ones – has arisen through a complex process of observation of nature. But the character and meaning of observation is not a matter of passively recording sensory data. Observations are always interpreted within the context of the existing state of knowledge of a domain.[63]

Science thus develops through a give-and-take interaction between the methods with which it approaches nature and what it learns about nature, or at least claims to know on the basis of the best reasons it has available. Included in that interactive development are, as we have seen, the subject-matter, the problem-structure, the standards, and the goals of science: in all these aspects, science is subject to change. And it has learned to make those changes, wherever possible, in the light of reasons – reasons which, for us, consist of observations of nature ... The traditional doctrine of conceptualism was thus partly right: we do extract our concepts of nature through observation of nature. But we do not simply 'abstract' those concepts by perception and reflection thereon. Rather, learning through observation, we gradually forge concepts which reflect what we have found to be the case, or at least believe to be the case on the basis of the best reasons we have available; and then we seek to learn further about nature, and perhaps will be led to further revision of the concepts we have forged, and so on. Thus the present view may be termed 'Bootstrap Conceptualism'.[64]

The basic problem with Shapere's argument is that while he rightly wishes to avoid any use of given and unalterable meta-scientific standards of what constitutes scientific practice and the legitimacy of results, it is in danger of slipping into the relativism and scepticism that he wishes to avoid. If the internalization principle is taken to an extreme it could be seen as a position very similar to those of Foucault and Feyerabend and the pragmatists. In their case, what constitutes a reason for holding a belief about nature is not that it corresponds in any, however complicated, sense with the reality of nature but that it coheres with the concepts and untested beliefs of the framework or discourse.

If relativism and scepticism are to be avoided then some notion of realism and the truthfulness of correspondence seems to be necessary. Therefore the most important point to glean from Shapere's approach is the concept of domain, for with it we have a way of reconciling the rationality of science with realism. In the process of building a science, he says,

items of information come to be associated together as bodies of information having the following characteristics:
(1)   The association is based on some relationship between the items.
(2)   There is something problematic about the body so related.
(3)   The problem is an important one.
(4)   Science is 'ready' to deal with the problem.[65]

The association between the items is well grounded in domains so that the subject-matter is seen as unified mainly in terms of the compositional and evolutionary theories that pertain to it. Compositional problems require theories and explanations of the constituents of the individual entities or elements of the domain and the laws governing their behaviour and interactions, and evolutionary problems require theories and explanations of the development of the entities or elements.[66]

The process of domain constitution depends upon the dual processes of theoretical reasoning within scientific fields and gradual discovery of what Shapere calls relevance-relations among the objects and powers of the natural world. Those relevance-relations should be seen, I believe, as structural causal relations that are naturally delineated. Domain construction and development thus ultimately depend on the ways in which the world is discovered to be naturally structured, and discoveries are dependent upon appropriate methodologies and theories. The appropriateness can only be determined historically *ex post facto* and thus methodologies and theories are contingent. The methodology of the domain is dependent upon the subject-matter of the domain, for it must be appropriate for making compositional and evolutionary discoveries at the level of the particular subject-matter. But of course nature is not given in some simple, easily apprehensible form. Shapere is very right to draw attention to the inadequacies of common sense, and we should go further, for nature has been found to be completely counter-intuitive in its complexity. Therefore methodologies evolve under the impact of further discoveries of the complexities of nature and the subject-matter evolves under refinements, reappraisals, and reconstructions of the methodology. There is no external principle by which methodologies are appraised or improved. Revolutions in which the old methodology and form of understanding of the subject-matter are abandoned, do not seem to occur. But the constant interaction between methodology and subject-matter as the complexities of nature are further investigated leads to rearrangements and reconstructions within the domain. Incremental stages of long-term progress can be observed within sciences, with the occasional change of direction and unification of separate domains. New understanding and knowledge within science are able to incorporate and re-interpret older understanding and knowledge, so that contemporary theories and explanations can be seen as genetically related to earlier ones.[67]

If social structural historiography is to develop a distinct domain of enquiry it is by being delineated through the interaction of the relatively unified nature of its subject-matter with its methodology. For a domain to be said to exist a body of shared information has to be assembled about the composition and evolution of a class of entities so that the entities have relevance relations of a realistic character. The initial establishment of relevance relations is not a question of simple observation but a complex process of metaphorical, analogi-cal reasoning.[68] Therefore in order to be definable as such the domain must have a definable subject-matter that can become the object of a distinct kind of enquiry. 'Definable' here means 'capable of being rationally abstracted from the totality of which it is a part'. A rational abstraction is one that has some discovered or hypothesized foundation in reality and so is capable of being given an objective definition. In other words, there are good reasons, which can be shared by social scientists, for believing that the abstraction of social structures is based on features of concrete reality. If social structures have a form of existence that is relatively autonomous (or at least their reality can be studied as if it were relatively autonomous, that is, without the abstraction of structures from the social totality being too injurious to the totality) then they can be abstracted and studied as a domain of enquiry. All domains of enquiry are based upon such abstractions because the totality of all there is in the world is both a totality in the sense of being fundamentally systemically integrated but also being divided naturally into sub-systems and sub-structures. Dis-coveries of these more or less natural divisions have allowed and prompted the development of separate domains of enquiry. Of course the history of ideas shows that some abstractions on which domains or proto-domains have been based have been construed wrongly or, to put it more accurately, certain proto-domains can be incorporated, following further research and theorizing, into other domains. As I indicated earlier, this is a central feature of the history of the sciences – the tendency to reduce the number of domains by uniting them through the use of encompassing general concepts and theories that operate at a deeper and wider level. (I believe the supposed domain of ec-onomics can now be seen as in part falsely or at least too narrowly construed and should be included within the domain of social structural enquiry. Many economists themselves now believe this too.)

THE IMPORTANCE TO SOCIAL SCIENCE OF A POLICY OF REALISM

Philosophical debates over the reality or otherwise of the objects of enquiry are clearly crucial to establishing the nature of scientific enquiry and knowledge and therefore for generalizing from mature to immature sciences. As I just pointed out, Shapere's domain conception depends for its power on showing its congruence with realism. Philosophical realism is not quite the same as the social ontology of realism that I alluded to in figure 1.1 and the associated discussion, but they are closely related in that philosophical realism provides epistemological underpinning for the social doctrine.

Philosophical realism is the broad and much-debated doctrine, with many internal variants, which holds that knowledge is true or false (or perhaps plausible versus implausible) according to how the external world really is, independent of our ways of knowing.[69] One variant is metaphysical or ontological realism, which asserts that there is a fairly sharp division between, on one hand, our explanatory frameworks, theories, and observations, and, on the other, the external world independent of mind. It starts with the metaphysical presupposition of a certain form of real existence of external, ordered, discoverable, reality, which then becomes the dominant principle of explanation. Another variant – epistemological realism – starts with the methodological assumption that assertions about causation and reality have to be tested according to well established and seemingly successful procedures, which, over time, with the aid of a certain form of reasoning, have been found to furnish knowledge through discoveries about external reality. This is clearly a more plausible doctrine than ontological realism because of its grounding in the history of discovery rather than in an a priori assertion. Indeed, for the same general reason, epistemology has rightly come to dominate ontology as the core of philosophical argumentation. A third variant is transcendental realism, which regressively argues from the fact of successful science, as measured by ability to intervene in nature, to make a claim about the necessary reality of the structures and mechanisms of the world in order for science to be possible. Such a transcendental argument licenses, at least, a *policy* of realism as a commitment underlying judgements of the plausibility of theories.[70]

Philosophical realism contrasts with rationalism (including idealism), phenomenology, and instrumentalism, all of which deny in various ways that the explanatory task can be to make objective discoveries about an independent real world. They all want to view subject-matter as constituted in various ways through processes of belief, thought, and conceptualization, and not as existing real structures independent of mental processes. For rationalists, knowledge is the product of reason that determines and reflects upon experience. For phenomenologists, the world can only be discussed and understood from a particular viewpoint and when the viewpoint changes so do the phenomena. The process of observation, understanding, and concept formation is partly constitutive of that being understood. That is, the world is constituted as available for knowledge through language. For instrumentalists, the object of enquiry takes the form of data produced by a methodology or technique, and they do not purport to examine 'reality', which has no meaningful content for them.

In practice, philosophical realists have combined elements of metaphysics and epistemology. One thing that divides them is the question of wherein lies the essence of reality – in the ordered appearances of the world or in some hidden counter-intuitive structure of the world to which appearances are not a reliable guide? This is the basis for the division between empirical or common-sense realism and critical or scientific realism. Both say the universe is independently real, but the first says that our senses are a good guide to its nature whereas the second says its nature has to be discovered or inferred by science in spite of appearances.[71]

The pragmatic version of realism that draws on epistemological and transcendental presuppositions – policy realism – says that realism should be employed only as a broad policy that directs research rather than as a strong claim about reality and the truth or falsity of theories.[72] The status of theories is, in this approach, more complicated and negotiable than the simple bivalence of true/false. Plausibility rather than truth is the aim. This is mainly because all knowledge is dependent on its framework to some extent and so assertions about reality and causation always come from particular rather than universal standpoints. But unlike relativism, in policy realism it is accepted that frameworks do change and improve under the impact of discoveries about the world, thus confirming that the external world has power to modify the ways in which we understand it, just as our knowledge is able to be applied to intervene successfully in the structure and operation of parts of the world. One advantage of policy realism over more metaphysical versions is its accordance with the history of science, which reveals a series of jerky forward movements in the direction of greater and greater discoveries, as confirmed by the increasing power of engineering in open systems. No claim about absolute truth is necessary to such a policy. All knowledge is provisional but some is more confirmed, plausible, and reliable than others.[73]

A policy of sociological realism presupposes that society and culture are independently real entities that are neither artifacts of the theorist's or actor's creation nor reducible to characteristics of individuals or patterns of individual behaviour. Although social structures and cultures cannot be sensed they are deemed to exist in virtue of their causal powers to influence the behaviour, beliefs, and understandings of persons, and they are knowable through the behaviour, products, and utterances of persons. But just what forms the social and cultural realities are thought to take is a matter for conceptualization, theory and research.

Sociological realism is not synonymous with sociological holism, although this mistaken equation has often been made in spite of cogent arguments that have been presented against it.[74] Holism is only one of two broad realist conceptions of society. A holist conception defines society as a self-contained and virtually autonomous unitary entity, sometimes endowing it with a spirit or quasi-mind of its own, which exists through the thought and actions of people within it. But society can also be defined as a looser, less integrated structure of rules, roles, and relations, all of which exist apart from the particular people who employ or occupy them, and which has a dialectical and changing, rather than strictly determining, relationship with human thought and behaviour. Nevertheless, it is still real, although its reality is less autonomous than that of a holistic system. I shall try to show later that the decisive advantage of a structurist conception[75] of social reality is that it enables the development of a plausible scientific theory of the origins and dynamics of social structures out of the historical intercausal relationships between society and human thought and action. Figure 1.2 attempts to sum up the inter-connections of all these concepts.

Excellent philosophical support for a realist conception of society can be found in Maurice Mandelbaum's *Purpose and Necessity in Social Theory*. He shows how the dichotomies of individualism/holism, purpose/necessity, and chance/choice, have to be transcended in order for there to be a social science. All of these concepts are necessary to social, psychological, and historical explanation and, as many other structurists have argued, their combination precludes the use of ahistorical theory based on rationalist rather than empirical reasoning. Mandelbaum's invaluable contribution to the question of establishing the parameters of the domain of the science of structural history will be discussed in detail in chapter 4.

EVENTS, ACTIONS, AND STRUCTURES: ON THE METAPHYSICS OF
THE SOCIAL WORLD

I contend, given the foregoing realist epistemological argument, that in order to establish the validity of the domain of structural history there has to be established the validity of employing a general conception of social structures as being non-phenomenally real and a conception of events (including actions) and structures as constituting a symbiotic duality rather than a dichotomy. The difference between dualist and dichotomous sociological conceptions is that in the former individuals and society are both relatively autonomous, with their own irreducible powers yet inseparably linked, whereas in the latter they are opposites and almost mutually exclusive in their designated powers in that the autonomous reality of one excludes the autonomy of the other. Social realism and a dualist conception of events, actions, and structures should imply each other.

This is an argument about social metaphysics, the resolution of which is fundamental to methodological debates. But, as I have pointed out, a realist onto-logical position that is counter to empiricism, idealism, and phenomenology

Figure 1.2 Basic types of social methodologies and theories

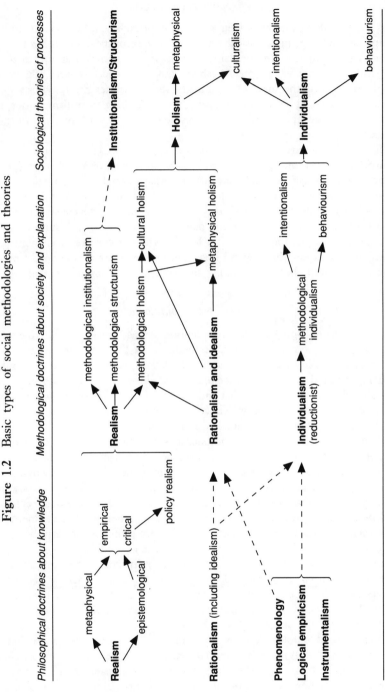

was arrived at only after a long process of proto-scientific and scientific activity, so that the metaphysical argument is a reconstruction of results made possible by inductively generalizing from a process of research and theorizing. (I shall say more in chapter 4 about this difference between the process of discovery and the logic of arguments about abstract metaphysics.) Nevertheless, all ongoing social enquiry, whether subscribing to realism or not, must employ some general ontological notion about the fundamental nature of the object.

Is social structure merely a statistical aggregation of singular events and individual persons and their actions, that is, an artifact of a technique (perhaps expressed as an instrumental concept) or perhaps merely a taxonomic category, having no intrinsic properties and powers of its own? Or does it have irreducible properties and powers? If so, are they such as to constitute it either as a holistic closed system with the power to control its own history and effect changes in other entities? Or is it a less integrated structure of elements, relations, and processes that depend upon persons for their production, reproduction, and history, but that causally influence the actions of agential persons?

Basic social ontologies

An individualist ontology directs attention almost solely to the role of the nature, powers, and behaviour of individuals. In this ontology, society is not something extra-individual in the sense of relations, rules, shared understandings, and meanings that are not reducible to individuals. Society, rather, is either a set of observable positions that individuals create and occupy, such as work positions and family roles, which cease to exist when not occupied, or it is just a pattern of individual actions and events.[76]

A holist ontology emphasizes autonomous structural existence and evolution. Society, in this account, is supposed to be a supra-individual organic entity or organization of rules, relations, and/or meanings, the sum total of which has properties and powers greater than its parts, particularly the powers to maintain and reproduce itself through dominating the choices and actions of individual people within it. The various kinds of holism all rest on the idea that society or culture or economy or nation are somehow objectively existing, external entities, which can be conceptualized and studied as though they are more or less unchanging things. The role of individuals here is as the passive carriers of collectively generated social forces. Change somehow mysteriously comes from the social whole and is implemented by individuals. This ontology is the least coherent of the three because it cannot generate a viable account of the genesis and history of structures.[77]

A structurist ontology directs attention to the structuring interactions between (on one hand) individual and collective human beliefs, intentions, choices, and actions and (on the other) the externally real enabling and constraining structural conditions of thought and action. In this model *social structures are the emergent ensemble of rules, roles, relations, and meanings* that people are born into and which organize and are reproduced and transformed by their thought and action. It is people who generate structures over time and initiate change, not the society itself, but their generative activity and initiative are socially constrained. This ontology denies the legitimacy of the action/society polarity that the others are based on and attempts to conceptualize action and society as being an interpenetrating duality in the sense advocated by Jean Piaget and Anthony Giddens. There is a duality of causal power in this model, with humans having structuring power and structures having enabling and constraining power.[78]

The tacit or deliberate adoption of one or other of these ontologies tends to determine the concepts of society and action and the general methodology for examining structural history that are adopted. This is not to say that general ontological concepts are always prior to concepts of social structure and action and to methodologies. All of these are usually closely related and should reinforce each other conceptually. Together they afford the construction of substantive theories but are not themselves theories, strictly speaking. Theories are general, putative, causal explanations that are in need of testing and confirmation in particular instances and may never reach the stage of being well confirmed. Theories are constructed using general concepts, models, and previously well-confirmed knowledge in order to try to deal with a domain of subject-matter that has certain problems about structure, causation, and evolution.

General sociological concepts – the macro-micro problem

The relationship between the macro (structure) and micro (action) levels of society is perhaps the fundamental problem for social theory.[79] Dichotomous approaches to concept formation emphasize the primacy of either the macro or the micro over the other, that is, one or other pole is seen as the site of crucial determination. Micro determination is generally synonymous with individualist conceptions of social phenomena. These have a long history in social enquiries, going back at least to Hobbes,[80] and now take several forms in sociology, economics, and history. Perhaps the most prominent and important are rational action, behaviourist, and exchange theories, all of which are closely related to each other.[81] Being individualist, they emphasize instrumental individual rationality and purposive behaviour. People are conceived as more or less autonomous individuals and the imperatives to action are sought largely within the natures, dispositions, consciousness, and decisions of people. Social structure, insofar as it exists, is conceived as the phenomenal outcome of large numbers of individual interactions and takes the form of collective patterns of observable behaviour. Social events are conceived as collective behavioural phenomena. Structure is ontologically dependent on rather than prior to action. This kind of conceptual scheme underlies neo-classical economics and is well articulated in the work of James Coleman, who has developed, refined, and applied it over a thirty-year period.[82]

Holist concepts of actions, events, and society start from the pole opposite from individualism, that is, from the pole of the social whole. Here society, or social reality, or the social totality, is conceived as an integrated unity with temporal, geographic, and cultural cohesion and integration. Humans have no individual autonomy or identity apart from that bestowed on them by the whole. Thus people are the personifications or the carriers of categories such as 'nation', 'race', 'class', and so on. Holist conceptions have taken many forms in social and historical theory, ranging through functionalist social-systems theory, structuralism, and phenomenological conceptions of the social life-world. In all these cases, the totality constitutes, motivates, and/or gives meaning to individual and collective action.

Dualist or structurist conceptions of the social realm have been developed as conscious attempts to transcend the older, polarized, individualist and holist traditions. These conceptions have an ancestry going back over a hundred years and in recent years there have been several new and extended articulations of them. Three of the most important conceptions are those of structurationism, networks, and figurations. All of these conceptual schemes focus on the decentred person as the agent of reproduction and transformation of pre-existing social institutions that in turn structure semi-autonomous action and consciousness.

The event/structure duality (rather than dichotomy) and the dynamic structuring process mutually implied by it form the necessary structurist ontological basis for the *history* of social structures fundamentally because this general conception has a central role for a causal agent within a structured, irreducible but evolving social context. This will be discussed extensively in chapter 3.

THREE ALTERNATIVE METHODOLOGIES FOR STRUCTURAL EXPLANATION

Unfortunately, what should be an event/structure duality has long and pervasively been considered a dichotomy. By emphasizing either the decisions and activities of persons or the determining powers of social entities the social studies have given rise to two main competing explanatory methodologies – individualism and holism. While these are not necessarily consciously or coherently adopted they can still be found strongly influencing the explanations of many or most practitioners in the socio-historical sciences.[83] Fortunately, there is a third possibility – structurism – which attempts to transcend this dichotomy.

Pulling together the foregoing discussion of ontologies and general concepts we can articulate the following methodologies.

Methodological individualism attempts to explain social phenomena and processes, behaviour, and consciousness by reference to individual motivations and actions, that is, it attempts to explain what are conceptualized as macroscopic

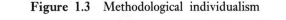

Figure 1.3 Methodological individualism

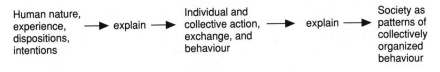

Figure 1.4 Methodological holism

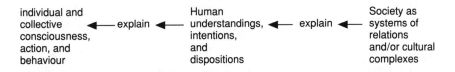

phenomena and entities by attributing their causation and even existence to their microscopic components (see figure 1.3). This does not necessarily rule out the existence of the macroscopic *per se* but it does deny it any inherent causal power on its own level, thus calling its ontological status into question. Reductive explanation is not necessarily reductive ontologically but it at least points in that direction. Reductive explanations are common in the physical sciences but even there they are far from universally applicable. Many macroscopic physical systems can only be explained *as systems* and the behaviour of their components can only be explained as parts of systems. This is even more the case in the biological and ecological sciences. The fundamental barrier to successful attempts at reductive explanation, which is also evident in the social studies, is the irreducibility of certain macroscopic systems with emergent properties and powers.

The opposite to individualism is methodological holism, which attempts to explain structures, behaviour, consciousness, and social change by reference to holistic categories such as 'social system', 'epoch', 'culture', 'nation', 'race', 'class', and even 'the spirit of the age'. The supposed entities referred to by these categories are assigned causal powers of their own, whether exercised pervasively through the consciousness of the actors who supposedly embody them or through some functional, teleological feedback relation upon action. Methodological holism is not ontologically reductive, for it recognizes the discrete existence of both wholes and parts, unlike methodological individualism, but its explanations do not go in both directions. The micro is seen as causally dependent (see figure 1.4).

Being methodologies, however, neither individualism nor holism is necessarily committed to a corresponding social ontology and set of concepts. Nevertheless, there is usually an implicit ontological assumption in each methodology. Methodological individualism usually implies sociological individualism, in the sense

Figure 1.5 Methodological structurism

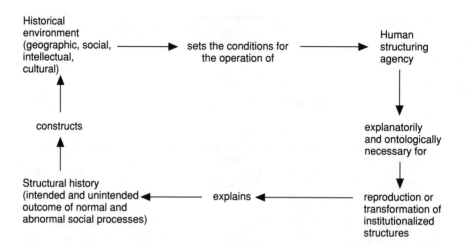

that social entities and processes are reducible to the individual people, events, and actions that supposedly constitute them; and methodological holism implies sociological holism, in the sense that social wholes have some form of real existence independent of individual people and events. Individualist methodology tends to overemphasize human autonomy and event distinctiveness while holism tends wrongly to impute autonomous power to social entities. Individualism does provide a coherent way of approaching the genesis and transformation of society, but its implied concept of society is impoverished. Holism cannot provide a coherent approach to social change because there is no place for an agent.

A third alternative says that social and behavioural explanations both have to be approached from the dual perspectives of action and structure. Methodological structurism approaches explanation by developing concepts of the separate real existence yet mutual interdependence of individuals and institutional structures (see figure 1.5). Structures *qua* structures have structural properties such that those properties are not merely the aggregate of the powers and behaviour of the individual people who are supposed to constitute them. On the other hand, those structural properties are not independent of the structuring practices of people. Thus methodological structurism is explicitly based on an ontology of the social that recognizes two nodes of causal power. However, the kinds of causal power that persons and structures exhibit are different, as we saw in the previous section. Persons have agential power, structures have conditioning power. The conception of persons as agents is the fundamental difference between this methodology and the other two.

The term 'methodological structurism' is not widely employed but the more common term 'institutionalist approach' seems to mean almost the same thing.[84] In fact there have been earlier intimations and versions of structurism going back more than a century.

This grid of ontologies and methodologies can be summarized, as in table 1.1.

Table 1.1 Methodologies[85]

	Ontology	Methodology
Individualism	Only individual events and people and their actions and beliefs are real. Society is an aggregate of individuals. The term 'society' is only instrumental.	Aggregative – builds up an analysis of society by studying individuals and their motivations for action.
Holism	Society is a closed, supra-individual system with powers of self-regulation. It dominates individuals who receive their life-courses and beliefs from the whole, which acts through them.	Conceptualizes and studies the whole as a totality that structures everything within it. Searches for the internal determining mechanisms and/or essential meaning of structural evolution.
Structurism	Society is a real structure of rules, roles, relations and meanings that has to be produced, reproduced, and transformed by individuals while causally conditioning individual actions, beliefs, and intentions.	Conceptualizes and studies the structuring process over time by examining the causal interactions of individuals, groups, classes, and their structuring social conditions, beliefs, and intentions.

EVENT HISTORY AND STRUCTURAL HISTORY

If economies and societies can be understood as dynamic, non-phenomenal yet real structures then all those who study the history of economies and societies (defined in a wide sense to include families, firms, markets, communities, political systems, and mentalities) are, *ipso facto*, social structural historians. If social structures are not being directly studied then this label should not be used. If the objects of enquiry are primarily events, actions, and/or the behaviour of groups, then that is not social structural history in the proper sense of the term but event history. However, structures and events are not somehow ontologically separate things, a mistake that tends to be made by some structuralist historians and sociologists. The basic problem is to try to establish the ontological relationship between structures and the phenomena of the social world. Each is completely dependent on the other but it is possible to construct a social methodology that emphasizes one or the other for explanatory purposes. Structures have a superhuman, non-phenomenal existence through time, even for centuries, and they are the context and object of events, actions, behaviour, and thought. Structures can be conceived as the systems of social rules, roles, relations, and symbols in which events, actions, and thought occur and lives are lived. But structures have to be reproduced continually in thought and through action and cannot exist apart from collective thought and behaviour. The division of labour in their study should be within a methodological structurist explanatory framework that emphasizes the symbiotic duality of event/structure rather than a dichotomy.

This argument about structures and events entails that 'historical sociology', 'societal history', 'social history', and 'structural history' should all be alternative names for the same discourse, whereas 'action and event history', even if it is mistakenly called 'social history', is distinct from but dependent upon structural history for its explanations, just as the converse is true. At times it seems that most historians and most kinds of history writing are now claiming to be 'social' because it is fashionable to be so. But mere labels and rhetoric are not sufficient. 'History from the bottom up' is intrinsically no more 'social' than 'history from the top down'.

If the study of social history is to be seen as having a distinct object of enquiry, as many of its supporters have strongly advocated, then that object must be the history of society as a definite real, continuous, structural entity. Some so-called 'economic' and 'social' historians, however, do not in practice study economies and societies as real structures and so do not rightly fall into this category. And some political, cultural, and intellectual historians are in fact primarily studying structural change, so they too should rightly be seen as structural historians. Indeed, political and cultural structures should be included. The analytical division should not be between the economy, society, and class structure, on one hand, and politics, ideas, beliefs, psyches, and so on, on the other. There should not be a material/mental methodological division, but rather a structure/event heuristic division. The material, social, and mental are all structured. Events and actions of all kinds are motivated, impelled, channelled, and organized by structures, partly towards reproducing and transforming them. If social history is to have an object of enquiry and methodology distinct from the traditional history of events and actions it has to be possible both to study structures relatively separately from the actions and events that they determine, and which in turn determine their history, and to study events and actions in new, untraditional, theoretically informed ways.

I emphasize that I am arguing against the complete collapse of all the socio-

Figure 1.6 The field of the social studies

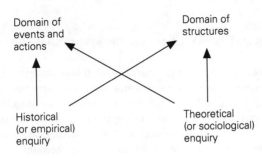

historical studies into each other. There needs to be a rational division of labour between the domains of event history and structural history within the single broad field of socio-historical enquiry. In other words, there is a sound basis for some separation between branches of the field, but the existing dichotomies of history/theory and past/present are not soundly based, and the separations should not be dichotomous.[86] These distinctions that I am advocating are ultimately based on the realist argument about the ontological status of events, thoughts, and structures, and the possibility of a correspondence truth relation between theory and evidence. I shall develop this philosophical argument in detail later.

These considerations lead to a summary description of the connections between all the socio-historical studies, which sees the broad field as consisting of four interrelated quadrants or branches, as in figure 1.6. This shows that there are two domains of enquiry delineated by the fundamental ontology of the social world. The establishment of this ontology is the outcome of two hundred years of enquiries. Those enquiries have been of two basic kinds, historical and theoretical.

A rational division of labour in the social studies would see enquiries concentrating on one or more of theoretical (i.e., sociological) or empirical (i.e., historical) enquiries into events or structures without ever losing sight of the influence of the others and seeing each enquiry as contributing to the overall understanding of a total historical social process. The best social scientists, such as Clifford Geertz, Barrington Moore, Emmanuel Le Roy Ladurie, Alain Touraine, Charles Tilly, Allan Pred, Ernest Gellner, and others, combine in their work the perspectives of all four quadrants. In that case we should call them social scientists, rather than any of the more particular labels of historian, sociologist, historical sociologist, anthropologist, or social theorist. Indeed, they usually reject such labels. But even in their work it is possible to identify analytically the four quadrants as separate kinds of analysis. In fact this identification is possible in the work of a great many historians and sociologists, but some of the quadrants are often poorly developed in their work. The rich development of all four makes the work of the social scientists mentioned compelling and powerful.

Having now discussed at a very general level the philosophical parameters of the putative or proto-domain of structural history I turn now to a considera- tion of some of the problems that are at issue in constructing explanatory accounts in structural history. Some of these problems arise because of the as yet vague state of the philosophical and methodological framework of the domain and others are inherent in all explanatory accounts.

Causal explanation

Some historians have been ambivalent about whether establishing causation is their aim and there is a glaring lack of agreement about what the establishment of causation involves. This ambivalence and confusion spring ultimately from a lack of agreement among philosophers about the nature of causal explanation and the relationship between generalization and particular cases. However, as I have argued, there is a growing current in the philosophy of explanation that rejects the characterization of scientific inference as conforming to the canons of deductive logic and attempts instead to develop more complex and em- pirically grounded accounts of the logic of causal explanation in different sciences. Scientific explanation, it is now argued, employs a complex structure of theoretical hypotheses, empirical generalizations, particular descriptions, analogies, metaphors, and models. It makes intuitive leaps and unsupported assertions. (These points will be developed further in chapters 4 and 6.)

The point here is that the interrelationship of hypotheses, analogies, models, general theories, and so on, to evidence is a central methodological problem for the causal explanation of structural history, as in any form of empirical enquiry. If causal explanation is not thought to be the goal, then the problem of giving a convincing account of an alternative goal is seemingly insurmount- able. It is difficult if not impossible to see what another goal could be because however the commencement of empirical enquiry is justified (as by a desire for 'understanding') it must boil down to a desire to answer questions of 'why' and 'how' as well as 'what' and 'when'. The understanding of what and when cannot be divorced from temporal and structural relationships of a causal kind. So-called 'hermeneutical understanding' and 'interpretive description' should be seen as incomplete forms of the complex form of causal explanation just mentioned. If they simply provide chronologies then perhaps they do not explain, but this is rarely if ever the case. Even supposed non-explanatory descriptions in fact involve some explanatory element, so it is not a choice between explanation or understanding or description. These are all parts of one enquiry. The problem is to try to penetrate to the causal relations between the moments of complex social structures in order to make a judgement of the relative strength of these relations. This involves a process of theoretically informed and organized empirical research. Construction of the problems and objects for enquiry takes place within theories, which are within domains, but theories must be responsive to empirical findings that they help to uncover and interpret. As Max Weber pointed out long ago (but it has been ignored too often),

the formulation of propositions about historical causal connections not only makes use of both types of abstraction, namely, isolation and generalization; it shows also the simplest historical judgment concerning the historical 'significance' of a 'concrete' fact is far removed from being a simple registration of something 'found' in an already finished form. The simplest historical judgment represents not only a categorically formed intellectual construct but it also does not acquire a valid content until we bring to the 'given' reality the whole body of our 'nomological' empirical knowledge.[87]

Conceptual and theoretical thoroughness

Ideally, causal explanations should not leave loose, unexplained ends. A basic working assumption should be that all phenomena and aspects of society are loosely interrelated and so in principle explainable by one general explanatory structure of theory and analysis. This means that in order for sociologists and historians adequately to explain any of the 'moments' and 'levels' of social totalities – actions, utterances, events, productions, behavioural patterns, cultures, structures, and so on, and changes in patterns, cultures, and structures – they first need concepts and theories of all these and of how they relate causally to each other in very general terms.[88] However, that is not to say much, because even when such concepts are present it is the content of the concepts and theories that is obviously crucial. For example, we can see that the behavioural approaches of James Coleman and George Homans, which are forms of individualist theory, and the structural functionalism of Talcott Parsons, which is a form of holism, all offer, in different senses, a complete approach to social and historical explanation, in that they have theories and explanations of all these aspects. But, in my view, their conceptualization and theorization are inadequate to the complexity of society.

Conceptual and theoretical adequacy

Conceptualization and theorization must be adequate to their objects. That is, all the 'moments' and 'levels' of a particular totality must be treated as causally efficacious. It is here that individualism and holism are fundamentally flawed by their explanatory concentration on one or other component of the structuring process. One or other of the components of individuals or structures remains causally passive or, even worse, epiphenomenal. Behaviourism attempts to explain social phenomena solely by reference to the motivations of individual behaviour, while structural functionalism, although purporting to be an action theory, in effect explains action solely by reference to its supposed functional relation to a holistic social system.

Against these, structurism tries to tie the micro and macro levels of social analysis together, without subordinating either to the other, by giving an account of how human personality, intentions, and actions interact with culture and structure causally to determine each other and social transformations over time. In order to do this it is essential that there be a model of humans as social agents. Agential persons have innate causal powers to affect intentionally and unintentionally their own actions and bring about changes in the world. This conception thus leaves no epiphenomenal danglers while incorporating all aspects into the explanation. Individualism and holism have impoverished conceptions of persons. (I shall say more about agency in chapter 3.)

Subjectivism versus objectivism

There is no doubt that social enquiry has a subjective element in that we partly rely upon the verbal and written statements of actors for our knowledge of society, and social enquirers cannot divorce themselves from society to the same degree that natural scientists are external to their subject-matter. Society is to a degree phenomenologically constituted by both actors and observers. What this means is that our subjective point of view of society affects the way we and others act and our actions in turn help to constitute the way society is. Because society is far from being absolutely objective in its existence there is a constant interaction between our socially constituting thought and actions and the pre-existing social structure. Nevertheless, social scientists are not natives of the societies they are studying, except in their own local communities and institutions, and so they can and must have a degree of detachment. The distinction between observer and native is always present, for no matter how much we try we cannot become completely native of that which we are not, so the possibility of an entirely empathetic understanding is ruled out. Social explanation cannot be a matter of getting inside the natives' skins and telling it as they see it, but rather it is a matter of enquiring into the natives' points of view as well as examining the structures in which they live, of which they may in any case have a very imperfect and distorted understanding.

The difference between natural and social reality has been seen as crucial by the advocates of the necessity of subjective interpretation since Vico at least. Society requires, these people argue, a subjective and phenomenological approach. On the other hand, the objectivity of society has been emphasized by several theoretical schools, including positivism, structural functionalism, Marxism, and Francophone structuralism. The task, as many historians and sociologists now realize, is to try to reconcile and transcend this age-old polarity

of objective structural determination and human subjective and socially constitutive action that structures the world within existing structural limits. As
Abrams and others have pointed out,[89] there are now valuable attempts being
made to overcome this polarity.

The presentation of historical accounts and arguments

We must distinguish, as Karl Marx and Max Weber did, between the rhetorical or artistic presentation of results and the logical structure of enquiry.[90]
The structure of socio-historical analyses is no different in essence from that
of other sciences but the presentation is usually different because of the role
played by storytelling or narrative. A false dichotomy is sometimes drawn (as
Lawrence Stone did) between narrative and analytical, statistical (sometimes
misleadingly called 'scientific') presentations of histories.[91] Both always have
a part to play, their roles depending upon the task in hand. Narratives are
more or less putative and incomplete causal accounts of a colligatory kind
and statistical accounts are incomplete, structural, causal explanations. Both
are analytical as well as descriptive to varying degrees. In fact, narrative seems
to be unavoidable for all historians because of the temporal dimension of
historiography. Events and actions follow events and actions in a continuous
jerky flow of time that takes place within a gradually evolving structural
context that enables them to happen. None of the *Annales* structuralists and
not even the economic cliometricians entirely eschew narrative in the way that
Stone seemed to believe. A glance at their work shows this and, as it also
shows, description is unavoidable. Perhaps some descriptivists do manage to
avoid giving causal analyses, in which case they are offering only chronologies
or shallow journalism. But even the shallowest of journalistic reporting implies
some explanatory causal sequence. The examples of early narrative that Stone
cites, such as Thucydides, Gibbon, and Macaulay, and biographies, all contain
putative or elliptical causal analyses. Moreover, the 'revival of narrative' insofar
as it exists is not a return to simple narrative, as Hobsbawm and Abrams
pointed out,[92] but contains an increased awareness of the epistemological scope
of narrative by combining explanatory colligation with theoretical explanation.
Philosophers of history have long discussed this question and many have
shown convincingly how narrative can be explanatory.[93]

The problem for historians in this regard, as many of them now recognize,
is how to combine structural analyses (employing theories, statistical data, and
qualitative evidence) with narrative presentations. Structural historians cannot
avoid examining aggregate patterns of events, actions, and utterances of all
kinds, because it is only through them that structures of rules, roles, relations,
and meanings become available for analysis. The task is not to reject *histoire
événementielle*, as some *Annalistes* have advocated (but not practised), but first
to grasp the ontological relationship between structures and events. Neither is
reducible to the other but neither can exist without the other. Structures

eventuate in events and are reproduced and transformed through events. So the presentation of structural history must take a partly narrative form and in fact always does so. Lawrence Stone's own work contains good examples of this.[94]

The role of comparison

If socio-historical explanation requires a complex web of different kinds of inference between analytical constructs and empirical evidence then there should be a central role for comparison of cases. Comparison is central to all the macro historical sciences – including cosmology, geology, biology, ecology, geography, anthropology, and sociology – where the subjects of study are complex, highly differentiated, and evolving structures that share features as well as having unique aspects. In these sciences every structure has to be compared either with ideal, typical classificatory categories and models or directly with other cases in order to be comprehended. Comparison can be all-encompassing, multiple, or just between pairs. There has to be a comparison between cases, categories, and models in order to arrive at an adequate explanation of any case. Comparisons can draw upon analogies, similes, and even metaphors, as well as simple descriptions. No two cases are exactly alike and no case exactly fits a model, so any attempt to explain deductively from a general law or principle is bound to be misleading. Nevertheless, general concepts, categories, hypotheses, analogies, and models are still necessary in all these sciences in order to think about, classify, and compare structures and kinds of entities and thus to begin to explain structures, functions, and history.[95]

THE RELATIONSHIP OF STRUCTURIST METHODOLOGY TO STRUCTURIST THEORY

A methodological doctrine does not logically have to imply or entail a socio-logical theory, but in practice there is a close coherence between the two levels of concepts. Methodological individualism usually mutually implies sociological individualism in the sense of a general theory of society consisting fundamentally or only of individual people whose behaviour is impelled by internal causes of an intentional and/or psychological kind. Methodological holism usually mutually implies a general theory that society is determinate on some macro level and within which people have little or no autonomy. Neither methodological doctrine would cohere easily, if at all, with the opposite social theory, but methodological individualism would not necessarily rule out a form of sociological structurism. This seems to be the argument of Jon Elster.[96]

　　Methodological structurism mutually implies the general theory of sociological structurism. As I indicated previously, with some examples, this type of theory rejects the poles of individualism and holism as concepts of social reality and the social process. For structurist theorists, society exists in a dual sense as agential people and the institutional structures that constrain people, which are the products of people collectively. In other words, this is a general theory that is resolutely historical in that it refers to the dialectical process in which the structure of society's institutionalized system of rules, roles, and relations is produced, reproduced, and transformed through human thought and action, which over time it enables and constrains. Society is both a structure and a historical structuring process of structurally oriented (rather than individually oriented) action.

Thus, without a structurist theory of society and action there is no proper place for history and without history there is no genuine sociological explanation. There can be many particular forms of the general theory of sociological structurism, depending on the explanatory tasks and objects for which they are required. However, there is a lack so far of well confirmed basic or pure theoretical propositions about the powers, causal relations, and history of the entities of the domain of structural history. Neo-classical economics does have some interesting basic propositions but they often seem of little use to structural historians because of their abstractness, concern with behaviour rather than structures, and ahistorical character. On the other hand, institutionalist economics has been a rich source of appropriate general historical hypotheses, found, for example, in the work of Karl Marx, Max Weber, C. P. Kindleberger, Douglass North, Mancur Olson, and others. Some historical sociologists and social anthropologists, such as Weber, Ernest Gellner, Michael Mann, J. A. Hall, Clifford Geertz, Benjamin Nelson, Barrington Moore (to name but a few) have attempted to establish basic theoretical propositions but none has been well confirmed. At the moment theoretical pluralism reigns and is seen by many structural historians, sociologists, anthropologists, and a few economists, as a virtue, even a necessity.[97]

TOWARDS A SCIENTIFIC DOMAIN FOR STRUCTURAL HISTORY

In the context of this wide range of metaphysical, methodological, and theoretical issues an outline of a putative domain framework for social structural history can now begin to be constructed. The first task in establishing the specifications of the domain is to establish a broad conception of the domain entities, that is, historical social structures. It is contended here that this involves, among other things, showing the validity of including both economic and social history as correctly construed. The study of economic and social history should be one domain of enquiry fundamentally because economies and societies are not separate kinds of entities but are the same sorts of relational structures. Thus, the concepts of 'economy' and 'society' should be considered merely as definitions of parts of the same broad subject-matter rather than descriptions of substantive natural differences in the entities and structures being dealt with. Can these alternatives indeed be transcended or perhaps synthesized to create a unified domain?

The fundamental questions about the domain's entities concern

(a) composition:
- the nature of economic and social (or socio-economic) structures;
- the relationship of structures to actions, events, and consciousness;
- the degree of autonomy of structures from patterns of events and from conscious understandings;

(b) evolution:
- the diachronic and synchronic powers and tendencies of structures;
- the agents of structural history;
- the real history of structural evolution.

Good answers to these questions can really be developed only through empirical research and theory-building, but all research can be conducted only within a framework of concepts and methodology. The relationship of a domain's specifying concepts and methodology to empirical enquiry is obviously crucial. As I have indicated, establishing a coherent and consensual domain framework is the result of a long process of empirical enquiry, theory-building, and concept formation. The process of discovery of the nature of structures, action, and historical processes cannot be the same as the deductive argument that reconstructs the logical relationship between the domain framework, theories, and empirical findings, once the process of their establishment has occurred.

A coherent and consensual domain framework and a well-confirmed general theory of structural history have not yet been established, but answers to the fundamental questions should take into account the following general considerations.

The nature and interrelationship of societies and economies

There are many schools of thought about the fundamental natures of and connections between societies and economies. I have already mentioned the theoretical diversity with regard to social structure, which has been conceived in many individualist, holist, and structurist ways. In economics, the dominant neo-classical tradition has conceived of the economy primarily as an autonomous realm of choices, action, and behaviour. Such a conception has led economists to try to model and/or explain the phenomena of production, distribution, exchange, and consumption as if they were organized patterns of individual and collective decisions, actions, and behaviour in which transactions or exchanges occur between rational sovereign individuals and groups in order to try to maximize the satisfaction of material desires. In the tradition of classical liberalism, people are theorized as freely moving monads, devoid of institutional, social, ideological, or cultural prior determination. As such, being based on a form of methodological individualism, neo-classicalism suffers from the attendant problems of such an approach. In particular, the major problems have been how to account for the aggregate socio-behavioural pattern by reference almost exclusively to individual choices (and a narrow range of those) and how to account for structural change. Individualism has adopted theoretical assumptions of rationalist and behaviourist psychological postulates and so directed its empirical attention to series of data about patterned behaviour and collective phenomena. The deductivist and instrumentalist epistemology that underlies this methodological individualism was derived from 1950s logical positivism and, in keeping with the tenor of that era in most disciplines, drove out any realist structural alternative. Theories are constructed as abstract, formal, mathematical models, which are often not intended to be descriptive or analytical of the real economy.[98] The power of unobservable but real structures of institutional relations or intellectual and cultural complexes, the complexities of human choice, decision-making, agency, and social relations, and the historicity of economies are all ignored in pure neo-classical theory. Behavioural postulates are axiomatic rather than problematic.

The major alternative to liberal, individualist, economic orthodoxy over the past two centuries has been a broad stream of realist sociological and institutionalist theorizing. This stream has conceptualized the economy either as an organic system of relations and interactions or as a social structure consisting of positions, rules, roles, and relations in which economic behaviour occurs. The major problems here have been how to account for the actual connections between systems or structures, decisions, and behaviour, and how to explain systemic or structural change.

The German historical economists of the second half of the nineteenth century had a realist institutionalist conception of the economy in which national economic and political interests, institutions, and policies played a prominent role. They opposed the abstraction, deductivism, and ahistoricalism of Menger and other Austrians. However, their account of action and human agency was severely underdeveloped. Similarly, the contemporaneous English historical economists also wished to study the real world of institutions and their history, but again they lacked a viable theory of action that was alternative to the utilitarianism of classical economics and the emerging neo-classicalism of their time.

Marx's version of socio-political economics conceived of the economy as a structure of social relations centring on historically specific forms of property ownership and the power that flows from property relations. Economic phenomena and technological change were determined by the structure of socio-political institutions, including property relations and social classes, which in turn were the result of prior technological, institutional, and political developments. He had a well-developed concept of agency, in which the key role was played by classes acting as collective, self-conscious entities to further class interests. An ongoing transformational process was at the heart of Marx's theory, so that for him there was no distinction between theoretical abstractions and the historicity of societies.

Like Marx, Max Weber had a relational conception of the economic structure, but his theory of motivation and action went further than Marx's socio-political model of persons to incorporate cultural determination. For Weber, people are rational actors whose individual decisions must be studied by the sociologist and the economist, but rationality is socio-culturally determined and not exogenous to the analysis. This approach has inspired a large following, including the modernization school of economic development theorists, who have studied economic transformation as a complex, psychological, socio-cultural, and political process.

Institutionalist economics was long overshadowed or marginalized by neo-classicalism but it has recently been revived.[99] The American institutionalists of the late nineteenth and early twentieth centuries, notably Veblen, Commons, Mitchell, and Ayres, also rejected the abstraction and simple behaviourism of classical and neo-classical economics and opted for studying the legal, ideological, socio-political, cultural, and organizational framework of economic behaviour. For them, the economy was the institutional framework and not some thing separate from it. In recent decades new versions of institutionalist economics have been developed, firstly by Karl Polanyi in the 1940s and 1950s.[100] He defended and employed in a series of empirical and theoretical works the idea of the economy as an instituted process that was embedded in society and had significance only through these wider structural and functional relationships. The non-economic context is as important for the operation of the economy as the economic activities and relationships themselves.

What is now called by some commentators the 'new institutionalist economics' tries to combine aspects of the old version with neo-classical rational action theory. This version is best called 'neo-classical institutionalism'. Douglass North and Mancur Olson,[101] for example, draw a distinction between economic behaviour and the institutional structure, that is, the institutions affect the economy but are not the economy itself. This means that the economy is defined, as in neo-classicalism, as a realm of individual rational decisions and actions, but they are shaped by the institutions of ideology, property, and socio-political systems. Economic institutions are for them the rules of individual and collective rational behaviour and not sociological structures of positions, roles, relations, or classes.[102] This distinction between rational action and institution is incoherent because it seems to assume that action somehow occurs separately from the institutional structure. But if institutions exist and play a role in moulding or determining behaviour, then behaviour must be considered as at least in part institutionally oriented rather than utilitarian, and then the behavioural foundation of neo-classical economics would be undermined.

An ultra-new version of institutionalism that can best be labelled 'structurist institutionalism' has recently been proposed, mainly by Geoffrey Hodgson,[103] who has rejected the polarity between action and structure that is inherent in neo-classicalism. He wishes to replace 'rational economic man' with a more complex theory of motivation and action drawn from cognitive psychology, which includes a role for ignorance, irrationality, habits, customs, and traditions. In his approach, economic systems of institutions are produced and reproduced in a dynamic evolving manner through the behaviour that grows out of this kind of sociological motivational complexity. People are social beings rather than narrow economic beings.

The economics 'discipline' has depended for its autonomy on assuming either that the economy is a natural kind of entity or system with relative autonomy from the wider society and which can be modelled by the use of abstract concepts and mathematical formulae (i.e., an abstractionist move) or that all kinds of behaviour can be subsumed under or explained by concepts and theories drawn from economic discourse (i.e., a reductionist or a subsumptionist move aided by deduction). In both cases economics is taken to be the key social science around which all the others gravitate. This is part of the dominant ideology of the modern age. The fundamental problem with this ideology is that it rests on a contradiction, which the neo-classical institutionalists attempted to remedy but could not. The contradiction is that economics is in fact not a social science but a behavioural science (or putative science) and so cannot provide the core for a social science. Neo-classical economics brackets or rejects social analysis in favour of trying to explain collective behavioural phenomena. But it fails to explain satisfactorily those phenomena for it lacks adequate social and psychological causal theories, a defect the neo-classical institutionalists understood but could not overcome, for they too retained the unjustified distinction between behaviour and institution. Most practising neo-classical economists rely upon largely unexamined behavioural postulates or assumptions and concentrate on making statistical correlations of behavioural aggregates rather than genuine socio-structural causal analyses. To make such analyses requires a framework of structural concepts and general theories of action and structure and their dynamic, historical interactions.

I am not claiming that there is no such thing as economic activity or economic relations or economic systems but rather that they should be understood as a subset of social activity, relations, and structures. Economic behaviour, like all behaviour, cannot be but social in its origin, orientation, and determination. The concept of the splendidly isolated, heroic (Robinsonade) actor moulding the world through rational choices and actions, although meant to be abstract, has been an irrational and unwarranted abstraction. Action is always structurally located, oriented, and impelled. Economic behaviour and structures have to be studied sociologically and not in abstraction from the wider social structure. Methodological individualist and reductionist neo-classical economic theory has flourished, nevertheless, first because of its support for the egoism and aggressive material acquisitiveness of capitalism, which has successfully broken down or moulded to its own purposes all non-economic institutional barriers to economic accumulation, and second because of its apparent theoretical success in building an operational paradigm that seeks to explain aggregate economic growth. But the aggregates it examines are of course statistical artifacts of the economist's theory and methodology. In themselves such aggregates pose no necessary problem for the construction of a science of structural history, providing they are not taken to represent structural reality. The explanatory success of orthodox economics is illusory because of the persistent failure to predict structural change and explain past structural change. The desire for prediction is not matched by results and the attempts at *post hoc* explanation are in fact *ad hoc* as well as radically incomplete, because of the abstraction of the economy from the wider sociocultural and political context.[104]

One of the central problems resulting from economic abstraction and the desire for positive science is the static conception of its subject-matter. The inherently dynamic and historical character of economic and social structures and behavioural patterns is bracketed in favour of static equilibrium analysis. This is not to deny the development of neo-classical, Schumpeterian, and Keynesian growth theories. But the problem of growth in the orthodox framework has been admitted largely by relaxing certain central assumptions of the equilibrium model rather than by being made the centre of analysis. Long-run structural change remains a great difficulty for orthodox economics, as underlined especially by the curiously ahistorical attempts to deal with it by the neo-classical institutionalists. The historicity that the eighteenth-century Scots, nineteenth-century Germans, and late nineteenth-century English historical school understood as being central was lost in the twentieth-century attempt to establish a positive science. Economic history became for a time a separate discipline. Now, unfortunately, in some places it is being reincorporated into economics as a form of applied theory rather than economic theory being subordinated to historical analysis. The North and Olson type of work shows the dangers of simply looking at the past from a standpoint resolutely in the present, trying only to explain outcomes rather than the realities of historical episodes and processes. History written only from a standpoint in the present loses its historicity and becomes instead merely applied theory. Applications of epoch-specific theories, such as the concepts of capitalist rationality, entrepreneurship, and property rights, to earlier epochs rest upon an untested and probably false assumption of rigid socio-cultural continuity across eons.[105] Anthropology and ethnographic and post-structuralist historiography should have disproved this assumption to the satisfaction of most people.

The failure of economistic approaches to explain economic and other social phenomena and structures and their dynamics leads to the conclusion that there has to be a socio-institutional, historical approach to and theory of the economic substructure. I have already mentioned the important revival of institutional economics. There have also been several conspicuous attempts from the 1950s onwards to merge economics and sociology, that is, to develop a sociological economics and an economic sociology.

Versions of sociological economics

There are two basic strategies for unifying the discourses of economics and sociology, that is, incorporating either into the other to produce economic sociology or sociological economics. These are certainly not the same, although many commentators tend to confuse them. Economic sociology, strictly speaking, should attempt to apply the forms of reasoning of orthodox economics to socio-political phenomena and processes. The utilitarian rational action model, market exchange theory, methodological individualism, and deductivism are all brought to bear on what is usually considered as non-economic behaviour, such as voting, marriage, family relations, education, and crime.[106] The effect of this approach is actually to conceive of all behaviour as economic. The whole of social life is examined as if 'economic rationality' prevailed everywhere.

Sociological economics, strictly speaking, should study economic phenomena and processes in a sociological manner. The economic realm is considered as part of the social structure and so is characterized by the same kinds of institutions, organizations, social relations, social interactions, and historical social processes as the wider society. Nevertheless, there is considered to be an economic substructure or subsystem that is oriented towards certain kinds of material production, which can be abstracted to some extent from the totality but is not ultimately explainable apart from the totality. Just as there is no dominant paradigm in sociology, unlike economics, so there is no broad consensus on methodology and theory in sociological economics.

Disregarding the misleading labels sometimes used, it is possible to identify several approaches to constructing a sociological economics. As with so much in social science, Karl Marx's was probably the first, in that he developed a social relational conception of the economy, but he was influenced in this by Adam Smith and the other members of the Scottish school. Economic relations and interactions were characterized by inequalities of social power that were institutionalized as class and property relations. Max Weber also had a sociological conception of the economy in which culture, class, and status dominated individual decisions and actions. Both Marx and Weber have inspired and continue to inspire many forms of neo-Marxist and neo-Weberian sociological economics.

Perhaps the first major new version of sociological economics after Marx and Weber was that of Talcott Parsons and Neil Smelser, whose *Economy and Society* (1956) with Smelser's later work developed a theory of the relationship of the economy as a subsystem to the wider social system. The goal-seeking orientation of actors was the key causal element. This attempt was very influential and inspired a strong movement in the sociology of development from the 1950s, centred mainly on the modernization school and the journal *Economic Development and Cultural Change*. These people, including Bert Hoselitz, Wilbert Moore, and S. N. Eisenstadt, drew on Weberian, Parsonian, Schumpeterian, cultural anthropological, and orthodox economic sources to construct their approach.[107] One of those influenced by this approach, but who moved away to develop a more anthropological and cultural approach to understanding the economy, was Clifford Geertz, whom I shall discuss in detail in chapter 3.

In recent years, Arthur Stinchcombe has systematically developed a new sociological economics, which he and other commentators call 'economic sociology'.[108] He has drawn on Marxian, Weberian, Polanyian, ecological, and other sources to construct a new paradigm that he and others hope will supersede both orthodox and institutional economics.

The argument I am trying to make here is in essence that the structural reality of the social world is not captured in theoretical conception by reductionist economic approaches or by any other form of reductionism or methodological individualism. Structures should be understood as social, that is, as the shared rules, roles, relations, and meanings in which people necessarily live their lives and which, as generalized structures, exist before individuals and groups and organize their behaviour. Actions, events, and patterns of behaviour cannot be understood and explained except by reference to such structures, as well as to problematic individual intentions, beliefs, and psychological imperatives. 'Social structure' in general subsumes so-called economic and political structures, but within social structures there are many types of action and substructure, including economic and political ones, which are concerned with more specific objects, productions, and goals.

The relationship of structures to events and actions – the micro–macro problem

Any approach to explaining the history of social structures should deal with the crucial issue of micro–macro interdetermination. Economists and anthropologists have long seen the micro–macro nexus as crucial and developed general concepts of the micro and macro levels of their subject-matter and their interconnection. Some sociologists and political theorists have been deficient in this area and traditional historians have been on the whole particularly so. But now there is a great interest in the question from many quarters of social studies, for the problem has come to be seen, quite rightly, as central to all social enquiry.[109] The question is crucial because it bears directly upon the problem of social dynamics. What is the source of dynamism – of innovation, change, evolution, history – in societies?

Fundamentally, there are three broad approaches to providing theoretical solutions to the problem of the micro–macro connection – individualist, holist, and structurist. Individualists have defined the macro in ways that either deny its ontological reality or place it in a completely dependent relationship with the micro. For them the micro level consists of powerful, autonomous actors – whether they be persons, integrated small groups, or legal entities such as firms – who interact with and strive to make exchanges with other actors in order to satisfy wants. In doing so they individually and collectively bring into being structured macro patterns or organization of behavioural interaction. In the simplest theory, when action and interaction are not occurring the macro pattern does not exist and so the structure does not exist. Strictly speaking, few theorists if any subscribe to such an ontological view, but this pure form of reasoning is implicit in the work of some individualists. More common is the idea that methodologically only the micro individual level is studied in order to grasp the macro, which is dependent for its very existence on the constant creativity of individuals. Common in economics is the idea that while the macro phenomena of the whole economy must be studied they can only be understood as a collectivity of micro decisions and interactions by individuals who have stable dispositions and preferences. The source of dynamism in such an approach obviously has to come from the power of creative individuals who re-create the social world on a constantly ongoing and moment-by-moment basis. Any change in their pattern of behaviour comes from internal mental processes and conscious decisions to alter behaviour. The collective behavioural outcome is the result of a large number of decisions. The problem with this is that the account of how beliefs, understandings, and decisions are arrived at is deficient without an account of prior mental structures or forms of consciousness and understanding, which have to be shared and linguistically based. Once that is conceded, there arises the problem of the social origins of language and consciousness. 'Social origins' implies prior existing social conditions that affect individuals. 'Social conditions' implies a form of social power, which is difficult to incorporate into an individualist approach.

On the other hand, holistic social reasoning is fixated on the nature of social power. The macroscopic social system is enormously powerful in the holist orientation, so much so that it determines the micro level more or less completely. Actions, events, and the mental processes of individuals derive their existence and character from their place and role in the system. Dynamism within such a system is aberrant, for the system has a powerful tendency toward static equilibrium. Actions and consciousness function to maintain the system and have significance only within that context.

With a structurist approach the problem of dynamism and history is central to the very conceptualization of the macro and micro levels and their nexus. The macro structure is conceived as the rules, roles, and relations that are the intended and unintended production over time of the conscious routine action and interaction of people conceived as social agents. Both macro and micro levels have power to influence the other but only people are genuine agents; they have power to mould and alter the structural world.

Given the foregoing definitions, it follows that in the structurist conception structures have a form of relative autonomy from events, actions, and consciousness, and therefore also relative temporal continuity. In the individualist approach, structures have virtually no autonomy or temporality, and in the holist approach they have enormous autonomy and temporality. If the study of social history is to develop a coherent framework which delineates structural history from action history then the relative autonomy of structures and their spatial and temporal continuity have to be conceptualized adequately. There has been much progress toward achieving this, examples of which will be discussed in the next two chapters.

If social structures, as the structurist methodology contends, are emergent systems of social rules, roles, and relations into which people are born and which must collectively be reproduced and occasionally transformed by human agents, then they themselves are not agents. They do not have power to act to try to bring about derived outcomes and they do not have consciousness. However, in the cybernetic sense, they have a 'memory' in that they have a powerful tendency towards maintaining temporal and spatial continuity. The fundamental power that they have, which is the basic index of their reality, is to mould and/or condition human action and thought. Humans cannot exist, act, or think except within structural contexts that enable and constrain their very existence, as well as their action and thought. Structures, not being agents, cannot make their own history, although they are all historical. Their historical powers and character arise through the actions and thought of human agents. Structures have within them a continuously shifting balance between diachronic and synchronic forces.

Thus humans individually and (much more so) in groups, classes, and institutions, are the agents of social structural history. This may seem very obvious but unfortunately structural history is sometimes studied and 'explained' as if humans are the mere carriers and/or victims of social forces completely beyond their ken and control. This is a mistake, for it ignores the collective and unconscious structuring power that all people possess in all times and places in virtue of the social co-operative arrangements in which they live. The self-consciousness of agency and the deliberate exercise of structuring power collectively to build new institutions and social organizations may be rare, at least before the advent of modern society, but the exercise of agential power does not need to be conscious. People necessarily structure the social and geographical environment in their daily lives. Agency does not imply political action, for the latter is but a heightened, conscious form of the former.

The real history of structural evolution

Last in this sketch of components of the domain of structural history is the part devoted to studying the real history of structural evolution. It is here that general empirical concepts and scientific theory have their place, all the foregoing being concerned with methodology. Scientific domains are characterized by, among other things, encompassing theories that are able to explain, to the satisfaction of most people, the entities in the domain. Social structural history does not yet have a well-confirmed, widely accepted general theory. Rather, there are many competing theories that do not share the same general concepts and hypotheses of causal relationships. Most of what follows is concerned directly or indirectly with elaborating the claims made for structurism and therefore establishing the general concepts and methodology of the domain of structural history.

2
A Critical Survey of
Structural History Approaches

The writing of economic and social history is now a multifarious, voluminous, and cacophonous business. While economic historiography and historical sociology have long been with us, so-called 'social history' writing in its various forms is more recent and now appears to be ubiquitous. It sometimes seems as if all historians now want to climb onto the bandwagon of social history's popularity. It is becoming part of popular culture and, like all elements of popular culture in the electronic post-modern age, it has a fluid, intangible, constantly changing character. The popularity of social history is significant for many reasons, one of which is its role in providing meaning in an anomic, competitive age. With the decline of community and family there arises a counter tendency to recover the past of communities and families, with the hope of reconstructing them or at least producing new ones. Another aspect of significance is the political, oppositional character of much social history writing. With the decline of organized party opposition to bureaucratic corporate centralism in most industrial societies opposition has arisen instead at a local, non-class level, and the appropriation of history has been made as a form of or a contribution to grass-roots political ideology. A third aspect, which is to some extent counter but also complementary to the others, is a desire for global comprehension in order to understand how the local is enmeshed in the totality of world structures at all levels.

Self-styled social history writing, then, covers the spectrum from local to global, from personal to structural totality. Is it any wonder that it is perceived as being not just another branch of history or sociology alongside all the others but as attempting to incorporate them all? However, just as it has come to this position of incorporation it threatens to fly apart. The tensions between microcosmic and macrocosmic inclusiveness, between the local particularities and the structural generalities, are difficult to reconcile. A few heroic efforts have been made, such as those by Braudel, Le Roy Ladurie, Tilly, Pred, and Hobsbawm, and they point the way perhaps, but they are very difficult to follow. In fact some thinkers about these questions hold that we cannot unite the social studies at all because the study of events and the actions of individuals and groups is different from the study of large-scale structures.[1]

This chapter offers a critical survey of the existing methodologies for writing economic and social history. There are in fact a great many approaches being used, not all with coherence and conceptual rigour, and many of them cannot truly be said to offer explanations of economic and social structural history, in spite of their names.

The old and crucial problems of the relationships between individuals and structures and between the material, social, and mental aspects of society, were the subject of the important but regrettably short-lived debate between Lawrence Stone, Eric Hobsbawm, and Philip Abrams in *Past and Present* in 1979–80.[2] In his opening paper in 1979 Stone claimed to diagnose the ending of an era in historiography, marked by the apparent abandonment of the attempt to produce 'a coherent scientific explanation of change in the past' by the so-called 'new historians'. They were now leading the way to a 'revival of narrative'. By the term 'new historians' he meant those social historians interested in mentalities, whom he separated from traditional historians. Their shift, he said, was from the 'analytical' to the 'descriptive' mode, which was made necessary by a major change in attitude about subject-matter so that mentalities were brought to the centre of focus. In turn, he saw this shift as depending on prior philosophical assumptions about 'the role of human free will in its interaction with the forces of nature' so that it is people rather than structural circumstances that are studied. Therefore, he said,

Historians are now dividing into four groups: the old narrative historians, primarily political historians and biographers; the cliometricians who continue to act like statistical junkies; the hard-nosed social historians still busy analysing impersonal structures; and the historians of *mentalité*, now chasing ideals, values, mind-sets, and patterns of intimate personal behaviour – the more intimate the better. (p. 21)

Stone was not actually advocating that all historians join the 'revival of narrative' or become students of mentalities and he did not develop a case for its superiority. But he did imply at least that the claims of scientific history were ill-founded. While neither Eric Hobsbawm nor Philip Abrams explicitly defended the notion of 'scientific history' they did argue that historians and sociologists should be, and often are, attempting to break down the divisions between *mentalité*/action/structure and history/sociology. They did not see a methodological turning-point occurring in social history, only a shift in subject-matter.

Overall, the Stone/Hobsbawm/Abrams debate was disappointing because it did not really deal with the central issue of how we can systematically and objectively study the history of societies in all their complexity and multifaceted reality. All three participants understood this to be central but stopped short of developing a survey of existing methodologies or, more importantly, a constructive criticism of approaches that showed the way forward. Abrams did offer some pertinent suggestions but these were not developed in his article.

AIMS OF THE SURVEY

As a step towards opening up the methodological debate again this chapter offers a survey based on a critical analysis of the philosophical and methodological concepts employed by practising economic and social historians and historical sociologists. There have been surveys before[3] but none I think that attempts systematically to examine the various philosophical and methodological assumptions and commitments that underpin practices.

My first aim in this chapter is abstracting and clarifying the methodological assumptions that are now tacitly used by economic and social historians. In order to construct my survey I have drawn upon the discussion of general philosophical concepts and issues in the previous chapter.

My second aim is to provide the basis for going beyond the survey to present in the next chapter a detailed argument with extensive examples about how I believe the study of the history of society should be advancing. In fact, no methodological survey can be developed in isolation from a particular viewpoint. I shall be developing and illustrating as I go certain ideas sketched in the previous chapter to the effect that studies of events must be united methodologically at a deep level with studies of structures. I want to argue that the study of historical social structures is the core task for social enquiry, properly so called. In other words, structural history rather than events, action, behaviour, or individuals as such is the process that gives social enquiry its raison d'être. And the appropriate methodology for structural history is methodological structurism, as instanced in the work of, among others, the writers I shall discuss in some detail in the next chapter.

My third aim is to begin to set the scene for my argument, against Stone and many others, that structural history can indeed be a science but in a sense quite different from the usual arguments for and against it. The argument about the nature of the science of structural history is developed in more detail in chapter 4. Stone said that various arguments for a scientific approach were untenable but his views were not grounded in an examination of the concept of scientific history. Of course it does not really matter whether we call structural history 'scientific' or not but arguments about this term have a direct bearing upon practice. It is explanation that matters and attention to methodological questions, including the question of science, does affect explanation. Explanations must be constrained by philosophical, methodological, and empirical criteria (not to mention cultural and political criteria), so that some explanations are seen as better than others. Without a notion of better and worse explanations and hence explanatory progress according to these inter-subjective criteria the whole enterprise of socio-historical enquiry (and socially oriented action) becomes philosophically meaningless. We are not free to say whatever we like about society because along that relativistic route lies radical individualism, hence unargued and irrational force, and ultimately perhaps a descent into tyrannical, Hobbesian society. That social collapse does not happen, even under conditions of state collapse, except perhaps very rarely and temporarily, shows the deeply contradictory nature of both radical individualism and the denial of the need for more or less shared, objective methodology.

THE STRUCTURE OF THE CRITICAL SURVEY

The many approaches to writing structural history are grouped here into five main 'traditions', which are defined primarily by their philosophical commitments to certain concepts of society and of explanation. The aim is definitely not to provide a survey or a detailed criticism of the work of particular writers (although some examples will be given) but to construct a set of categories through which to view particular texts. These categories are not meant to be descriptions of actual methodologies that are used but heuristic types for the task of methodological criticism and explanatory progress. Many texts and writers do not fit neatly into a particular category and most writers do not in fact have clearcut methodologies. The work of most social historians straddles approaches, unselfconsciously drawing upon several philosophical positions. While eclecticism and conceptual diversity may enable an element of methodological richness to pervade such work, these are not necessarily helpful. Eclecticism and syncreticism often lead to impoverished explanations. There is clearly a desire among historians, economists, and sociologists to construct better explanations, but how to get there is the problem. These categories should help comprehension of the methodological panorama that exists and point out in general terms why some texts contain better explanations than others.

The criticism of approaches draws upon the philosophical and methodological points made in parts of chapter 1. Let me summarize six of the relevant points made in those sections.

1 There are three ontologies and methodologies that are assumed or explicitly adopted by structural historians – individualism, holism, and structurism.
2 The subjectivist/objectivist dichotomy is false because it ignores the structuring interaction between consciousness, action, and real structures.
3 The relationship between causal explanation and hermeneutical understanding should be a close and mutually supportive one, rather than oppositional.

Table 2.1 Methodological approaches to structural history according to their philosophical foundations

	Individualism	Holism	Structurism
Empiricist and individualist approaches	• traditional biographical history • empiricist historical sociology and demography • traditional economic history • orthodox empirical social history • neo-classical cliometrics • behaviourist individualism • neo-classical institutionalism		
Systemic-functionalist approaches		• functionalist history • functionalist modernization sociology	
Interpretist approaches		• traditional historical interpretism	• sociological and anthropological interpretism • people's history

mentalité, socio-economic
history)
- ecological history
- Marxist structuralism
- post-structuralism

- *Annales* totalizing
  structurist history
- Marxist socio-cultural
  history
- totalizing Marxist history
- Marxist historical
  sociology
- Weberian historical
  sociology
- Elias's historical sociology
- Tilly's historical sociology
- structurationist geography
- social network approach
- Touraine's historical
  sociology

Relational structurist
approaches

The task is to provide causal explanations, but they are not well described by the covering law model of explanation.

4 Both analytical–statistical and narrative modes of presentation are required in order to provide adequate accounts of historical processes.

5 The comparative method is virtually indispensable for structural historical enquiry even though each structure is unique in some respects.

6 Structural history needs a better conception of science that is able to provide epistemological support for the less than absolute structurist ontology and methodology advocated above.

Table 2.1 summarizes the survey that follows.

EMPIRICIST AND INDIVIDUALIST APPROACHES

Empiricism and its cousin positivism are much misunderstood and abused terms that have changed considerably in meaning during the past 150 years.[4] In general usage, 'positivism' refers to a programme of unifying all empirical enquiry on the supposed foundation of the method of natural science, particularly physics. If an enquiry cannot in principle be conducted in a factual, objectivist manner that attempts to uncover the laws governing phenomena, then supposedly it cannot rightly be called a science, or a potential science, and so its findings do not have the status of genuine knowledge. A sharp demarcation is drawn between knowledge and belief.

More recently, logical empiricism was developed as an account of the philosophical foundations of advanced scientific reasoning. The basic tenets of logical empiricism as formulated by philosophers of science in the 1960s and 1970s[5] are:

1 Logicism – the attempt to show that objective confirmation of scientific theory should conform to the canons of deductive logic.

2 Empirical verificationism – the idea that only propositions that are either empirically verifiable or falsifiable (i.e., synthetic propositions) or are true by definition (i.e., analytic propositions) are scientific. Propositions about unobservable 'structures' are at best instrumental, that is, they are merely convenient fictions and do not have truth content. Synthetic a priori propositions, which are statements of fact made prior to any experience of the world, are ruled out entirely.

3 Theory and observation distinction – the idea that there is a strict separation between theoretical propositions about unobservables and observations. Observations are the testing grounds for theories but are not determined by theories, being theoretically neutral.

4 The Humean theory of causation – establishing a causal relation is a matter of discovering the invariant temporal relationships between types of observable events.

Now, this precise formulation is not often consciously employed or even unconsciously followed by self-styled empiricist practitioners in socio-historical studies. This rational reconstruction by philosophers is supposedly drawn from physics and many self-professed empiricist historians deviate from it in various ways. An earlier form of empiricism underlay the mid-nineteenth century attempts by Buckle and von Ranke to develop a scientific history.[6] Their different methodologies shared the idea of the priority of observational evidence and the importance of induction for arriving at explanations. In the mid-twentieth century, empiricist and positivist philosophies reached their apogee in the work of Carl Hempel and Rudolf Carnap.[7] They influenced attempts by some practitioners of history and sociology to construct a science, notably the cliometricians and the behaviourist exchange theorists. Less orthodox or in-complete versions of empiricism, influenced more by Rankism and 'common-sense' empirical thinking than by logicians or philosophers, have also underlain the work of other kinds of individualist social historians, notably some of the work of 'traditional' Anglophone historians such as Peter Laslett, Richard Cobb, and Theodore Zeldin. Such work tends to be influenced by the older tradition of 'common-sense' inductivist history which sprang ultimately from Hobbes and Locke but more recently from people such as Buckle, J. S. Mill, Acton, the Webbs; or early economic historians such as Rogers and Cunningham; or Trevelyan and Namier.[8]

In fact there is a wide range of empiricist and individualist historical methodologies running from traditional empirical history which eschews sociological generalizations, through consciously empiricist sociological approaches, to fully fledged cliometrics and behaviourism. What unites all historical empiricist approaches is overt commitment to the autonomy of 'factual' evidence and methodological individualism, and they sometimes have a tacit commitment to psychological behaviourism, which is itself based on empiricism. They all reject notions about the reality or autonomy of social structures as real structures with irreducible powers, and the theory-ladenness of observations about structures and actions. Their task is carefully to reconstruct the past from factual evidence rather than to offer general interpretations. Let us look briefly at each of seven groups.

Traditional biographical history has been advocated by G. M. Trevelyan[9] and sometimes practised by Richard Cobb and Theodore Zeldin.[10] What generally characterizes the intentions and productions of these historians is a concentration upon examining the actions of individuals and their personal motivations. They are actively opposed to sociological theories and statistical generalizations, preferring to try to see each person as basically independent and actions as explicable by reference to 'common-sense' notions about mentality and behaviour. These largely unexamined common-sense notions sometimes include the idea that humans are rational egoists who always seek personal or familial advantage. Such history is often presented as large-scale exercises in generalized biography writing, whether of important or unheralded individuals. When it is unheralded individuals or small groups who are examined it is sometimes said that history is being done from the bottom up.

Empiricist historical sociology and demography, unlike the first approach, actively seeks to explain social structural change. Its concept of social structure tends to be individualist and the methodological relationship between theory and evidence is empiricist. Structure is modelled as a set or aggregation of observable occupational and familial positions or roles and the collective pattern of behaviour of a large number of individuals that takes place within that set. In order to examine structure it is a question of examining supposedly objective evidence about categories of behaviour and individual persons to test hypotheses and develop generalizations from it. These generalizations then constitute knowledge of structural change. Some of the work of Lawrence Stone, Peter Laslett, E. A. Wrigley, and Alan Macfarlane[11] has tended to be of this sort, although they have considerable differences over theory and research techniques. They have all employed sampling and statistical methods to deal with large bodies of atomized 'objective' data.

Traditional (or 'old') economic history is a self-consciously empiricist approach in the inductive mode and originated in the late nineteenth century, partly as an attempt to investigate the economic origins of social inequality and working-class degradation resulting from industrialization. Writers such as Toynbee, the Webbs, and the Hammonds[12] were among the first to study the English industrial revolution from this viewpoint. In the 1920s and 1930s the tradition began to lose its sociological element and the more narrowly focused, economistic, and empiricist form of enquiry into past economic action and processes became dominant. This form at first employed simple but later sophisticated economic theory and 'common-sense' psychological theory, but always retained theory-neutral evidence as central. Narrative played and still plays a considerable part in the presentation of results. Concerns with wider questions of the role of demography, classes, social institutions, and ideology in economic history still exist in the discipline.[13] These characteristics set it apart from the 'new' economic historians, or cliometricians, who parted company over these methodological and sociological issues.

Orthodox empirical social history is a rather vague label for an amorphous approach that is probably the major form of social historiography in the Anglophone world. The approach has largely grown out of old economic history, sharing methodological assumptions with it, and it has developed since the 1950s largely as a consequence of a growing disenchantment with the narrowness of the subject-matter of economic and political history rather than because of serious methodological objections or innovations. These historians agree with economic history's traditional concerns with questions about such things as the standard of living, social classes, and the processes of production. They wish to go further in that direction and include all kinds of enquiries about daily life. Their methodology is usually opposed to the use of sociological theory in any strong, organizational sense, and, although some attention is paid to general structures and structural processes, the main emphasis is given to careful empirical enquiry into particular actions, events, classes, and social movements. There is little conceptual development about society and what there is tends to be commonsensical.[14] The questions of methodology and theory have not been raised explicitly by most of them and they remain resolutely committed to the autonomy of historical enquiry from social science. While counting has become important, they have not adopted statistical techniques in the way that some other empiricists have done. Their empiricism remains largely unreflective. This is not so with the fifth approach, the 'new' economic history, or neo-classical cliometrics.

Cliometrics is a slightly misleading name for the group which bears it because accurate measurement is only part of what characterizes their methodology. More importantly, *new economic historians*, who are really applied economists, tend to employ large-scale quantification, econometrical techniques, neo-classical economic theory, and nomological deductivist epistemology.[15] All of these characteristics set them apart from the three previous groups who are either less enamoured of econometrical techniques or reject them entirely, employing only a vaguely defined behaviourist theory to explain action and develop inductive generalizations. The cliometricians have been directly influenced by recent logical empiricist epistemology, especially as propounded by Carl Hempel, which has taught that only nomological deductive explanations can be considered as scientific. Neo-classical rational action theory provides the laws from which deductions about behaviour are made. This is a form of dispositional behaviourism which directs research toward the particular observable environmental stimuli and conditioning of the utility-maximizing disposition that is supposed to be present within all people. According to original behaviourism the only steps in the causal chain are observable environmental stimuli and observable behaviour. No supposedly independent mental or social factors can be included in the causal account of behaviour. More recently, dispositional behaviourism has allowed that fixed psychological dispositions (or human nature) intervene between stimulus and behaviour. There appears to be little place in neo-classical economics and cliometrics for variability of human nature, or the intervention of independent, unpredictable intentions, or a role for unobservable but irreducible social and cultural structures. Since this epistemology requires an equation of explanation and prediction cliometricians believe they have to rely upon a fixed, determining law of behaviour.

Behaviourist individualism is directly defended and exemplified in the work of George Homans and James S. Coleman.[16] Like neo-classical cliometrics, with which their work shares methodological ground, their sociological writings are methodologically explicit. They contain an aggregational (or reductionist) notion of structure so that the concept is largely instrumental, not meant to refer to a real entity with properties and powers. Society is conceived as systematic patterns of behaviour and the task is to search for the stimuli that influence the operation of the human rationality disposition. But these sociologists have produced little historical work.[17]

Recently some economists and economic historians have become disenchanted with the narrowness of new economic history and have widened their theories to include institutional and ideological components. *Neoclassical institutional economists* have produced an impressive body of work on the general problem of the long-run rise and decline of economies and nations as I indicated in the previous chapter.[18] Their basic philosophical commitment is to the rational individualism of neo-classical economics.

I think it can be seen that all these approaches more or less share fundamental empiricist notions about the priority of empirical observations; the instrumental nature of structural concepts; and the sharp distinction between theories and observations, the latter being epistemologically privileged. A narrative presentation which in effect tacitly adopts a Humean idea of causation as a succession of events is adopted by the first four groups, and although the others are not essentially narrativists they have a similar idea of causation, rejecting the idea of realist structural causation. They also oppose the idea that human action is at base intentionally rather than psychologically caused and propose various forms of psychological dispositionalism to help explain action. Humans are thought to act from relatively fixed, given, dispositional drives which are prior to reason, dominate intentions, and are triggered by observable environmental events.

SYSTEMIC–FUNCTIONALIST APPROACHES

Systemic–functionalism also operates in a positivist framework but is clearly opposed to many aspects of empiricism. Most notably, it not only postulates the existence of society as an organic, real structure but claims that there are causally efficacious functional relationships binding society together into a tightly integrated holistic system.

The ambiguous legacy of nineteenth-century positivism has made it possible for both holistic functionalists and individualists to claim to be positivists, offering different ways of constructing a positive science of society. What sets systemic–functionalism apart in this regard is its ontological holism and a different comprehension of the structure of scientific reasoning. Under the influence of logical empiricism, it has adopted a nomological deductivist approach to theory confirmation, rather than the inductivist route to generalizations of the traditional empiricist historians.

Systemic–functionalist social theory grew out of a confluence of Darwinian biological theory, evolutionary sociology, functionalist anthropology, systems theory and cybernetics, and deductivist positivism.[19] Talcott Parsons, Edward Shils, Marion Levy, and Neil Smelser constructed a new framework on these foundations in the 1950s.[20] It was immediately influential, particularly in the United States, partly because of its all-encompassing scientific claims and its apparent refutation of Marxism in a Cold War climate. It was employed, among others, by those economic development theorists (such as Bert Hoselitz, Wilbert Moore, and Joseph Spengler) who were attempting to construct an anti-Marxist, pro-capitalist theory to explain modernization and to implement capitalist development strategies in the Third World.[21]

In brief, the main tenets of the systemic–functionalist approach to socio-economic history are, first, an organic concept of structure – society supposedly has powers of self-maintenance, self-regulation, and a self-adjusting equilibrium. Each element of the whole has an integrating functional role within it. Although Parsons and Shils developed an 'action theory', genuine human action actually plays a dependent or stunted role in their work. Humans are in fact what has been accurately described as 'oversocialized' and 'cultural dopes' in their theory.[22] Apparently the only real actor is the whole society. Second, there is a central role for general theories and model-building in directing research and interpreting empirical evidence. Third, there is the adoption of an evolutionary theory of social change that directs attention toward societal growth through adaptation and differentiation, leading to higher stages of equilibrium.

Talcott Parsons was never a historian, remaining as an abstract grand theorist of social change, insofar as he considered the question of change at all. His theory was quasi-Darwinian in that it directed attention to the role of social 'mutations' in promoting the adaptive ability of particular societies within a hostile, competitive environment made up of natural conditions and other societies. The result of this process over time was the gradual differentiation of societies in terms of their internal structure. Furthermore, certain mutations were considered to be universally significant, leading to a general development of all human societies because of the adaptive power of these mutations and their subsequent spread to all societies.[23]

This general theory has been applied to actual historical research by functionalist historians such as Neil Smelser and Mark Gould,[24] and the functionalist modernization sociologists such as Bert Hoselitz, Daniel Lerner, and Everett Hagen.[25] Smelser analysed the evolution of British working-class actions and institutions as a process of differentiation and adaptation. He expressly employed a functionalist evolutionary theory and model to write what he called 'sociological history', which was a form of applied social theory. Similarly, the modernization theorists employed a simplistic model of 'traditional' and 'modern' societies with a theory of the process carrying some societies from the first to the second state resting on the crucial role of 'deviant' entrepreneurs. Some of these writers investigated in great detail the psychological sources of such deviance in the child-raising practices of marginalized groups.[26]

INTERPRETIST APPROACHES

So far, we have seen how the empiricist tradition concentrates on individual actors and their dispositional motives, and how the functionalist tradition concentrates on holistic social systems and the socialization of actors within them. Some exponents of each tradition claim to be constructing a positive science of history. Conversely, the defenders of the third kind of approach to social history – interpretism – reject any notion of a scientific approach to human enquiry. Humanistic explanation (or understanding) for this third approach is hermeneutical, although they do not always use this term. They see their task as imaginative interpretation and reconstruction of past acts, events, episodes, cultures, mentalities, and even epochs. For pure interpretists, such objects of enquiry do not have an objective existence and so are not susceptible to an objective analysis of their structures. Only hermeneutical understanding can grasp them as a whole gestalt entity.[27] Descriptive narration is the only appropriate method of presentation of results of such an enquiry, and every narration will be different because the story is always told from a particular point of view. These historians rely upon insight and intuitive grasping of the meaning of actions, beliefs, and epochs which come from a total immersion in and attempted rethinking of the ways of thinking of a milieu. There are three broad streams of historical interpretism.

Until recently *traditional historical interpretism* has been the main historical methodology in Anglophone countries this century. Exemplars include some of the writings of Hugh Trevor-Roper and G. R. Elton.[28] They eschew present-oriented sociological and psychological theory and rely upon 'common-sense' interpretations of constellations of events and epochs. These writers have been indirectly influenced by the ordinary language school of philosophy emanating mainly from Cambridge and Oxford in the 1950s as a reaction against logical positivism. This school saw the task of explanation as being the linguistic situating of common-sense meanings and their comprehension as part of everyday language use. It was not their task to analyse the underlying structure or the social grounding of language or meaning. Accordingly, traditional interpretive historians see their task as being to understand the meaning of past social epochs, events, and lives, as expressed in the recorded utterances and actions of important individuals. Concepts of society as an independent structure with causal power play no part in their work but they do usually have a vaguely holistic concept of the *Zeitgeist* or 'character' of an epoch.

Sociological and anthropological interpretism does have a central role for theory in historical explanation while also still seeing the hermeneutical method as essential. These writers have been influenced by Max Weber, recent German phenomenological and hermeneutical philosophers such as Schutz and Gadamer, American symbolic interactionist sociologists such as Mead and Goffman, and the findings of cultural anthropology. Accordingly, they have a quasi-phenomenological concept of society as having only a partly objective, external existence, always being mediated by and known through forms of consciousness, but a consciousness that is shared to some degree. Because these writers wish to go beyond pure phenomenology and relativism to analyse the dialectical interrelationships between forms of consciousness and real social structures, they have attempted to link micro enquiries about beliefs with macro structural enquiries. One of the ways they have attempted to do this is by employing the dramaturgical model of social action. In this model social structures and situations are like scripts of a drama which people perform before an audience. Social reality is something that is constructed only in the context of the play and the audience interacts with the cast so that the distinction between them is blurred and their positions are sometimes altered. The script is also being constantly tinkered with and occasionally rewritten, especially by powerful individuals.[29]

Some prominent examples of sociological and anthropological interpretism, which can also be called 'symbolic realism' or 'anthropological history', are found in the work of Clifford Geertz, Robert Darnton, Natalie Zemon Davis, and Peter Burke.[30] Their work places them among the leading representatives of Stone's 'new historians' who deal with mentalities. They have a close affinity with the *mentalité* stream of the *Annales* school of historians, and their interest in mentalities coincides with that of some of the biographical historians, such as Cobb and Zeldin. These theoretically informed interpretists try to retain a central place for both the structuring social power of people and the power of cultural structures (or symbol systems) to influence action. Although they are ambivalent about the degree of independence and the power of social structures and cultures, this ambivalence is not necessarily a weakness, because most of them have sensitively and extensively explored the fundamental problem of the complex interrelationships between subjective human understandings, action, and objective structures. The work of Geertz will be discussed in more detail in the following chapter.

The third stream of interpretism may seem out of place in this general category. *People's history and oral history* are rightly referred to as 'movements' because they have a political, proselytizing zeal, attempting directly to link their historical work to grass-roots social criticism.[31] Biographical, feminist, and local history are often seen by them as ways of recapturing control of self and community. The political aspect of interpersonal relations is asserted, sometimes through examining the historical origins of local power structures in order to overcome oppression in everyday life. One of the aims of these movements is to recapture the full complexity of the lives and social situations of ordinary, powerless people; to rescue them, as Edward Thompson put it, from the condescension of posterity. While such enquiries should be and often are informed by structural theory, they frequently rely essentially upon a hermeneutical method through which the historian closely questions the subject to establish a circle of understanding. In a purely hermeneutical enquiry a close, shared understanding (akin to a psychoanalytic diagnosis) is established, which draws its authenticity from the fact of agreement and not from a priori theory or inductive generalizations based on 'factual' data. These movements are not purely hermeneutical but, as in all the streams based on this methodological tradition, explanatory primacy is given to actors' understandings and perceptions of their situations, experiences, and motivations. But in contrast with traditional historical interpretists and orthodox social historians they are usually more theoretically informed and structurally aware.

STRUCTURALIST APPROACHES

'Structuralism' is a many-faceted and much used term. All adherents to a structuralist methodology, properly so-called, are opposed to individualism, empiricism, and hermeneutics. Structuralists attempt to uncover the nature, effects, and history of social structures as independently real entities. This they share with systemic–functionalists, who are also sometimes called structuralists. There are many forms of structural theory in philosophy, sociology, and anthropology. The most influential form, and the one that most people would immediately associate with the term 'structuralism', I shall call Francophone structuralism because of its origins.

Unlike systemic–functionalism of the Parsons kind, with which they share much, and empiricist structuralism of the Homans kind, most *Francophone structuralists* hold that structure is not an observable system governed by cybernetic, cultural, or psychological mechanisms. Rather, for them structure takes one or other of two quite different forms. First, it can be (as in the work of Ferdinand de Saussure, Claude Lévi-Strauss, Jean Piaget, Roland Barthes, and Louis Althusser) a set of abstract principles, susceptible perhaps to logico-mathematical formalization, that are inherent but hidden within observable languages, cultures, ways of knowing, and social structures. Or second, structure can be (as in the work of Marc Bloch, Fernand Braudel, and some other *Annales* historians) a large-scale set of geographic, economic, and social relations and behavioural patterns that link multitudes of people together in definite ways and determine the events of observable history.

Francophone structuralism has therefore given rise to two overlapping streams of historical work, both loosely associated with the journal *Annales*. The first stream, which originated with the writings of Émile Durkheim and Lucien Febvre, concentrates on *mentalités*, forms of collective belief, understanding, and representation that causally influence action and thus help to explain action and social change. The usual task here is to uncover and articulate the fundamental and little-changing linguistic and cultural principles governing ways of thinking in past epochs.[32] The second stream, which originated with the writings of Francois Simiand, Henri Pirenne, and Marc Bloch, examines large-scale socio-economic structures over long periods of time. Such structures are theorized as multi-layered with multi-temporal dimensions. Their study is distinguished sharply from the history of events – i.e., from *histoire événementielle*.[33] But there is a serious doubt regarding the nature of these sorts of structure because they are usually not well conceptualized. Braudel, for example, seems to hold that behavioural patterns rather than the social rules, roles, and relations that constrain behaviour are the elements of structure. In that case, structure is conceived as the observable pattern of human life, which runs counter to the epistemologically dominant principle of Francophone structuralism.[34] The method of *structuralisme*, as developed by Saussure, Lévi-Strauss, and Piaget, is predicated upon an ontology of unobservable elements and layers requiring a non-empiricist science. There is a tension in Braudel's books between his massive data collecting about the observable patterns of daily life and his almost *ad hoc* assertions about the existence of structural layers and his neglect of mentalities. In spite of his claims that it is the long-term history of structure that he was primarily concerned with, his concept of structure remained underdeveloped.

A metaphor that is often used to characterize structuralist methodology is that of archaeology. The task of the archaeologist is to sift carefully and incorporate a vast amount of evidence in order to piece together the architecture, lifestyle, culture, politics, and economy of a past epoch. The ideal result is a *total* reconstruction. Many *Annalistes* (including Braudel and Emmanuel Le Roy Ladurie) see their approach as totalizing – all structural levels, cycles, phases, events, and transformations must be incorporated into a total history.[35] But the actual achievement of a genuinely totalizing result is rare for it requires at least the employment of both mentalistic and geo-socio-economic concepts of structure. Le Roy Ladurie has approached this complexity in *Carnival in Romans*,[36] which I shall discuss in more detail in the next chapter.

Another important question about Francophone structuralism concerns the agency/action/structure interrelationship. For example, Braudel's books have little place for structuring human agency in spite of his concern with the activities of daily life and the supposedly autonomous, creative role of international capitalism. Structures are apparently remarkably stable and persistent across epochs and the surface pattern of events and actions disturbs them little. On the other hand, Le Roy Ladurie has achieved in some of his work a remarkable synthesis of structuralism (*à la* Lévi-Strauss) and historical agency. Such work shows what a totalizing, multi-layered, multi-temporal, approach can achieve. He gives a central place to sudden ruptures in structural evolution brought about by collective action of the sort analysed in *Carnival*. The dialectic of continuity and transformation is, as Piaget taught, a fundamental reality of all structure and at its best Le Roy Ladurie's work attempts to address that reality.[37] As a consequence he goes beyond *structuralisme*.

One further aspect of the *Annales* school needs to be mentioned – the important role given to theories in their work. Some of them are sophisticated employers of theory of various kinds – geographical, ecological, sociological, psychological, economic, linguistic. As such, they can be seen, at their best, as interdisciplinary social scientists – drawing on a wide range of theory and evidence to try to explain the empirical complexities of actual structural processes, actions, and events.

The nearest equivalents to *Annales* structuralism in the Anglophone world are those books which have employed a long-term *ecological perspective* on social change. As with many of the *Annalistes*, some of the writings of W. G. Hoskins, W. H. McNeill, A. Grenfell Price, and A. W. Crosby,[38] for example, see the interaction of people as biological and social beings with the natural environment as being crucial to structural change. This is not really methodologically different, only a particular theory within the broad structuralist methodology – the structural constraints in this case being human biology and/or the geographical environment. Unfortunately, the methodological basis of ecological history has not been well articulated by these historians. The relationship of the ecological approach to social history and to historical geography needs to be explored. Of course the awareness of the importance of ecological structures in a wider socio-historical framework has been well recognized by many others apart from the *Annalistes*, such as Clifford Geertz and Ernest Gellner.[39]

The *Marxist* philosopher Louis Althusser has been a vigorous defender of the epistemology of structuralism, claiming that Marx was the original structuralist. The core of his defence is the notion of 'totality'. Society is a totality that makes possible and structures everything within it, notably actions and events.[40] This is a holistic ontology that is similar to that of Talcott Parsons, except that for Parsons social relations are a visible cybernetic hierarchy, whereas for Althusser the causal relations are invisible and knowable only through their effects as relations of social dominance and subjection. Similarly, Immanuel Wallerstein's Marxist approach to the history of the modern world system is structuralist in the sense that the world totality determines the particular modes of production that exist in particular places at particular times. He asserts the existence of a holistic system which controls and structures the economies within it.[41]

Wallerstein's work contains one attempted way out of the problem that both holistic structuralists and systemic evolutionists get themselves into. That problem is to account for change. His solution is to posit a reified collective agent – a carrier of history (the bourgeoisie) – within the structure. Althusser's solution is to posit the structure as its own cause. Braudel's solution is a tendency to ignore transformation in favour of describing continuity and cycles. Parsons seeks the genetic mutations and selection conditions within organic systems. None of them has an important place in their theory for the relative autonomy of human thought and action.

Another proposed way out of the structuralist problem is represented by the *post-structuralism* of Michel Foucault.[42] His solution is in effect to deny the existence of history as a process. For him specific discourses, world views, epochs, do not evolve into new ones. Rather, there are complete ruptures of one into another, without continuity or progress. The problem, then, as he sees it, has not been to account for change but to uncover archaeologically and reconstruct the essential structure of these particular discourses and epochs and to show the power relations that exist within them. In order to do this he attempts to transcend all preconceptions, especially of a historical kind, so that he can grasp each system of knowledge in its own terms, there being no external criteria of truth or progress. He seems to advocate a radical relativism while adopting a transcendent position for himself.

It is important to emphasize that historical structuralism does not have to be holistic. Piaget argued strongly against the idea that structures were either unchanging or somehow changed themselves. Many histories written in the *Annales* totalizing tradition, including works by Febvre and Le Roy Ladurie, have had their social structures populated with real agential people, making their own history within structural conditions and constraints. In fact this kind of structuralism, which emphasizes the reality and effectiveness of structures at the same time as denying them a holistic character, is a form of what I have called 'methodological structurism', to contrast it with 'methodological holism'. There are also other French sociologists and historians (not to mention many writers from other countries), notably Alain Touraine and Pierre Bourdieu, who have developed other forms of structuralism free from holism.[43]

RELATIONAL–STRUCTURIST APPROACHES

A broad structurist tradition of structural history writing can be identified, which is far from being a school or a single coherent approach but in effect unites some *Annales* historians, some Marxist historians and sociologists, some Weberian and quasi-Weberian historians and sociologists, the figurational sociology of Norbert Elias and his followers, the action sociology of Alain Touraine and his group, and some others who neither owe conscious allegiance to nor fit easily into one or other of these groups. The hidden unity of their work can be understood as based partly on their employment of the methodological structurism I have articulated in the previous chapter. This methodology is closely related to what is now widely known as the 'structurationist' framework for social explanation. This comprehensive framework for approaching the explanation of the person/action/society/time complex of interrelationships, which was recently articulated by Anthony Giddens and Philip Abrams, contains a set of concepts about ontology, methodology, and theory. In fact the framework has existed in embryonic form for a long time, most notably in some of the historical writings of Marx and Weber and as the core of Piaget's philosophy, but Giddens, who coined the term, has been less than assiduous (unlike Abrams, who called it 'the problematic of structuring') in tracing the history of structurationism or in uncovering its tacit existence in the work of many contemporary social historians and historical sociologists. The lack of an empirical, historical dimension in his work weakens his claim to have provided a new framework rather than the articulation of an existing one. Nevertheless, we must be grateful for his convenient formulation of the tenets of this approach.[44]

Giddens's account of structurationism can be summarized in five points:

1   A central ontological and methodological place is given to the conscious but decentred human agent who has social structuring power.
2   Neither the human agent nor society is considered to have primacy; each is constituted in and through recurrent practices.
3   Institutions are theorized as structured social practices that have a broad spatial and temporal extension. Structure as institutionalized relations is the outcome of the social practices it recursively organizes.
4   Social conduct and social structure are conceived as fundamentally temporal and specifically environmentally located.
5   The forces for social change have to be looked for in the causal interrelationships between action, consciousness, institutions, and structures.

This means that those who employ such an approach have a realist ontology of society as consisting fundamentally of institutionalized and historical structures of social relations, and a theory of persons as social agents who structure the social world through time. Social structure is usually modelled as a set of 'levels' or 'networks' of relations, that provide the structure for the rules, roles, and practices that institutionalize those relations. Structure and action, then, are not the poles of society but two moments in a dialectical duality. 'Society' is not a reified holistic entity. Indeed, for these writers it does not exist in the traditional ways that it has been understood. Rather, societies are structured, fractured, complexes of manifold, discontinuous, and overlapping sets of relations.

Giddens's structurationism and the methodological structurism I have been developing here are not quite the same set of ideas. Structurationism is a broader and more detailed framework, incorporating ontological, methodological, and theoretical elements. It purports to be a total framework for sociohistorical explanation, offered in opposition to structural functionalism and Francophone structuralism, in particular. Methodological structurism can be seen, on the other hand, as a component of the broader structurationist framework, but not necessarily having meaning and significance only within that framework. It is logically possible to employ methodological structurism with ontological individualism, but in practice I know of no examples, and there are various forms of structurist theory that are compatible with the structurist methodology.

The concepts 'structurationism' and 'methodological structurism' are not employed by any historian, as far as I know, but their main elements are in effect employed in various explicit as well as implicit ways by many historians.

They have become part of our way of thinking without everybody being well aware of it because of the pervasive, unacknowledged influence that Marxian, Weberian, and Piagetian theories have had on the social sciences in recent decades. (I shall discuss the historical background of structurism in the next chapter.) However, within their underlying unity around the ideas of real structures of social relations, the power of the structuring process, and the methodology of structurism, the approaches and theories of these historians are quite diverse. In regard to a theory of social structural change, for example, although they often have an abstract model of structure as consisting of several 'levels' or 'spheres', they are certainly not all historical materialists. They do not all see the technological or economic 'level' or 'sphere' as explanatorily primary. Even among those who have varying degrees of allegiance to Marxism there are some who in effect reject materialist explanations and among the Weberians there are some weak materialists. In other words, Marxism and Weberism are neither monolithic schools of historians nor theories applied consistently. It is possible to identify the following overlapping streams within this broad tradition, which are differentiated mainly according to their general concepts, uses of theory, and emphasis upon different aspects of the social totality. Identifying the similarities between these streams is the first step toward constructing a more synthetic structurist approach and in fact there is already a good deal of consciousness of the similarities between the contours and content of each of these streams.

Many Marxist historians have been opposed to structuralism and economistic reductionism. Perhaps the best-known *Marxist socio-cultural historians* belong to the vaguely defined British Marxist school, including Christopher Hill, Edward Thompson, and Raymond Williams. What primarily sets their work apart from other similar Marxists is their emphasis on the mental or cultural structures of past social life, a concept of social class as social practice rather than rigid structure, and an examination of the actual historical life experience of representative individuals, small groups, and social movements. Overt theory and comparison play little role in most of their historical work.[45]

Another stream of Marxist history writing is more structurally oriented in that it primarily investigates the history of social, economic, and political structures, but without neglecting events and the actions of individuals, groups, and classes. This kind of *Marxist totalizing history* is similar to some of Le Roy Ladurie's work. All aspects of the social totality are investigated for their mutual influence and causal relationships. Explicit theory and comparison play a larger role than in the former approach, but this is still not a form of applied theory. A leading practitioner is Eric Hobsbawm. Other examples are found in the work of Victor Kiernan and R. S. Neale.[46]

Marxist historical sociology is explicitly theoretical and comparative and studies the history of structures with little attention to the details of ordinary individuals and everyday events. This is probably the major form of Marxist social science but, like the two former approaches, it is not dogmatically wedded to

Marxism, drawing on theories from other traditions as well.[47] It has many well-known practitioners, including Barrington Moore, Rodney Hilton, Perry Anderson, Theda Skocpol, Robert Brenner, and Geoffrey de Ste Croix.[48] Unlike the structuralist Marxists, with whom they share some important concepts, these people give a central place to the structuring activities of powerful individuals, groups, and classes of people. They do not see the social totality as being a systemic whole that strongly determines the activities of all those within it. In fact, all three of these streams of Marxism reject economic reductionism, or what is known as vulgar Marxism, but they do more or less subscribe to the central idea of historical materialism that the social 'base', however it is defined, has causal primacy in the long-run history of society.

Weberian historical sociology, like its Marxist counterpart, with which it shares a good deal, is highly theoretical and comparative. But there is also a lot of theoretical diversity, reflecting Weber's ambiguous legacy – a legacy perhaps even more ambiguous than that of Marx. Those influenced by Weber are even less tightly integrated as a group than the Marxists and less loyal to his ideas. As can be seen from the thematic variability of the work of Reinhard Bendix, S. N. Eisenstadt, Clifford Geertz, Ernest Gellner, John A. Hall, Michael Mann, Albert Hirschman, and Benjamin Nelson,[49] for example, those influenced by Weber disagree about the degree of objectivity of social structures and the precise role of material, cultural, and ideological influences in social change. Contrary to popular opinion, it is even possible to be a Weberian historical materialist, a position that has considerable textual support in some of Weber's historical writings, such as *The Agrarian Sociology of Ancient Civilizations*. What their works tend to have in common is Weber's emphasis upon reconciling the objectivity of structure and sociological enquiry with the subjectivity of structuring action and the enquirer's point of view.

Norbert Elias drew upon some Comtean, Marxist, and Weberian themes to construct his figurational approach, in which social structures were theorized as being formed of complex networks with particular patterns according to local historical and power relations. Each social situation was characterized by peculiar figurations, so he was opposed to constructing ideal typical categories of the Weberian sort, preferring the role of theory to be that of inductively developed generalizations from comparisons of social figurations, something he believed historians generally failed to develop.[50]

Charles Tilly has attempted to construct a comprehensive approach to the historical study of large-scale, long-run structural change *qua* structural change. Perhaps more than any other writer, he has attempted to construct an approach that tries to study all kinds of social structures simultaneously without collapsing them together into a single or holistic category. This framework explicitly rejects the concepts 'society' and 'social change' as reified, generalized, entities. Moreover, like Elias, he rejected a priori social theorizing divorced from historical observation. General theory about large-scale structures such as nation states and capitalism and concrete historical enquiry into small-scale structuring processes complement each other. A long series of empirical works[51] reveals the power of this approach, particularly its ability to explain the relationships between state-building processes and local collective action.

An essential part of the historical structuring process is the social transformation and the socially constraining power of the physical environmental space and context of social interaction. Many writers have argued for a *structurationist approach to historical geography*, the foremost being Allan Pred. In many works[52] he has attempted, as Giddens and other social theorists have argued ought to be done,[53] to incorporate time and space into the centre of social theory and historical explanation. For Pred,

Women and men make histories and produce places, not under circumstances of their own choosing but in the context of already existing, directly encountered social and spatial structures, in the context of already existing social and spatial relations that both enable and constrain the purposeful conduct of life. In other words, the scope for human agency is enabled and constrained both by already existing power relations and their associated social logics, rules of behavior, and modes of regulation (social structures) and by the full array and relative location of features humanly built into given geographical areas, by spatial patterns of transformed nature (spatial structures).[54]

Here we have an excellent statement of a methodological structurism that rightly goes beyond social relations and which should force a thorough re-examination and re-incorporation of geography into the centre of social science. We shall see in detail in chapter 3 how the ecology of physical and human spatial interaction has also been developed in the work of Le Roy Ladurie and Geertz. Pred's work could equally well be seen as an exemplar of such social science.

Some recent versions of the *social network approach* to explaining social structural composition and change can be understood as employing methodological structurism. The neo-network school of social structural analysis[55] connects with several other streams of methodological structurism in that this school is arguing for and demonstrating how an improved network concept, methodology, and technique should underpin all kinds of social structural analysis. They are arguing for the ontological significance of micro networks of social ties and relations as the basic building block for large-scale social structures. This kind of network analysis rejects both individualism as being too reductive and structuralism as being too holistic. They argue that all human social interaction and social structuring takes place through small-scale networks of interpersonal relations that connect with other small-scale networks, which ultimately form a vast, complex, unevenly integrated and sometimes fractured structure in which interpersonal power relations exercise a central causative role.

The *action sociology* that Alain Touraine and his group advocate is similar to that of Giddens and Abrams in that it emphasizes the dialectic between action and structure,[56] but unlike Giddens he has actively pursued empirical research (in collaboration with others), in his case into the origins, structures, and activities of contemporary new social movements by actually taking part in the movements themselves.[57] Touraine's sociology of action is really historical sociology or social history of the present, but of course historians cannot normally participate in the activities of the people they study. Philip Abrams also did similar work.[58] Their research serves to remind us that any distinction between past- and present-oriented enquiries is methodologically unwarranted.

In the following chapter I shall support my contention that structurism is employed by many contemporary historians by examining in more detail the work of some structural historians who employ versions of the methodology.

3
Methodological Structurism in Historical Explanation

The methodology of structurism that the relational, structurist tradition employs can be formulated as a description of the implicit assumptions and logic of certain explanations rather than of the surface texture and actual content of those writings. Structurist historians do not necessarily give the same explanations for the same kinds of phenomena and processes. Methodology operates at a deeper level than concrete explanations, for explanations also vary according to the content and use of theory, the particularities of evidence, and differences in the questions being asked. There are indeed variations in the kinds of explanations that these writers have developed. Nevertheless, it seems that there is a deep methodological unity between them which sets them apart from those who adopt individualism and holism and which strongly influences the kinds of explanations they give. In chapter 1 structurism was briefly outlined and in chapter 2 various approaches that employ it were mentioned. The central point of this chapter is to make a more detailed analysis of the work of some historians, work which, it will be argued, contains versions of methodological structurism even though no historians employ this term to describe their methodology. In order to demonstrate the explanatory role of structurism in certain writings some discussion of its content will help focus the analysis.

THE DEVELOPMENT OF STRUCTURIST METHODOLOGY

While the terms 'structurism' and 'structuration theory' have only recently been extensively articulated and contrasted with versions of individualism and holism, there have been several earlier attempts to articulate such a position. It is not true, as has recently been claimed,[1] that 'structuration theory' originates in the writings of Anthony Giddens. The central idea of structurism and structuration theory – that humans are the reproductive and structuring agents of the social world – had its origins in the European Enlightenment.

We can find it in rudimentary form in the thought of the Scottish histor-ical school. As with most aspects of the social sciences, the influence of Karl Marx and Max Weber was pervasive in the early development of structurist methodology and theory. Marx's famous aphorisms in *The Theses on Feuerbach* and *The German Ideology* about the centrality of human praxis, and in *The Eighteenth Brumaire* that it is men who make history but not under conditions of their own choosing, are canonical statements but were not explicated in any detail by him. For Marx it was social classes as institutionalized collective structural actors who, acting largely in their collective material interests, were the prime agents of social history. Much of his work embodies this idea, especially texts such as *The Eighteenth Brumaire* that analyse complex episodes and eras of rapid structural change. The methodology is less immediately obvious in his accounts of long-run macro-structural change such as the origins and development of capitalism, but there too it can be uncovered as in the 'Pre-Capitalist Formations' section of *Grundrisse*. Marx's historical materialism is not a form of deterministic methodological holism but contains an early (perhaps the earliest) version of methodological structurism.

Weber, being a scientific social theorist where Marx had been a radical social critic, extensively developed theories of rational action, the forms of social organization of action, and the interrelationship of action, consciousness, and structure. He advocated a combination of hermeneutical interpretism and causal explanation in his explicitly methodological writings, and he was opposed to a historical materialist theory of structure and history. But in some of his works of social structural history, such as *The Agrarian Sociology* and *General Economic History*, we can see a form of structurist methodology being employed. Perhaps most importantly, Weber inspired a broad stream of socio-historical enquiry that has centred on the power of ideational and cultural frameworks for structuring individual and collective action, rather than Marx's emphasis on ideologies as forms of false consciousness about real material interests. Nevertheless, in recent years the complementarities rather than contradictions of their methodologies and macro-social theories have begun to be well under-stood.[2]

Weber's contemporary Georg Simmel was one of the first thoroughly to think through the problem of the boundaries of the domain of sociology as a distinct science. His argument remains of fundamental importance to the articulation of a structurist framework. He extensively defined and defended the notions of 'society' and 'sociation' as the basis of comprehending the relationship of individuality and society. Society for him is a structure that is both the emergent product and the presupposition of social interaction. In his book *Sociology* (first published in German in 1908) he wrote that:

The concept of 'society' has two denotations which scientific treatment must keep strictly distinct. The first designates society as the complex of societalized individuals, the societally formed human material as it has been shaped by the totality of historical reality. The second denotes society as the sum of those forms of relationship by virtue of which individuals are transformed into 'society' in the first sense of the term . . . When using 'society' in the first sense, the social sciences indicate that their subject matter includes everything that occurs in and with society. But when using the term in the second sense, social science indicates that its subject matter is the forces, relations, and forms through which human beings become sociated. Studied separately, these forces, relations, and forms show society in the strictest sense of the term. And this, of course, is not altered by the fact that the content of sociation (that is, the special modifications of its material purpose and interest) often if not always determines its specific form . . .

There is no such thing as society 'as such'; that is, there is no society in the sense that it is the condition for the emergence of all these particular phenomena. For there is no such thing as interaction 'as such' – there are only specific kinds of interaction. And it is with their emergence that society too emerges, for they are neither the cause nor the consequence of society, but are, themselves, society. The fact that an extraordinary multitude and variety of interactions operate at any one moment has given a seemingly autonomous historical reality to the general concept of society.[3]

A little later in the book he dealt with the problem of the individual and social relationship:

The processes of consciousness which formulate sociation – notions such as the unity of the many, the reciprocal determination of the individuals, the significance of the individual for the totality and of the others and vice-versa – presuppose something fundamental which finds expression in practice although we are not aware of it in its abstractness. The presupposition is that individuality finds its place in the structure of generality, and, furthermore, that in spite of the unpredictable character of individuality, this structure is laid out, as it were, for individuality and its functions. The nexus by which each social element (each individual) is interwoven with the life and activities of every other, and by which the external framework of society is produced, is a causal nexus. But it is transformed into a teleological nexus as soon as it is considered from the perspective of the elements that carry and produce it – individuals. For they feel themselves to be egos whose behavior grows out of autonomous, self-determined personalities. The objective totality yields to the individuals that confront it from without, as it were; it offers a place to their subjectively determined life-processes, which thereby, in their very individuality, become necessary links in the life of the whole. It is this dual nexus which supplies the individual consciousness with a fundamental category and thus transforms it into a social element.[4]

Together these passages contain a clear statement of what Giddens later articulated as the duality of the agent–structure interconnection. Simmel was a highly original and insightful thinker who was partly responsible, along with Weber, for founding sociology as a separate discipline in Germany before the Great War. But there is not and never has been a school of Simmelian sociology as there has been with Marx and Weber, perhaps because he made no strong intervention in the methodological debates of the time over positivism and hermeneutics and because the potential of a structurist framework was neglected in those debates.

Jean Piaget's genetic epistemology and psychology has been a major contribution to the development of structurist methodology and theory. Piaget's book on *Structuralism* (1968) is perhaps the most important text in the development of structurism before those of Giddens because of his emphasis on the genesis and transformation of structures and the duality of the structure/structuring relationship. Piaget wrote that 'if the character of structured wholes depends on their laws of composition, these laws must of their very nature be *structuring*: it is the constant duality, or bipolarity, of always being simultaneously *structuring* and *structured* that accounts for the success of the notion of law or rule employed by structuralists.'[5] The central problem, then, of this approach to structures, is that of '*construction* and of the relationship between *structuralism* and *constructivism*'.[6] Far from the subject's disappearing or dying in this sort of structuralism, as some post-structuralists have asserted, it is rather decentred. That is, for Piaget,

the subject's activity calls for a continual 'de-centring' without which he cannot become free from his spontaneous intellectual egocentricity. This 'de-centring' makes the subject enter upon, not so much an already available and therefore external universality, as an uninterrupted process of coordinating and setting in reciprocal relations. It is the latter process which is the true 'generator' of structures as constantly under construction and reconstruction. The subject exists because, to put it very briefly, the being of structures consists in their coming to be, that is, their being 'under construction'... *There is no structure apart from construction*, either abstract or genetic... The problem of genesis is not just a question of psychology; its framing and its solution determine the very meaning of the idea of structure. The basic epistemological alternatives are predestination or some sort of constructivism.[7]

The contemporary development of structurist sociological methodologies in Anglophone countries owes a good deal, often unacknowledged, to the pervasiveness of the ideas of Marx, Weber, and Piaget, in particular. Somewhat outside this macro-sociological stream, the ongoing work of Rom Harré has also been influential. He has concentrated on the social psychological roots of micro-social interactions that have produced small-scale webs of social situations and episodes. He has drawn upon the social constructionist, dramaturgical, and phenomenological streams in social psychology, as developed by, for example, Schutz, Mead, Goffman, and Burke. But Harré has stepped back from propounding a macro-sociological approach on the mistaken phenomenological grounds of the supposed unreality of macro-social entities.[8] Roy Bhaskar, an erstwhile student of Harré's, does not share his ambivalence about either the reality of macro-social structures or the duality of the structure/individual relationship. He has extensively explored the importance of the interrelationship of concepts of structure, structuring agency, realism, and science at a high level of abstraction.[9]

The contribution of Anthony Giddens to articulating the 'structurationist paradigm' was discussed in the previous chapter and need not be repeated.

From the point of view of the explicit development and exemplification of an empirical, historical methodology the work of Philip Abrams, Norbert Elias, Charles Tilly, and Allan Pred is more valuable. Abrams has not only espoused a form of structurism in the crucial book *Historical Sociology*, but he has also employed it in sociological analyses.[10] Norbert Elias's figurational notion of society can also be seen as a form of structurism, for he posits the nexus between individual consciousness and action and prior social figurations as fundamental to society.[11] Charles Tilly has extensively articulated a structurist methodology in numerous texts, most notably *As Sociology Meets History* and *Big Structures, Large Processes, Huge Comparisons*. And Allan Pred has shown in detail, especially in *Making Histories and Constructing Human Geographies*, how a structurist historical geography overlaps with and indeed is essential to the structurism employed in sociology and history.

There are also important contemporary French contributors to the development of versions of structurism. Pierre Bourdieu's concepts of 'practice' and 'habitus' and his work on the problem of social reproduction are relevant here,[12] as are Alain Touraine's studies and theorization of the dynamic interrelationships of action, consciousness, structures, and history.[13]

AGENCY, POWER, AND REALISM

A central theme recurring in the work of structurist historians and theorists is the role of human agency in social structuring processes. The idea of agency is an essential notion in methodological structurism and is closely allied to the idea of social realism. Rather than focusing on the motivation, behaviour, and power of individual persons or the holistic systems in which people are supposedly enmeshed, structurists focus on the dynamic processes of structuring action. Such individual and collective action has as its largely unconscious object the reproduction and maintenance of structures and occasionally their transformation. The concept of 'agency' is very different from the various individualist concepts of the person and of action, such as rationalism and behaviourism, which emphasize abstracted individual autonomy, and from structuralist and functionalist concepts which emphasize the structural determination of action so that the only apparent role for action is carrying and instantiating the social relations and meanings of the totality.

'Agency' in general has two related meanings. First, it is the relatively autonomous power that an entity or part of a system has to produce an effect, that is, to be an agent of a change or phenomenon. Second, it is the power that a person has to act on behalf of another, according to a certain remit or instruction, to try to bring about a result or outcome desired by the principal. The concept of 'social agency' combines elements from these two definitions so that it means, first, the power that persons in general have to be the active, change-inducing, relatively autonomous component within social structures that existed before each individual or group. All complex systems that are charac-terized by evolutionary or historical forces, such as ecosystems, insect and animal societies, and human societies, have agents for change within them. Second, it means that people individually and collectively are agents on behalf of 'social principals' that take the form of pre-existing structures, norms, institutions, and so on, which require actively to be reproduced if they are to survive. However, the process of intended social reproduction gives rise to gradual and sometimes sudden transformations because of the necessity to re-produce the material basis of society by transforming the environment. This is the inherent non-subjective teleology within social systems. The duality of social agency is apparent from this – people both reproduce and transform their social structural environment, as well as transforming their geographical and ecological environment.

Thus 'social agency' implies the ability of persons to choose courses of action and, acting upon their choices, to bring about certain structural changes because of their capacity to do so.[14] Choice is clearly not unconstrained and neither is action and its consequences. The constraints upon choice and action are the structural boundaries (ideological, cultural, social, political) of con-sciousness and action. Consciousness, choice, and action are, by necessity, largely oriented towards social reproduction. Transformation is usually the unintended consequence of attempted individual and collective reproduction rather than of unconstrained, freely acting, self-conscious political movements. Nevertheless, the latter force has on occasion brought about great upheavals, the ultimate results of which were largely unpredicted.

Therefore, agential persons should be conceptualized as beings with collective social structuring power who work upon pre-existing materials and within largely pre-existing patterns and relationships. A concept of social action is needed that does justice to the socially constructing power of subjective persons and the uneven distribution and effectiveness of their power. Indeed, the distri-bution of power is so uneven that many ordinary people believe that they have no power either to control their own lives or to influence social situations. For much of human history they have been virtually right in this belief, that is, social structures have correctly appeared to dominate their lives completely.

It is important to make several points about social power. Power is indeed unevenly distributed so that in all societies most people have little power to control and alter their own life patterns, while a few people have a great deal of power to control their own lives and the lives of others, and to manipulate and transform social situations and structures. The social embeddedness and class distinctiveness of power seem undeniable.

But most people do not understand that actually and potentially they have more power than they believe they have; that is, they have a distorted consciousness of the potential collective strength of their social position and influence. This distortion is a result of three main things: social control through the pervasiveness of ideologies (including idealism, structuralism, and functionalism) that have the effect of hiding the possibility of social power and blocking its realization; social autonomism which has precipitated irrational individualist action, often resulting in the strengthening of repressive social structures; and a failure by all people until very recent times to understand the mechanisms of social transformations that result from intended social reproduction. This internal dialectic of social life springs from the necessity for social production and reproduction through transformation of the physical and social environment.

Following the last point, ordinary people do have the potential for collective structuring power, a potential that history reveals has been realized in semi-conscious and fully conscious group and class actions at many moments in history. At such moments ordinarily powerless individuals take on great structuring power through their collective action, the outcome of which is usually unpredictable but certainly socially transformative.

Therefore it is essential to uphold the notion of general human agency and social power against those who would argue that very few if any people are agents. Agency and power are not human characteristics that have to be manifested constantly in order to exist, as the behaviourists have incorrectly argued. They are capacities which may be manifested only at rare moments. On the other hand, all people unintentionally, constantly, and gradually structure the social and geographical world in their daily lives, so in that sense human power is always being exercised. People have the power, that is, the ability and the capacity, to be agents both consciously and unconsciously.

So there are several kinds of social action, all of which can have some intended effects and some unintended results and which exhibit the variability of power. First, there is personal interaction in small group situations, which are partly structured by that short-lived interaction. Second, there is collective or group action in which individuals act in shared patterns to achieve individual goals. Third, there is patterned action in which individuals act in routinized shared patterns to achieve individual goals. And fourth, there is political action which has as its deliberate aim the maintenance or transformation of the structures and patterns of a society and culture in which all other action takes place. Political action can be individual or group-based or class-based. All kinds of social action have intended and unintended results, and people are often unable to realize their goals through social action. The unrealized consequences of intentions and aims should be an important component of the explanation of social interaction.[15]

Concepts of human structuring agency and power imply the existence of real structures of rules, roles, and relations that are the emergent results, objects, and conditions of human choice, action, and thought. But this implication has to be defended against those ontological individualists who argue for either instrumentalist or phenomenological ideas of structure. In both cases structure is a mental construct, existing only in the thought of observers and/or actors. Nevertheless, these theorists concede that the idea of structure has a powerful influence upon action, even if its independent reality cannot be established.[16]

A realist social ontology can be based upon two arguments. First, there can be a transcendental argument about society's necessary existence prior to and independent of individual and collective understandings at any particular moment. A transcendental argument takes the form of a regression from an assertion of certainty about the world to an assertion that something else which is unknown must be indispensable for that certainty to be the case. Given that behaviour is patterned and ordered, and social relations and roles are apparently institutionalized and more or less stable, there must be sets of rules that govern it. These rules, roles, and relations do not depend on either knowledge of them by particular individuals or the existence or actions of particular individuals, that is, they cannot be reduced to consciousness or to individuals. But they do depend for their continued existence on collective, socially productive, interactive behaviour. Social structure does not exist prior to social interaction in general but is the historical product of it. Nevertheless, there has never been a primordial moment when 'society' was 'awaiting' creation or emergence.

The second argument for social reality says that causal power rather than physical being or sensory apprehension is the vital index of existence. But the causal power has to result in empirical effects before we can ascribe reality to it. In this case, social power is real if it results in observable human actions, utterances, and institutionally organized patterns of behaviour and production. The way to establish at least in theory the existence of social power is to argue that actions spring in large part from knowledge and beliefs about social structures and situations that are shared by groups of people. Intersubjective social knowledge and beliefs about the real coercive power of social rules, roles, and relations structure behaviour into strong patterns. Moreover, rules, roles, and relations structure behaviour and knowledge independently of consciousness, decisions, or choices. Freedom to choose does not mean freedom to act. Therefore, rules, roles, and relations are among the causes of behaviour and so must be real. (In chapter 4 I shall flesh out this argument for social realism.)

MENTALITY, SOCIAL STRUCTURE, AND HISTORY

The complex interrelationship of mental processes and structures (defined in a wide sense), the observed behavioural phenomena, and economic and social structures is the fundamental problem for socio-historical science. Whereas there used to be fairly sharp distinctions between studies of culture, social structure, economies, and politics, so that there were separate disciplines concerned with each one, these divisions have broken down increasingly in recent years. The undermining of the traditional disciplinary boundaries has come largely from anthropology, which has always been more 'interdisciplinary'. Anthropologists have usually been interested in the question of the relationship of mentality or culture to the wider society. The distinctiveness of humans as cultural beings is the anthropological problem *par excellence* and the role of cultural constructs in the socially structuring process has come to be seen as crucial by structurist historians.

What is the general relationship of mentality or culture to society? Is there a general relationship? Does the mental realm play a vital role in social transformation? In order to discuss these questions, we should first raise the question of the meanings of the concepts 'ideas', 'ideology', 'culture', and 'mentality'. Each of these has been used to help designate a sub-field of historical enquiry or a theory of structure and its history. They are not alternative definitions of the same phenomena. 'Ideas' usually refers to publicly stated, recorded, and shared explicit concepts, which are taken to have a history that can be studied. The history of ideas or intellectual history was thus traditionally the study of the development and social influence of certain key concepts in formal philosophical and social scientific discourse. There is often an unexamined assumption of progress in these studies.[17]

'Ideology' usually refers to a constellation of ideas of a socio-political kind that states a world-view about history and society and is an impetus and guide to political action. The study of ideology is the study of socially significant systems of ideas, not all of which are explicitly stated and consciously subscribed to; indeed, they may remain largely tacit. For theorists of ideology the problem is to account for the origins and political role of these ideational systems, which are usually taken to have a distorting effect on social understanding.[18]

'Culture' is a more encompassing concept than the two earlier ones and has several related meanings, depending on the intent and theoretical background of the user. First, it traditionally means formalized artistic expressions of societies and groups – that is, semi-official or 'high' culture. Second, it has come to include wider constellations of belief systems, implicit world-views, forms of understanding, rituals, and popular artistic expression. A third meaning is wider still in that it includes forms of productive life, including material products and tools.[19]

'Mentality' is a term that is usually used interchangeably with the second meaning of culture, that is, it means the 'popular' culture of ordinary people: how they understand themselves and the world, and how they express themselves through religion, rituals, dress, music, and so on, in short, the external manifestations of mental life, a level of life that is concerned with making sense of the world.[20]

To return to the question of the role of mental life of all kinds in social action and social change, in the 'mentality' sense it cannot neatly or even messily be separated from economic, social, and political life; or at least, the onus is on those who wish to use such abstractions to show the explanatory significance of doing so. Social, economic, and cultural life can be abstractly defined, to be sure, but are these abstractions helpful in explanation? All these spheres of social life interpenetrate but they are definable separately. In modern society these abstractions perhaps have more reality than in traditional society, but even here they are not descriptive of radically separate real levels or spheres of structural reality. Culture is certainly not completely coterminous with social structure, economic organization, or political practice. This is one of the prime distinguishing features of modern society – the abstraction of spheres of social life and the growing separation of the spheres so that they can be out of phase, as it were, with each other. Traditional societies seem not to be so abstracted.[21] In other words, there does not seem to be a general ahistorical relationship between culture and social structure. Nevertheless, it is generally conceded, even by historical materialists, that the mental sphere plays a vital role in motivating, channelling, and even dominating human agency.

A refusal to draw sharp divisions between supposed branches of the social and historical studies and an anthropological orientation towards action and society have gone hand in hand with a structurist methodology. For example, Clifford Geertz is usually considered to be an anthropologist or ethnologist, primarily examining the mentalities of particular societies and groups, especially in Java, Bali, and Morocco, but also in modern Western society. But while doing this he has also explored the social, political, and economic structures of his chosen societies, as well as examining their histories. Robert Darnton, while ostensibly a social historian, has been strongly influenced by anthropological understanding, including Geertz's, when studying the mentalities, or structures of understanding, of eighteenth-century France. Emmanuel Le Roy Ladurie has employed economic, social, psychological, cultural, political, and geographic perspectives and theories to explore the history of French agrarian society from late medieval times to the nineteenth century. Ernest Gellner, another ostensible anthropologist by institutional location, has written extensively about the processes of the rise of modern capitalist societies and cultures and their relationships with agrarian traditional societies, as well as about social theory and epistemology and the nature of modern society and culture. Similar but differently nuanced claims could be made for the work of Norbert Elias, Barrington Moore, Philip Abrams, Natalie Zemon Davis, R. S. Neale, Paul Veyne, Alain Touraine, Michel Vovelle and others.

It is no accident that such putative structurists are often either anthropologist or strongly influenced by anthropology. They see that the social structuring processes which give rise to pervasive structures of material, social, and mental relationships linking large numbers of people together into extensive societies and/or cultures have their origins as much in the beliefs, rituals, and ideologies of people as in the material, political, and geographical connections between them. Anthropology as a mode of thought and enquiry has been in its many manifestations the methodologically and theoretically most comprehensive, subtle, and developed of the social sciences. This is perhaps because of its extensive encounters with 'alien' societies, beliefs, and forms of understanding, and the consequent necessity of developing ways of reconciling Western scientific rationalism with traditional non-scientific forms of explanation and understanding.[22]

In recent decades anthropologists have extended their range to enquire into present Western cultures and societies, rightly seeing them as also requiring theoretically rich analysis and interpretation beyond the more traditional approaches of sociology and economics. The 'current situation' of the anthropologist's own society can be just as 'alien' as that of traditional, pre-modern societies. The falsity of the simple 'traditional = anthropology' and 'modern = sociology' equations in social science has been well understood at last. This new understanding raises the question of the proper object of anthropological enquiry. In the broadest sense it deals with the nature of humans as sociocultural beings and as such it should reject the abstraction of people from their economic, social, and political contexts in order to study only their cultural contexts. The humanness of humans is not just to be found in traditional societies or in culture. An anthropological perspective on any society can bring to bear a combination of hermeneutical interpretation and scientific enquiry.[23]

Historians, too, must deal with 'alien' societies and events, although this is not always obvious from their writings. The past is indeed another country, requiring explanations of its structural processes no less difficult to formulate, perhaps more so, than those of anthropologists examining living 'alien' societies. The adoption of an ethnographic attitude by all historians (as well as sociologists) would help to improve their explanations, for it would serve to limit the distortions of theoreticism and so-called 'common sense' derived from present-centred attitudes. Of course historians must always be tied to the present and to a particular milieu but an attempt critically to quarantine the particular viewpoints of the milieu is essential if the realities of 'alien' times and places are to be investigated.[24] But it is the very possibility of this quarantine that the relativist philosophers and theorists have rejected. While they too have supported an ethnographic attitude they have claimed that all investigations are subjective. Structurists cannot agree with this, although they are sympathetic to it. Objectivity is still fundamental to their work. For them social reality is not deconstructed by the theorist but persists in spite of the theorist. Nevertheless, social reality is constructed in and through the activities of structuring agents who have conscious and tacit understandings of the nature of their social and cultural milieu, which help to constitute their structuring activity. Activity is constrained, though, by prior existing structures (including cultures) within which agents operate to reproduce and transform their social life.

Economic historians can also be ethnographic and structurist. Insofar as they are methodologically warranted in their focus on the economy, they should employ theories of the relationship of economic action, institutions, and processes to the wider social, political, and cultural context. None of the putative structurist writers discussed in this chapter ignores or brackets the economic aspects of the totality and none of them adopts a present-centred attitude of projecting a narrow notion of economic rationality onto the past, a central feature of neo-classical economic history. The mentality, including the form of economic rationality, of past epochs, is a question that can only be answered empirically, not theoretically.

THE PROBLEM OF MODERNITY AND MODERNIZATION

The broad problem of the character of modernity and its preceding states and of the broad process of modernization is a central preoccupation in one form or another of many of those who have been concerned to construct structurist explanations. Whether it be, for example, Le Roy Ladurie's early modern reformation and the origins of rural capitalism; Geertz's socio-cultural change in post-colonial Indonesia and Morocco; Darnton's pre-Revolutionary break-down and the loss of mental, economic, and social legitimacy of the *ancien régime*; Moore's origins of capitalism and the modern working class; Hobsbawm's development of the capitalist world imperial system and of bourgeois society between the eighteenth and the twentieth centuries; or Gellner's interest in disenchantment and social change in Christian and Islamic civilizations; they are all concerned to study the processes of social and cultural dislocation attendant upon the rise and/or penetration of modern rationalism and capitalist relations in complex traditional societies. Indeed, these concerns are the heart of the contemporary social anthropological and historical sociological discourses, for they began in a context of the new European and American imperial expansion and the triumph of bourgeois modernity in the late nineteenth and early twentieth centuries. Prior to that, European interest in 'primitive' peoples tended to be Darwinian or physiological in focus and Euro-centric in its attempt positively to demonstrate the biological and cultural superiority of the white races. Gradually through the twentieth century anthropology and historical sociology have come to focus increasingly on the questions of the universality, temporality, and specificity of the structures of humanity's socio-cultural arrangements and the great transformation of traditional into modern.

EXAMPLES OF STRUCTURIST HISTORIOGRAPHY

The claim that structurist methodology, as formulated through the discussion in this and the previous chapter, informs the work of many structural historians must now be demonstrated. This will be done in two ways, first, by mentioning briefly particular works, and second, by discussing the entire corpus of two exemplary historians.

Works of structurist historical writing can be seen as falling more or less into two overlapping broad categories – studies of long-run, large-scale structural change and studies of particular historical episodes of structuration. Both are concerned with the dynamics through which the forces of agency, mentality, and structure interact in the structuring process to reproduce outcomes of social structuration. But outstanding studies of micro structuration – local episodes or 'windows' of structuring – through which the structuring process in general can be grasped better are relatively rare in historiographical literature but more prevalent in anthropological writing for they are more difficult to construct from historical sources. Insight into local mentality, which is required among other things, is difficult to ground without excellent literary sources, in the absence of personal testimony and the possibility of interrogation of subjects. On the other hand, long-run, large-scale structuration is more easily studied and depicted using literary and quantitative sources. Of course the two kinds of study fade into each other and ideally draw upon each other. It is the focus upon the dynamic structuring interaction of micro and macro determination and human agency as the essential social process that fundamentally characterizes a structurist methodology.

Examples of structurist studies of episodes include many of Clifford Geertz's essays about Javanese and Balinese village life, among them the justly famous article 'Deep Play: Notes on the Balinese Cockfight' (1972), in which he studied the complex layers of significance and causality beneath common cultural events. Emmanuel Le Roy Ladurie's work includes two outstanding examples of intensive, penetrating, complex studies of episodes – *Montaillou* (1980) and *Carnival in Romans* (1981) – which will also be discussed in more detail in a moment. Both of these writers attempt to weave together local and large-scale studies of structuring processes to illuminate each other. Similarly, there is Robert Darnton's work on eigteenth-century France, which has been particularly concerned with the social roles of mentalities and other more articulated and systematic ideologies in structuring actions, behavioural patterns, material production, and social hierarchies.[25] Being a historian, he is not directly concerned with drawing general theoretical conclusions (nor with applying general theories for that matter) about social and cultural structures and change. Rather, he sees the task as more hermeneutical and empirical, but this does not prevent him from striving for objective explanations of structuring processes.

In the category of long-run structural studies many examples could be included, e.g., Barrington Moore's *Injustice: The Social Bases of Obedience and Revolt* (1978),[26] in which he attempted to construct a multi-level analysis of structural changes and, moreover, charted the interpenetration of the economy, class structure, politics, and culture. A complex of moments of social reality – personality, action, ideology, culture, and structure – were examined through theories of how these multiple realities intersected to produce the phenomena of socio-political consciousness and behaviour by the working class of Germany in the late nineteenth and early twentieth centuries. In a somewhat different manner Eric Hobsbawm's work, including his three-volume *magnum opus* on the history of the modern world from the late eighteenth to the early twentieth centuries – *The Age of Revolution* (1962), *The Age of Capital* (1975), and *The Age of Empire* (1987) – and his historical studies of labouring classes, analyse the layered complexity of society and the causal interrelationships of actions, events, and structures.[27] Both Hobsbawm and Moore pay close attention to the causal relationships over time between macro levels of the social totality, but, although their analyses of these relationships are informed partly by some of the concepts of historical materialism, this theory does not determine their empirical findings about the hierarchy of social forces and motivations in particular instances.

In another example, some of the work of R. S. Neale, it can be seen how a version of Marxism can be at once a pervasive influence on explanation but at the same time a non-determining one. Some of his writings, especially *Bath 1680–1850: A Social History* (1981) and *Writing Marxist History* (1985),[28] contain a combination of a materialist understanding of society, a set of Marxist categories about class, production, and ideology, and detailed empirical and interpretive enquiries into processes of class structuring and the production of material and mental culture. These enquiries reveal the complex structuring process of early modern England, undergoing transformation from an agrarian, aristocratic society to an industrial, bourgeois one.[29] Of course it is possible to be a theoretically explicit historian, even an applied historical sociologist, and not be influenced to any significant extent by Marxism. This is the case with the historical writing of Emmanuel Le Roy Ladurie, Norbert Elias, Reinhard Bendix, Ernest Gellner, and Charles Tilly, for example. Bendix, Gellner, and Tilly have been influenced by Weber. Ernest Gellner's philosophical writings are inseparable from his anthropological and sociological concerns. His work as a whole provides a good example of an attempt to combine these aspects of modern Western thought into one synthetic framework for understanding the origins and complexity of modernity as a great divide from traditional society. *Thought and Change* (1964), *Saints of the Atlas* (1969), *Muslim Society* (1981), and *Plough, Sword, and Book* (1988) all carry forward this project of grasping the essential constellation of structures and ideas that set the modern world apart from the traditional one.[30]

Charles Tilly, a long-term defender of what amounts to structurism and a sophisticated employer of social theory drawn from different sources, including Weber and perhaps more so Durkheim, has also opposed the use of broad ahistorical categories and theories, such as 'modernization'.[31] He has been particularly concerned, for example, in *The Contentious French* (1986), with the pivotal role of sudden collective acts, such as riots and revolts, which he has examined for their long-run ideological and structural causes and consequences; and at the most general with the process of state-making across millennia, particularly with the role of war-making as a structuring process, as in *Coercion, Capital, and European States, AD 990–1990* (1990).

Finally, we could cite the work of Allan Pred, which spans the local and the global, the past and the present, and more than one continent. As I have indicated earlier, he has sucessfully attempted to bring geographical structures into the centre of the structuring process, but that process involves language, culture, social class, economic relations, spatial transformations, and, of course, time. This complexity is shown most strongly perhaps in the synthetic collection of essays in *Making Histories and Constructing Human Geographies* (1990).[32]

There are several others who could also be cited among those who have offered similar analyses of socio-historical processes employing such multi-level, multi-moment perspectives. At their best, all these writings show that a social structural historiography that strives to be empirically and theoretically adequate to the complexities and multiple realities of society also expresses intuitively grasped truths through insight and interpretation. The power to compel assent depends on both kinds of criteria, as I have tried to argue above when discussing the relevance of hermeneutics to science. Let me now try to establish this point in greater detail by examining at some length the work of Clifford Geertz and Emmanuel Le Roy Ladurie.

CLIFFORD GEERTZ: THE SCIENTIFIC CULTURAL HERMENEUTICS
OF STRUCTURES

Clifford Geertz is one of the most widely respected anthropologists and sociologists of recent decades. Born in San Francisco in 1926, he was educated at Antioch College and Harvard University, where he studied in the Department of Social Relations headed by Talcott Parsons. He held positions in several American universities, including MIT, the University of California at Berkeley, and Chicago, before becoming a professor in 1970 at the Institute of Advanced Study, Princeton, where he has remained. In 1973 he wrote that the American university system, which at that time was 'under attack as irrelevant or worse', had been for him a 'redemptive gift' by providing an ideal setting for scholarly work.[33]

Geertz's work shows the influence of several streams of ideas prevalent in twentieth-century social thought. Perhaps the strongest influences came, first, from functionalist sociology and anthropology, especially via the writings of Malinowski and Parsons's idiosyncratic new synthesis of functionalism and Weberian macro-sociology. Second, there was also Weber's sociology of religion. Third, there was a strong influence from the stream of ethnography that had been influenced by Wittgensteinian ordinary-language philosophy as espoused by Ryle, Winch, and Evans-Prichard. Fourth, there was a strong influence from the semiotic theories of Kenneth Burke and Suzanne Langer. And finally there was the influence of hermeneutic theory as developed by Ricoeur and others. But it cannot be said that Geertz's work belongs to a particular school. In fact he has rejected various labels and has attempted to develop a new synthesis of the social sciences.[34]

In trying to come to grips with Geertz's entire corpus, six main aspects of his work can be identified. These are not discrete categories but aspects of an integrated evolving approach, which is focused on the general problems of understanding and explaining social order via understanding the role of meaning in social life and, more particularly, on explaining the complexities of modernization.

The first aspect is his early Javanese anthropology and socio-economic studies, published in the years 1956–65. These writings were partly the result of fieldwork in Java in 1953–4 and 1957–8 and together they were a self-conscious attempt to provide an interdisciplinary analysis of a society. As he wrote in *Agricultural Involution* (1963), he tried to 'establish a fruitful interaction between biological, social, and historical sciences'.[35] This involved examining the religion, culture, manners, social structure, economic system, and ecological interaction of a Javanese town, and the history of all these over the previous century or so. Not all the works of this period on Java achieve all these integrated aims at once, but they all attempt an integrated analysis to some extent. For example, his earliest essays in the years between 1956 and 1959 on the contemporary Javanese economy gave a central place to the role of religion, culture, and social structure in influencing economic behaviour.

In the 1950s the study of economic underdevelopment had become a major geopolitical, strategic, and academic problem, especially in the United States with its Cold War climate of opinion. On the whole, approaches to the problem of how to stimulate development were less narrowly economistic than they later became and more influenced by social, psychological, and cultural theories, including the work of Weber and Parsons, particularly Parsons's interpretation of Weber. While Geertz was never really part of the modernization school of theory centred on the work of Hoselitz, Moore, Higgins, Stigler, and others, there was some influence on his early work from this school. Some of his earliest writings were published in their journal, *Economic Development and Cultural Change*. The school took the general line, as the title indicates, that economic development could not be explained or promoted without reference to cultural change. But their understanding and use of the simplistic traditional/ modern dichotomy and their theories of culture, the role of entrepreneurship, and the importance of free-enterprise capitalism in promoting the welfare of economically underdeveloped peoples, were not followed by Geertz to any great extent. While they adopted a Western or America-centred perspective that tended to divide the world into a few simple categories, Geertz took a more local ethnographic or nativist point of view. He wrote in *Peddlers and Princes* (1963) that

the method of anthropology – intensive, first-hand field study of small social units within the larger society – means that its primary contribution to the understanding of economic development must inevitably lie in a relatively microscopic and circumstantial analysis of a wide range of social processes as they appear in concrete form in this village, or that town, or the other social class; the theoretical framework of the economist almost inevitably trains his interest on the society as a whole and on the aggregate implications for the entire economy of the processes the anthropologist studies in miniature. (p. 4)

Thus he produced a series of writings on Javanese cultural anthropology in this period, including *The Religion of Java* (1960) which was the definitive work up to that time. However, his writing was not without significant traces of the dominant American socio-economic theories, notably functionalism, modernization theory, and even the Rostowian 'take-off' concept. Nevertheless, he was critical and sceptical about the usefulness of these theories.

A new phase in Geertz's published work began in 1959 with the results of his Balinese research. He first did fieldwork in Bali in 1957–8 and that began a continuing interest in and engagement with Balinese society, culture, and history. The Balinese research served partly as a foil or comparison with the Javanese work, as in *Peddlers and Princes* (1963), and he later added a Moroccan perspective. But it is Bali with which Geertz is most closely associated. His Balinese writings and themes contain the quintessence of his interpretive, historical anthropology, his anthropological methodology, and his theory of society. These themes are interwoven in, for example, his seminal essays 'Person, Time, and Conduct in Bali' (1966) and 'Deep Play: Notes on the Balinese Cockfight' (1972) and his book *Negara: The Theatre State in Nineteenth Century Bali* (1980).

Geertz opened a third part of his work with his fieldwork in Morocco in 1964–6. This interest resulted in two of his most important works, *Islam Observed: Religious Development in Morocco and Indonesia* (1968) and later, with Hildred Geertz and Lawrence Rosen, *Meaning and Order in Moroccan Society* (1979), as well as informing many of his subsequent writings. *Islam Observed* is an ambitious attempt to 'lay out a general framework for the comparative analysis of religion and to apply it to a study of the development of a supposedly single creed, Islam, in two quite contrasting civilizations' (p. v). This is a task of Weberian proportions, reminiscent of Weber's sociology of religion but not on the same scale.

Overlapping with the Javanese, Balinese, and Moroccan aspects of Geertz's work can be found another – generalized writings on the broad problem of economic development and underdevelopment in what came to be known as the Third World or what he sometimes referred to as the 'New States'. Indeed, this was always part of Geertz's perspective, even when he was writing in fine ethnographic detail about his three source cultures. But he always remained an ethnographically oriented observer, building from the particular village to the global situation rather than the reverse. As an anthropologist, he wrote in *Islam Observed*, he was attempting to 'discover what contributions parochial understandings can make to comprehensive ones, what leads to general, broad-stroke interpretations particular, intimate findings can produce' (p. vii).

Now we come to the fifth, and perhaps most important, aspect of his work for, as he said, he was not content to remain at the parochial level but was rather concerned to discuss very general issues to do with human nature and its relationship with culture and society. We can label this aspect as discussions of the problem of the methodology of interpretive anthropology, cultural hermeneutics, the cultural concept of humankind, and the culturalist concept of society. Such discussions were first published as early as 1962 and have remained a central theme through his work ever since, the best example being his central essay on 'Thick Description' (1973).

Finally, there is a sixth, related theme – discussions of modern Western thought, its relationship with other cultures, and problems of the philosophy of social scientific knowledge. Here the central works are some of the essays collected in *Local Knowledge* (1983) and the lectures in *Works and Lives* (1988).

Looking at Geertz's work as a whole it is possible to discern a coherent structure in his thought, so that each aspect – philosophy, methodology, theory, and empirical enquiry – is closely interconnected with the whole, as in figure 3.1. Like all summarized reconstructions of the thought of particular writers and schools, it must be understood that this diagram makes Geertz's work seem very coherent and systematic – more so than it really is perhaps – and indicates an apparent hierarchy of ideas and implications that are not all well delineated and traced out in his work. And of course, even if such a reconstruction is well warranted in his work, it doesn't mean that this structure of ideas sprang well-formed and complete from his mind in one creative act. It must be remembered that such an *ex post hoc* reconstruction attempts to establish a coherent model or system of ideas with which to grapple in a critical way. Nevertheless, Geertz's corpus of work does naturally have an unusually high degree of coherence, which he has himself written about on occasion, and this makes the reconstruction a fairly objective one.

Geertz's philosophical and methodological framework

As figure 3.1 indicates, he has attempted to steer a course between the poles of objectivism and relativism in his philosophy of explanation. The powerful idea that we can never, as anthropologists, historians, sociologists, or common-sense observers, fully apprehend and understand another culture, society, or era as the native does seems to lead to relativism, but this is not to say that we cannot apprehend and describe at all. He believes that it is not only possible but essential to marry hermeneutics and social science and that many writers do so. To write 'the social history of the moral imagination' is to try, he says, to penetrate the tangle of hermeneutical involvements,

to locate with some precision the instabilities of thought and sentiment it generates and set them in a social frame. Such an effort hardly dissolves the tangle or removes the instabilities. Indeed, . . . it rather brings them more disturbingly to notice. But it does at least (or can) place them in an intelligible context, and until some cliometrician, sociobiologist, or deep linguist really does solve the Riddle of the Sphinx, that will have to do.[36]

Figure 3.1 The structure of Geertz's thought

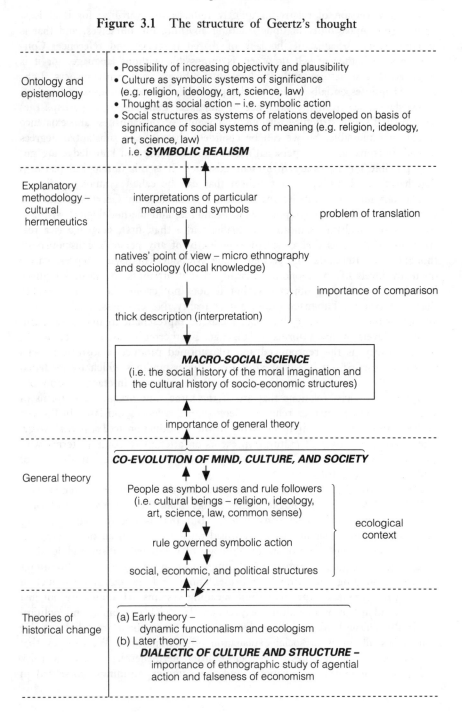

Any strong version of relativism quickly reduces to absurdity, for it at least implies the impossibility of understanding anything but ourselves, and that is also impossible because of the lack of shared language and reference. Consciousness, whether of self or other, is impossible without language, for it is language that structures and develops in symbiosis with consciousness. Language is quintessentially social, so the possibility of social understanding and knowledge arises from the existence of language. Language is a (perhaps the) fundamental social structure without which human consciousness and existence would be impossible. So we can be confident that at least substantial degrees of both personal and interpersonal social understanding and knowledge are not only possible but necessary to human existence. It is this ontological platform that has to be built upon, a platform that can be called symbolic realism.

The ontology of symbolic realism is a central idea in Geertz's work. We encounter it in his ethnographic, socio-economic, and methodological writings. By 'symbolic realism' is meant the dualistic idea that, first, language is a real structure of symbols that exists independently of any person's consciousness, thought, and utterances, and second, being symbolic, language is representative on many levels of an autonomous reality that it attempts to grasp. Language is real in the sense of objectivity, but it does not create the external reality that it represents. Language grows out of reality. Nevertheless, reality is only apprehensible via language, but reality can be represented in many ways and on many levels by many forms of language. Furthermore, social reality, unlike natural reality, is the reproduced and transformed product of historical social interaction carried out in a context of social understandings which are mediated linguistically or symbolically. For Geertz, forms of social interaction grow out of systems of social relations that are at the same time organized as forms of symbolic meaning, such as religion, ideology, art, science, and law. 'In the last analysis, then, as in the first,' he wrote in the introduction to *Local Knowledge*, 'the interpretive study of culture represents an attempt to come to terms with the diversity of the ways human beings construct their lives in the act of leading them' (p. 16).

Geertz subscribes to a sort of weak relativism that is actually better labelled as 'localism' or, as he also put it, seeing things 'from the native's point of view' because meaning is socially constructed.[37] But that is not the only point of view. The complexities of the social world must be seen in all their complexity.[38] A social science based on an ontology of symbolic realism and localism *à la* Geertz requires hermeneutical interpretation of systems of meanings through examining the symbolic representations and the cultural conduct of people who carry and reproduce these meaning systems. Meanings are not just to be found in forms of cultural expression. If social, economic, and political life is also cultural life any sharp distinctions between them are ruled out. He approaches all forms of social explanation ethnographically. We can say that for him social science relies upon socio-cultural hermeneutics to make a 'thick description' of episodes, situations, and the complex meanings embedded in and helping to determine social life. Ethnography is faced with 'a multiplicity of complex conceptual structures, many of them superimposed upon or knotted into one another, which are at once strange, irregular, and inexplicit'.[39] Grasping and rendering these is a difficult task of semiotic translation, so that it is like 'trying to read (in the sense of "construct a reading of") a manuscript – foreign, faded, full of ellipses, incoherences, suspicious emendations, and tendentious commentaries, but written not in conventionalized graphs of sound but in transient examples of shaped behavior.'[40]

The methodology of social science must be, then, a combination of micro-ethnography, thick description, and macro-empirical, historical enquiry that attempts to transcend ethnocentrism. We are not trapped in our own culture, unable to grasp others in their complexity. There must and can be a degree of objectivity and universality. Indeed, the value of being able to understand diversity is that it allows us to understand ourselves as well as the social world. It is the asymmetries, he says,

between what we believe or feel and what others do, that make it possible to locate where we now are in the world, how it feels to be there, and where we might or might not want to go. To obscure those gaps and those asymmetries by relegating them to a realm of repressible or ignorable differences, mere unlikeness, which is what ethno-centrism does and is designed to do . . . is to cut us off from such knowledge and such possibility: the possibility of quite literally, and quite thoroughly, changing our minds.[41]

For the ethnographer as for all social enquirers there are fundamental problems of translation and the use of theory. While we undoubtedly share our humanity and we all have languages, there is a persistent worry that we might not be able to understand those whose languages (in both the linguistic and cultural senses) we do not share. Translation is problematic in social science as well as in everyday life. To be at all possible translation must involve im-mersion in the thought world of the society whose language and culture are being translated. For Geertz this has meant the necessity for micro-ethnography – studying the small-scale social life of villages, local customs and culture, and local political and economic activities – in order to build up to macro analyses. But he is not advocating a simple empiricism of fact-gathering:

The bulk of what I have eventually seen (or thought I have seen) in the broad sweep of social history I have seen (or thought I have seen) first in the narrow confines of country towns and peasant villages. A number of people . . . have questioned whether this sort of procedure is a defensible one . . . of course . . . it is invalid . . . Anthropologists are not . . . attempting to substitute parochial understandings for comprehensive ones, to reduce America to Jonesville or Mexico to Yucatan. They are attempting (or, to be more precise, I am attempting) to discover what contributions parochial understandings can make to comprehensive ones, what leads to general, broad-stroke interpretations particular, intimate findings can produce. I myself cannot see how this differs, save in content, from what an historian, political scientist, sociologist, or economist does, at least when he turns away from his own version of Jonesville and Yucatan and addresses himself to wider problems. We are all special scientists now, and our worth, at least in this regard, consists of what we are able to contribute to a task, the understanding of human social life, which no one of us is competent to tackle unassisted . . .

Like all scientific propositions, anthropological interpretations must be tested against the material they are designed to interpret; it is not their origins that recommend them.[42]

Here the role of theory takes its necessary place, for it is theory that enables generalization and sets a framework for employing concepts developed from particular cases for other cases and for making sense of particular cases in the first place. As he says in *Peddlers and Princes* (p. 142), particular local studies of economic development enable more intensive probing of general dynamics and of the social and cultural context in which development occurs. The 'gross dichotomies and over-systematic ideal types' that have been employed in development studies can be avoided and some greater flexibility introduced. But this doesn't imply an atheoretical, 'every case is different' attitude. A balance must be sought between broad categories and local variations (pp. 146–7). *Peddlers and Princes* attempts to achieve this by developing a middle-range sociological theory of development.

Geertz's book *Negara* contains perhaps his most sustained theory-building attempt. There he tries to construct a framework for studying the structural history – ecological, ethnographic, sociological – of the Indic-Indonesian form of civilization. In order to do that he had to have an appropriate model of socio-cultural processes in such civilizations. In constructing this theoretical model he employed a combination of some knowledge of developmental sequences of civilizations elsewhere, an ideal typical formulation isolating central features of the form, and detailed ethnographic analysis of a current case that is assumed to have a familial resemblance to other cases.[43] But he puts the ethnographic component at the centre of the theory-building process. Having constructed a model of the *negara* or theatre state as a political order it could be applied experimentally. The model is

a conceptual entity, not a historical one. On the one hand, it is a simplified, necessarily unfaithful, theoretically tendentious representation of a relatively well-known sociocultural institution: the nineteenth century Balinese state. On the other, it is a guide, a sort of sociological blueprint, for the construction of representations, not necessarily or even probably identical to it in structure, of a whole set of relatively less well-known but presumably similar institutions: the classical Southeast Asian Indic states of the fifth to fifteenth centuries.[44]

The use of such theoretical models is essential in writing structural history. Historical enquiry can only be done from the present but that does not mean there is an inevitability linking past and present.

Geertz's general theories of society and history

The ethnographic and anthropological methodology of social explanation implies the rejection of various forms of reductionist arguments. The complexity of societies and their history cannot be grasped by an over-simplifying theory that tries to see everything in economic or social class or cultural terms. The following slightly artificially articulated passages serve to convey what we can call Geertz's anthropological–ecological model and theory of complexity.

What we [the authors of *Meaning and Order in Moroccan Society*] all hold is not any particular interpretation of any particular aspect of Moroccan society, . . . any overarching 'theory of society', or even any shared attitude toward the moral and political implications of what we imagine we found out (save, of course, that there are some). What we all hold is the view that the systems of meaning, whether highly explicit like Islam or rather less so like hospitality, in terms of which individuals live out their lives constitute what order those lives attain. We see social relationships as embodying and embodied in symbolic forms that give them structure, and we are concerned to identify such forms and trace their impact. (p. 6)

The interplay of environment and culture is one of the basic themes to which anthropologists have devoted themselves. If their studies have established anything, it is that the environment is no mere given, no neutral constant, no passively enduring condition. Rather, it is an integral part of man's life-world, as deeply shaped by social conditions as social conditions are mediated by it. The natural setting is more than a context to adapt to, a store of resources to draw on, or a stage on which the drama of social life is played out; the ways in which a civilization works out its relation to its setting over a long period of time makes the environment a vital aspect of that civilization itself. To explore the irrigation of land use patterns of people of bled Sefrou is to explore how its inhabitants use the available resources, how they make the resources a part of their own social drama, and how their ecological adaptations relate to other aspects of their culture. (p. 8)

What is perhaps the central theme of his work – the necessity to take the complexity of social reality seriously and not reduce it to simple formulas – is strongly evident in many of his works. The anthropological–ecological model ties together the personal, ecological, cultural, social, economic, and political aspects of human life in such a way as to make sense of each of them within what seems at first glance to be a holistic frame, which is probably what Geertz would call it but which should more accurately be described as a structurist frame. From his earliest work in the mid-1950s onwards he has been concerned to examine the interconnections between these traditionally defined but often abstracted aspects of the totality in order to explain economic and social change, cultural phenomena, and the nature of humanity.

The anthropological–ecological model has several components. First there is the idea of people as cultural beings whose actions, behaviour, and interrelationships are culturally structured. People's actions are rule-governed and employ symbolic forms as well as being symbolic. The outward forms of actions and utterances, whether they be formal structures such as religion, law, and science, or artistic expression or political ideology or just so-called common sense, are all symbolic in that they are culturally embedded forms that symbolize structures of belief and meaning.

Second, rule-governed symbolic actions and interactions structure the world of economic, social, and political institutions. Social structures are systems of relations and interactions developed on the basis of the significance of systems of meaning such as religion, ideology, science, law, common sense, and art. Third, systems of meaning, social structures, and forms of social interaction all take place within a physical, ecological, and geographical context which sets certain limits, at least temporarily, to social arrangements and economic development. Finally, Geertz rejects the idea of long-run determination by any of the aspects of the social totality. That is, he rejected culturalism, materialism, and economism, in favour of the idea of the co-evolution of mind, culture, and society, with none being historically determinant.

This implies of course the rejection also of an overarching general theory of structural history. But the anthropological–ecological theory of society establishes certain parameters for theorizing social change in general and for developing theoretical understanding of the history of particular societies and social forms. Partly under the influence of structural functionalism, the dominant approach in 1950s American sociology and developed primarily in the Harvard Department of Social Relations where Geertz had studied, he employed a synthesis of dynamic functionalism and ecologism in his early Javanese writings. The essential features of this theory were, first, a revision of functionalism to make it more capable of dealing with social change. He did this by developing an analytical distinction between culture and social structure and treating them as independent variables that have mutual interdependence. They can then be seen as capable of a wide range of forms of integration with each other rather than just simple isomorphism. This then gives the possibility of incongruity and tension between them and with the pattern of motivation, so that transformations in any of them can occur.

The second feature is the idea that the dynamic interactions between culture, structure, and motivation always occur within an ecological framework. By 'ecosystem' he meant 'the material interdependency among the group of organisms which form a community and the relevant physical features of the setting in which they are found'.[45] An ecological enquiry investigates 'the internal dynamics of such systems and the ways in which they develop and change' in order to see not what is there but what is happening (p. 3). And what is happening 'is a patterned interchange of energy among the various components of the ecosystem as living things take in material as found from their surroundings and discharge material back into those surroundings as waste products' (p. 3). The inclusion of people in an ecosystem does not change the basic relationships. But an ecological social analysis is not reductionist, for it tries to determine 'the relationships which obtain between the processes of external physiology in which man is, in the nature of things, inextricably embedded, and the social and cultural processes in which he is, with equal inextricability, also embedded' (pp. 5–6).

Geertz later dropped the functionalist aspect of his theory of social change as the local ethnographic and social orientation became more central in his work. In *The Social History of an Indonesian Town* (1965) he studied the interaction of ecological, economic, social structural, and cultural factors over a period of a century or so in order to discover the processes of social change. In order to do that he carried out a 'theoretically controlled analysis' and constructed several arguments about the historical processes. In other words this is not a 'history' in the orthodox, traditional sense of history writing but a work of what could be called 'historical sociology' or more accurately 'social history' in the structural sense defended throughout this book.

The central theoretical argument of Geertz's analysis in *Social History* and in much of his work is based on the idea that

all societies, unrealized ones included, have a characteristic order, a particular sort of structure, even if that order and structure are incomplete, contradictory, and ... vague and inconstant in outline.
To discover and present that order, or a reasonable approximation of it, I have had recourse to a somewhat unusual sort of analysis of the main conceptual categories in terms of which the inhabitants of the Modjokuto of 1952–1954 themselves perceived their society – of the principles of social grouping. (p. 8)

Here we have perhaps the clearest statement of Geertz's methodology and general theory that inform all his work. A society and its history are investigated ethnographically in the present to reveal the structure of order, employing a general theory that links local understandings, culture, social structure, economy, and ecology, and present with past. *The Social History of an Indonesian Town, Islam Observed, Meaning and Order in Moroccan Society,* and *Negara,* are the central texts of Geertz's corpus of work, for they are the synthetic places where all the aspects of methodology, theory, and empirical enquiry come together to produce works of scientific structural history. The empirical validity of his arguments or explanations in those texts is a separate question. The importance of the texts for helping to establish a domain framework for structural history enquiry is independent of such validity.

Geertz's explanations of structural change

Now that we are able to grasp the intellectual apparatus that Geertz has brought to bear upon the task of explaining particular socio-cultural phenomena and processes of change and the more general problem of attempting to unravel, from particular cases, the very knotty problems of the nature of people and their historical social arrangements and dynamics, we can appreciate the particular explanations of structural change that he has developed.

Much of Geertz's early work up to the mid-sixties was concerned with the problem of the post-independence economic development of Indonesia. In *Agricultural Involution* (1963), *Peddlers and Princes* (1963), and *The Social History of an Indonesian Town* (1965), he attempted to explain the contemporary structural processes occurring in parts of Java and Bali, compare them, and come to some conclusions about their significance for Indonesia as a whole. He argued, using Rostow's concept of 'take-off', that Indonesia was in a pre-take-off phase – between having lost its traditional equilibrium and not yet having attained the dynamic equilibrium of an industrial society.[46] Following the Weberian prescriptions that economic development is inevitably part of broader changes in society and that development or modernization is fundamentally a process of economic rationalization brought about by entrepreneurs, and based on his two case studies of a Javanese and a Balinese town, he proposed the following six hypotheses for further testing:

1. Innovative economic leadership (entrepreneurship) occurs in a fairly well defined and socially homogeneous group . . .
2. This innovative group has crystallised out of a larger traditional group which has a very long history of extra-village status and interlocal orientation . . .
3. The larger group out of which the innovative group is emerging is one which is at present experiencing a fairly radical change in its relationship with the wider society of which it is part . . .
4. On the ideological level the innovative group conceives of itself as the main vehicle of religious and moral excellence within a generally wayward, unenlightened, or heedless community . . .
5. The major innovations and innovational problems the entrepreneurs face are organisational rather than technical . . .
6. The function of the entrepreneur in such transitional and pretake-off societies is mainly to adapt customarily established means to novel ends.[47]

The pre-take-off stage of the eco-social structure of the wet rice-growing (Sawah) areas of Java and Bali was characterized as suffering from 'involution', brought about by the Dutch-imposed culture or cultivation system which caused a dual agricultural economy to develop between export plantation crops and subsistence wet-rice growing. 'Involution' is a concept that refers to the process of inward over-elaboration of an established form or system so that it becomes rigid (*Agricultural Involution*, p. 82). He argued that wet-rice cultivation as an ecological and social system was able to absorb into the existing pattern of production and land tenure almost all the large additional population that western intrusion indirectly created without a serious fall in per capita income or a structural upheaval (p. 80). From the mid-nineteenth century the Sawah system was characterized by increasing tenacity of basic pattern; internal elaboration and ornateness; technical hair-splitting, and unending virtuosity. And this 'late Gothic' quality of agriculture increasingly pervaded the whole rural economy: tenure systems grew more intricate; tenancy relationships more complicated; cooperative labor arrangements more complex – all in an effort to provide everyone with some niche, however small, in the overall system. (p. 82)

The dual economy impinged on the pattern of village life, in Geertz's account, to bring about involution there too. The village

faced the problems posed by a rising population, increased monetization, greater dependence on the market, mass labor organization, more intimate contact with bureaucratic government and the like, not by a dissolution of the traditional patterns into an individualistic 'rural proletarian' anomie, nor yet by a metamorphosis of it into a modern commercial farming community. Rather, by means of 'a special kind of virtuosity', 'a sort of technical hair splitting', it maintained the over-all outlines of that pattern while driving the elements of which it was composed to ever-higher degrees of ornate elaboration and Gothic intricacy. Unable either to stabilize the equilibrated wet-rice system it had autochthonously achieved before 1830, or yet to achieve a modern form on, say, the Japanese model – the twentieth-century lowland Javanese village – a great sprawling community of desperately marginal agriculturalists, petty traders, and day laborers – can perhaps only be referred to, rather lamely, as 'post-traditional'. (p. 90)

The involution thesis has proven to be highly controversial and a large literature has developed on the topic, which need not concern us here.[48]

Geertz's extended essay *Islam Observed* contains a comparative historical sociology and an attempt to comprehend present Islamic beliefs, practices, and significance in Morocco and Indonesia. It is, therefore, an attempt to explain several centuries of cultural change, how the past grew into the present. He dismissed four common 'strategies', or what we could loosely call methodologies, for approaching the problem – the indexical, the typological, the world-acculturative, and the evolutionary (pp. 57–9). They shared the common defect, in Geertz's eyes, of merely describing results of change rather than its mechanisms, and not analysing the causes. To uncover causes requires attention to processes (p. 59). The basic process that he identified in the religious history of Morocco and Indonesia in the past 150 years was a progressive increase in doubt about the depth or strength of religious belief. The main causes of this process he identified as being three related developments:

The establishment of western domination; the increasing influence of scholastic, legalistic, and doctrinal, that is to say, scriptural Islam; and the crystallisation of an activist nation state. Together these three processes, none of them yet concluded, shook the old order in Indonesia and Morocco as thoroughly, if not so far as productively, as Capitalism, Protestantism, and Nationalism shook it in the West. (p. 62)

In religion the impact of the West on these countries was first to provoke a strengthening of Islam, for that became oppositional to Western Christianity – people were now Muslims as a matter of policy (p. 65). An 'oppositional, identity-preserving, willed Islam' flourished, whose content became scripturalism – 'the turn toward the Koran, the Hadith, and the Sharia' (p. 65). The new movement directed its criticism not towards Christianity but towards the older Islamic doctrines and practices, Maraboutism in Morocco and illuminationism in Indonesia (p. 65). This process culminated in our time in a 'tense intermixture of radical fundamentalism and determined modernism':

Stepping back in order better to leap is an established principle in Cultural Change; our own Reformation was made that way. But in the Islamic case the stepping backward seems often to have been taken for the leap itself, and what began as a rediscovery of the Scriptures ended as a kind of deification of them. 'The Declaration of the Rights of Man, the secret of atomic power, and the principles of scientific medicine', an advanced Kijaji once informed me, 'are all to be found in the Koran', and he proceeded to quote what he regarded as the relevant passages. Islam, in this way, becomes a justification for modernity, without itself actually becoming modern. It promotes what it itself, to speak metaphorically, can neither embrace nor understand. Rather than the first stages in Islam's reformation, scripturalism in this century has come, in both Indonesia and Morocco, to represent the last stages in its ideologization. (pp. 69–70)

Geertz as structurist

Geertz's empirical explanations have sometimes proved controversial, especially the involution thesis, but his methodology has been increasingly influential on the enquiries that are striving to reintegrate the various strands of the social sciences so as to be able to grasp complex structuring processes.[49] Placing the human agent as the centre of social analysis necessitates developing an adequate methodology and general theories of the conditions, motivations, and structural consequences of agential action. This further necessitates an adequate conceptualization of structure and its generation. Geertz's work provides all these, as I have tried to indicate. His methodology directs attention to the complex structuring processes involving all the moments and levels of society. His general theory emphasizes the role of mentality in the structuring action of agential people. This is crucial, because agency implies choice and power, and choice is reflective thought made out of a background of understandings of self, society, and the world. Understanding is culturally conditioned and constrained, so mentality must play a vital social role, even in modern, supposedly rational, society. Human action is empowered partly by the positive, collective integration of mentality and action. Of course it is not often so integrated, because of the coercive power of certain social arrangements.

EMMANUEL LE ROY LADURIE:
THE GEOLOGY OF STRUCTURAL HISTORICAL TOTALITIES

Emmanuel Le Roy Ladurie is widely considered to be the outstanding member of the third generation of the *Annales* school. The school was founded in the late 1920s at Strasbourg by Lucien Febvre and Marc Bloch, who created the journal *Annales d'histoire économique et sociale*, which later moved with them to Paris in the mid-thirties. After the war the journal was re-created. The school was institutionalized in 1947 as the sixth Section (Economic and Social Sciences) of the École Pratique des Hautes Études under the leadership of Fernand Braudel, the doyen of the school in the post-war decades. But the school was still outside the established university system until after 1968, when the sixth Section was re-created as the École des Hautes Études en Science Sociales and given degree-granting rights.

Le Roy Ladurie was born in 1929 in Calvados, the son of an official who became Minister of Agriculture in the Vichy regime. He repudiated his father's politics and as a youth joined the French Communist Party, which he later left. He was educated in a Paris *lycée* and the École Normale Supérieure. He taught at Montpellier University in the early sixties and was part of the sixth Section in the late sixties. He became an editor of *Annales* in 1969, a Professor of Geography at the University of Paris VII in 1970–3, and Professor of History and Modern Civilization at the Collège de France in 1973, in succession to Braudel.

In order to gain a general understanding of Le Roy Ladurie's work, we need to know something of the *Annales* approach to history and society. When Bloch and Febvre began their work in the 1920s the dominant tradition of historiography in France, as in Britain, America, Germany, and elsewhere, concentrated on the designation and interpretation of singular events and actions, particularly political actions, events, and institutions; on elites; and on 'national characters'. Bloch and Febvre wished to re-orient historical enquiry towards socio-economic structural change and the history of groups, classes, and communities, particularly the long-run history of agrarian societies. Accordingly, historical geography and social theory were important influences on their work, as was psychology, because they also wished to study the history of the collective mentalities of communities. In short, they were interested in the history of material, social, and mental structures.

But the *Annalistes* were not interested in writing theoretical history. They were resolutely empirical – what Febvre called 'archaeological' – in their methodology. This is a metaphor that has recurred down the years among *Annalistes* and it seems to mean that they wished to try to investigate and comprehend a civilization in the totality of all its aspects. Theories of various sorts were employed throughout, but always sceptically. They were strongly historicist in their attitudes to the past and to the use of theory. Their aim was to attempt a total sifting of all possible evidence in order to try to bring to life the material and mental milieu of a group, community, region, society, or epoch.

'Total history' was strongly espoused and exemplified in the work of Fernand Braudel, editor of *Annales* from 1956 to 1968 and the leading second-generation *Annaliste*. His three major works – *The Mediterranean and the Mediterranean World in the Age of Philip II*, *Civilization and Capitalism*, and *The Identity of France* – exemplify his and the school's interest in the long-run history of structures. His structures are the virtually unchanging geographic and economic continuities and cycles of the material life of pre-industrial Europe and the world. Braudel was not very interested in either mentalities or politics. The first- and second-generation *Annalistes* were dismissive of political-event history – *histoire événementielle*. Events were important to them only insofar as they carried the deep structures of material life.

Le Roy Ladurie's early writings[50] were strongly influenced by Braudelean structural history. His youthful period of teaching in Montpellier impelled him towards a life-long interest in Languedoc, which had earlier been known as Occitan or Pays d'Oc, that area of south-west France where the Romance language Oc had been spoken until the nineteenth century and even into the twentieth in some places. His first studies were of the social structural and ecological history of that region – its climatic and agrarian history – which resulted in a two-volume *doctorat d'état thèse* on *The Peasants of Languedoc* (1974), first published in 1966. The following year he published a path-finding book on the history of climate – translated as *Times of Feast, Times of Famine* (1972). These works immediately established his reputation as one of the outstanding younger *Annalistes*. The books exemplify the totalizing and structuralist approach of *Annalisme* at that time. His book on the peasantry of Languedoc is a massively detailed quantitative study of a whole socio-economic and cultural evolution across a long period of time. He was concerned to establish the connections among geography, economy, social structure, institutions, forms of consciousness, and class struggle. As he said, he endeavoured in *The Peasants of Languedoc*

to observe, at various levels, the long-term movements of an economy and of a society – base and superstructure, material life and cultural life, sociological evolution and collective psychology, the whole within the framework of a rural world which remained very largely traditional in nature. More particularly, I have attempted to analyze, in their multiple aspects, successive phases of growth and decline. These phases, taken together in chronological sequence (lift-off, rise, maturity, and decline), imply a unity and serve to describe a major, organized, secular rural fluctuation spanning eight generations.

To put it more simply, my book's protagonist is a great agrarian cycle, lasting from the end of the fifteenth century to the beginning of the eighteenth, studied in its entirety. I have been able to delineate and to characterize it thanks, naturally, to the price curves, but more particularly thanks to demographic studies (of taxpayers and of total population), to indices of production and business activity, and to the series of charts reflecting land, wealth, and income distribution. (p. 289)

Associated with his interest in structures, cycles, continuities, and total history, Le Roy Ladurie became an early enthusiastic employer and advocate of large-scale quantification and the use of data analysed by computers. But unlike the parallel development in the 1960s of cliometrics in the United States, he did not see the task as being the application of a present-oriented theory to historical data. He was not an econometrician who manipulated data to answer preconceived questions about abstract variables. Rather, one of the main points of quantification was to reveal the serial and cyclical nature of society over long periods – the continuities, repetitions, and fluctuations of patterns of behaviour, institutional arrangements, economic relationships, ecological conditions, and so on. It could also reveal hitherto unsuspected changes in large-scale collective social phenomena. Against a critic who would say that human beings are neglected in such an approach, he wrote in *Times of Feast, Times of Famine* that, if Marc Bloch's dictum that the historian is 'like the ogre in the story: wherever he smells human flesh he recognizes his prey' were taken literally,

it would mean that the professional historian would systematically neglect a whole category of serial or qualitative documentation, such as early meteorological observations, phenological and glaciological texts, comments on climatological events, and so on. A strictly human historiography could take such documents into consideration, but never to work out completely and for itself their intrinsic climatic content, only to check some usually minute point in human history or local or specialised knowledge. (p. 191)

Within this context, large-scale and machine-assisted quantification cannot in itself answer questions and solve problems, as the cliometricians sometimes seem to believe, but it opens up new problems by providing long series of data. These days, such an understanding is commonplace but we tend to forget the novelty of computers and the hostility with which they were greeted by many historians and some sociologists in the sixties. Le Roy Ladurie saw their potential very early. In the essays contained in *The Territory of the Historian* (1979) he vigorously defended their use and gave examples of it.

In the 1970s he developed a parallel stream of work which, while not altering or abandoning his general structural and quantitative orientation, focused on the history of mentalities, or what might be called forms of collective consciousness or semi-conscious cultural structures, and how mentalities have influenced collective behaviour. This has resulted in several powerful works, most notably *Montaillou* (1980), *Carnival in Romans* (1981), and *Love, Death, and Money in the Pays d'Oc* (1984). These are works of great complexity and richness. The first two focus upon particular episodes of social upheaval and spread out from there to analyse whole milieux. Layers of significance and structure and circles of influence are revealed by a combination of empirical enquiry, theoretical complexity, and hermeneutical insight. *Love, Death, and Money* reveals more clearly than his other work, and indeed almost more than anywhere else in the *Annales* tradition, the underlying influence of Lévi-Straussian structural anthropology and linguistics. Lévi-Straussian concepts are employed by him to explore the cultural meaning and significance, in the anthropological and literary senses, of an Occitan eighteenth-century novella. As in the other books, his analysis spreads wider and wider to examine the whole social milieu of which the text is both a pregnant signifier and potentially a socially integrative force.

Le Roy Ladurie's methodological foundations

Le Roy Ladurie has discussed his own explanatory foundations on several occasions and he has taken a strong interest in methodological questions, as have many *Annalistes*. Indeed, the *Annales* movement and the sixth Section were explicitly founded in methodological opposition to established orthodoxy, so the basis for their attempted subversion of history and sociology disciplines had to be articulated clearly.

As the quotation above from *The Peasants of Languedoc* indicates, Le Roy Ladurie saw himself as engaging in the writing of total history. What did this mean in practice? It meant at least three things together. First, there was the idea that none of the structural 'levels' or 'spheres' of an actual society in the general overall sense – the economic system of material production and distribution, the form of social interaction and hierarchies (which is more than the class structure), the form of mentality or culture and beliefs, and the form of ecclesiastical and state administrative institutions – could be grasped, understood, or explained in isolation from all the others. Here a geological rather than archaeological metaphor is central for he saw societies through it as being stratified or, perhaps more accurately, as sedimentary, being an accumulation of layers of institutions, practices, and beliefs. Second, there is the idea that total history requires attention to the totality of available empirical evidence (or as much as possible), especially about the economy. Every possible source of data must be combed. Third, the notion of totality includes the structuralist idea of transformations, but in the peculiar *Annaliste* sense of the deep structure of cycles and conjunctures. This leads to the apparent paradox of *l'histoire immobile* (or 'History that Stands Still') which was actually the title of his Collège de France inaugural lecture in 1973.[51] How could there be history if there were no change? His short answer is: because there were cycles and conjunctures within a more or less structurally static geo-eco-demographic totality that persisted across many centuries. But this answer is unsatisfactory as it stands. We need to examine his concept of *l'histoire immobile* further, for it is central to his and to *Annales*' distinctive contribution.

The concept of a history that stands still could only apply, if at all, to a particular kind of society – an agrarian, pre-industrial, traditional society with a Malthusian relationship between environment, technology, and population. France between the end of the Middle Ages and the beginning of the eighteenth century was conceptualised as such a society, but its national integration was almost non-existent. This area and milieu was the particular focus of most of *Annales'* attention. For Le Roy Ladurie, this society was an object, 'the statistical dimensions of which, despite some sizeable fluctuations, always tended to return to a fixed level which acted as a ceiling'.[52] The rural demographic and ecological system was able to deviate but always reproduced itself in such a way that it returned to the same main parameters (p. 21). However, this kind of structural continuity obviously did not last. It began to break down after about 1720 and the way he explains why and how it did so is significant for understanding his structurist methodology and the role of theory within his work.

Francophone structuralism[53] has had three overlapping streams or locations – linguistics and anthropology; epistemology and psychology; and social structural history. The *Annales* historians, most notably Braudel and including Le Roy Ladurie in his *histoire immobile* incarnation, have embodied this third stream. Braudel argued that such an approach to history was concerned with the *longue durée* of structural continuity, as revealed through the cyclical rhythms of material life. Structural history was for him the core of social science. However, the great problem with his work is the difficulty he had in both theorizing and explaining structural change and transformation. The role of social agents in the form of powerful individuals, groups, and classes, is extremely minimized, as is the influence of mentalities. Geo-economic structural determinism is the focus of Braudel's totalizing work, and his achievements in such enquiries are outstanding, notwithstanding the weakness in his writings regarding transformation.

Le Roy Ladurie's totalistic studies are not so deterministic and, furthermore, he shows in his books on mentalities – *Montaillou* and *Carnival* in particular – that the event and the long term, the continuities and the ruptures, must be brought together. As he went on to say in his inaugural lecture, France after 1720 began to experience a great transformation in its geo-eco-social structure:

The forces of renovation included the State, the modernized Church, the educational system – all more repressive and more efficient; a more plentiful money supply; a more sophisticated nobility and bourgeoisie; better-run estates; greater literacy everywhere; a more rational bureaucracy; more active trade; and urbanization at what eventually became an irresistible rate, forcing nations (whose productivity was not keeping pace) to produce more peasants in order to feed the new mass of townspeople. Wisdom or folly – who knows? But it opened Pandora's box, forcing the agricultural population out of its eco-system, breaking the old medieval norms, unbreached until the death of Louis XIV. The breach stood open through the age of the Enlightenment and of course during the following nineteenth century. In 1328, the French population stood at 17 million; it was 19 million in 1700 – still about the same. But by 1789, it had reached 27 million and had risen to almost 40 million by the time of the Franco-Prussian war of 1870. In other European countries, the advance was even more rapid. The demographic upswing, accompanied by the disappearance of famine, made it necessary and inevitable that simultaneously there should be some growth in the gross agricultural product – not to mention the superior methods of transport for grain and foodstuffs. The increase in production of the now generally available fruits of the earth had, if hunger was to be satisfied, to be at least equivalent and probably superior to that of the country's population.[54]

(This passage is not only important methodologically but also theoretically, as I shall show in a moment.)

So Le Roy Ladurie's total history is not the deterministic holism of Braudel. It does not transcend all events and transformations. If structural history writing could truly be transcendent of the particular it would perhaps be very satisfying, but of course the historical process is not, as he wrote in another essay, entirely logical, intelligible and predictable.[55] Events and ruptures cannot be exorcized even by a totalizing 'science' that attempts to grasp all within an encompassing framework. But as I have argued, 'historical science' is a defensible notion if it is not considered in this quasi-positivist or indeed positivist way. Braudelean structural history, in spite of its great empirical and theoretical strengths, in the end cannot adequately explain its object because of its holistic construal of society and its history, and so it fails the basic test of social science. As Le Roy Ladurie rightly says,

a trend or a structure can quite easily be unmasked. All that is required is a little patience, a great deal of work and plenty of imagination. But the aleatory transition from one structure to another, the *mutation*, often remains, in history as in biology, the most perplexing zone, where chance appears to play a large part. Once one has reached this zone, factors which are often mysterious delineate the poles of necessity within the field of possibilities: once they have surfaced, their existence is obvious – but a moment before their appearance, they were as unpredictable as they were unprecedented.[56]

In other words, what we have to explain is not structural continuity but structural rupture, and a concentration on continuity not only disguises the ruptures but hinders explanation of them.

Thus the structural location but transformative (or what might be called 'agential') character of certain ideas, actions, events, groups, and people, were the subject of Le Roy Ladurie's parallel streams of work, which concentrated on those aleatory transitions that were so hard to explain. *Montaillou* and *Carnival* are excellent examples of such work. The concentration on significant micro-social events and groups does not imply that he was returning to narrative history of events and neglecting structures. The two had to be combined, as in these books. Each deals with a small series of significant events that are upheavals or ruptures in the processes and structures of their place and time. These events are not only narrated from several points of view but investigated for their own deep structures. They are then placed in their complex structural situations and processes – ecological, economic, political, cultural – and shown why they are significant both historically and methodologically. In the manner of landslides and tectonic rift forces these ruptures lay bare the geological strata of their societies. Consequently these books are at once narrative stories, historical geographies, anthropological and sociological analyses, and economic and political histories.

In analysing the processes Le Roy Ladurie concentrated on the role of mentalities in motivating and explaining social change. *Montaillou* deals with the social influence of Albigensianism and the mental world of fourteenth-century peasants in a Pyrenean village. The first half deals with the ecology of the village – its households and the peasant economy. The second half deals with what he calls the 'archaeology' of the village, by which he means its mentality or culture in the sense of the beliefs, rituals, customs, social relations, and morality. *Carnival* has a somewhat similar structure but greater complexity, in keeping perhaps with the greater complexity of a sixteenth-century town with its complicated social structure and powerful economic and religious tensions. Although the violent upheaval that surrounded the carnival of February 1580 was, as he wrote, a local incident, it is greatly significant for the historian because it 'represents a deep probe into the geological stratifications of a dated culture. It informs us about a specific city and a particular province. More generally speaking, it elucidates the urban dramas of the Renaissance, at the time of the Reformation, the beginning of the Baroque age, and the rise of the Catholic Counter-Reformation.'[57]

The combination of such integrated, simultaneous, enquiries into structures, events, and transformations with the use made of theories in Le Roy Ladurie's work can be seen, I argue, as together providing an example of structurism in the dual methodological and sociological senses. Before discussing that further we need to know something about his use of theory.

Le Roy Ladurie's use of theory

Like all *Annalistes* Le Roy Ladurie explicitly and implicitly refused to distinguish between historical enquiry and theory construction and application. Each was necessary to the other. In many places in his work he explicitly employed theories and in several places discussed and defended their relevance. For example, he wrote in *Times of Feast, Times of Famine* that the historian of climate must begin by learning all there is to know from the researches and theories of meteorologists, glaciologists, geographers, biologists, geologists, dendochronologists, archaeologists, and even physicists. There must also be a reciprocation between these scientists and the scientific serialist historian in order to explain climatic history (pp. 20–22).

In his inaugural lecture he wrote of the relationship between history and theoretical social science in the following illuminating way, which is worth quoting at some length:

Until the last century, knowledge was based essentially on the dialogue between two cultures: the exact sciences and the humanities – mathematics versus intuition, the 'spirit of geometry' and the 'spirit of discernment'. History, from Thucydides to Michelet, was of course included in the humanities. And then along came the 'third culture', unobtrusively at first, but soon becoming visible to all: the social sciences. For a long time, they coexisted quite cheerfully with the historian: in the line running from Marx to Weber, Durkheim and Freud, there was a constant exchange of concepts and much crossing of frontiers between the two. More recently, however, old Chronos came under attack. The social sciences, wishing to preserve a reputation for hardness and purity, began to operate a closed shop against history, which was accused of being a 'soft' science. The attack was characterized by a great deal of ignorance and not a little gall on the part of the attackers, who affected to forget that since Bloch, Braudel and Labrousse, history too had undergone a scientific transformation. Clio had stolen the clothes of the social sciences while they were bathing, and they had never noticed their nakedness. Today at any rate, the move to exclude history seems to be almost over, since it is becoming clear that it has no future. Everyone has eventually bowed to the obvious: it is no more possible to build up a human science without the extra dimension of the past, than it is to study astrophysics without knowing the ages of the stars or galaxies. History was, for a few decades of semi-disgrace, the Cinderella of the social sciences, but it has now been restored to its rightful place. Indeed, it now appears to have chosen just the right moment to withdraw, refusing to become a narcissistic mental activity, rotting away in self-absorption and self-congratulation; while the death of history was being loudly proclaimed in certain quarters, it had simply gone through the looking-glass, in search not of its own reflection, but of a new world.[58]

What theories did Le Roy Ladurie invent, borrow, employ, and reject in his search for hitherto neglected worlds? What knowledge and use of social theories do his historical writings display? There isn't space here to discuss all the various employments and rejections of theory that his work reveals, but a few examples will suffice. First, the analysis of the independent peasant household (the *domus*) and village life that he carried out in *Montaillou* was strongly influenced by the work of Karl Polanyi and A. V. Chayanov (see pp. 353–4). Second, *Love, Death and Money in the Pays d'Oc* is an anthropological and sociological work that has been strongly influenced by Lévi-Straussian structuralism (see pp. 401–3). Third, in one of his remarkable regional histories, on the Rouergue (or the modern *Aveyron département* in Languedoc) he wrote that the theories of neither Marx nor Weber had anything to teach about its history:

In 1800, the majority of the Rouergue population consisted of rural proletarians, with a minority of self-employed farmers (about 50,000 to 40,000, according to Béteille). By the end of the nineteenth century, these proportions had been reversed in country areas. Rural society, as organized by the *ostal* system, was becoming not ideal (far from it) but distinctly better balanced and less wretched – and that, after all, is what matters.

No marks for Marx then, but no marks for Weber either, with his Anglo-Saxon-Germanic obsession with the regenerating and fertilizing effects of Protestantism. The Rouergue was blithely ignorant of such things. Until recently it remained part and parcel of an essentially Catholic culture: the Pope's little acre in the Occitanian south, a Catholic enclave like Poland or Ireland, but more fortunate than either of these. The Rouergue benefited from an appreciable rise in living standards, accounted for by its whole-hearted participation in the career of a comparatively privileged and highly developed country like France. The Catholic culture of the Rouergue produced a remarkable number of local vocations to the priesthood or to convents, thus making it easier for the *ostal* to pass to a single heir, from one generation to another.[59]

And fourth, there is the example, mentioned above, of the use of a range of scientific theories in his book on *Times of Feast, Times of Famine*. That book comes closest of all to being a work of applied theory rather than historical enquiry, but even it remains on the level of attempting to explain the complex, fine-grained reality of a real process.

The most important questions about Le Roy Ladurie as socio-historical theorist concern his basic theory or model of society and of its dynamics. How did he conceptualize the structure of pre-industrial French society in particular and how did he account in theory for its transformations? Another way of looking at these issues is to ask if Le Roy Ladurie's work contains, as perhaps Braudel's does, a version of historical materialism; or does it contain a rival conception, a form of historical culturalism perhaps? What is the general relationship that he sees, if any, between ecology, economy, society, politics, the state, and mentality? In fact, Le Roy Ladurie does not propose either explicitly or implicitly a general theory of social structural history in the way that some *Annalistes* do, Braudel in particular. A case can be made that all Braudel's work is informed by a version of historical materialism. He relies upon a kind of half-articulated geographical determinism to explain structural change over long periods.

As I argue in chapter 5, historical materialism is a theory of social history that rests upon a model (which is not a description) of society as being structured in 'levels', 'strata', 'layers', or 'spheres' that have relative but overlapping autonomy. There are 'lines' or 'currents' of influence, contradiction, and/or determinism that link the levels in various ways in this model. But what the levels are and how they interrelate is not prescribed in advance by such a general model, so they can be conceptualized in many ways. Historical materialism, then, is a theory, employing this model, which says the material level or levels is/are the prime locus of historical causation, in the sense that the impetus for changes on other levels and in the whole social structure comes primarily in the long run from the material aspects of the structure.

Le Roy Ladurie's work is certainly strongly informed by a dynamic 'geological' model of society, as the following passage from *Carnival in Romans* shows:

An isolated incident, the Carnival in Romans illuminates, reflects on the cultures and conflicts of an era. These include strictly urban struggles, municipal problems which set the craftsman and the butcher trade in opposition to the patrician ruling group; traditional peasant agitation moulded into an assault on a system of land-holding that was becoming aggressive, capitalistic; the violent rejection of the government and taxes, both revealing of social conflict. There was also a place for the Catholic, medieval, Renaissance, and soon to be baroque folk traditions of festivity; the bourgeois, semi-learned and semi-egalitarian ideologies drawing inspiration from classical authors . . . The Carnival in Romans makes me think of the Grand Canyon. It shows, preserved in cross section, the social and intellectual strata and structures which made up a *'très ancien régime'*. In the twilight of the Renaissance it articulates a complete geology, with all its colours and contortions. (pp. 338–9)

The passage from page 289 of *The Peasants of Languedoc* quoted above also reveals his debt to the 'base–superstructure' model. But he does not take the next step into historical materialism. That is, he does not explain structural change, in any of his writings as far as I can ascertain, by reference to the causal influences of changes in the relatively autonomous material levels of society, such as climate, geography, and technology. On the contrary, he refuses such explanations. The passage from page 25 of *Mind and Method* that I have quoted above (p. 121) clearly indicates the contrary. He finds the forces for social transformation in a long list of locations – such things as the state, church, money supply, nobility and bourgeoisie, literacy, rational bureaucracy, trade, and urbanization. Perhaps it could be said that such a list indicates that there is in fact no explanation offered, because if everything is used to explain everything then nothing is explained. I do not believe he is guilty of this, but the point here is that when he came to consider the question of general explanations of all historical processes he could find none. Each process had to be explained separately, partly by reference to chance events and partly by reference to the overlapping, complex interconnections of the various levels, none of which had priority. The levels model directs attention to the sites of possible determination but does not indicate what those determinations are. The aleatory transitions that he refers to elsewhere could not be explained by some overarching structuralist theory. This can be seen clearly from his detailed studies of structural history and transformations.

I think it can be seen from the foregoing discussion that Le Roy Ladurie's work as a whole contains a form of methodological and sociological structurism. Methodologically, his work contains a notion of the reality of social structure as a complex system of 'levels' or substructures that causally interrelate with each other. The structure is not a monolithic system with holistic powers of self-generation and self-maintenance. Actions and events by individuals, groups, and classes are the moving force of history. This means that explanations have to be made simultaneously on both the micro and macro levels of society. Explanations of actions, events, consciousness, and structural change all require reference to all the others. Sociologically, the theory of society is that social phenomena and social structures have this dual, historical, character and so require an appropriate methodology. Society is an ongoing structuring process on all its levels. There is in Le Roy Ladurie's work a series of overlapping dialectics between continuity and transformation, action and structure, material and mental. Such complexity is the basis of a claim that Le Roy Ladurie's structurism is moving in the direction towards being adequate to its object – the complexity of human society.

TOWARDS A SCIENCE OF STRUCTURAL HISTORY

At the end of chapter 2 I pointed out how the relational–structurist tradition in history writing employed methodological structurism, which has been summarized late in chapter 1. In the present chapter I have tried to articulate further the content of this methodology and demonstrate its existence and employment in the work of some historians. But of course, as I emphasized at the beginning of the chapter, methodology does not directly determine the content of theories and explanations, although it does constrain them and it does rule out some theories such as an ahistorical materialist conception of history.

From all this discussion we can draw the following essential points about the structurist methodology for structural history. The methodology emphasizes the necessity of studying two nodes of causal power – the conditioning power of social structures of all kinds and the agential power of persons acting collectively. Explanations of structural change and of action must take full account of their complex intercausality. And the full complexity of all the moments of the social process has to be incorporated so that there are no loose ends, that is, no nomological danglers at the end of causal chains. Neither intentions, nor biological drives, nor social structures, nor cultures, are prior to any of the others. Our conceptual apparatus must be able to integrate them into a coherent framework of reasoning that enables explanations of social complexity. At the beginning and the end of the reasoning is the human agent, a historical actor who is not a heroic moulder of the world, outside history, but embedded in a complex evolving structure of rules, roles, relations, and meanings that must be collectively reproduced in daily life. Through that reproduction process structural transformation and hence history occurs.

Thus the fundamental test of the value of a methodology for socio–historical enquiry is whether it is able to direct theoretical and empirical attention to studying how action, thought, and structure causally interact over time. I have tried to show in chapter 2 and in this chapter how methodological structurism can provide a framework for such an explanation. The philosophical assumptions of individualism and holism are unable to support a sufficiently powerful methodology for doing this. Individualists and holists overemphasize one side of the social process to the virtual neglect of the other. They therefore tend to miss half of the causal interconnections. In fact many of the individualist historians cannot rightly be called social or structural historians at all because they do not share what should be one of the most important concepts of the domain of structural history, that is, the idea of the reality and irreducibility of social structure. All the others are more or less sociological realists, although most interpretists and some relational structurists are ambivalent about the degree of objectivity of society.

As we have seen, among all those who subscribe to social realism there is a division between holists and structurists. Holists, in turn, are divided between systemic holists, who believe society is a powerful, self-regulating, integrated system, and cultural holists, who believe society is a gestalt of meanings. Both groups seem to have little place for the structuring power of persons and groups. Structurists, on the other hand, accord a central place to human agency. Society for them is a structure of rules, roles, practices, and relations that causally condition social action, and it is the intended and unintended result of past collective structuring action and thought. In practice many social historians have come to see, sometimes only semi-consciously, that this is the right methodological framework. A glance through the issues of recent years of social history journals will reveal this immediately. Nevertheless, holism continues to guide some practitioners, especially some structuralists and traditional historical interpretists. And individualism is still prevalent in empiricist and behaviourist sociology, traditional history, and cliometrics.

Furthermore, explanation for methodological structurists is not a question of developing strictly logically and/or statistically derived conclusions, as it often is for empiricists and sometimes is for Francophone structuralists of the Lévi-Strauss sort. The arguments of, for example, Le Roy Ladurie, Geertz, Moore, Hobsbawm, Tilly, Pred, or Touraine, cannot be reconstructed in nomologically deductive terms. They contain, rather, a complex web of reasoning that includes imaginative hypotheses, theories, models, metaphors, analogies, inductive empirical generalizations, and deductions. Their aim is neither to give a simple statistical or narrative account nor to give a logically justified account. Rather, their achievement of an increasing degree of plausibility comes from a combination of theoretical richness, empirical complexity, explanatory narrative, and methodological structurism. Structural history done in this way is at least potentially scientific because like other sciences it is based on a realist ontology of structures and a commitment to discovering the complex multi-level structural reality of the world. The ideas of empiricist objectivity and absolute truth that have been associated with science are bypassed in this better account of science, and the questions of experimentation and prediction are irrelevant.

In chapter 4 I shall try to establish that scientificity comes, rather, from a combination of:

1   The employment of a complex *web structure of reasoning*, which is found in all sciences, that links hypotheses, theories, models, metaphors, analogies, and data.
2   The general *adequacy of domain concepts* to their object of enquiry (which can only be established through research).
3   Adoption as a research rationale of the *discovery of structural reality and history*.
4   Adoption of a *combination of coherence and correspondence ideas of truth* such that there is a gradual convergence between them as the structural reality of the world is discovered. Short-term pragmatic coherence is acceptable within the framework of the long-term policy of discovery.
5   The central significance of *empirical evidence*, but evidence that can never be entirely theory-neutral.

As many students have shown in recent years, science is not a discourse that fundamentally either aims at or achieves absolute objectivity. Rather, it is a socially constructed and socially relative set of practices, but practices that nevertheless attempt progressively to discover the causal structures of the universe. Whether they are always successful is not the most important question. Clearly they are not for much of the time, although the fact is that the natural sciences have made progress. The important question here is: what makes a science adequate to its task? I believe I have sketched a way to show how a science of structural history (which must be the core of a wider science of society) can be adequate to its task. The employers of methodological structurism are candidates for the label of 'scientific' structural historians because they go a good deal of the way towards meeting the criteria mentioned above. Progress in explaining the history of societies can be and has been achieved by basing the scientific domain on methodological structurism.

4
Realism and Structurism as the Foundations for a Science of Structural History

The fundamental philosophical issue that the social studies still face is that of the possibility of objective knowledge or, which is another way of putting it, the possibility of scientific knowledge. However, given the multiplicity of notions of what a science of society and history should be like, is there anything to be gained from still discussing it? I believe there is, as I have indicated in chapters 1 and 3, because of major advances that have occurred in the philosophy of scientific realism in the past decade or so. In the second section of chapter 1, I argued that realists have convincingly shown that the reasons for the success of science lie in a combination of the implicit use of critical realism, scientific internalization, a reflexive network of reasoning, and the development of theories that are able to analyse the world into its natural kinds, the success of which is confirmed by engineering in open situations.

LOGIC OF DISCOVERY VERSUS LOGIC OF ARGUMENT

Realist discussions about social explanation have tried to steer a course among the multiple hazards of common sense, relativism, hermeneutics, structuralism, behaviourism, and empiricism, to arrive at a destination that promises to place social explanation on a new basis of explanatory strength. This new philosophical basis is intimately bound up with and mutually supports methodological structurism, as I shall argue in this chapter. What gives the argument linking structurism and realism such potential force is that the logic of the deductive argument that links them is in a sense the mirror image of the inductive logic of the discovery of the connection between them. That is, the connection between realism and structurist empirical research that was initially established through a process of discovery that led through successive steps of generalization to greater and greater abstraction, ending in philosophical realism, can

Figure 4.1   The connection between realism and structurist research

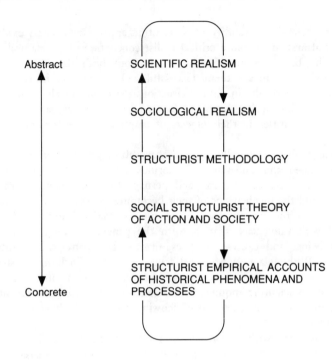

be expressed *ex post facto* as a series of deductive steps from abstract to concrete, as in figure 4.1.

The presentation of the argument about the connection of realism to structurist empirical accounts could only come after those accounts had been developed, at least in a rudimentary form to begin with, and subsequently confirmed in methodological and theoretical senses by writers such as Geertz, Le Roy Ladurie, Tilly, Pred, and others. Structurist accounts could only be made at first, of course, within some prior proto-structurist framework, and we saw in chapter 3 how structurism has gradually developed during a century and a half. All advanced sciences exhibit this sort of history, in which successful explanatory methodologies and general theories emerge and crystallize over periods of time, reinforcing themselves as they develop through the ongoing research process, thanks to their explanatory power. It is only later that we can construct the steps in the argument that conceptually links abstract to concrete. The process of discovery was an inductive, generalizing one rather than a deductive one. This chapter presents an argument about the possibility of a science of structural history rather than an account of the process of discovery of the general concepts and general theories which help to form the framework for the science.

NATURAL AND SOCIAL REALISM

In order to defend the validity of a scientific approach to social explanation, it is essential first to uphold a critical realist conception of the natural sciences as being the best account of what it is about both the world and their methodology which makes them successful and progressive in the discovery and application of results in natural situations. Realism can also show how the potential methodological unity of all forms of empirical explanation could be based upon similarities in their objects of enquiry and the structures of their reasoning.

Scientific realism generally argues[1] that, although particular phenomena can be described and understood in various ways, it is the task of science to attempt to reveal the general, and perhaps hidden, structural features of phenomena and the mechanisms of their becoming. Science is not on the whole concerned with the unique features of phenomena and entities. Science is concerned with universals, that is, with the general defining characteristics, modes of being, and causes, of types, classes, and patterns of entities and phenomena. Without a notion of real types of entities (including systems and structures), which have discoverable dispositions, powers, and potentialities, there can be no scientific enquiry, because such enquiry consists fundamentally of uncovering such properties and of showing how actual phenomena relate to those properties.

Science operates with a concept of multi-layered depth. The observable behaviour of entities has to be explained by uncovering the shared nature of those entities, as well as by uncovering the relationships in which entities exist and have their being. Therefore, without a theory of the real and relatively enduring nature of social entities as entities there cannot be a science of society which is not reducible either to a science of individual behaviour or to a hermeneutical study of intentions and actions.

However, realism gives rise to a major problem of epistemic access because it does not remain on the level of phenomena. If it is held that reality is layered and some layers are not available to sense perception, and so must be modelled and inferred from effects before being known, then the question of how we move from our base in the sensory world to uncover these hidden layers must be of central concern to scientists of all kinds. The unobservable nature of aspects of physical reality, such as energy, force fields, subatomic particles, and viruses has not prevented scientists from discovering these realities. Similarly, the unobservable nature of the social realities of rules, roles, relations, and meanings is not an insurmountable barrier to scientific knowledge. However, the difficulty of social science is obviously compounded by the impossibility of developing a mechanical gauge of unobservables which is analogous to a bubble chamber, a gas spectrometer, a radio telescope, a Geiger counter, or a compass. We cannot so detect and measure mental states and never will be able to, even if we have a complete knowledge of neurophysiology. The intentionality of actions and the socially constituting power of beliefs and understandings are always going to remain to some extent personal, ambiguous, and opaque to shared knowledge. But society does also have a real and relatively enduring structural existence which can be the object of a scientific enquiry, but one that must take account of expressed understandings, intentions, reasons, and meanings, although not restricting itself to them. Indeed, they must be criticized by science.

Thus realism does not deny the importance of the investigation of common-sense understandings, reasons, and intentions, or of emotional and 'irrational' motivations for action. They too must be investigated in a scientific manner, using theories, models, hypotheses, and empirical investigation. The employment of a scientific methodology does not entail subscribing to a theory of action as fatally or physically determined. Furthermore, it is not the case that scientific history and sociology must dispense with creative imagination in favour of some wholly inductive or deductive method. Imaginative conjectures, metaphors, analogies, and intuitive leaps seem to be necessary in all empirical enquiry, especially for the framing of new hypotheses and models. But they are by no means the only or basic method, being rather an essential part of scientific enquiry itself.

This is not to say that the different branches of science have an identical structure of reasoning, only that there is a certain basic similarity that unites them as sciences and differentiates them from other kinds of discourse. The strict demarcationists drew the boundary much too sharply, but there is nevertheless a distinction worth drawing between science and non-science (even though they shade into each other) on the grounds of attempted objectivity, realism, structural enquiry, and progress of knowledge. In what follows I shall try to present abstract models of science that are not meant to be precise descriptions of actual forms of scientific reasoning but which can serve to show that the study of society and its history are open to scientific enquiry.

THE STRUCTURE OF REASONING IN NATURAL SCIENCE

A plausible account of the structure of reasoning in any science must take account of the key problem of epistemic access. How do enquiries into the structures and workings of the physical world proceed? The dominant tradition in the philosophy of science until recent years – logical empiricism, epitomized by the 1950s and sixties writings of Braithwaite, Carnap, Hempel, and Feigl – argued that the standard form of scientific explanation ideally conforms to the canons of deductive logic.[2] Deductive inference from covering laws to general causes, combined with knowledge of specific conditions of observable events, should become, it was claimed, the standard form of explanation in all the empirical enquiries, if they are to be taken seriously in their attempts to explain their objects. The problem of gaining access to what we wish to know about causation was thought to be a matter of observations of regularities between types of events, the formulation of hypotheses about constant causal conjunctions between those types of events, empirical testing by observation or experimentation, and ultimately the presentation of results as proven laws from which further deductions could be made. Furthermore, for these philosophers there should be a strict separation of theoretical and observational statements. The former refer to hypothetical entities and causes, the latter to discovered and confirmed entities, events, and causal correlations. Theories are not explanations and do not govern observations, which are taken to be epistemologically neutral.

For most empiricists, then, truth was a matter of correspondence with observable reality. The senses were taken to be the basic guide to reality, so that scientifically aided observation through experimentation and measurement was the ground on which scientific truth was assessed. But for some others, 'reality' was a metaphysical notion about which nothing could actually be known. They preferred to speak only of laws, theories, hypotheses, data, and not about truth. Their theories were only instruments for generating and making correlations between data.

Most empiricists were also reductionists in that they wished to reduce supposedly macroscopic entities to their constituent elements and to try to explain macroscopic complexes by laws governing constituent events. For them societies were ideally to be explained as aggregates of individual behaviour and behaviour in turn by psychophysical laws. There was no place in the science of such empiricists for levels of emergent reality of a systemic kind (such as minds and social structures) with their own laws of composition, operation, and evolution, which were not reducible to their physical constituents. Nor was there a place for causal powers of a social relational kind. For the strict empiricists there was no further alternative between physicalist science and dualist and pluralist metaphysics. However, some philosophers, such as Karl Popper, who share the deductivism of most of the logical empiricists, do not agree with instrumentalism and reductionism, nor with the epistemological absolutism of truth and falsity of most empiricists.[3]

I argue that logical empiricists were wrong about the actual practice of science on three main epistemological grounds: logicism, empiricism, and reductionism; and correspondingly wrong about the ontology of the natural and social worlds. Therefore, any argument about the possibility of a science of society which bases itself upon logical empiricism is bound to be misleading. With a better account of the structure of reasoning in natural science the question is reopened.

In developing a better account, the first thing to be clear about is the correctness of the idea that the social studies should look to natural science for philosophical guidance. The empiricist positivists were right about that for one good reason and several bad ones. The good reason was that the natural sciences, particularly physics and chemistry, are more advanced and may have methodological lessons to teach. But the lessons are not those that were drawn by the pseudo-empiricist practitioners in the social studies, such as the cliometricians and some behaviourists, who wished to reduce social phenomena to atomistic events and 'explain' those events by subsuming them under psychological covering laws. The first correct lesson is that, insofar as science is successful in explaining and manipulating nature both inside the laboratory and in open situations, it is because it operates with a multi-layered realist conception of the world. Its subject-matter is of two general sorts – the generative mechanisms of a dispositional kind that are inherent in the composition of kinds of things, and the forces which inhere in the relations between kinds of things. Another way of putting this is to say that the world is an ensemble of powers, propensities, and forces, which inhere in the ways kinds of things are composed, structured, and related to each other within systems. These powers, propensities, and forces can be given abstract formulations as laws, but those laws are used to help refer to and explain real complex situations, events, and processes. Laws are not descriptions or summaries, but without real situations the universal character of powers, propensities, and forces would not exist and would not have been discovered. They do not 'exist' in the abstract or as Platonic forms or essences but are real universals that exist only in and through particulars. Furthermore, some sciences are not able to formulate universal laws, but in order to explain particular events and processes they do require the essential help of lower-level generalizations about causes. It is the discovery of the real powers, propensities, and forces of the world that gives science its explanatory (and in some cases its engineering) power.[4]

Realism also argues that new levels of reality emerge from the combination of particulars into systems. Science in fact has to make explanations of causation on several levels without attempting always to make reductions to lower levels. Moreover, if reality is taken to include structural powers of both strictly physical and emergent kinds, then the problem of epistemic access in science is quite different from the one understood by the empiricists. It is not a matter of seeking constant conjunctions of observable events but of modelling hypothesized mechanisms and inferring their necessary existence, within emergent structural systems, from their effects.[5]

Within a domain framework of philosophical and methodological commitments of the sort discussed in chapter 1, science operates with a complex web of reasoning, some parts of which are neither inductions nor deductions. Chief among these non-logical aspects are metaphors, analogies, similes, and models. These are necessary to scientific reasoning because it is constantly trying to move from a base in sensory perception and partial understanding to uncover unobserved and hypothesized entities, powers, systems, and structures. These unknown things have to be thought about in terms of and inferred from what is already known. Therefore metaphors, analogies, similes, models, and so on, must take the place of concrete descriptions and detailed analyses. Such forms of thought all rely upon using what we already know to construct new concepts and provisional models about what we do not know or only partially understand.[6]

This is the creative task of science, a task no less imaginative and creative than that of literature or painting. And like literature and painting, the power of scientific creation depends upon its relationship to what we suspect, intuitively feel, or know to be the truth, and that may be closely related to its aesthetic appeal. But unlike the arts, science must constantly test and revise its hypotheses to move closer and closer towards uncovering the causal structures of the world. At least that goal serves as a powerful regulator of scientific practice, as Karl Popper rightly argued.[7] It might be argued that the arts also do this in that they too are searching for structural truths of a sort, and good art appeals more strongly to us because we perceive or share its insight. But its methodology is radically different from science. Artistic insight could not have discovered universal laws of nature, for example, which have proved to be counter-intuitive. Similarly, the general causal structures of cultures, economies, and societies are opaque to common sense and artistic insight.

So, science and the arts both contain a hermeneutical element because they depend on establishing a circle of agreement between explicit statements within the discourse and the background framework of ideas shared by the community of scientists or artists. That background framework helps initially to conceptualize the objects and procedures of enquiry and/or expression.[8] Many defenders of the hermeneutical character of the human and social studies have not understood this necessity for such an understanding in the sciences and so have wrongly drawn a distinction between science and the arts on this ground.[9] Nevertheless, the hermeneutical element in science can be overstated greatly. Science must move well beyond such circular understanding to a criticism of knowledge and understanding *vis-à-vis* discoverable reality. A central role for the correspondence theory of truth must be retained.

I pointed out in chapter 1 how scientific theorizing and practice operate within a background framework of general problems and questions, concepts, source models, and hypothetical ontologies about the subject-matter of the domain, and a general methodology for approaching explanation.[10] Understanding the importance of this framework is crucial to comprehending the partly hermeneutical way in which science operates, but it is also important to see that frameworks gradually change under the impact of empirical enquiry.

The structure of reasoning in natural science can be modelled as in figure 4.2. (It and figure 4.3 are taken from my *Explanation in Social History* and partly draw upon some ideas of Rom Harré.) This diagram attempts to show that science has a complex structure of reasoning that ideally constitutes a coherent network or web of concepts, beliefs, theories, and justified inferences. All parts are necessary to the web, although some are explicit and some are tacit. This web of ideas articulates with the world via observations, experiments, and engineering, which have the power to force modifications of the web.

Figure 4.2   The structure of reasoning in natural science

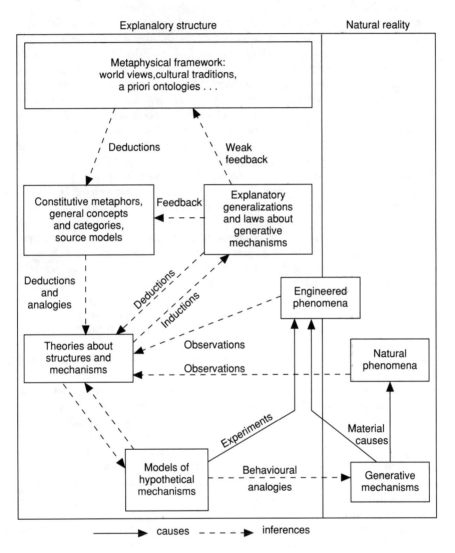

If the foregoing comments and this diagram are more or less correct about scientific reasoning, then the claims of logicism, empiricism, and reductionism can all be disposed of. First, science does not always operate strictly logically.[11] For example, in the framing of hypotheses and tentative models of unknown entities, powers, and forces it often proceeds in logically unjustified ways. Sometimes there are intuitive leaps to conclusions, which are then used as foundations for experiments and discoveries, which can retrospectively prove the correctness of the original intuitions. Logically unwarranted assertions, partially supported hypotheses, inductively justified beliefs, and deductive arguments are all central components of scientific reasoning. Second, science is not empiricist in that it postulates the existence of real causal powers, forces, and structures, which do not and cannot have an empirical form. Causal power is the prime index of reality, not sensory perception, according to the realist account. The world exists and is ordered independently of our perception, which we have discovered through science. Perception has proved unreliable and even misleading as to the deep structural character of reality. And, third, science is not always reductionist, in that many forms of science do not seek always to reduce each macro level of reality to its constituent micro elements. Rather, they seek for the emergent compositional structures and laws of systemic entities. All natural sciences, even particle physics, in effect adopt a structural, systemic, and universalist ontology.

THE STRUCTURE OF REASONING IN SOCIAL SCIENCE

How does this account of scientific reasoning compare with both what is and what could be the situation in the social and historical enquiries? Clearly, the self-perception of many sociologists and historians is that their enquiries are not and cannot be like the sciences of nature. Many philosophers also see the structures of reasoning in these enquiries as in fact being quite different and necessarily so. But given the account of science I have outlined, could social enquiries be, in general terms, like natural science as just described, if they are not already? (Obviously there is and must be a great deal of variation in methodology in the whole field of socio-historical studies.) In fact, much of my answer has been sketched in the previous section, where I argued for social realism. But more support needs to be adduced.

I believe the social and historical enquiries should be trying to explain three kinds of things: first, particular actions and events; second, human behaviour in general (including speech); and third, the origins, development, and dissolution (i.e., the history) of the institutions and social structures in which actions, events, and behaviour take place, such as families, firms, organizations, institutions, social movements, kinship systems, classes, and economies. The explanations of these things can be approached in a variety of ways each of which should try to come to terms with the central problems of the reality and effectiveness of institutions and structures, and the causal interrelationship they have with actions, events, and behaviour.

If the explanation of the history of real social structures is required of all socio-historical enquiries into actions, events, and behavioural patterns, and if those structures persist through time and have conditioning powers, then such an ontology permits, even necessitates, a structure of reasoning similar to but not identical with that of natural science as described above. Social structures as structures of rules, roles, and relations, like the powers, dispositions, and forces of nature, cannot be directly sensed, so perception is no direct guide to their existence and powers. They have to be inferred and studied via their effects. Therefore, metaphorical, analogical, modelic reasoning, among other things, is required for their analysis. And social scientific enquiry, like natural science, always takes place within frameworks consisting of ontologies, methodologies, general source models, and general theories, which help to conceptualize objects of enquiry and the form of explanations.

The major differentiating element that separates the subject-matter of social from natural science is human intentionality, morality, and meaning. It is a fundamental characteristic of humans that they are agents – they have intentions, choose courses of action, act to achieve preconceived goals, try to realize plans, at least much of the time – and they also endow their own acts, goals, relationships, and the world generally, with a multitude of meanings. Parts of the background motivation of action are the meaning, symbolic, and moral systems through which people view the world and their place in it. Furthermore, the social world of rules, roles, relations, and behavioural patterns is the intended and unintended product of individual and collective action over time. If we are to explain the history and effectiveness of structures we must allude to the roles of meanings, intentions, understandings, and practices in producing them. Structures cannot produce or reproduce themselves. Socially productive and reproductive behaviour is always performed in a context that includes understandings about society and people.

Nevertheless, even with this important complicating element, the reasoning in social science does or should have a structure similar to natural science because of the necessity to explain the causal relationships between general and continuous social and cultural structures, psychological propensities, intentions, understandings, and behaviour. It is the existence of social continuities and generalities that underlies this similarity in scientific reasoning. But it is obviously important to add that the space–time invariance and persistence of social and cultural structures is considerably less than in nature. It is because of the structuring process that occurs in society that the natural science model has to be modified. As Bhaskar and others have shown, our social realism has to be circumscribed in important ways.[12]

Figure 4.3 attempts to summarize this reasoning. Its differences from figure 4.2 will readily be apparent. In particular, the place of experimentation and engineering has been taken by expressed intentions. In most natural sciences

Figure 4.3   The structure of reasoning in social science

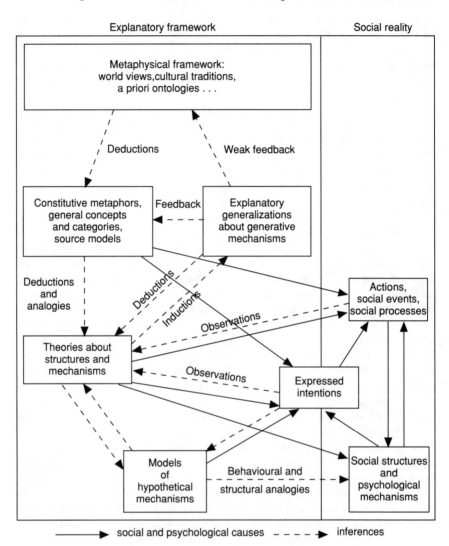

engineered phenomena straddle the realms of reality and explanatory structure and are in effect the result of an intervention in reality by the explanatory structure. (Of course some natural sciences, especially astronomy but also geomorphology, taxonomy, and ecology, cannot conduct experiments into the operations of their systems either. They employ the experimental findings of physics and chemistry but are themselves basically historical and observational sciences.) In social science intentions are the result of cultural, social, and psychological imperatives as well as personal understandings of reality, and those intentions in turn have a causal effect upon social reality through the actions that result from them. Obviously, in such two-dimensional diagrams the vital interactive and temporal movements cannot be shown. But the diagrams attempt to model in a simplified shorthand way a complex, multi-dimensional, fluid process.

It can be seen from both diagrams that scientific reasoning has a network of ideas and inferences, all of which are necessary to its existence and all of which are ultimately focused upon the goal of causal explanation of the phenomena of the world. While there is an important, complex, background framework of ideas for explanation, that framework is ultimately dependent upon its relevance to furthering the goal of increasingly better explanations. The goal of progress in explaining the world is always the ultimate rationale, if not achievement, of scientific enquiry. Nevertheless, it has seemed to many observers that internal coherence between all the parts of the network is an important consideration for scientists and some have held that coherence and problem-solving have overridden the goal of progressive empirical explanation.[13] However, this relativist position is ultimately incompatible with the realism I have been defending so far, but it is important to retain something of the coherence notion of truth. Correspondence and coherence must be combined in a convergence theory of truth.

A CONVERGENCE THEORY OF TRUTH

It has long been thought by many practising social scientists, especially since Vico's distinction between science and conscience, that the ideals of plausibility and truth in the human and natural studies are quite different. The human studies supposedly operate with a relativist, coherence theory of plausibility, there being no objective external test of validity. On the other hand, the natural sciences are supposedly objective studies operating with an inter-subjective external test of truthful correspondence of claims and judgements with empirical reality. But much recent work in the history and philosophy of science has had the effect of breaking down this dichotomy and showing how in fact science operates with a notion of truth that in effect combines elements of the coherence and correspondence notions of validity. This also allows the possibility of closing the gap between the ideas of plausibility applicable in natural and social science.

The coherence and correspondence notions of truth are philosophically opposed. The coherence notion says in essence that statements or judgements are true or false according to whether they cohere with a system of other statements or judgements. A system of concepts about the world can be said to be coherent because of certain assumptions about the meanings and references of the concepts which together imply each other. Any new concept or statement about the world can then be judged for its truth, according to whether it coheres with the system. The correspondence notion says that the truth of statements or judgements or propositions about the world is determined by the facts with which they purport to deal. Agreement with or correspondence with the independent facts is the essence of the theory. There has been a long history of debate about the many complicating aspects of these notions, which need not detain us. Realism by its basic nature subscribes to the correspondence notion because it rests the case for the validity of its statements and judgements about the world on what can be discovered about the world independently of our conceptual frameworks. This obviously contains, at least to begin with, a metaphysical claim about the independence of the world from knowledge of it. But then it goes further to argue that the metaphysical assumption is retrospectively justified by the success of science as revealed by progress in discovery, which comes about because of progress in building theories about the world and means of studying it to reveal its causal structures.

Relativists such as Kuhn and Feyerabend have argued that there is no rock-bottom inter-theoretic reference between words and the world, such that there can be a gradual convergence of theories upon truthful explanations. There has been no genuine progress in discovery according to them.[14] But a line of reasoning stemming partly from Quine and including (in different ways) Putnam, Harré and Madden, Shapere, Boyd, and Hesse,[15] has cogently shown that, although our investigations of both the world and our ways of knowing about it always have to be made from within particular ways of knowing, there has clearly been progress in discovering the causal structure of the world. People collectively over time have been able to improve their understanding of nature and society and to exert some control over them accordingly. But people do not simply mirror the world in their thought, in spite of some evolved isomorphic capacities to do so. Explanations always remain bound by frameworks, but our frameworks improve through feedback from empirical observation, experimentation, and engineering.

A network account of the framework/theory/observation interrelationship (as represented in figures 4.2 and 4.3) argues that each part of the network exercises an influence over the other parts. There is a degree of implication between most parts but the network should not be thought of as an integrated paradigm *à la* Kuhn or as a perfectly coherent system. The lack of complete coherence is crucial for allowing and necessitating scientific change of both incremental and revolutionary forms. This account of science does not collapse into relativism providing we retain the notion of 'logical' support for networks of an inductive and analogical kind and empirical support of a probability kind; that is, the network directs empirical research into its subject-matter. A body of empirical evidence is gathered from which certain generalizations can be drawn. These generalizations bear upon the usefulness and validity of the models and analogies that are used to think about and gain access to the unknown or little understood entities, powers, dispositions, and forces that are being searched for or investigated. The more empirical support that is adduced for hypotheses and theories, the greater the probability of their validity. There is never an absolute correspondence with reality, only increasing degrees of plausibility regarding empirical claims. Empirical evidence has the power to force alterations to parts or all of the network. As Mary Hesse has pointed out, in this network model of scientific reasoning,

science retains its empirical basis, because the criteria of learning the correct use of descriptive terms in the natural language are empirical, and the self-corrective feedback process depends essentially on recognition of the success or failure of empirical predictions. The account therefore retains also the essentials of the correspondence theory of truth, but without the assumption of a stable observation language unpermeated by theoretical interpretation. The view of truth is, however, also essentially instrumental, since it derives from situations of prediction and test, and its relation to theories is indirect. Since the thesis of under-determination of theory by data is built into the model the sense in which 'truth' can also be predicated of theoretical frameworks remains undetermined.[16]

Thus the correspondence and coherence notions of truth can be combined by retaining realism. While this account does remove the possibility of a timelessly true objective basis for knowledge, it does rest on the idea that in the mature sciences at least most analytical descriptions of kinds of entities according to what has been discovered about their causal structural properties are correct, although particular descriptions within systems of classifications and particular referential meanings may be false. Neurath's famous raft metaphor[17] can be adapted to express this: we float on a sea of sensory evidence on a raft of concepts and descriptions whose planks we replace one by one as we go. There is no particular set of planks that has to be retained throughout but we must always retain sufficient within the correctly ordered structure of planks to 'survive'. Thus we never escape the network of coherence conditions but we do add to and gradually alter it. All the while we actually remain afloat on the sea of facts because of the basically correct assumption that our understandings of kinds of entities, powers, and forces correspond correctly to the way the world is. But there is still much to learn, of course, especially about how entities interrelate in systems. However, this degree of progress has not been achieved in the immature sciences. The powers, structures, and dynamics of persons, cultures, and societies are still little understood and so we still lack reliable rafts.

In all mature sciences, then, discovery is a result of, first, the coherence of networks of reasoning, which produce concepts, analogies, models, and hypotheses about the entities and processes under study, and, second, a correspondence between existential claims and evidence. What counts as evidence and how it is assessed is always strongly influenced by the network, but evidence has a degree of neutrality and the potential, therefore, to force changes in the network and usually, sooner or later, to decide disputes between competing theories. There has been a gradual, jerky, convergence between coherence conditions of networks and their degree of correspondence with reality. In short, as Hesse put it, 'that the truth-value of an observation statement is relative to coherence conditions is a matter of epistemology, but the concept of truth that is presupposed is a matter of ontology. That is, of a relation between existents.'[18] Thus both hermeneutics, in the sense of shared understandings about basic meanings, references, and classifications, and the provisional objectivity of references to structural reality are necessary to science.[19] The philosophical, cultural, and social embedding of scientific reasoning should not be denied but neither should the history of its successes. Those successes are not the result of empiricism but of the (tacit?) adoption of realism and the possibility of truthful explanation as basic regulators of scientific practice.[20]

REALISM AND STRUCTURISM:
THE IMPORTANCE OF MANDELBAUM'S CONTRIBUTION

Powerful support for the argument that realism, in both the philosophical and sociological senses, and a theory of the role of human choice and agency, are crucial to constructing a scientific domain for the explanation of structural history can be found in the work of Maurice Mandelbaum. An examination of his contribution is helpful in developing this position. He was one of the most consistent and determined defenders of philosophical and social realism, and what he called 'methodological institutionalism', which contains a theory of human agency and a theory of how the social world comes to be institutionally structured, that is, a structurist theory. In a very important series of works stretching across fifty years he continually, and with remarkable consistency, criticized empiricism, relativism, individualism, and holism, as well as the notion that there should be a strict separation between analytical philosophy and substantive theorizing and research.

Mandelbaum's defence of social realism

Mandelbaum's defence of social realism was developed through a series of works from the late 1930s onwards.[21] In his first book of 1938 on *The Problem of Historical Knowledge* he defended a rather simplistic version of historical objectivity on the basis of empirical realism. In the 1950s he improved on this by arguing for the irreducibility of social concepts and the necessity of scientific social laws for social and historical explanation.[22] Irreducibility does not mean that society is independent of all human beings, only that references to social as well as to psychological influences are necessary for both behavioural and social explanation. A sensory perception theory of knowledge is unable to provide an explanation of non-phenomenal social causes, and methodological individualism is ruled out if reduction to psychology is impossible. The denial of reductionism and individualism does not imply holism, as I have emphasized and as Mandelbaum was at pains to explain. Society, in his view, is a set of semi-autonomous institutions rather than an integrated organic whole with a single law of functioning. Psychological and intentional explanations are required, as much as sociological ones, for social structures and processes.

The form and role of laws in explanation became a central issue in all branches of the philosophy of explanation in the 1950s and sixties, following the work of Karl Popper and Carl Hempel. Their argument was that the deductive covering-law model of scientific explanation was the only viable one for all explanatory disciplines, including history and sociology. Unlike the relativist and hermeneuticist critics of the relevance of covering laws, Mandelbaum's position was that there should not be demarcations between scientific, historical, and sociological explanation.[23] Rather, they should indeed be epistemologically united, but on the basis of a conception of causation and laws different from that propounded by Popper and Hempel and the logical empiricist tradition. Rather than seeing laws as statements about universal sequences of constant conjunctions of events, he argued that scientific laws are statements about 'uniform connections between two types of factor which are contained within those complex events which we propose to explain'.[24] He rejected the logical empiricist theory because it cannot explain natural or social events due to its failure to distinguish invariant sequences of events from actual causative conditions for events. It attempts to deduce the causes of events from laws, whereas historical realism attempts to discover them within the structure of the complex systems of which they are part. The real causes are the necessary and sufficient conditions of events. Those conditions include the natures and states of particular systems and structures and the law-like generalities governing their internal structures and functioning. All causal explanations require such realist, abstractive, generalities, as he argued earlier in regard to history.

Mandelbaum's most sustained defence of critical realist philosophy of explanation and attack on empiricism was made in *Philosophy, Science, and Sense Perception* (1964). Critical realism is also called scientific realism, because it is a philosophical description and defence of the actual presuppositions of practising scientists. As I argued earlier in the chapter, and as Mandelbaum and many others have also argued, science builds upon and goes beyond common-sense descriptions and understandings of the world to try to uncover hidden properties and structures beneath phenomena. The core problem here is of perception, which many philosophers have seen as an epistemological problem only. Mandelbaum rightly saw it as a scientific problem, i.e., how to move from perception to reality, because some of the perceivable qualities of objects have been found to be unreliable guides to structural properties. This is not a rejection of all perception, for that would lead to a senseless world (literally and epistemologically) but a criticism of common-sense perception in terms of discoveries of the more important aspects of objects. Thus common-sense experience is not abandoned but criticized by science so that through the two perspectives a detailed knowledge of the nature of objects is developed.

The relationship of critical realist philosophy to methodological and sociological structurism, although implicit in some of Mandelbaum's earlier work, was not properly argued by him until his last book, *Purpose and Necessity in Social Theory* (1987), which I shall discuss in a moment. In his earlier criticisms of methodological individualism and holism he defended a position that he termed 'methodological institutionalism'. In this, social institutions, which make up the structure of society, require *sui generis* sociological 'laws' as well as psychological 'laws', in conjunction with knowledge of the actual conditions of the specific human behaviour and events that bring institutions into being and transform them. (The question of the relationship between this institutionalism and structurism will be discussed in a moment, but on the face of it they seem to be very similar.)

Mandelbaum on causation and truth

'Structurism' and 'institutionalism' in both their methodological and sociological conceptual forms rest upon a particular concept of social causation. Mandelbaum argued[25] that the causes of events are not separable antecedent events, but the complex structure of functional relations that are the conditions that gave rise to the event. They are often not prior to the event but coterminous with it. The role of laws or other weaker generalizations is not to provide an explanation by themselves, that is, making a causal explanation is not a matter of deducing it from a causal law. He said that 'to give a causal analysis is to trace an ongoing process that terminated in the specific effect we wish to explain; this involves describing a particular set of interconnected occurrences. In formulating a law, on the other hand, one is concerned not with a particular effect, but with an effect of a specified type; the object is to show on what factor or factors an effect of this type always depends.'[26] That is, laws are not about regularities of sequences of events or even of types of events, but are about types of factors within complex structures and processes.

There is a continuity between simple crude generalizations from everyday experience, through law-like historical and sociological generalizations, to invariant scientific laws. Generalizations are necessary to all causal explanations but they are not explanations in themselves. In socio-historical studies they serve as useful tools with heuristic rather than precise explanatory power, because no truly lawful basic propositions have yet been established, notwithstanding the attempts of historical materialists, structural–functionalists, and structuralists.[27] Generalizations include views about the nature of persons, the nature of society, and the factors affecting social stability and change. Their role is 'to help explain why two or more independent series of events that intersect at a particular place and time produce the results they do'.[28] But 'it is on the basis of the connections inherent in the evidence with which historians work that they can propose concrete causal analyses of the events with which they deal . . . It is not, then, on the basis of general laws that causal connections are authenticated; it is on the basis of evidence as to what actually occurred.'[29]

This brings us back to realism and the correspondence theory of truth. Why sociological structurism needs such a realist theory of causation can now begin to be seen. If society is an ongoing process of institutional structuring through patterns of behaviour, the explanation of social events and processes must employ a causal theory that attributes patterned behaviour and institutional structuring to the pre-existing and coterminous social systemic historical process itself. Causation is neither external to the system nor a sequence of types of events but the concrete interaction of real psychological, cultural, and social forces present within particular societies. Precise general laws of behaviour and social processes are desirable but not available. Less precise generalizations, especially about particular social systems, are necessary but not sufficient for historical and sociological explanation.

Mandelbaum on purpose and necessity and the philosophy/ theory connection

Mandelbaum's book on *Purpose and Necessity in Social Theory* (1987), which draws together, summarizes, and updates some of his themes to present a synthetic argument that encompasses the history and methodology of social theory, is worth examining in more detail for what it can offer my defence of structurism and the scientificity of structural history. The book is an outstanding demonstration of the potentially close connection between philosophy and fundamental social theory because the methodological argument rests upon and reinforces the general conception of social reality. His general social theory in turn is inspired by his philosophical commitments to realism and the correspondence theory of truth. Thus there is a coherent circle of reasoning, as shown in figure 4.4.

Six closely related themes can be identified in Mandelbaum's book, which together help to constitute this circle of reasoning. I shall briefly say something about how he treated each of them before going on to discuss a little more extensively and in more general terms the questions of social reality, truth, causation, and change. In this way we can begin to evaluate his arguments for realism and structurism, towards which all of these themes contribute.

Figure 4.4 The circle of Mandelbaum's philosophical coherence

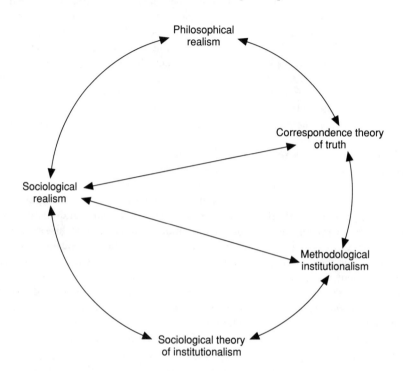

First is the defence of the importance of philosophical and methodological criticism. All social theories contain presuppositions of a normative and theoretical kind. The latter tend to take the form of pairs of opposite categories, such as purpose and necessity, individualism and holism, and psychologism and historicism. These presuppositions play important but often hidden methodological and substantive roles in all social explanation. The task of analysing social thought is to uncover them and show their influence. This involves recourse to philosophical criticism of epistemological and ontological kinds. He saw little distinction between epistemology, ontology, social philosophy, methodology, and fundamental theory. Philosophy therefore has a critical and continuous role in aiding social explanation.

Second is the demonstration of the pervasiveness of the three pairings of categories or concepts of individualism/holism, purpose/necessity, and chance/ choice throughout the history of social theory. It is clear following Mandelbaum's revealing discussion that these dichotomous concepts, together with a few others such as realism/instrumentalism and freedom/determinism, constitute the deep structure of social theory. That is, all social theorising has employed some combination of these concepts as its presuppositions or foundations. He

Figure 4.5 Mandelbaum's view of the pervasive dichotomies of social theory

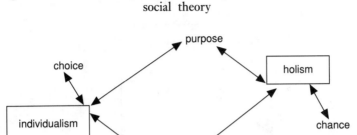

argued that they have been understood as related to each other in a particular way which can be represented in figure 4.5. In this figure each of the arrows shows the alternatives apparently open to a social theorist who starts with any of the six concepts, particularly with individualism or holism, which have been the basic concepts of society. For example, if a holist conception was seen as basic then there were supposed to have been three alternative possibilities (necessity, chance, or purpose) available explanatorily to support the presupposition of holistic reality. Social wholes arise and exist either as a social necessity, due perhaps to human nature, to chance happenings, or because of teleological purposiveness. Similarly, individualist explanation has been open to three alternatives – necessity, purposiveness, and choice – but construed in different ways from the holists. Society is a collection of individuals who relate to each other because of their individual psychological drives and needs, or their inherent purposiveness as social individuals, or their conscious choices.

The third theme is the criticism of the legitimacy of these dichotomies. The argument is that these polar opposites are false and rather than having to choose between each pair, as social theorists have been doing for three centuries, they should be trying to combine them in various ways without obliterating them in order to explain social reality. The reason for this comes from the nature of social reality itself, which cannot be explained except by using all the categories of 'individual', 'whole' (in the sense of institutional structure), 'purpose', 'necessity', 'chance', 'choice', 'psychology', and 'history'. (But 'purpose' and 'necessity' have to be interpreted in non-teleological and non-metaphysical ways.) Therefore, his argument about the correct relationship of the concepts can be shown by figure 4.6. As this implies, his argument about the categories therefore rests on his ontological theory of social reality and causation, to which the categories have to correspond adequately.

The fourth theme is the theorization of social reality. This takes two parts – an argument for the *sui generis* reality of society as distinct from behaviour and culture, and an outline of the universal factors in all social organization.

Figure 4.6   Mandelbaum's synthesis of categories

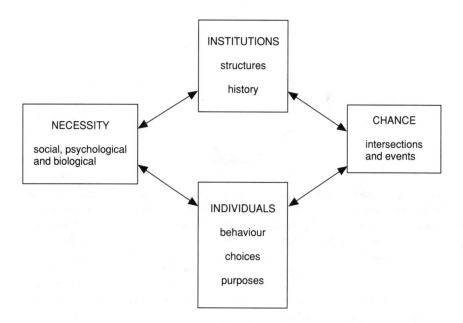

Against the early individualist tradition that began with Hobbes, which identified society with groups of individuals as individuals, he said that:

> the characteristics on the basis of which societies are to be identified are various
> patterns of learned behavior to which persons occupying different positions in a society,
> and playing different roles in its activities, are expected to conform. It is these
> normative patterns themselves, and not the individuals who behave in accordance
> with them, that must be taken into account when one wishes to describe the nature
> of a society and what constitutes its essential parts. However, those who have searched
> for what have been called 'rock bottom' explanation in the social sciences have held
> that it is only in terms of individual behavior that the nature and functioning of a
> society can be understood. In short, they mistakenly treat social organization as a
> by-product of individual behavior, not as a major determinant of it . . . It has been
> widely assumed . . . the basis for such explanation is to be found in one or more
> universal and unchanging characteristics of human nature. That assumption has most
> often been challenged on the ground that there are no such characteristics, but my
> objections to it lie elsewhere. I reject it because any explanation of the nature and
> functioning of an actually existing society cannot be concerned solely with whatever
> characteristics may be common to all persons. Of themselves, such characteristics could
> not explain the very different forms of behavior expected of individuals living in
> different societies.[30]

The holist alternatives are equally unattractive, whether they be the organic type, such as those developed by Herder, Hegel, Burke, de Maistre, Savigny, and Ranke, or the institutionalist type developed by Comte and Marx. The organic holists viewed each nation and period as an intuitively grasped whole and did not attempt to analyse historically the components of cultures and societies to explain the origins and character of different institutions. The institutionalist holists did attempt to do this in order to establish universally applicable laws about social structure and change.

Individualism was revived in the late nineteenth century and in recent decades attempts have been made to conflate individualist and institutionalist approaches under the guise of the 'behavioural sciences'. It was partly because Mandelbaum found no important attempts to reject this conflation (a view which ignores much recent work in Britain, France, and Germany by, for example, Giddens, Abrams, Elias, Touraine, and Bourdieu) that he wrote his book. While neither pole is satisfactory their obliteration is also unsatisfactory. A distinction must be retained between 'what can be explained in terms of psychological concepts and what must be explained with reference to the societal context in which individuals act'.[31] When it is society that has to be explained rather than behaviour it is the structure of rules governing institutions that have to be studied. He wrote:

Every social institution involves a patterning of relationships among individuals: if their behavior were not to a large extent regulated by commonly recognized rules, so that each person had a notion of what was to be expected with respect to the actions of others, there would be no institutions and no organized social life. Since one cannot speak of institutions without speaking of rules according to which individuals behave, it would seem that we should regard societies simply as a congeries of individuals who behave in a certain way. This, however, would be a mistake. For example, the rules defining the nature of a game are not identical with the behavior of those who play that game: they play *according to the rules,* and the rules are not simply summary statements of how they actually behave. This is clear every time a foul is called in a game, and every time an individual breaks a law, committing a crime. It is therefore a mistake to think of society in terms of the actual behavior of individuals, even though it is clear that were it not for the existence and activities of individuals, the society would not exist. That the individuals themselves are not to be considered the elements constituting a particular society becomes evident when we consider what is involved in describing a society: we proceed by describing its various institutions and their relations to one another, rather than by referring to the individuals who participate in its life . . . Conversely, when we describe any individual, we do not simply describe his physical appearance, his capacities, his character and temperament, but we also refer to his status within his society.[32]

Are there fundamental principles or rules governing institutional origins and structure? Is there a deep structure to social organization, limiting its possibilities? Many social theorists and historians (notably Marx, Weber, Radcliffe-Brown, Parsons, and Althusser) have claimed there are, seeking them in the nature of people or in the needs of social systems as organic or structured wholes. Mandelbaum's proposal was to seek for the requirements of society as an organization analysed in terms of a number of different psychological, biological, and social factors rather than as the needs of a system as a whole. Thus it would attempt to uncover what is functionally essential if people are to live together in organized social groups.[33] This is not to say that people can live without society. Social organization is necessary to human life and even the life of some other animal species. The socially functional necessities usually reinforce each other, but this does not mean that they lead to society being an organic, coherent, and stable unity, because chance and choice play important roles, and these universal requirements are not always met.[34] This is crucial for the explanation of social change.

The fifth theme in the book, which follows from the third and the fourth, is the relationship between sociological, psychological, and cultural explanations. He rightly wished to keep all these distinct because of the relative autonomy of behaviour, culture, and social structure. Society is the result of institutionalized rules of behaviour and not behaviour itself. Nevertheless, to explain social organization the motivations of behaviour have to be explained and that in turn involves some reference to social organization, because individuals and their behaviour are shaped by society as well as by their innate nature. Psychological and social explanation are both necessary but separate tasks.[35] Similarly, culture is distinct from social institutions. Culture includes such things as languages, technology, customary habits, and systems of belief. These are transmitted from person to person by imitation and example. Institutions, on the other hand, define the relations, status, and roles of people. Obviously culture and institutions overlap, but Mandelbaum saw as the basic difference, that institutions and not culture define the social position of people and regulate their behaviour, obligations, rights, and privileges. Culture and society are not only different in character, but also they are not coterminous. Thus society cannot be studied through culture, consciousness, or behaviour but must be studied in itself.[36]

This is a very significant argument because there are strong tendencies in psychology, sociology, anthropology, and common sense to conflate these three kinds of explanation or at least to try to explain and reduce social structure to one or other of culture, behaviour, or social mores. Mandelbaum argued convincingly that society is to be understood neither as a system of beliefs nor as a pattern of behaviour, so it cannot be studied through them alone. Nevertheless, social study requires attention to both of them. Going beyond behaviour and cultural and ideological perceptions are crucial steps for social science if it wishes to uncover interpersonal structures of institutionalized rules, roles, and relations which may not be well understood by the actors that inhabit them.

Nor can the social sciences do without history. This is the sixth theme of the book. All social explanation involves the (usually tacit) use of generalizations about basic principles of economic, political, and social life in conjunction with knowledge of specific conditions. How these generalizations are developed is obviously an important question. As Mandelbaum rightly pointed out, unfortunately it has been abstract analysis rather than attention to history that has been the main way ever since sociology was founded. Marx was an early conspicuous exception because he derived theories of social formations from empirical enquiries. All science needs descriptions of particular events and their conditions and all descriptions need generalizations, so the ideographic and nomothetic elements need each other. There is always going to be a tension between concepts that are ahistorical and the fine distinctions between even very similar social structures. Historical explanation needs sociology and psychology, and sociology needs historical data.[37] Why a society is the way it is can only be answered historically, 'and its history will have been channeled by necessity and by chance, as well as by the choices of individuals who, at specific times, learned what they did learn and made the choices they actually made'.[38]

Now we are at last in a position to see why Mandelbaum believed the categories of 'individual', 'whole', 'purpose', 'necessity', 'chance', and 'choice' are all necessary to social explanation and therefore why the pervasive dichotomies must be broken down. The doctrine of individualism cannot account for the social conditioning of behaviour, just as holism cannot account for the origins and history of institutional structures. Studies of the causal interaction of behaviour and institutions as relatively separate levels of social existence are required for explanations of both behaviour and institutions. Thus we can defend a conception of the social totality as being a structure of institutions rather than a supra-individual metaphysical entity. But the institutionalist methodology, which rightly rejects the poles of individualism and holism, is not fully translated by Mandelbaum into a theory of social causation and social change. In the terminology I have employed earlier, he has only hinted at how methodological institutionalism might be translated into a sociological structurism that can develop an account of the genesis of history of structures.

How institutions arise and change is one of the main things that structural history should be attempting to explain. Part of the explanation involves giving due weight to the necessary universal requirements for social organization, for satisfying human needs, and for internal social consistency. This kind of necessity is not the same as metaphysical determinism. Such a complete determinism would rule out chance and choice in human affairs. Necessity operates, rather, at the level of essential structural conditions, which set the parameters for behaviour and institution building, and not at the level of causation *per se*. The denial of metaphysical determinism does not imply that events are not caused, only that some are chance events in the sense that they result from a coincidence of different, independent, lines of causation, particularly of an institutional kind, which could not have been predicted. Neither does such a necessity rule out human purposive choice, within the constraints imposed by institutional structures and human personalities. Individuals vary and so therefore does their power to influence society. Purposiveness does not have to imply teleology in the holistic, metaphysical sense, but operates at the level of individual choice and behaviour. Individual behaviour is teleological in the sense of being goal-oriented, and some institutions may also be so, but social systems cannot be.

The argument of *Purpose and Necessity* and the totality of Mandelbaum's work support the contention that in the task of developing scientific socio-historical explanations three basic problems are equally important, the answers to which should conceptually reinforce each other:

- the problem of social reality and truth,
- the problem of social causation,
- the problem of social change.

Each of these bears directly upon the others, so that if a particular socio-historical theory is constructed primarily on the basis of a particular approach to one of them it should more or less completely determine what can be said consistently about the others. Thus if a theorist begins with an explicit or tacit concept of social reality it should greatly constrain what can then be said consistently about causation and change. However, it is unfortunately the case that not many social theorists, sociologists, economists, or historians have fully grasped this synergy. In what follows I want briefly and very generally to try to establish why all three issues are equally basic for structural explanation and how they should conceptually reinforce each other.

THE PROBLEM OF SOCIAL REALITY AND TRUTH

Much of Mandelbaum's *Purpose and Necessity* is about the age-old meth-odological problem of defining social reality. Wherein does the social lie? Is it inherent in the mental and physical nature of individual people – some sort of impulse to be socially co-operative in complex and meaningful ways? Or is it the extra-individual sets of relationships of manifold and overlapping kinds that people are born into, which mould their lives, which they simply reproduce and perhaps transform, but which have existed since time immemorial and have a life and history of their own? Is it meaningful at all even to envisage humans apart from society? Are sets of social relations, if they really exist independently, more or less unchanging systems or are they fluid, shifting, and able to be manipulated? Do social structures in fact have any rigidity? Perhaps social 'reality' is a mental construct – a set of beliefs, norms, and understandings about how people should act and interact and which therefore determine how they do. Such mentalities may even be little or not at all consciously understood by those who carry them. Perhaps 'social reality' is a misnomer because its 'construction' may be a result of each person's social theory or lay understandings.

In any case, three things seem indisputable. First, society, like nature, is multidimensional and multifaceted and which dimensions and facets are seen and discussed are partly a matter of choice, social position, and social insight. Social (and natural) scientists cannot explain everything at once because societies are not unitary entities, although there can be greater or lesser degrees of generality in analysis. Levels and aspects of analysis have to be chosen. Second, societies and cultures change and so do social theories and understandings. The fact that all of these have shown a persistent if variably paced tendency to change, as well as a degree of continuity, should make us at least very cautious about absolute and universal social concepts. Third, human understandings of behaviour and society help to constitute behaviour and society. Therefore social understandings and theories have been an important contributor to the nature of social reality itself over time. But one must be careful not to commit the genetic fallacy of confusing the observer's understanding with the causal social process. Societies are the institutionalized aggregate products over time of a host of beliefs, needs, choices, behaviours, accidents, and already existing social and physical environmental influences, so that the understanding that particular persons have at a particular moment cannot at that moment be the constituting cause of what the observer is observing and reflecting upon. Holist and individualist conceptions of social reality are untenable because they are unable adequately to explain observable social phenomena as the outcome of this complexity of causes.

As I have argued, a powerfully persuasive tradition in the philosophy of explanation, exemplified in differing ways by Mandelbaum, Quine, Hesse, Putnam, Boyd, Harré, Shapere, Bhaskar, Salmon, and Hooker, has shown how the task of empirical enquiry is to criticize and explain the appearances of the world by reference, through the use of conceptual frameworks and theories, to the underlying unobservable causal structures which inhere in and help to generate the objects and phenomena of the world. This approach sees no essential difference in principle between the philosophical foundations of explanation in the natural, social, and psychological sciences. Cultural explanation may well require certain important differences of foundations but even there it is not a question of a fundamental gulf between it and science. Given this argument, the correspondence–realist theory of truth in the convergence form I have advocated above cannot be avoided by those who seriously wish to explain the causes of observable human behaviour, utterances, and products.

When examining the issues of realism and correspondence, the most important questions for us are 'correspondence with what?' and 'how do we assess the truth of a correspondence claim?' What is the reality that social concepts, theories, and explanations supposedly correspond with and how can we be sure of this words-to-world relation? After all, references to and ideas about the world can only be made via ways of thinking about the world. There is no extra-world standpoint, no cosmically neutral position of omniscience.[39] The core of the answer given to these questions by the physical and most biological sciences is provided by experimentation and engineering. The validity of natural science explanations is constantly tested, at their margins at least, in open, natural situations. Truth claims in those sciences are ultimately validated (provisionally at least) by a correspondence relationship between knowledge claims and the success of interventions in and observations of natural situations beyond the laboratory control and intellectual consensus of scientific groups and institutions. Truth is not claimed to be absolute but, as Karl Popper has cogently argued, we go only so far into the realm of the hitherto unknown as is presently possible and is required to support our present arguments and claims. Scientific theories are not simply true or false but provisionally so and always against a background of real-world testing.[40] A policy of realism and correspondence, rather than an absolute claim about them, drives a scientific mode of enquiry and proof. A gradual increase in scientific understanding of reality is thus confirmed in an incremental, constantly refined, and pragmatic fashion.

Of course many natural scientific understandings and theories remain un-tested in any direct sense and are the subject of tacit agreement and convention. Nevertheless, as I argued earlier in this chapter, natural sciences are total but loosely integrated networks of theories, knowledge, reasoning, and institutional arrangements, which depend ultimately on applications in and observations of uncontrolled natural situations and stand or fall in part, and occasionally as net-works, on these continuing applications and observations. Repeated failures of experiment, engineering, and prediction lead to rejection of part or all of the body of theory and knowledge on which they rest. In this way discoveries are built up in a jerky progression. Without success in the crucial tests of precisely controlled open-system applications the validity of the science would be in doubt because its correspondence relation would be in doubt. The external reality of the natural world is thus confirmed by the ability of engineers and scientists to manipulate the world successfully in preconceived ways and by the power of the external world to prompt changes in our ways of understanding it by its failure to conform to prediction. There is an inter-causal relationship between theories, experiments, and observations. (Precise scientific theory is not necessary to engineering of a more primitive kind, as the buildings of ancient and mediaeval societies reveal. Nevertheless, even there at least some tacit mechanical theory was necessary.)

Such an argument about the role of experimentation, engineering, and prediction does not apply well to social science. No special kind of scientific theory and research is necessary consciously to manipulate social institutions and to 'engineer' enduringly the social world, at least in a broad, ameliorative sense. Although unscientific social interventions have many more unforeseen consequences than do more precise, scientifically inspired ones, they all have that character to some extent. (This is also true of natural science.) Rather, what is required for social manipulation and creation is social power and a degree of social insight and, unlike the power of physical engineering, power and insight rarely if ever spring from scientific knowledge. They come instead from some combination of individual personality; position within social groups, institutions, and hierarchies; access to and control of information; control of the apparatus of institutional power; and control of the symbolic and cultural sources of legitimacy. Social scientific knowledge can aid institutional construction but general social structures are not the outcome of controlled, conscious engineering. Rather, they are the result of complex historical processes without a teleological subject. The task for social science, then, is to try to grasp the full complexity of those processes. *Post hoc* explanation rather than prediction, control, or engineering, is therefore the prime aim. Some natural sciences, such as cosmology, geology, and evolutionary biology, have a similar aim in that they too attempt to explain the historical developmental processes of large-scale systems that are beyond scientific experimental control as systems. To develop explanations they employ knowledge from experimental sciences as well as observation and theory.

How can we know that our explanations correspond with the reality of historical social processes if we are denied experimental and engineering tests? Social realists at their best provide a complex answer containing the following mutually reinforcing elements. None of these elements is of much value apart from the others. First, the basic ontological premise is that causal power is the prime index of reality so that social structural reality has to be inferred from its effects on behaviour, production, and speech. Second, attention to the history of socio-historical theories and research programmes shows that they have grown in conceptual complexity and methodological richness over the past three centuries. Since society and its history have been revealed, by the use of these methodologies and theories, to be complex, dynamic structures, this is an essential symbiotic development if theory is to be adequate. Third, there has been a steady accumulation and tabulation of data from documentary and other material sources about past and present societies. Fourth, data is assumed to be largely (but not entirely) theory-neutral and so can be used cautiously to test rival theories. Fifth, social theories have grown in precision and testability as the amount of usable data has grown. Sixth, there has been a gradual convergence in the meaning and reference of concepts and theories between rival schools of explanation. Mandelbaum's book demonstrates this to some extent, both in what he expressly says about different theories and how his argument converges with those of many others whom he does not mention.

This argument and studies in the history of science together support the contention I made earlier that 'truth' is not an absolute but should be seen in more pragmatic terms as the growing plausibility that results from a gradual convergence between our philosophical and methodological frameworks, our theories, our hypotheses, and data. Coherence between all of these is highly desirable but never fully attainable. Truth is neither just a matter of conceptual and theoretical coherence nor of empirical correspondence alone. The intersection between, or networking of lines of conceptual, theoretical, and empirical reasoning is the site of the greatest plausibility within networks of scientific thought which refer to but separate themselves from external reality.[41]

So, notwithstanding the differences in forms and degrees of validation between different forms of empirical explanation, we are still justified in speaking of a science of society. This is so because of some things more important that all forms of science share and which basically set them apart from non-science. As I have tried to indicate, what makes a science a science is not its form of validation but the structure of its reasoning, its policy of realism, its notion of epistemological convergence, and some version of the correspondence-realist concept of truth.

The phenomenological tradition in social explanation rejects the idea of an objective, discoverable social reality and the possibility of a convergence between methodologies, theories, and empirical explanation. It claims that social concepts, understandings, and explanations are essentially contested. There is apparently no way in which we can translate social understandings into some meta-language of concepts and data in order to analyse, compare, criticize, and judge their validity. This is not the same as saying that social science is simply immature and will develop a meta-language or paradigm at some future date. That possibility is ruled out by phenomenologists on ontological and epistemological grounds. The basic premise here about the fundamental nature of society is that society has no fundamental nature! Rather, societies are phenomenologically constituted by actors through their understandings and behaviour. There are no social data that are theoretically or culturally neutral. In order to study societies the particular interrelationships among behaviour, utterances, understandings, and culture have to be investigated. That requires a hermeneutical method of reasoning and enquiry. There is no rock-bottom explanation possible.

Such an approach has to come to grips with the powerful argument advanced by Mandelbaum and others in defence of the objectivity of patterns of observable behaviour and cultural forms that in turn rest upon certain factors that govern the persistence of certain kinds of institutions within and across cultures, societies, and milieux. The meanings, local understandings, and significance of these patterns and factors may be in doubt, but phenomenological social theorists cannot do without some at least tacitly adopted structural or institutional notions about languages, beliefs, and customs. All social groups and organizations, as such, are held together by shared languages, beliefs, customs, experiences, and institutionalized patterns of behaviour. Actors' understandings are not necessarily a good guide to either their existence or their effects. However, it is important to agree with the phenomenologists to the extent that actors' understandings do have collectively a socially constituting role over time and that every individual is therefore a social agent to some extent. But this does not deny the reality of societies as structures of rules, roles, and relations, which must be studied. As Mandelbaum argued at length, society exists independently of every individual's perception, understanding, and behaviour, but not of the totality of behaviour and beliefs of all those within it.

THE PROBLEM OF SOCIAL CAUSATION

As we have seen with the question of reality and truth, analysing social causation involves a nest of problems. There is the philosophical problem of causation in general – what it means to make a causal statement or a causal explanation. What sort of relationship is believed to exist between supposed cause and effect? Is it sequential, conditional, structural, or something else? There is the problem of the extent to which social causation is like that of nature. Is the causal structure of society completely different from that of natural systems and events or is there an underlying similarity? What is it that analyses of social causation have to explain – behaviour, culture, structure, structural change, or all of these? What are the causal relationships between human action, culture, structure, and social change? Is social structure perhaps epiphenomenal – the merely apparent but non-existent result of human thought and behaviour? We must distinguish between general concepts of causality and causal attribution, on one hand, and theories of social causation, on the other.

There are at least four general concepts of causation. First, there is the metaphysical idealist concept, which asserts that the phenomena of the universe are products of or emanations from an omnipotent being or some such final cause. In order to know about such causation divine revelation must be received and/or human contemplative reason employed.

Second, there is the empiricist (or Humean) regularity concept, which is based on the idea of causation being a matter of constant conjunctions of events. Events are taken to be the causes of subsequent events and the universe is characterized by discoverable regularities between types of events. Only events can be studied within this approach, so empiricists have to disaggregate and reduce processes into what are taken to be their constituent chains of events. Just how universal laws of the sort 'Bs are always caused by As' are arrived at is a central controversial question for empiricists.

Third, the functional/teleological/consequential concept says some types of events and processes are caused by their own (expected?) consequences through some sort of feedback relation. In this case these events and processes are goal-directed so that goals are causes. An obvious difficulty with this approach is how to discover what the goals are and how they influence events and processes.

The fourth concept is the realist, structurist, and dispositional approach, which sees relational structures and internal dispositions as the causes of phenomena. Things and processes are said to occur because it is their nature to behave in certain ways and to influence other things in certain ways, depending on their actual structural interrelations. Causal laws are statements about structures, dispositions, relations, and processes, rather than events. Events and processes are always structurally located, conditioned, and caused, so they cannot be isolated from structural complexes. Here the central problem is one of epistemological access to structures if observable events are not taken to be the causes of other events.

Within these general concepts of causation we can identify five particular theories of social causation. First, there is emanistic holism, which says that society is an emanation of a super-social force. Second, the empiricist regularity theory says that social causation, like natural causation, is a matter of antecedent events. Human behaviour, whether individual, patterned, or grouped, must ideally be explained by prior environmental and neurophysiological events, such as decisions. The most radical and reductionist version of this theory rejects the idea of the existence of irreducible social and mental structures, which instead are taken to be merely epiphenomenal products of brain processes. The result is an atomistic and behaviourist social theory. Less radical versions would concede the existence of irreducible psychological states and drives and see them as the fundamental causes of individual behaviour.

Third, an intentionalist theory of social causation gives the central role to the conscious and intentional states of individuals and their culturally conditioned ways of understanding. This is also a form of individualism, but here the individual is the conscious and cultured source of motivation, understanding, and social interaction. Society is not something that can ever have an independent, causally powerful existence apart from individual and shared understandings about it and the behaviour that they motivate. Understandings play the prime causal role, so the problem for social explanation is to investigate human consciousness and intentions and their cultural roots. Culture here is the idea of historically developed shared belief systems, customs, and languages. The task for investigators within this theory is a hermeneutical one – to understand understandings and intentional behaviour.

Fourth, there is functional and structural holism, which claims that social events and processes are caused by their systemic relationships within tightly integrated social systems. The parts of the system are subordinate to the whole and are governed by their dedication to reproducing and maintaining the system. Obviously such causation can only operate within historical, social, and engineered systems and it depends crucially on a teleological mechanism. While there is no doubt that much human behaviour is indeed goal-directed, the basic problem for this approach is how to establish that social systems as systems do have holistic, autonomous, and goal-directed characters.

Fifth, there is the structurist and institutionalist theory. Here equal emphasis is given to the powerful structuring role of individuals and groups and the conditioning role of institutional structures to mould behaviour and consciousness. People are the prime agents of society. They have dispositional (including teleological) propensities to behave in certain ways, as well as conscious intentions. Their behaviour is therefore taken to be the result of a combination of causes – psychological dispositions, intentions, social structural and ecological imperatives, and conscious rational and irrational choices. Society as an integrated structure with conditioning power is the outcome of these forces over time, but there never has been a time without society.

With the help of Mandelbaum I have been defending a correspondence–realist notion of truth and a structurist theory of social causation. Therefore the task of explanation is to uncover the real causes of the origins and history of behavioural patterns and institutions within the complex contemporary and pre-existing social structural conditions for behaviour and institutions. Social causes are not sequential chains of events but social conditions in the form of structural complexes. They have to be abstracted and analysed into their parts to find the relations of cause and effect, but these relations are never singular and rarely linear. Social events rarely have pre-existing events as their efficient causes. And causal analyses should not be attempts to reduce social structures to supposedly independent components because those components are not in fact independent. Neither are they deterministically related. All this makes virtually impossible the accurate measurement of the causes of social events (and even more so of processes) and their presentation in the form of precisely specified functional equations. Correspondingly, it reinforces the hermeneutical component of social explanation. Observation, measurement, and interpretation must all play a central role.

THE PROBLEM OF SOCIAL CHANGE

Given the argument so far about the categories of social enquiry, we should look for the basic source of social change in the conflict between social necessity and individual attitudes and choices. Necessity's role is in the basic requirements for a social structure's existence in that every society must satisfy certain functional conditions (see note 33 of this chapter). These also establish the limits of what is possible, that is, institutions must together satisfy the physiological and psychological needs of many individuals and be mutually consistent. If they fail in either of these ways their existence is in jeopardy. Change thus comes about because sufficient numbers of individuals are dissatisfied or find themselves in stressful situations of conflict caused by the incompatibility of institutions and they are able to do something about altering their situation. People begin to evade their institutional responsibilities or reinterpret them in ways that result in institutional change.[42] The rules, roles, and relations governing choices and actions are ignored and altered.

Why situations emerge that cause conflicts between institutional structures and individual attitudes and actions can be a result of both chance and choice. Changes in the physical environment – climatic, ecological, epidemiological, for example – can be important chance events. The choices of powerful

individuals and groups can have far-reaching consequences, planned or un-
planned. Furthermore, each institution has to some extent its own history and
these histories intersect at unpredictable points with unpredictable results.
History is not a continuous stream leading up to the present. Rather, as
Mandelbaum wrote, we should see the past as 'a highly complex reticulated
network in which the history of each society will to some degree be independent of the others'.[43] The cross influences between them are often a matter of
chance. Similarly, the choices of individuals intersect with some degree of
chance and have intended and unintended consequences. There is an important
distinction here between freedom of choice and freedom of action. The first
does not imply the second. The ability and power to act upon choices varies
with social role, personal power, and institutional constraint. They are also
constrained by history, which is a further form of social necessity, for the past
constrains the present in that it cannot be undone. The present institutional
structure is a result of past processes, so what is possible in the present is
constrained by what happened in the past. Moreover, change itself always
necessitates further adjustments. Thus, wrote Mandelbaum,

adjustments that take place in order that a society may better satisfy one or other
human need will create a situation which could threaten the stability of the society if
those adjustments are not offset by changes in some other institutions that had been
affected by them. Yet, once such adjustments have occurred, a new situation will have
emerged, and any future actions will have to take account of that situation if they are
to succeed. Thus, insofar as individuals are in a position to bring about some change
in social organization, the choices they make will have many unforeseen consequences.[44]

In the final analysis, then, it is human needs and actually existing institutional
and environmental conditions that are the parameters of the choices and actions
of socialized individuals in bringing about new institutional arrangements.
Social structural necessity, chance, choice, and individual purpose all play a
role.

Within these parameters many developments which will lead to social change
are possible. The balance between necessity, purposiveness, chance, and choice
is highly variable. But such a set of parameters cannot possibly be studied with
methodological individualism and holism. Individualism denies any role to
social necessity and holism denies any role to individual choice and purposiveness.
There have of course been many general individualist and holist theories of
social change developed down the years. Against these, a structurist approach
leads to the denial that there can be a valid general theory of social change
which is trans-historical or even trans-societal. Rather, all theories of social
change can only legitimately refer to historical and contemporary social structuring
processes within particular societies. But there is a (perhaps unavoidable)
tension here between theories (or laws) of change in specific societies and
general concepts about societies and forces for change within all societies.

Theories cannot do without general concepts because theories by their nature contain generalizations about classes or types of events, structures, and processes. There is an essential role for general concepts and theory in making socio-historical explanations of specific cases.

It bears repeating that theoretical generalizations are not themselves explanations. This common confusion bedevils all the sciences, especially the social and historical sciences. It leads to what has sometimes been called 'theoreticism' – the employment of general, a priori, rationalistic, theoretical pronouncements about societies and their histories instead of careful empirical enquiry. Often in sociology and history the gulf between theory and empirical enquiry is so great as to lead to mutual incomprehension and sometimes to the hurling of what are meant to be condemnatory epithets such as 'empiricism', 'positivism', 'historicism', 'structuralism', and 'theoreticism'. Fortunately, this gulf is beginning to close and in much work now, especially in economic and social history and in historical sociology, there is a close mutual dependence of theory and empirical enquiry, although many of the theories are inadequate. Mandelbaum's book is an important contribution to showing why and how this should occur. He also shows that the diverse history that social theorizing has had is partly a consequence of the failure of many theorists to pay sufficient attention to empirical historical work as a source and testing-ground for generalizations. This is a philosophical failing, traceable, among other things, to a failure to adopt a correspondence notion of truth. Without some version of that there really is not a sufficient check on the rationalistic, abstract system-building tendencies of social theorists.

Now we can return to where it was said that answers to the three problems of reality/truth, causation, and change, should conceptually reinforce each other. I think that now we can see how that should happen. Table 4.1 (overleaf) attempts to sum up the discussion of the last three sections, rearranging the concepts employed there and in figure 1.2 to show their conceptual implications. Of course this does not mean that the correct implications are always drawn.

The institutionalist/structurist stream offers itself as the only viable way forward fundamentally because of its synthetic theories about structures and empirical evidence about action, behaviour, and events, and the effects of institutional structures upon these. The strength of such a combination (which is not a syncretism) of psychology, sociology, economics, anthropology, and history, has begun to be widely understood in the social sciences in recent years, but the extent of this sharing itself has not yet been well understood.

Table 4.1   Streams of conceptual implication

Concept of social reality	Theory of truth	Theory of social causation	Theory of social change
idealist or rationalist wholes ⟶	intuitive coherence ⟶	emanistic holism ⟶	idealist emanation
socio-cultural wholes ⟶	critical coherence ⟶	functional or structural holism ⟶	socio-cultural evolution
institutional structures ⟶	critical-convergent empirical correspondence ⟶	sociological structurism/ institutionalism ⟶	structurist history
behaviourist individuals ⟶	empiricist correspondence ⟶	socio-psychological individualism ⟶	behaviourist history
intentional or phenomenological individuals ⟶	hermeneutic coherence ⟶	intentionalist individualism ⟶	interpretist history
instrumental individuals ⟶	logical empiricism ⟶	epiphenomenalism	?

(brace linking socio-cultural wholes and institutional structures) }realism

(brace linking behaviourist individuals, intentional or phenomenological individuals, and instrumental individuals) }individualism

5
Historical Materialism and Structurism

Historical materialism is one of the oldest and most important attempts or series of attempts to provide a general explanatory theory and/or methodology for the domain of structural history. As I argued in chapter 2 when outlining the history of structural history writing, Marx and Engels were well ahead of their time, and of many of their subsequent interpreters and defenders, in developing a methodological approach to structural history that contains versions of realism and structurism. For nearly a century many Marxists were unable to grasp the centrality and importance of these features of their work.

THE PROBLEM OF THE ESSENCE OF HISTORICAL MATERIALISM
AND ITS VALIDITY

The edifice of Marxian historical materialism as a coherent approach is now beginning to crumble from within under the weight of large numbers of reconstructions and transformations proposed by sympathetic, often erstwhile Marxist critics. But, of course, attempts to reconstruct historical materialism in order either to save it or transform it have been made ever since it came into existence. Even Marx's and Engels's theory was an elaboration, synthesis, and reconstruction of earlier, half-formed versions of the theory that were first developed in Britain and France in the second half of the eighteenth century and in France and Germany in the early nineteenth century. And Marx and Engels were aware that they were not the only historical materialists of their time, acknowledging the work of, for example, L. H. Morgan, Maxim Kovalevski, and Joseph Dietzgen. Soon after the work of Marx and Engels, partial reconstructions and amendments were made by Eduard Bernstein, Georgi Plekhanov, and V. I. Lenin; and Max Weber's work can be seen as an attempt to build on, criticize, and go beyond Marx's materialism. In recent times many writers have made more or less sweeping attempts to amend Marxism or make its foundations compatible with some other philosophical system in order to save it or the other system. These reconstructors of the foundations of historical materialism can be seen as either rescuers or transformers.

The rescuers, such as Louis Althusser, G. A. Cohen, Jorge Larrain, and Derek Sayer, wish to save what they believe is the essence of Marx's historical materialism from distortions or obscuring and irrelevant glosses. Although often describing their work as reconstructions, they are really not so much reconstructors as rescuers, trying to provide a better interpretation of the theory from within what each of them takes to be its original assumptions. Unfortunately, each provides a different construction and Marx's texts are ambiguous, so any claim to be offering the definitive Marxist construction is difficult if not impossible to evaluate. The transformers, on the other hand, such as Claude Lévi-Strauss, Jean-Paul Sartre, Jürgen Habermas, Raymond Williams, Jon Elster, and Anthony Giddens, wish to change historical materialism into something else, usually through marriage, so that what is good in it can perhaps be united with some other theory.

What separates these two approaches is largely a matter of degree – the first sees historical materialism as essentially valid and powerful, the second as at best only partially valid and containing fundamental weaknesses. Both are of course opposed to historical idealism, but whether the transformers actually remain materialists is debatable and depends very much on the meaning of 'material', as we shall see. The simplistic idealist/materialist dichotomy is one of the things that all these critics (rightly) wish to transcend. Another thing that unites these critics and many of those who have written explicitly about historical materialism in general ever since the 1890s[1] is the assumption that it is synonymous with Marxism. This is a serious error that blinds them to important variations in the theory. It also prevents some of them from seeing that an attack on historical materialism is not necessarily an attack on Marxism. It is at least possible, despite some statements by Marx and Engels that their theory was materialist, that they in fact may *not* have developed such a theory at all! It is possible to interpret Marx's theory of history in a non-materialist way, as some Marxists have recently done. So I emphasize that this chapter is not mainly about Marxism, because I do not wish to enter the debate about its character.

This prompts the questions of what is the essence of historical materialism that apparently needs rescuing, restating, updating, or transforming; and what are its strengths and weaknesses? There is little agreement among writers on answers to these questions and a good deal of dispute has occurred. This chapter is partly a comparative consideration of the ideas of several recent reconstructors, some of whom wish to rescue historical materialism in various ways and some of whom wish to transform it and go beyond it. After discussing their ideas I shall turn to the question of the validity of historical materialism and try briefly to develop and defend structurism as a *post-materialist* approach to developing structural historical explanations.

Towards a defence of structurism as post-materialism

This defence of structurism *vis-à-vis* historical materialism centres on:

1 The affirmation of five components that have been common to some (especially Marxist) historical materialists:
   (a) the centrality of human practice for structuring the material, cultural, and social worlds;
   (b) the social-relational theory of society, material production, and culture;
   (c) the abstract model of the social totality as having several 'levels' or 'spheres' of activity and structure;
   (d) the abstract model of persons as having several 'levels' of interests; and
   (e) the notion of the historicity of all social forms.
2 The necessity of three main additions to these existing components:
   (a) a theory of action as motivated primarily by a combination of personal intentions, psychological dispositions, and socially and culturally conditioned understandings and interests, rather than mainly by material interests;
   (b) a central rather than a lagging role for meaning, culture, and ideology in the social totality; and
   (c) an epistemology based on philosophical realism, supervenience theory, and a provisional/convergence notion of truth.
3 The denial of any general primacy to the material aspects of society, no matter how 'material' is construed.

I do not, however, wish to replace materialism with some version of idealism or culturalism. Rather, what has been fundamentally wrong with historical materialism is the dogmatic materialist part. There seems to be no sustainable reason for retaining it. Materialism is not generally necessary for the explanation of action, socio-economic structure, culture, or ideology, nor for the explanation of social structural change, although it may be valuable for such explanations under certain limited circumstances. But we must not replace it with another dogma, hence the importance of the point about a provisional/convergence notion of truth, which I will elaborate later. The value of materialism as a theoretical explanation of any particular process or phenomenon is empirically contingent.

Before launching into the discussion it is important to pause a moment to consider one possible objection to any denial of the primacy of the material in social explanation. This objection is the idea that because there is only a material reality in the universe – the doctrine of substance monism – all causation is material. I agree with this general ontology but it is important to add that it does not rule out property pluralism – that there are emergent properties which are not reducible to their physical base level and are not some other form of substance. It is the emergent properties of society – such as social rules and relations, cultures, ideologies, and so on – that are in need of explanation and which have a contentious relationship with the physical substance of society. In any case, historical materialism is not the same as philosophical materialism, although it is related to it. So the issue here is not whether social and cultural properties are material. They are in the sense articulated by Donald Davidson, Mario Bunge, and Jaegwon Kim, among others, to the effect that they have a supervenient relationship with the physical world, as I argued in the previous chapter.[2] The issue is: what is the relationship between, on one hand, the social, cultural, and ideological properties, and, on the other, the physical substance of the material societal totality?

By way of introduction to this argument I want first briefly to illustrate (without justifying) the contention that historical materialism as a theory of history was not invented by and is not confined to the writings of Marx and his followers. If we are to extract the essence of the doctrine we must first know something about the history and variability of historical materialist theories.[3] I emphasize that I am not talking about materialism in general or about methodology but only of those theories that pertain to social history and social structure. I think it is possible to identify at least ten different prima facie versions of the theory that have been presented over the past 250 years. Not many of them were called 'historical materialism' and in the next section I shall discuss the labelling of them.

1   The original rudimentary form of historical materialism was developed in the second half of the eighteenth century by the Scottish historical school centred on Adam Smith, Adam Ferguson, and John Millar. They argued that socio-economic, political, and legal history had evolved through a series of stages, with the dynamic element provided by the mode of material subsistence or what we would now call the economy. The other 'levels' of the social totality were dependent in some sense upon the economy.

2   From the 1840s German historical economics was developed by a group of writers, such as Roscher, Knies, Bücher, Schmoller, and Sombart, who reacted against the abstraction of English classical and Austrian marginalist economics. They defended a form of economic holism and evolutionism in which economic progression through stages played the leading historical role.

3   Classical Marxism, as developed by Marx and Engels, was the first fully-fledged historical materialism theory, in which the influences of the Scottish School and classical economics were strong. (They also developed the first methodology of historical materialism.)

4   As an outgrowth from classical Marxism there was dialectical materialism – or what can be called Marxism–Leninism – as propounded mainly by Lenin,

Luxemburg, Bukharin, and Stalin. This is a much more mechanical version of historical materialism than that of Marx in that it proposed a simpler, more deterministic relationship between the economy and other aspects of the social totality.

5 English positivist history, notably that of T. H. Buckle and Herbert Spencer in the 1860s and seventies, espoused a basic materialist cause of history while marrying that idea with a positivist conception of universal historical laws.

6 Materialist anthropology, as developed from the 1870s mainly by some American, British, and Russian anthropologists such as Morgan, Maine, and Kovalevski. These writers influenced the late anthropological writing of Marx and Engels without there being a reciprocal relationship. They had an economic interpretation of the evolution of preliterate cultures.

7 Some of Max Weber's work can be seen as historical materialism, which is perhaps surprising for some people, given the subsequent interpretations of his work. In some of his writings on historical sociology, especially on the ancient world, he developed a theory of history that gave primacy to economic interests and economically defined social classes.

8 While history did not play a central role in classical economics, from the 1880s and nineties there began to be developed, especially in Britain and America, the modern form of economic history, which in the twentieth century has been directly influenced by neo-classical economics. This neo-classical economic history, while not being a school, nevertheless rests upon certain shared assumptions about the primacy of economic interests and institutions for motivating economic and social behaviour. This has been made very explicit in more recent times by the cliometricians and other economic reductionists.

9 Meanwhile, in France a version of historical materialism was developed by some of the *Annales* school, such as Bloch and Braudel, who saw a central role for ecological and economic influences on social change.

10 Finally, there is recent ecological anthropology and history, developed partly under the influence of Marxism by writers such as Marshall Sahlins, Marvin Harris, W. G. Hoskins, W. H. McNeill, and A. W. Crosby, who argue for the centrality of ecological and biological influences on social and cultural history. The influence of ecology from these kinds of sources and from the *Annales* school is now also having an influence on neo-Marxist theories.

DEFINING HISTORICAL MATERIALISM

Given all these supposed versions of historical materialism theory, can something that is common to them be found that we can call its essence or core? This question can be answered in either an analytic or a synthetic sense. Analytically, a definition could be constructed that would depend upon the meaning of the terms 'historical' and 'materialist' and then the uses of the term could be compared to see if in fact various doctrines measure up. There could be established a priori what a minimal and a maximal historical materialism would have to be committed to. Synthetically, a concept could be inductively generalized from the various doctrines that claim or seem to offer a version of the doctrine. As far as I know that has not been done thoroughly, although there have been partial attempts, such as the one by Seligman long ago.

However, the major difficulty with both these approaches is that the meanings of terms change over the centuries according to the theoretical backgrounds of the users. So, any overly rigorous a priori construction made now is bound to miss some of the particular complexities of earlier theories, and an inductive generalization would have to remain on a fairly vague level in order to incorporate all the varying uses of the concepts over the centuries. I shall try to employ a combination of the two approaches, so that definitions of terms can be modified according to historical usage.

Therefore I start with a broad minimal definition of historical materialism as being

a theory of history (not a methodology) that explains the long-run evolution of social, political, and ideological structures in general by reference to the causal influence over time of the material aspects of the social totality.

This definition does not say anything explicitly about how the social totality is structured, or about particular social structures, or what the material aspects are, or how they causally influence social evolution or the motivation of human actions. However, there is a strong implication that society is at least analytically divisible into material and non-material aspects, so there is an implied theory of structure. There is also the assumption that human societies are a real entity or series of entities that have a history.

A moderate definition of historical materialism would go a little further and specify to some extent the social structure and the material aspect, that is, it would become more than just a theory of history but also a methodology containing general concepts of society and an implied epistemology as well. An example is the definition given by Frederick Engels in *Socialism, Utopian and Scientific* in 1892:

that view of the course of history which seeks the ultimate cause and the great moving power of all important historic events in the economic development of society, in the changes in the modes of production and exchange, in the consequent division of society into distinct classes, and in the struggles of the classes against one another.[4]

A maximal definition of historical materialism would include strong statements about causation, social structure, the material and the mental, action, and consciousness. One possible maximal definition might be that it is a theory of society, socio-political action, and social history that models society as a 'layered' structure in which the material-economic 'layer' causally determines the other 'layers', including consciousness, politics, and ideology, both synchronically and diachronically. This causal connection therefore produces a history of both social structures and forms of socio-political action, which pass through a definite progressive series of stages. All societies and social events are its product and therefore explicable by it.

Different versions could replace the economic definition of the material with a technological, geographical, or some other definition, and the directly causal connection with a so-called 'functional' connection.

Employing the minimal definition, I think we can say that all ten versions outlined in the previous section would be covered by it. This is because they can all be seen as offering a theory of history depending in some sense or other on the material aspect of the social totality. But they defined 'material' in different ways and even those who had an economic conception of the material conceived of the economy in different ways. Few of them, and none before Marx, had a worked-out methodology of historical materialism. They did not have explicit and general concepts about social reality, practice, structure, causation, and history, nor about how to study them. But this does not mean they are not historical materialists. It is possible both to try to explain particular social events and processes in a materialist way without being aware of general implications for all social explanation, and to try to explain structural history in a materialist way without adopting some sort of dialectical conception of the social totality *à la* Marxism.

A maximal definition, however, would probably not fit many of these versions. Whether it does or not depends to some extent on the particular interpretation that is made of each of them. Marxism, for example, has been variously interpreted in technological determinist, culturalist, and pheno-menological forms. Some neo-classical economic historiography can also be seen as containing a very different maximal version of historical materialist theory, resting on an individualist rather than structurist social ontology and methodology.

A BRIEF CRITIQUE OF SOME RECENT RECONSTRUCTIONS

Having discussed various aspects of the question of the essence or core of historical materialism I can now begin to discuss the more important question of its strengths and weaknesses. Here I come back to the six key concepts I mentioned in the first section. I want to employ them, and others, to consider very briefly some of the recent attempts at reconstruction to see what they consider to be the strengths of historical materialism and how they attempt to overcome what they consider to be weaknesses.

The constructions of Cohen, Miller, Larrain, and Sayer

First, there have been recently many different constructions of historical materialism which purport to offer improved and defensible versions of Marxism, most notably those of G. A. Cohen, Richard Miller, Jorge Larrain, and Derek Sayer. The first thing to note about them is their undefended conflation of Marxism and historical materialism. None of them discusses whether historical materialism could take a form quite different from Marxism. Each of them sees Marxism primarily as containing an *analytical* methodology and macro theory or theories of history which are empirically testable. Their careful analytical construction of Marxian concepts and theories contrasts with earlier approaches by people more influenced by the Hegelian, phenomenological, and structuralist traditions, who all read Marxism in terms of its supposed holistic nature as an a priori philosophy of praxis, experience, and history which has to be accepted in total. This means in practice that Marxism is a discrete language and cannot be criticized from a supposedly 'bourgeois' standpoint of analytical concepts and orthodox logic.

In *Karl Marx's Theory of History: A Defence* (1978) Cohen makes a careful exegesis of Marx's texts but claims to find only one theory of history in them – the technological determinist thesis. According to this, Marx explained the history of social relations and politics by reference to their functional relationship with the technological mode of production. The forces of production, in this reading, have a long-term autonomous tendency to develop. The role of social relations and politics is, *inter alia*, to facilitate this development in the long run – that is, they function to further or occasionally to fetter the development of the forces.

Cohen's reading takes us back some of the way to earlier readings of Marx, notably that of Plekhanov, but he was the first to bring to the forefront the latent functionalism that undoubtedly exists in Marx. However, it is certainly not the case that this is the only theory of history in Marx's ambiguous texts and it is strongly debatable that it is the best, as Cohen claims. The constructions by Miller, Larrain, and Sayer offer alternative, more subtle and better textually supported readings.

Richard Miller's book *Analyzing Marx: Morality, Power, and History* (1984) is one of the most persuasive ever written on Marx. In contrast with Cohen, who is concerned to extract and develop a single, internally coherent thesis about history, Miller has paid full attention to the complexities, ambiguities, and contradictions in Marx's texts. Out of all that he extracts various possibilities and shows why some readings are more textually supported and plausible than others. He constructs a version of the narrow economic determinist theory of history and then proceeds to show why it is not supported in Marx's writings. In opposition to it he defends what he calls a 'mode of production interpretation', or what I would call 'relational materialism', in which basic, internal economic change arises (whenever it does, in fact, take place) on account of a self-transforming tendency of the mode of production as a whole, that is, the relations of production, the forms of cooperation and the technology through which material goods are produced. Because of the nature of the mode, processes that initially maintain its characteristic relations of production eventually produce their downfall. This change need not overcome any barriers to material production. It may do so. Change may be based on developments in the forms of cooperation or in technology, giving access to enhanced productive power to an initially subordinate group, and motivating their resistance to the old relations of production because the latter come to inhibit the further development of that new productive power. But, in this broad mode of production theory, change may also be wholly internal to the relations of production. The patterns of control in the old relations of production may make it inevitable that an initially nondominant group will acquire the power and the desire to overthrow the old relations. (pp. 172–3)

As Miller rightly says and shows, this theory fits Marx's practice as a historian, which cannot be said for technological and economic determinism. What is less certain is his claim that this is a defensible theory of history, irrespective of Marxism. I shall discuss relational materialism in more detail in a moment. There is no doubt that it is the most plausible version of historical materialism but it is still a materialist theory.

Like Miller, Jorge Larrain has also provided a careful and textually rich interpretation of Marx in *A Reconstruction of Historical Materialism* (1986). He attacks economic determinist, Hegelian, existentialist, and structuralist readings and argues for the central importance of human practical subjectivity within a structural context. Rather than Marx's 1859 preface being the canonical text, he takes the *Eighteenth Brumaire* as central, in which Marx said that it is men (we should read, 'people') who make history but always under conditions not of their own choosing. Larrain rightly says that

it does not make sense . . . to concede 'primacy' to a social result, be it productive forces or relations of production. Primacy can only be attached to human beings' practical production and transformation of their material life. Of course, this practice necessarily involves both relations of production and productive forces as *results* and *preconditions* of material reproduction. But change cannot be fully explained as a structural effect of these social results. Change is only conditioned by them but not fully preordained. It is human beings with their practical activity that bring about change within a set of limited options. It is true that human beings do not choose freely their productive forces and relations of production – they are handed down to them by the preceding generation – but this does not make them absolutely powerless to change them nor does it preclude various possibilities in attempting to change them.

The tensions in Marx and Engels' conception of social change must therefore be resolved in favour of practical political activity and class struggle. (p. 116)

With this conclusion Larrain is close to abandoning historical materialism altogether, something that is reminiscent of the work of many supposedly

Marxist historians such as Christopher Hill, Edward Thompson, Eric Hobsbawm, and Barrington Moore, who have not allowed general base/superstructure and economic determinist formulas to dictate their explanations of actual processes. Perhaps we should think of their work as examples of post-materialism.

Similarly, Derek Sayer argues in his textually rich and persuasive book, *The Violence of Abstraction* (1987), that social historians such as Hill and Thompson, who employ historical materialism in a fluid and dynamic fashion, are closest to Marx's 'guiding thread'. Sayer's non-rigorous, non-abstract, metaphorical, reading of Marxism owes much to the defences by Engels after Marx's death and to Thompson's use of it to explain history. He believes that Marx's 'shifting, and theoretically treacherous, recourse to metaphor and analogy may be a linguistic signal of exactly the inappropriateness of attempting a closed and 'rigorous' formulation of theory at this level of generality' (p. 14). In particular, he sees as a mistake the attempt by 'traditional historical materialists' (including Cohen) to separate material production and social relations. He has much textual support to show that Marx's claim was not

that social relations are caused by material production but that it irreducibly involves them. They are part and parcel of it. It accordingly cannot be conceptualised, in any empirically adequate manner, independently of them. In particular, production cannot be conceived as a purely 'material' sphere, if material is taken to exclude social ... This vitiates Cohen's attempted distinction between 'material' and 'social' relations of production as substantially distinct kinds of relation. (p. 25)

One of the main things that follows from this is a different interpretation of the base/superstructure and economic determinism concepts from that propounded by the traditionalists. Sayer rightly argues that to see ideological spheres as somehow independent is a fetishized reification. For Marx, on the contrary, 'superstructures' are not levels of reality separate from the 'base' but forms of appearance. Therefore,

to construe the base/superstructure metaphor as a model of the relation between substantially discrete levels, practices or 'instances' within the social formation, and conceptualise that relation in causal (or functional) terms, is to replicate exactly the illogical illusion of superstructural separability Marx is above all concerned to refute. Such constructions spectacularly miss the central point of his argument. The base/ superstructure metaphor applies to the relation between social being and social consciousness, it is not a putative model of societal 'levels' at all. (pp. 91–2)

The only way to explain the history of society, then, in Sayer's account of Marx's historical materialism, is by a painstakingly empirical tracing through time. The use of a structural or functional logic or a general theory provides no short cuts (p. 96). Like the account given by Larrain, this has the potential, at least, to take us away from historical materialism to a post-materialist position that builds upon aspects of it, and again poses the question of the status of Marxism.

The ecological reconstructions of Stinchcombe and Godelier

Arthur Stinchcombe and Maurice Godelier have recently quite separately proposed adapting Marxism to wider conceptions of materiality that incorporate an ecological idea of the social totality and a more developed concept of social formations in which to locate the complexities of actual economies, class structures, and politics. Marx, being the restless, unsystematic thinker that he was, did not stop to develop clear, coherent concepts of modes of production or social formations, or, of course, of the notorious base/superstructure model. Nevertheless, these concepts are of central importance and clarifying their meaning and significance is still one of the main problems for Marxist theory. These two writers make persuasive attempts to show why Marxism must be reconstructed in an ecological and anti-economistic direction.

Stinchcombe argues in *Economic Sociology* (1983) that what was fundamentally wrong about Marxism was *not* that it needed a theory of politics to counterpose or add to its economic theory in order to avoid economic determinism. While a theory of how politics responds to economic conditions is needed, he believes that what is more important is a better economic theory. That requires a sociological theory of productive enterprises under different ecological, technological, cultural, demographic, administrative, and political conditions. He proceeds to show in some detail how all those aspects are interrelated in quite different ways within contemporary Karimojong society, eighteenth-century France, and the modern United States. He then argues that a mode of production has ecological, technological, organizational, and populational boundaries, and which is more important for the sociologist depends on what needs to be analysed (p. 243). These are not strata within a total social formation but different, equally important aspects (p. 245). The problem then is to analyse how all the modes of production of a particular society add up to the class dynamics of the whole. His answer is that there is no lawful way that they do. The outcome is always contingent (pp. 245–6). This, then, amounts to a rejection of the base/superstructure model and he provides a powerful case for widening historical materialism but not for rejecting materialism entirely.

Godelier develops in *The Mental and the Material* (1986) a concept of the social totality that allows for the possibility of the dominance of non-economic aspects in non-capitalist societies. He also argues for a widening of the notion of materiality to include the ecosystem with which people interact, and for a blurring of the nature/culture distinction. He is strongly opposed to abstract model building which reifies aspects or levels of the social whole, especially the material/mental or infrastructure/superstructure models. Material action necessarily involves mental activity and mental realities of various kinds. He writes that

since thought is not an instance separate from social relations, since a society has neither top nor bottom, since it does not consist of superimposed layers, we are forced to conclude that if the distinction between infrastructure and superstructures is to retain any meaning at all, it cannot be taken as a distinction between levels or instances, any more than between institutions. (pp. 18–19)

His proposal is to isolate relations of production from the totality and to see whether they are the most general category. They have three functions:

determination of the social forms of access to resources and control of the conditions of production; organization of labour processes and allocation of members of society to them; determination of the social forms of circulation and redistribution of the products of individual or collective labour. It is then possible to show that in certain societies kinship relations (the Australian Aborigines) or political relations (fifth-century Athens) or politico-religious relations (Ancient Egypt) also functioned as relations of production. (pp. 19–20)

He believes this kind of analysis allows a reformulation of the problem of domination by a particular institution, such as religion, or caste, or kinship:

For while in every society there exist social relations which organize the workings of kinship, the mechanisms of authority and of power, and the channels of communication with gods and ancestors, yet kin, political or religious relations are not dominant in every society. Why then should one set of relations be dominant in one place and a different set in another? I believe I have shown . . . that a set of social relations dominates when they function simultaneously as social relations *of production*, as the social framework and support for the material process of appropriation of nature. (p. 20)

This is reminiscent of a footnote in the first volume of *Capital* where Marx said that it was the mode of production that determined whether politics or religion dominated a particular society.[5] Godelier's idea of functions has the merit of empirical flexibility and plausibility and his refusal of abstract formulations allows his version of Marxism, what remains of it, to incorporate the findings of many non-Marxists. In fact, he too goes a good deal of the way towards a post-materialism.

Habermas's evolutionary reconstruction

In 'Towards a Reconstruction of Historical Materialism'[6] Jürgen Habermas has proposed reconstructing historical materialism to eliminate the supposed teleology and economic determinism that he professes to find in Marxism. His reading and reconstruction are at the most abstract level possible. He reads Marxism primarily as a general theory of history which needs a better theory of systemics and evolutionary mechanisms to make it work. Those mechanisms have to be found, he argues, at the level of learning and communication, not the economy. He sees society as an integrated, evolved, unstable system in which there is an endogenous growth of knowledge. The system continually throws up systemic problems. He argues that:

a. The system problems that cannot be solved without evolutionary innovations arise in the basic domain of a society.
b. Each new mode of production means a new form of social integration, which crystallizes around a new institutional core.
c. An endogenous learning mechanism provides for the accumulation of a cognitive potential that can be used for solving crisis-inducing system problems.
d. This knowledge, however, can be implemented to develop the forces of production only when the evolutionary step to a new institutional framework and a new form of social integration has been taken.

It remains an open question, *how* this step is taken. The *descriptive* answer of historical materialism is: through social conflict, struggle, social movements, and political confrontations (which, when they take place under the conditions of a class structure, can be analyzed as class struggles). But only an analytic answer can explain *why* a society takes an evolutionary step and how we are to understand that social struggles under certain conditions lead to a new level of social development. I would like to propose the following answer: the species learns not only in the dimensions of technically useful knowledge decisive for the development of productive forces but also in the dimension of moral–practical consciousness decisive for structures of interaction. The rules of communicative action do develop in reaction to changes in the domain of instrumental and strategic action; but in doing so they *follow their own logic.* (pp. 147–8)

Since the mid-1970s Habermas has worked on this project of examining the conditions and effects of communicative action. This could perhaps be thought to take us beyond materialism, rather than simply being a reconstruction of it. But the great problem with this text of Habermas is its holistic and systemic theory of society governed by a cybernetic hierarchy. While it is important to address the questions of knowledge and communication, their social role has to be examined in concrete rather than highly generalized and abstract ways. We are not dealing with a natural system with universal laws but social systems, characterized by human agency, structural contingency, and enormous local variation.

Giddens's contemporary critique

Finally, I come to the sustained attempt by Anthony Giddens, in *A Contemporary Critique of Historical Materialism* (1981 and 1985) to come to terms with Marxism from a sympathetic point of view and move beyond it to a more comprehensive and more powerful post-materialism. His 'structurationism' is an attempt to add to certain elements of Marxism a better theory of action, a theory of time, and a better, more complete account of history. He is strongly opposed to functionalism, evolutionism, technological determinism, and economic reductionism. He does not propose a new general theory as such but rather a methodology consisting mainly of a set of general concepts, such as 'agency', 'time–space', 'institutions', 'power', and 'structure'. This is similar in the programmatic nature of its conception to Max Weber's project in the first part of *Economy and Society*, and in terms of concept construction Giddens is attempting to be the Weber of our time, but he lacks Weber's knowledge of economic, social, and cultural history.

In summary, we have here a spectrum of so-called reconstructions, varying from the differing defences of Marxism by Cohen, Miller, Larrain, and Sayer, through the partial defences with considerable amendment by Stinchcombe and Godelier, to the wholesale restructuring and more or less abandonment of fundamental aspects by Habermas and Giddens. In fact the latter have ceased to be materialists and have developed what we could call post-materialist or post-Marxist methodologies and theories. While abandoning materialism they have not adopted idealism or individualism and they have retained certain key elements of Marxism.

THE INADEQUACIES OF SOME EXISTING FRAMEWORKS FOR
STRUCTURAL HISTORY

I have argued that minimal historical materialism must be construed as a general theory of social history, that is, all versions of it are theories that explain the history of society by reference somehow to the material aspects of the totality. Moderate and maximal versions also contain a general ontological model of social structure as being layered and real, and general concepts for analysing different social structures. Furthermore, the best existing form of historical materialism, as represented in the readings of Marx by Miller, Larrain, and Sayer, can be characterized as relational materialism because it sees the fundamental social reality as complex structures of social relations rather than actual material things or systems, such as technologies and forces of production. They rightly argue that it is systems of social relations and their representations in forms of consciousness that structure the ways people act and interact with the material world to mould it to their purposes, and the material world in turn helps to mould social relations and consciousness. In this dialectic an inanimate force cannot be the prime mover. Surely the prime social force can only be the mentalities and powers of people *qua* social people. But this element tends to be underdeveloped in relational materialist theories.

Because of its strength, it is this relational materialism that must be criticized. If it can be shown to be inadequate and transformable then simpler forms of historical materialism would therefore also become unattractive. In order to begin to assess its adequacy as a general theory and methodology for the social domain we need to see how it relates to certain methodological and theoretical criteria that together constitute the principles of adequacy for theories of structural history.

Criteria of methodological and theoretical adequacy

Drawing on the discussion of the previous chapters, we can say that an adequate approach to socio-historical explanations must implicitly or explicitly fulfil the following methodological requirements as a minimum programme:

1 It must have a coherent general model (or general conception) of social structure, one that views structure as real and not merely an instrumental figment of the theorist's view of the world.
2 This implies a social-realist commitment that holds non-observable systems of social rules, roles, and relations to be real and relatively independent of thought.
3 The model of structure must be sufficiently general and flexible to encompass the changing nature of structures and the enormous empirical diversity to be found.
4 There has to be a general conception of how individual and collective actions are intentionally, psychologically, and sociologically motivated, and therefore of how they relate to social structures.
5 There must be a general conception of how thought, including systems of ideas and mentalities, interrelates with actions and structures.
6 The general kinds of causes of actual structural processes and transformations have to be theorized.
7 The problems of the relationship of the social enquirer to social realities and the relationship of social phenomena to structures have to be examined and theorized. The epistemological problem of the relationship of observable evidence to theoretically specified non-observable 'layers' has to be specified so that the truth conditions (or plausibility conditions) for explanations are made clear.

The commitments and weaknesses of relational materialism

Within the ambit of these requirements, the significance of a relational materialist perspective of the sort adhered to in varying degrees by Larrain, Miller, Sayer, Godelier, Stinchcombe, and some other Marxist and Weberian historians and sociologists, lies in its commitment to five interconnecting principles, on which it must be judged:

1 It conceives of social reality as being fundamentally a structured set of relations, rules, roles, and positions that exist through time more or less independently of individual consciousness and action, and which have causal power to impel and constrain action.

2　Social structure is conceived as being organized into a system of semi-autonomous 'levels' or 'spheres' of structural relations and activity. This is not a descriptive but an analytical model or concept. The levels or spheres are not independent of the totality but each is in some way present in the others. The significance of the model lies in the power it gives to direct attention to particular, historically specific, causal and/or explanatory priorities in concrete analyses of structural history.

3　The production of material existence and material motivations for behaviour are theorized as having long-run (but not necessarily short-run) causal and explanatory priority (within a framework of social power relations) over other kinds of motivation, action, and thought.

4　Social change is theorized as the result primarily of structural contradictions that arise within production and the social totality, manifested partly as struggles between social classes defined by the relationship of their members to the material production process.

5　Social history in the long term is conceived as the progressive mastery of the material world and the progressive development of human productive forces and co-operative social capacities and arrangements.

While some other approaches to socio-historical explanation, such as Parsonian structural–functionalism, Weberian culturalism, and *Annales* structuralism, share many of these principles they do not have them all. But of course they might still be able to meet as many of the requirements of a good approach because the relational materialist approach is certainly not perfect. It is able to fulfil all the criteria of adequacy listed previously except points 4 (on individual motivation) and 6 (on the causes of actual historical processes). In those two areas it does adopt a position, but the particular way in which it addresses these problems is usually inadequate. Furthermore, despite the general strengths of this approach there are other serious weaknesses. Its third commitment, regarding materialism, and its fifth commitment, regarding the generally progressive nature of world history, are both empirically unsustainable and must be considered as a priori metaphysical assumptions rather than empirical conclusions. Such general kinds of assumptions are necessary to all sciences at some stage, but they have to be critically examined in the light of subsequent research, which some later Marxist historians have indeed done. The fourth commitment – the economic definition of classes and contradictions – is too historically specific to be elevated to a general theory of change.

The weaknesses of individualist approaches

Despite their weaknesses existing forms of historical materialism are more explanatorily powerful than methodological individualist approaches, such as behaviourist sociology and neo-classical economics, which I believe are inadequate on the following main interrelated grounds.

Their concept of structure is instrumentalist and so they are opposed to the idea of society as a real system of causally powerful social rules, roles, and relations. Rather, concepts of structure are either eschewed or inadequately based on individualist social ontologies. Society is thought to be a mere patterned aggregation of individual behaviour which is motivated by psychological dispositions alone. Social phenomena in the sense of social interactions and group behaviour are supposed to be the result of individual motivations in pursuit of individual goals of satisfaction.

As this indicates, their theory of human motivation and action gives little or no place to conscious intentions, social and cultural imperatives, or the gaps between psychological states, intentions, and actions. Rather, they adopt a dispositional behaviourist model which tends to see people as making learned responses to environmental stimuli. People supposedly have psychological dispositions always to behave in so-called rational self-interest, and what is perceived to be their self-interest depends largely on the opportunities presented by and learned about the environment. Motivation is then understood by the observer by inference directly from behaviour. There seems to be no place in analysis for unintended or unrealized effects of personal intentions.

Little or no place is given to non-environmental causes of behaviour or to unobservable intentional motives. Personal material interests, as construed from observable behaviour, are usually given explanatory dominance and the economy is seen as the realm of rational behaviour, which is more or less independent of the rest of society or, more radically, the rest of society is reduced to the economic sphere.

Epistemologically, these approaches are empiricist and positivist, therefore they do not employ realist concepts about non-empirical social and intentional realities. Society and psychological states supposedly have to be observable, or to result in observable behaviour and/or utterances, to be real. This requirement excludes from explanations unactivated intentions, unintended consequences, and social relations, and it puts reliance upon preconceived psychological dispositions, such as economic rationality, and upon observable behavioural patterns. In general, then, individualism misses a good deal of the discoverable reality of society and the causal complexes of behaviour.

The weaknesses of holist approaches

Holist approaches to social history conceive of the social totality as a supra-individual structural or cultural entity, apparently with powers of self-regulation and self-transformation that are employed through the control the whole exercises over the minds and behaviour of the people within it. The main problems with this approach include the specification of this holistic entity, which, especially by traditional historians, is usually underdeveloped. Vague notions about the 'character' of an epoch or society or milieu are substituted for clear analysis. Collective entities such as nations are sometimes given the power to determine functionally the behaviour that is in the 'interests' of the collective entity or even powers of decision-making and self-activation.

In the case of holistic structural theories where society is theorized as a tightly integrated system it is assigned powers of self-regulation and self-maintenance which operate through the functions of subsystems and patterns of human action. The system itself is the agent of its own integration and equilibrium through its supposed power over the behaviour of people within it. But no justification seems possible for such a concept of society as a supra-individual, organic entity. It is implausible at least that such macroscopic entities as nations and social systems could bring about their own history. The question of agency is not coherently addressed by holists.

Both individualism and holism rest upon a false dichotomy drawn between the individual and society; by concentrating on one side only they cannot really explain either. What is needed is a conception of the two sides of social reality as constituting a dialectical duality in which each structures the other. It is individual and collective action and thought that causally structures society and it is society that organizes and structures, but does not directly cause, action and thought. The duality is an evolving, historical process, so time is the essential third dimension of social reality.

BEYOND HISTORICAL MATERIALISM: TOWARDS A NON-MATERIALIST, STRUCTURIST THEORY OF STRUCTURAL HISTORY

The theory of sociological structurism is able to build upon points 1 and 2 of the relational materialist approach (which refer to the relational theory of society and the 'levels' model of structure, as well as the ideas of human practice and the historicity of all social forms) in two main areas: the theory of action, and the role of meanings, culture, and ideology. In addition, the theory is strengthened by an explicit recognition of the centrality of episte-mological realism.

From Marxism to an agential theory of action

A theory of action is certainly contained in an underdeveloped form in Marxism. It tends to be an interests theory which attributes action primarily to the pursuit of what are perceived to be material interests. But according to Marx conscious understanding of one's interests can often be false and this is usually the case if personal interests are placed above class interests. For Marx true interests are those that coincide with the historic advance of social classes. Action, then, is a product of conscious understanding (whether ideological or scientific) of one's own social position. (There can also be found in Marx an undeveloped theory of the unconscious, but its status and role in his work are at best uncertain.) The social understanding of actors is in turn largely determined by their social position. Many Marxists (especially dialectical materialists and structuralists) have therefore downgraded the role of general human agency and choice, especially in regard to the pursuit of supposedly objective interests. Consequently, history has been seen as taking place 'behind the backs' of ordinary people as a largely alien, incomprehensible, and usually oppressive process, determining their actions but not being produced by them, at least not until they develop revolutionary class-consciousness.

The discovery of the structural determination of action was a great advance by Marx that led him to formulate the outstanding theory of structural change of those developed in the nineteenth century and one of the best ever. However, we are now able to see that any theory of human action which denies general human agency is defective. This is because without it there cannot be a real mechanism of social structuring and social change under any social conditions.

There are two kinds of causal powers inherent in the structures of material things, material systems, and relational systems. (There is no evidence for the existence of other kinds of entities in the universe, and the existence of relational systems is denied by physicalists.) These are the powers of agency and conditioning. Agency is a power that emerges spontaneously from the physical structure of some entities and enables them to control their own behaviour and interactions and to alter their environment within the parameters of their intrinsic natures. As I argued in chapters 3 and 5, agency is the power to choose courses of action and influence the action of other entities. A human agent is able to monitor its own action, to monitor its monitorings, and to make adjustments to life courses within certain constraints. It is able more or less deliberately to enter into relations with other entities in order to form relational systems in which there emerge conditioning powers. Weaker, less conscious, and unconscious forms of agency exist in other animals, who also have the power and the compulsion to alter the environment to suit their own existence. Animals have little power as individuals but great power collectively within ecosystems. Human agential power varies according to consciousness, personality, and the conditioning power of social and ecological situations.

Conditioning powers, then, are those that set constraints on and impel in certain courses the actions of agents. Such powers emerge within physical and relational systems. They are also the passive powers to produce phenomena that naturally exist within physical systems that are constituted by smaller physical components.[7] Relational systems, which are animal and human societies and biological ecosystems, have conditioning powers to control their individual constituents. Such powers arise from the precisely organized way in which their constituents interact. In human social systems these interactions are a complex and precise combination of biological, geographical, psychological, cultural, economic, and political exchanges and relations.

Relational systems depend on the actions of their agential members (and blind genetic mutations within those agents and within the passive, conditioning elements of the system) for their transformations and therefore for their history. They cannot produce their own history. The imputation of agential powers to societies as holistic entities is an unwarranted (and unnecessary) reification that is unfortunately all too prevalent in the social sciences and everyday understanding. Only people, in groups and as individuals, are the moving forces of social history, so we must look to agential people to discover the causes of social change. That is why in the first place a well-developed theory of human action and consciousness is necessary to social science. But people must never be studied in isolation from their structurally conditioning social situations. Methodological individualism, as much as methodological holism, must be avoided.

Furthermore, as I argued in chapter 3, agency is a capacity that people have in virtue of being people. It is not an invariably determining disposition to behave in a (so-called) rational egoistic manner, as many writers in neo-classical economics and individualist psychological traditions seem to believe. They adopt an (often unexamined) behaviourism that views people as automatic responders to environmental stimuli which impinge on a limited range of psychological dispositions. According to that theory people are supposedly freely moving individuals, but they always seem to move in the same direction – towards individual material gratification. They are therefore not really agents, in spite of the theory's emphasis upon rational choice, because their behaviour is in fact pre-determined by pre-rational psychological drives. Agents, rather, make genuine choices after a more complex, partly rational, thought process. And their choices are not always just from the limited range seemingly available from their social situations. Their actions can be and often are transformative of their social situations.

In chapter 3 I showed how the theory of action and agency has been discussed and improved lately by many writers, including Charles Taylor, Donald Davidson, Rom Harré, and Anthony Giddens.[8] They and others have been converging on a new, rich, powerfully explanatory paradigm that denies the claims of the physicalist, behaviourist, psychoanalytic, voluntarist, and dualist alternatives. The heart of the new paradigm is a conception of the person as a socially powerful agent with intentions and abilities to choose reflectively and to structure society meaningfully, according to intentions and unintentionally. Persons are not strictly determined physically, nor psychologically, nor culturally, nor sociologically, nor do they possess minds that are independent of such determinations in total. Agency is always conditioned in these ways, but it remains in an important sense independent of them. If it didn't it would not be agency. But human action is meaningful because of its shared conditions and it cannot be understood apart from them. The dialectic between the powers of agency and conditioning is the core of the sociological and humanistic problem.

The importance of meanings, culture, and ideology –
against the idea of primacy

The second area in which the structurist theory improves on the existing relational materialist approach is in the place given to meanings, mentalities, cultures, and ideologies. One of Marx's most powerful theoretical devices was the analytical 'levels' concept of society. He did not entirely invent this idea – it had been a part of European thought for perhaps a century or more – but he gave it a greatly enriched content. Ever since, many of the leading social scientists (including, for example, Max Weber, Claude Lévi-Strauss, Talcott Parsons, Fernand Braudel, and of course most later Marxists and many Weberians) have adopted some version of the levels model or analogues of it. All agree that the levels of economy, politics, and culture exist as abstractly defined (but perhaps semi-autonomous) substructures, or subsystems, or spheres, or forms of activity. Many theorists add to the list other levels or sublevels such as ideology, law, and religion.

The point of these models is not to make descriptions. Rather, they are abstractions that serve to isolate putative causal or functional relations between types of social activity, social structures, and forms of social understanding. In the case of Marxism, primacy was assigned to the economic and technological level. Just what 'primacy' means has been hotly debated ever since, but this point has been the most basic feature distinguishing traditional Marxist materialism as a theory of history from non-materialism. Another feature has been the way in which Marxism has defined the economy as a set of relations of production and forces of production structured by internal property relations between the owners of labour power and the owners of surplus extracted from production.

The debate over primacy has served to highlight the problem of the role of culture and ideology in structural determination and action. Some Marxists have attempted to remedy this deficiency by developing theories of the 'super-structure' of society. Non-Marxist levels theorists, such as Weber, Lévi-Strauss, Parsons, and Harré, and many relational-structurist historians have also placed much more emphasis upon meanings, culture, and ideology. This is a necessary development. To conceive of human motivation as essentially economically oriented, as many Marxists did and still tend to do, is to mistake the appearance of human activity for the deeper reality of human nature. In fact, as Marx showed clearly in his early writings, human activity primarily has a group-oriented, cultural and psychological imperative that is sometimes forced under the exigencies of particular material and social conditions (especially capitalism and slavery) to take the form of constant materially productive labour. Under conditions where this is not necessary a concentration on cultural production is of greater social significance. Only in modern capitalist society is materialism dominant. As many anthropologists, cultural theorists, and social psychologists have argued, it is the creation of status, respect, moral careers, public personae, psychological domination, meaningful personal relationships, and above all meaning, that primarily motivate people.[9] Material interests and welfare, although obviously very important, are the mechanisms that bring about this cultural and psychological end. There is no constant, universal, overriding, economic imperative. There are numerous examples of individual and mass psychological, cultural, and ideological motives overriding economic considerations, even in modern, supposedly rationalistic, capitalist society.

Therefore a viable general theory for structural history must give a central place to the importance of the cultural, ideological, and social psychological aspects of social life to add to the already well-developed economic theory of the relational materialist tradition. Opting for a Weberian, or Geertzian, or Harréan approach wholesale is not sufficient, because of their failures to theorize adequately the importance of internal relations of production and hence the dynamic inherent within some types of economy as opposed to others. The link between the economy and other levels cannot be properly grasped unless internal relations of production are understood as manifest at the other levels in the forms of social class relations, law, ideology, and culture, just as these aspects are inherent within the economic structure. In short, what is required is a better theory of personality and the importance to people of psychological welfare and cultural expression to add to the social relational theory of material production. Sociological economics must also become psychological and cultural economics.

A relational–structurist approach, then, is not a materialist theory of history. It does not attribute some general determination or primacy to the technological or economic level, however the economy is defined. Rather, its theory of action says that in general human motivation is more complex. Action is more culturally and psychologically oriented than economically, even under capitalism. It has been a fundamental mistake of historical materialists, including many Marxists, to overemphasize human materially productive labour against cultural and social production. In fact structurism refuses to take a stand on this question of primacy, holding that the tendency and the manifestation of human motivation vary with the prevailing economic, social, and cultural situation. A general theory cannot tell us in advance what the real social situation is, although it can point our search in certain directions.

More emphatically, structurism is strongly opposed to economic reductionism. Marx was not guilty of it but some Marxists and neo-classical economists are. The methodological individualist and rationalist economic approach to socio-historical explanation cannot account convincingly for sociological and cultural imperatives to action or for irrational behaviour. People display a good deal of behaviour that is *not* directed to supposedly rational economic gratification and is even strictly irrational on any criteria. Human rationality is a variable, hidden, often unactivated capacity, rather than a determining disposition. Structurism, because of its sociological and psychological realism, is able to accommodate hidden capacities whereas positivist neo-classicism cannot.

6

Realism, Structurism, and History as the Foundations for a Unified and Transformative Science of Society

This final chapter attempts to pull the threads together in such a way as to reveal the normative significance of the argument about scientific structural history. The abandonment of the modernist project of building an intersubjective foundation for knowledge in the face of the obvious destructiveness and oppression wrought by the political defenders and employers of (vulgar) science or scientism has been a mistake. To abandon scientific reason is to abandon the only means of identifying and overcoming the causes of the degradation of the ecological, political, and social environment. But science can do its proper liberating work only in a rational, enlightened, democratic community. It is here that the normative level asserts itself as the ultimate justification for scientific methodology, theory, and enquiry. Science is ultimately justifiable as an enterprise by its critical and explanatory perspectives but it is not normative in itself, or at least it should try to bracket norms.[1] A scientific attitude of truth-seeking provides a framework for a culture of liberation. Once the content of social liberation is spelt out social science can lend itself to the judgement and validation of claims about the structural context of society and politics, and of attempts to relate normative values to social contexts. Science cannot validate the content of liberation but it can try to establish the structural conditions of liberation. The alternative to intersubjective critical validation is tyranny or nihilism.

THE POLITICAL NECESSITY FOR A HISTORICAL SCIENCE OF SOCIETY

The question of the proper methodological foundations for social, political, and historical studies is now seemingly in a greater state of intellectual contention than at any time this century. Perhaps this is a consequence of the incipient breakdown of neo-Enlightenment modes of thought, with their at least partial coherence around the projects of rational enquiry and promotion of progressive social justice. The propagation of new and ever more sophisticated versions of relativism now poses a serious threat to the whole possibility of intersubjective understanding and explanation, not just of society but of nature too. I fear that with that possibility goes another, of rational, democratic, emancipatory transformation of the social world. Social critique and rational emancipation seem inevitably to depend on some universalistic concepts, as well as on a commitment to the principles of equality and democracy.

The contemporary *Methodenstreit* has many similarities with that of the 1880s and 1890s in Germany and Austria, which Max Weber made such an impressive attempt to transcend. Today we also have our putative Max Webers – Jürgen Habermas, Pierre Bourdieu, Alain Touraine, and Anthony Giddens are obvious contenders. Perhaps we might also include Karl-Otto Apel, Niklas Luhmann, Peter Berger, Jon Elster, and others, according to our preconception of the nature of the problem. While these writers have made important and influential attempts to recast the general framework of social enquiry from different perspectives, some of them lack a fundamental component that was central to Weber's thought and to that of most of the nineteenth-century founders of social science – a strong commitment to and thorough understanding of general economic and social historiography. A lack of this structural historical dimension is a great weakness in any attempt to provide a way out of cacophonous philosophical and methodological debates. Its presence can help prevent the turn towards relativism.

Conversely, it is the commitment to historical enquiry that adds strength to those outside this *Methodenstreit* who see their primary task not as being explicitly to provide a new methodological framework, or general set of categories, or general theory of change, but to conduct research into the history of societies and cultures, using whatever methodological and theoretical materials are found to be useful. Historians such as Emmanuel Le Roy Ladurie, Barrington Moore, Eric Hobsbawm, Charles Tilly, Reinhard Bendix, Norbert Elias, R. S. Neale, Clifford Geertz, Robert Darnton, and Ernest Gellner have been advancing social understanding and knowledge in powerfully plausible ways, even though they have different theories. What is it about their methodologies and practices that enables them all to produce richly explanatory texts? I have tried to answer this question by attempting to combine an argument about social methodology and theory with articulations of methodologies drawn from structural historians, presenting a synthesis in such a way as to show the significance of each of these strands when woven into a coherent, historically oriented, framework for the social studies. In this way the sources of the richness and strength of the best structural historical work can be grasped better and so the practices not only of socio-historical enquiry but all social explanation can be improved.

A framework constructed in the historical and structurist manner articulated here is able to point the way towards resolving several persistent philosophical and methodological problems in the social studies. In particular, it shows that the following old problematic dichotomies can be transcended: positive science versus hermeneutics, explanation versus understanding, action versus structure, change versus continuity, and history versus sociology. In case it seems that this is rather too ambitious or flogging a series of dead horses, depending on one's philosophical background, I then tried to show that these problems are still very much alive in the social studies and that they may be susceptible to comprehensive resolution. I contend, as some other writers have done, that most of these problems have their origin in the failure to comprehend properly the structure of reasoning in physical science.

The social studies have been for centuries greatly influenced by philosophies of science, negatively and positively. The desire for positive, universal knowledge or the complete rejection of its possibility, both in a context of uncritical, naïve, and often distorted borrowings of the epistemological ideas of writers about science (including recently those of Carnap, Hempel, Popper, Kuhn, Feyerabend, and others) have led to several unfortunate courses of theorizing in the social studies, ranging from empiricist pseudo-scientific cliometrics and behaviourism, through functionalism, to interpretism. Moreover, scientism in its various forms has been both philosophically false and politically dangerous. Scientism is the wrong-headed idea that the scientific method is one of objectively dealing only with observable facts. Any putative science that does not employ 'the scientific method' is condemned as merely subjective and therefore not explanatory. Any enquiry that has to rely on subjective interpretation of evidence and whose objects are not observable entities, events, and processes cannot be a science. This idea can lead to one of two conclusions about human and social studies – they are irretrievably condemned as subjective or they have to become like natural science, especially physics, if they wish to be taken seriously in their claim to produce knowledge.

It is ironic and significant that scientism itself has taken two forms when applied to the social and human studies – holist and individualist. The former sees the task of a genuine science as the study of organic systems or wholes. This idea may be traced back to the positivism of Comte. It means that social science can only deal with supposedly objective collectives, systems, or holistic epochs. The individualist version sees science as employing a reductionist empiricism that deals only with atomistic data about objective, observable events and actions. This version may be traced to Hume and later to the Viennese logical positivists. Both versions reject the possibility of social explanation employing a phenomenological and hermeneutical approach or an approach that tries to develop explanations employing a combination of hermeneutics and objective empirical enquiry about non-holistic structures.

Both versions of scientism are false for two main reasons. First, the claim that there is only one scientific method to which all empirical explanations must conform if they are to produce knowledge is not borne out by studies of the actual methodologies of various natural sciences, let alone of social sciences. That the proponents of a unitary and objective scientific method have not themselves agreed over the years is a glaring flaw in the argument for methodological unity. Second, the logical empiricist account of scientific method, on which scientism has recently based itself, does not in fact seem to describe any branch of science. Furthermore, scientism is politically dangerous because it can lead to an attitude of passivity in the face of the supposed impossibility of objective knowledge about the social conditions of action, or to an irrational voluntarism inspired by the idea of the supposed non-existence of objective social structures and hence an absence of social constraints on action.

Nevertheless, in spite of these strictures I have tried to defend the idea that there is or should be a loosely unified form of scientific reasoning that does apply to all branches of empirical explanation and which serves to separate science from non-science. Positivists of various kinds have long striven to achieve such a unity and demarcation. This book tries to present an alternative to their account that both upholds the important differences between branches of science and maintains the possibility of scientific enquiry into society and its history against the defenders of the radical separation of so-called 'moral' or human studies. There have been other similar arguments recently[2] but the account of science I have proposed has some novel features.

The ultimate rationale for a science of society must be to rescue the possibility of rational, humanistic, democratic, social transformation on the bases of, first, increasingly truthful understanding of the history, structures, and process mechanisms of society and, second, an empirically developed conception of what a good society could be like in very general terms derived partly from a conception of persons as necessarily social beings.[3] The possibilities of emancipating action have to be understood and grasped, and this first involves transcending the dichotomies mentioned above. Attempts to do this have recently been made by Jürgen Habermas, Karl-Otto Apel, Roy Bhaskar, Maurice Mandelbaum, and others.[4]

Optimistic belief in the possibility of rational, affirmative, democratic social transformation requires a new foundation because positivism and evolutionism no longer seem to have optimistic explanatory power. Critics of positivism are apt to forget the optimistic, radical, and democratic character that it had in Austria and Germany in the thirties. The original logical positivists, such as Schlick, Carnap, and especially Neurath, saw their work as recasting philosophy to rid it of oppressive idealism, speculative metaphysics, and irrationalism (which could be seen as underpinning Fascism) and to provide the foundation for, among other things, an objective, value-free, social theory and a democratic politics in an irrationalist, totalitarian era.[5] But positivism was later attacked by some philosophers for its reductive empiricism and (wrongly) blamed for some right-wing social engineering carried out under the inspiration of positivist economics and sociology. Social evolutionism was also transformative in its intent in mid-to-late nineteenth-century Britain and Germany. But it became discredited because of its association with social Darwinism or, in its later structural–functional form, with a holistic and conservative theory that stressed the norms of social inertia and cultural and ideological hegemony. This is unfortunate because an evolutionary epistemology has much to offer social scientific enquiry, through its potential to reinforce a theory of institutional transformation as the dynamic consequence of attempted social reproduction.[6]

Theories of rational social construction (or 'social engineering' of a sort, to use a more problematic and redolent term) must have a central place in the social studies under one guise or another. Social enquiry has always received an impetus, directly or indirectly, from problems of political action, admin-istration, social control, social planning, and social justice. Even so-called 'alternative' political movements, such as the Green parties, need a social theory that purports to grasp correctly existing social processes and person/ society relationships on which to base a practical programme. This must not only be fully recognized but made the object of an internal scientific critique that affirms, against irrationalists, autonomists, cynics, conservatives, and pessimists, the basic project of actively promoting democracy, equality, and social progress on the basis of social knowledge. How to liberate people from oppressive structures and arbitrary power should still be on the agenda. A penetrative and critical science that is able to grasp the objectivity of social realities and the possibilities of progressive change is an essential requirement, as the eighteenth- and nineteenth-century founders of the social sciences knew. It is now possible to provide a more viable philosophical foundation for such a social science. And the core of such a science must be a structural, historical perspective.

While it is generally true that practising historians are usually concerned to make descriptions and explanations of particular actions, events, and processes, many of them believe that their approach to doing so is quite different from social science and natural science, involving a narrative method, imaginative interpretation, and the ability to be free somehow of social and psychological generalizations and theories. I call this position 'historicalism' to contrast it with scientism.[7] Practising historicalists have usually been complacent about the relevance of philosophical and methodological issues. Social and economic historians and historical sociologists, however, have not on the whole been complacent about such issues because they have been attempting to develop a new kind of enquiry, one which stands between history, as traditionally conceived, and the social studies. They often claim to be studying the social totality, but in what form it exists, how it could have a history, and how it should be explained, are not agreed.

One of the themes of this book is that social structural history should become the core for a unified science of action and society, past and present, which is like the sciences of nature but different in some respects. A new, much improved account of science derived from critical realist epistemology and ontology overcomes the problem of scientism by underpinning the diversity within the unity of the sciences.

In order for sociologists and historians adequately to explain any of the moments and levels of social totalities – actions, utterances, events, production, behavioural patterns, cultures, structures, and so on, and changes in patterns, cultures, and structures – they need concepts and theories of all of these and of how they relate to each other. However, that is not to say much about actual explanations, because it is the content of the theories that is obviously crucial. For example, we can see that the behavioural approaches of James Coleman and George Homans, which are forms of individualist theory, and the structural–functionalism of Talcott Parsons, which is a form of holism, all offer more or less complete approaches to social and historical explanation in the sense that they have theories and explanations of all these aspects. But what is more important is that individualism and holism are fatally flawed by their explanatory concentration on one or other side of the structuring process. Behaviourism attempts to explain social phenomena by reference to the motivations of individual behaviour while structural–functionalism, although purporting to be an action theory, in effect explains action by reference to its supposed functional relation to a social system.

Methodological structurism tries to tie the micro and macro levels of social analysis together, without subordinating either to the other, by giving an account of how human personality, intentions, and actions interact with culture and structure to determine each other and social transformations over time. In order to do this it is essential that there be a model of humans as social agents. As I have argued, agential persons have innate causal powers to affect intentionally and unintentionally their own actions and bring about changes in the world. Action is thus socially structuring. But structure pre-exists individual actions and conditions them. The generality of action through time is necessary for the creation, continued reproduction, and gradual transformation of structures which leads to the creation of new structures. The historical/transformative dimension is essential to the structurist methodology. Both individualists and holists tend to ignore it.

The versions of methodological structurism that have been argued for recently by several social theorists and methodologists, such as Giddens, Tilly, Touraine, Pred, Elias, Abrams, and Bendix, although not employing this term, recognize and agree with the basic tenets outlined above. All are explicitly concerned to theorize the dialectic between the structuring power of people and the enabling and constraining real structures of society. They have tried to establish methodologies for linking action and structural analyses and for explaining social structural history. All give a central place to the particular historical processes of active social reproduction and transformation.

STRUCTURIST HISTORY

With this approach we have a philosophical and methodological basis for showing the centrality to social science of the historical study of social structures. Methodological structurism has temporality as an essential component because the socially structuring process in which humans are constantly engaged has the (usually unintended) consequence of producing a history of structures. Therefore genuine social scientists should in effect be structural historians, irrespective of which label is attached to their practices. Conversely, to be good structural historians in the sense of the account of social science established here, structurism has to be adopted as a methodology.

I have argued that confirmation of the power of this methodological argument can be found in the writings that have been developed in this structurist and historical mode. Touraine, Elias, Abrams, and Bendix have not only explicitly developed versions of such a structurist methodology but also made rich explanations of particular social processes employing them. They and several others, most notably Geertz, Le Roy Ladurie, Tilly, Pred, and the other historians mentioned in chapter 3, can be seen as belonging to a vaguely defined but identifiable tradition of thought in the social studies that in effect is based on methodological and sociological structurism, what I called in chapter 2 the Relational-Structurist Tradition. The members of this tradition have all attempted to develop similar approaches to explaining how all the moments and levels of social reality relate to each other over time in a structuring manner.

Drawing on the discussion of examples in chapters 2 and 3 it is now possible to state in abstract the ideal type or model of the relational–structurist approach to socio-historical explanation that I believe they collectively contain or which is implicit in most of their work. I emphasize that this is not meant to be a precise description of all their methodologies and theories. This is a pure type from which they all deviate in various particulars. It contains the following elements:

1   A structurist ontology and epistemology, which implies a structurist methodology, that is, explanations of any moment or part of the social totality presuppose or imply explanations of all the others. In order to explain any moment or part it must be situated in its total structural context. This is because society is a non-reducible macroscopic structure in which there is a dynamic interaction, rather than a holistic determinism, between the parts. No part is necessarily dominant over the others, but only humans have structuring power within the social structure. Structures as such do not have any autonomy.

2   A realist–relational concept of social structure. Structure is seen as relatively autonomous of individual actions and understandings but not of the

structuring power of collective action over time. Structures consist of real sets of enduring social relations, rules, and roles that organize action and behaviour.

3   An abstract 'levels' model of the social totality along the lines of the economy/politics/ideology/culture set of 'levels' or 'spheres' of social reality, or something similar. But the reality and the relationships between the 'levels' are major points of debate with considerable variation in the theorization and roles assigned to these 'levels' and the hierarchical relations, if any, between them.

4   A model of persons as social agents, having self-activating powers of intentionality, rationality, reflexivity, and choice in a context of social and cultural constraint. It is people who are theorized as the makers of history but always within particular enabling and disabling social and cultural situations.

5   An important place is given to concepts of mentality and ideology. While the tradition accords a central place to systems of ideas in forming understandings of reality, it usually holds that ideas, actions, and social structures can be out of phase with each other. Mentalities and ideas have to be studied for their social consequences because of their formation of understandings and motivational effects and criticized for their adequacy as articulations of social structures.

6   An important place is given to the theorization and study of social hierarchies as organizers of consciousness and loyalties, but simple class models and theories are ruled out.

7   Unintended consequences of action and unrealized results of intentions are seen as highly significant for social change. If ideas, actions, and structures are not mutually reinforcing then gradual social change happens irrespective of the desires of individual actors and regardless of what other forces may be at work.

8   This leads to the final component – the idea that all societies are inherently changing and therefore fundamentally historical. The basic structurist idea – that society is continually being structured by agential actors, partly as a consequence of their intentions but also unintentionally, behind their own backs, as it were – is subscribed to by historians in this tradition. They therefore see the three fundamental moments of the historical process, all of which have to be analysed, as being:

(a)   given structural and cultural circumstances that motivate, enable, and constrain action and thought;

(b)   action that is historically significant for its structuring consequences; and

(c)   the intended and unintended consequences of action that turn into the objective structural conditions that motivate, enable, and constrain action and thought, and which often appear to be unalterable.

This approach to history therefore holds that persons and societies are highly complex but determinate entities requiring for the explanation of their composition, functioning, and transformations an order of enquiry which must go beyond pre-theoretical knowledge and common-sense observations and understandings. The use of explicit theory is indispensable to socio-historical explanation. This contrasts with historical writing done in the traditional interpretive and 'common-sense' mode, which subscribes to what I call 'historicalism'. Even many writers who call themselves social historians, which, on the face of it, should indicate that they are interested in explaining the history of structures as structures, do not employ a social scientific mode of enquiry.

TOWARDS THE REUNIFICATION OF THE SOCIAL STUDIES

Given the philosophically weak but institutionally strong disciplinary boundaries in our institution and culture generally, the best structural historians have a peculiar problem of disciplinary delineation, as many of them have recognized, since they wish to be at once historians, social theorists, sociologists, anthropologists, and sometimes economists. They wish both to distinguish themselves from historians of actions and events by enquiring into the social totality, and to transcend and supersede the explanatory practices of traditional historians. So their aim has to be not just theoretically and empirically to explain the relationships among social structures, cultures, actions, and events, but also to uncover and account for the history of real structures themselves. If their practice were to be based on the realist–relational approach it would provide a framework for simultaneously explaining particular acts, events, patterns of behaviour, consciousness, and structural change. Such a framework is therefore well suited to be the basis for structural history. Traditional historians do not use such a framework because they see themselves as explaining 'unique' individual acts, events, and processes largely by reference to 'unique' dispositions, purposes, and reasons, and not to general social, cultural, and psychological imperatives. But they are largely mistaken in this, or at least incomplete in their explanations, although intentions and reasons are certainly necessary to such explanations. It is because of the deeper relation of partly intentional behaviour to both the given structural conditions of behaviour and the production, reproduction, and transformation of structures, that action-oriented and structure-oriented history can be united on a more fundamental level. Such a unified science would ideally then incorporate all the existing empirical and theoretical social and historical studies.

The merging of existing historical and social discourses could be and has been argued for from several different (but sometimes overlapping) theoretical perspectives:

1   Cultural holism, which argues for unity on the basis that all individual actions and events have meaning as part of social and cultural wholes. This perspective aims at an explanatory subsumption of history, sociology, and anthropology under the phenomenological and interpretive study of constellations of meaning.

2   Francophone structuralism, which argues for the explanation of social phenomena as the manifestations and bearers of deep structures of minds, culture, and history, which have to be formalized as systems of rules of transformation.

3   Structural–functionalism, which sees all acts, patterns of behaviour, and culture as functionally related to the maintenance of the equilibrium of holistic, organic structures of relations and roles. This perspective aims at explanatory reduction of history, psychology, and anthropology to structural sociology.

4   Sociological individualism, which argues for unity on the basis that social phenomena are really only aggregates of individual acts and so attempts to make an explanatory reduction of social science to atomistic history or behaviourist psychology.

5   Sociological structurism, in which action, behaviour, culture, and structure are studied in an ongoing structuring context. Intentional and unintentional actions are seen as causally conditioned and enabled by structures; and structures of rules, roles, and relations are seen as the consequence of prior collective action.

Within this last perspective, the relational–structurist approach has the virtues of providing all-encompassing coherence without reduction. It makes it possible to retain a temporal dimension as intrinsic to any study of society, since structure, culture, behaviour, and acts are interrelated in a dynamic, transforming, historical manner. While this approach attempts to argue that particular acts and events can only be investigated for their causation, significance, and meaning within a structural context, it does not deny that there is merit in making a division of labour between, on one hand, the explanation of particular acts and events and, on the other, the explanation of patterns of behaviour and structures since, on one level, every act and event is different from every other and the precise mix of mechanisms or imperatives will vary in every case. Nevertheless, on another level, all acts and events fall under general descriptions and into general patterns and no particular act is the outcome of a truly unique set of mechanisms. The two kinds of history must be methodologically united on this deeper level, and able to take account of the relationship of particular acts and events to patterns of behaviour and social structures over time.

Any division between static and dynamic studies has validity only as a heuristic device. Since all societies are in a constant if gradual state of change, both internally and in their connections with their natural environment, any attempt to study them in isolation from either their changing material foundations or relational transformations must be abstract and one-sided. Such abstractions do, however, have their uses, but they are not confined to any of the existing sub-branches of the historical and social studies. While societies are constantly changing, it is often heuristically helpful theoretically to postulate them as fixed entities; and, in any case, the fact that structures gradually change does not rule out the possibility of scientific enquiry since they do have a relative continuity as structures. Without some continuity scientific enquiry would be impossible and so would social understanding, since language and meaning themselves would be impossible, and so would action because it is predicated upon an enabling social context and is mostly oriented towards reproducing that context. Even consciously transformative action requires a relatively stable social object to work upon.

To return to the claim made near the beginning of this chapter regarding the transcendence of those problematic dichotomies, I believe the discussion shows how they might be resolved. First, science and hermeneutics are not the opposites they were once thought to be, although there is still a distinction between them. There is an important hermeneutical element in all science, just as there should also be an element of scientific enquiry in the hermeneutical study of texts, art forms, and social practices. Therefore, second, explanation and understanding are not opposites but have an important area of overlap in the social studies. Explanation partly depends on personal interpretations and hermeneutical understandings of actions and social situations, but it must go beyond them, as historians such as Clifford Geertz, Barrington Moore, Emmanuel Le Roy Ladurie, and Robert Darnton have shown. Third, a sharp distinction between the studies of action and structure on the grounds of uniqueness versus generality or ephemeral versus continuous is untenable because of the structuring role of action and the conditioning role of structure. Each is dependent on the other. Fourth, following from the previous point, change and continuity are not distinct aspects of social reality but two intertwined moments of it. And finally, history and sociology cannot therefore be two distinct kinds of enquiry, one concerned with uniqueness and change and the other with generality and continuity. The dialectic between uniqueness/generality and change/continuity is the difficult multidimensional reality that social science has to try to grasp and represent through two-dimensional media and often inadequate linguistic and diagrammatical devices.

TOWARDS DEMOCRATIC TRANSFORMATIVE PRACTICE

Finally, to return to the significance of advocating a transformative scientific approach to society and history, what actually hangs on the use of the concept of science here? Why does consciously transformative practice require a scientific basis? While none of the methodologists and historians in this tradition directly state political lessons about the present from their historical enquiries, most of them see the contemporary political resonances at least of historical work, as would be expected of historians influenced by Marx and Weber. Indeed, some of them have engaged in discussions about the contemporary socio-political relevance of structural historiography.[8] They rightly believe that structural historiography must be a necessary component of scientific knowledge of the present. History must be rescued from the ideologues who appropriate it on the basis of individualist or holist philosophies in order to legitimize radical individualist political ideologies or repressive regimes that promote holistic cults of national character and destiny.

There has been a long, acrimonious, and sometimes arid debate, stemming mainly from Marx, about the merits of so-called scientific approaches to political action, but I believe it is worth raising again because of new arguments about scientific knowledge. But before pointing out the value of this new scientific terminology it is as well to point out some of the perhaps obvious dangers in any argument about the relevance of science, because the notion of science has been devalued. One is that it leads to political passivity, because if correct practice awaits absolutely correct social explanation then it will wait a long time. It is well known that this situation has been common among some Marxist groups who have awaited the development either of the 'correct situation' or the 'correct theory' before engaging in revolutionary acts and so have done nothing. It also exists among some academic theoreticians of revolution who have occupied themselves with interminable arcane debates over correct concepts and practices without ever examining concrete events and processes or engaging in piecemeal political or other socially transformative activity.

Another danger is that social transformation is seen as only a technical problem – a matter of implementing abstract knowledge in an instrumental, dehumanized fashion. This view is prevalent among those social scientists (especially economists) and politicians who are inspired by a scientistic, positivistic, and decisionistic outlook. For them, society is viewed as a set of rational individuals and their observable behavioural patterns, which can be manipulated by the right stimulus-reward regime to conform to the prior decisions of social managers. Underlying this approach has been an inadequate concept of science and false social and psychological theories, which tend to impute behaviour to a simplistic combination of a supposedly rational drive for gratification in a context of environmental stimuli and rewards.[9] Such an approach to social engineering is doomed to fail in its own terms and has had deleterious unforeseen consequences.

A concept of science as the absolutely truthful result of correctly structured logical enquiry is of no use either as an account of the existing sciences or as a guide to practice. Rather than being the entirely passive reflector of an unchanging external reality, all sciences, as cognitive networks, have to some extent a mutually transformative relationship with their theoretically specified objects. Observation and theory interact in the sense that theories determine to some extent what we choose to observe and study and how we understand it, and observations in turn determine to some extent the content of our theories. Piaget has persuasively developed the notion of a genetic, structuring, epistemology that weakens the place of absolute objectivity and truth. But this is not the same as advocating relativism or irrationalism. As I have tried to show, we must retain as central the idea of truth as a regulative principle of enquiry and as the provisional result of a gradual convergence between our frameworks, our activities, and the degree of correspondence between our theories and the hidden realities of the way the world is.

While it is true that without approximately correct 'common-sense' knowledge of the world we could not successfully live our lives (if at all), consciously transformative practice to achieve preconceived goals requires a much greater degree of penetrating precision about structural realities and historical processes than that of ordinary actors. And there do seem to have been some advances in the development of such knowledge during the past century. These limited advances are the result of the realism inherent within the social sciences. The reality of society is multifaceted, multilevelled, and historical, and it is beyond the capacity of pre-theoretical observation and understanding. Just as the understanding and explanation of human physiology require a science that goes well beyond personal understandings about our bodies, so social relations and the rules governing our social interaction and the exercise of social power are also in need of theoretical and structural knowledge.

Therefore if consciously transformative practice is to achieve its goals the structural realities on which such action has to work and which set the limits of what is possible have to be more or less correctly understood. Above all, this involves knowledge of the existing institutionalized and informal power structures and their historical origins. It also involves understanding how attempted transformation actually works and how in turn it feeds back upon practices to modify them. There is an interaction among structures, knowledge, and practice so that social science and political practice have to be continually reflexive. The main beneficial result of a genuinely scientific social knowledge, therefore, is to reduce the unintended effects of transformative action. The social sciences in this respect are not different from the natural sciences. The latter usually aim at least at engineering situations with such precision that they achieve only their goals and do not bring about unintended consequences. That requires precise scientific knowledge of the complexity of natural systems. But of course absolute precision remains as an often unrealized goal even in natural science and engineering, as we know full well from the failings of machines, medicines, and buildings, the destruction of ecosystems, and the general pollution of the environment on which we all depend. (These failings are of course made worse by ideologies of greed and sectional commitment.) The sea of ignorance still lies all before us and it is the scientific perspective that convinces us that that is so. It also convinces us that the boundary between our knowledge and our ignorance is gradually being extended into the realm of the unknown, but not always with beneficial consequences for human life.

A further potentially beneficial consequence of a historical structurist social methodology is its power to show that violent so-called 'voluntaristic' or 'autonomous' political behaviour and large-scale, violent social upheavals always have unforeseen, dangerously destructive consequences. 'Autonomist' behaviour is based on a belief that there is no objective social structural reality, only powerfully repressive individuals, and therefore action is thought to be ruled only by egoistic individualism. But a scientific approach shows that it cannot be so ruled, because society is structurally ordered and action cannot easily and wilfully break out of the order or destroy it. This realization, dimly perceived, often prompts disorganized political terrorism, which sometimes has the actual repressive result that autonomists supposedly wish to avoid but sometimes deliberately provoke. Similarly, organized violence of a totalitarian kind is also based on a belief that society can be reordered wilfully and rapidly if sufficient force is applied. This has proved to be partly correct in the sense that violent social reorganizations have sometimes been achieved by mass collective action or through the elite monopolization of administrative and coercive power. But never has it happened without massive unintended consequences. Military invasions, revolutions, and state-directed terrorism and repression have been recurring features of history and have always resulted in dislocations and outcomes that were not desired by the instigators.

Given the value, then, of such a scientific foundation for political action, what form should a scientifically based transformative politics take? I have argued for a conception of social science that draws on the work of the best practitioners of social historiography. Their work shows the power of a combination of realist epistemology, convergence theory of truth, agential concept of persons and action, historical and levels model of social structure, and methodological structurism. Using this as a framework for political action involves understanding at the outset that science is a methodology that does not guarantee absolutely correct knowledge of any system, so political activity on a social scientific basis certainly cannot be relied upon always to achieve its goals or avoid unintended consequences. And indeed, one of the consequences of this model of scientific reasoning is the realization of the importance of the dialectic between scientific understanding, social structure, and political practice. This should then prompt a political attitude that centres on:

- a radically egalitarian and democratic conception of the political process and the nature of the good society towards which practice should be moving;
- a theoretically and historically informed empirical understanding of social structure and social power;
- negotiation about the relationship between social theory and social goals;

- modest short-term political aims within the long-term perspective of egalitarianism and democracy; and
- rational decision-making about actions on the basis of the previous points.

Without these the risk of failure grows. Furthermore, this attitude excludes holistic, utopian blueprints of the future good or perfect society towards which practice should be directed. The model of science and of human consciousness outlined above and the principles of egalitarianism and democracy are incompatible with a priori utopian thinking and the imposition of grand ahistorical theories.

In the introduction I wrote that by the end I hoped to have established five theses. While 'established' is probably too strong a claim, I think that a case for the five has been made. These theses are on the level of philosophical arguments rather than scientific hypotheses or empirical claims about history and society, so their validity is not open to empirical confirmation in the same way. The cogency and persuasiveness of philosophical arguments depends largely on their coherence and their ability to bridge gaps between what are, on one hand, firmly held and widely agreed general views about the world and, on the other, new possibilities that are only partially and dimly understood. Thus the basic strategy here has been to present a general argument that moves from an understanding of the nature of scientific enquiry and the existing methodologies of structural history writing to argue that explanation of structural history can be and sometimes is methodologically similar to the sciences of nature. This similarity is based on the idea of establishing a domain of structural history enquiry on the premise that there is an ontological distinction between social structures and social events.

The domain of enquiry into the history of social structures needs, like all scientific domains, a unifying conception of subject-matter, about which there are fundamental problems of composition and evolution, and a unifying methodology. All mature domains also have a unifying general explanatory theory. Structural history, being still in the domain-forming process, lacks all these unifying elements in any but an inchoate and contentious sense. Movement towards delineating a domain framework that takes account of the arguments about composition and evolution that I presented at the end of chapter 1 can be detected on two levels. On one, conscious attempts are being made to provide a framework of methodology, general concepts, and theory, such as those by Anthony Giddens, Philip Abrams, Charles Tilly, Allan Pred, and Alain Touraine. On another level, there are conscious attempts to show how structural history should be approached, theorized, and written through practices from which are drawn general methodological conclusions, such as those by Clifford Geertz, Emmanuel Le Roy Ladurie, Ernest Gellner, Eric Hobsbawm, Charles Tilly, and Reinhard Bendix. Of course, many writers operate on both levels.

I have argued that all of these theorists and historians share a relational structurist conception of society and a structurist methodology. But not all structural historians share these methodological and theoretical foundations, so we cannot say that a genuine shared framework exists. As I have tried to indicate, the advantage of structurism as the foundation for structural historical enquiry arises from its emphasis on the structuring agency of people and taking social complexity seriously. Explaining structural history is a task that must employ appropriate methodologies and theories, but it is not in itself a methodological and theoretical enquiry. Rather, empirical enquiry must stress the real complexity of social processes and attempt to incorporate them into a comprehensive account that leaves no loose ends, no moments of the social totality that are inexplicable or left dangling. At their best, structurist historians of societies have achieved an exemplary level of explanatory complexity and persuasiveness.

Notes

INTRODUCTION

1 Cf. E. Gellner, *Legitimation of Belief* (1974), p. 28.
2 I. Wallerstein, 'Beyond *Annales*' (1991), p. 14.
3 As shown by some of the uncomprehending reactions by social historians to my *Explanation in Social History* (1986). See, for example, Asa Briggs's review article in *History and Theory*, 29, 1990, where he actually goes to the extent of inventing 'quotations' to support his unwarranted assertions and misunderstandings.
4 C. Lloyd, *Explanation in Social History*, ch. 1. See also pp. 47–50 of *The Structures of History*.
5 I have given an outline of it in *Explanation in Social History*. Here I shall develop a more extensive discussion.

CHAPTER 1   EXPLAINING THE HISTORY

1 Vico, *The New Science* (1968). There is now a vast literature on Vico. For an interesting discussion see L. Haddad, 'The Evolutionary Economics of Giambattista Vico' (1983).
2 R. Meek, *Social Science and the Ignoble Savage* (1976), chs 1 and 2.
3 Ibn Khaldûn, *The Muquddimah* (1958). See also Y. Lacoste, *Ibn Khaldun: The Birth of History and the Past of the Third World* (1984) and E. Gellner, *Muslim Society* (1981), ch. 1, for illuminating discussions.
4 K. Marx, *Grundrisse* (1973), p. 487.
5 See the excellent discussion of Smith and the Scottish School in Meek, *Social Science, passim.*
6 On Turgot see Meek, *Social Science* and P. Groenewegen, 'Turgot, Beccaria and Smith' (1983).
7 See H. Butterfield, *Man on his Past* (1969), ch. 2, and F. von Schiller, 'The Nature and Value of Universal History' (1972), originally printed in 1789.
8 Cf. Butterfield, *Man on his Past.*
9 See D. C. Coleman, *History and the Economic Past* (1987), ch. 3.

10 On the ideas and influence of Saint-Simon and Comte see G. G. Iggers (ed.), *The Doctrine of Saint-Simon* (1972); A. Comte, *The Essential Comte*, ed. S. Andreski (1974); and F. E. Manuel, *The Prophets of Paris* (1962).

11 P. Bourdieu, 'The Specificity of the Scientific Field and the Social Conditions of the Progress of Reason' (1975), and 'The Genesis of the Concepts of *Habitus* and of *Field*' (1985).

12 For a discussion of the German historical school see J. A. Schumpeter, *History of Economic Analysis* (1954), part IV, ch. 4.

13 There are excellent discussions of their work in Schumpeter, *History of Economic Analysis*, and B. B. Seligman, *Main Currents in Modern Economics*, vol. I (1962), ch. 1.

14 K. Marx, *Capital* (1971), *passim*, and *Theories of Surplus Value* (1963–71), part III, *passim*.

15 For Weber's relations with the historical school and the *Verein* see the essays in part I of W. J. Mommsen and J. Osterhammel (eds), *Max Weber and his Contemporaries* (1987). On the *Methodenstreit* see Schumpeter, *History of Economic Analysis*; M. Weber, *Roscher and Knies* (1975), and *The Methodology of the Social Sciences* (1949).

16 On Marx and Engels as realists see R. Bhaskar, *Philosophy and the Idea of Freedom* (1991), section 2.

17 English evolutionary sociology and anthropology are discussed in J. W. Burrow, *Evolution and Society* (1966), *passim*; and S. K. Sanderson, *Social Evolutionism* (1990), ch. 2.

18 On British historical sociology see J. A. Hall, 'They Do Things Differently There, or, The Contribution of British Historical Sociology' (1989).

19 On English historical economics see A. W. Coats, 'The Historist Reaction in English Political Economy' (1954) and 'Sociological Aspects of British Economic Thought (1880–1930)' (1967); D. C. Coleman, *History and the Economic Past* (1987); G. M. Koot, *English Historical Economics 1870–1926* (1987); A. Kadish, *Historians, Economists, and Economic History* (1989); S. K. Sanderson, *Social Evolutionism* (1990); J. Maloney, 'English Historical School' (1987).

20 For a discussion of the functionalist tradition in socio-historical theory and research see W. E. Moore, 'Functionalism' (1979).

21 See bibliography for Weber's main writings. There are excellent general discussions of his work in R. Collins, *Weberian Sociological Theory* (1986); S. Whimster and S. Lash (eds), *Max Weber, Rationality and Modernity* (1987); and D. Käsler, *Max Weber* (1988).

22 Weber's historical methodology and theory are discussed in G. Roth and W. Schluchter, *Max Weber's Vision of History* (1979).

23 See bibliography for relevant works of these writers.

24 For recent discussions of cliometrics see D. McCloskey, 'The Achievements of the Cliometric School' (1978), and *Econometric History* (1987).

25 On the new institutional economic history see G. Hodgson, *Economics and Institutions* (1988) and 'Institutional Economic Theory: The Old Versus The New' (1989); D. C. North, *Institutions, Institutional Change, and Economic Performance* (1990); A. J. Field, 'The Problem With Neo-Classical Institutional Economics: A Critique With Special Reference to the North/Thomas Model of Pre-1500 Europe' (1981); and K. Basu, E. Jones, and E. Schlicht, 'The Growth and Decay

of Custom: The Role of the New Institutional Economics in Economic History' (1987).

26 On the modernization school see B. F. Hoselitz, *Sociological Aspects of Economic Growth* (1960); B. F. Hoselitz and W. E. Moore (eds), *Industrialization and Society* (1963); and M. Nash (ed.), *Essays on Economic Development and Cultural Change* (1977).

27 The development and significance of the *Annales* school is discussed by, among many others, F. Braudel, 'Personal Testimony' (1972); T. Stoianovich, *French Historical Method: The Annales Paradigm* (1976); L. Hunt, 'French History in the Last Twenty Years: The Rise and Fall of the Annales Paradigm' (1986); and P. Burke, *The French Historical Revolution: The Annales School, 1929–89* (1990).

28 On the British Marxist school see H. Kaye, *The British Marxist Historians* (1984) and E. J. Hobsbawm, 'The Historians' Group of the Communist Party' (1978).

29 See the bibliography for the relevant writings of Boyd, Hooker, Bhaskar, Ellis and Salmon.

30 For recent discussions of the question of the scientificity of economic and social history see J. M. Kousser, 'Quantitative Social-Scientific History' (1980); J. M. Clubb, 'The New Quantitative History: Social Science or Old Wine in New Bottles?' (1980); A. Rutten, 'But It Will Never Be Science, Either' (1980); R. W. Fogel, 'The Limits of Quantitative Methods in History' (1975); R. W. Fogel and G. R. Elton, *Which Road to the Past? Two Views of History* (1983); S. P. Hays, 'Scientific Versus Traditional History' (1984); E. H. Monkkonen, 'The Challenge of Quantitative History' (1984); I. Winchester, 'History, Scientific History, and Physics' (1984); and L. Davis and S. Engerman, 'Cliometrics: The State of the Science (or is it Art or, perhaps, Witchcraft?)' (1987).

31 For Shapere's work see the list in the bibliography.

32 There is an excellent discussion of the relationship of science to non-science in E. Gellner, *Legitimation of Belief* (1974), *passim*.

33 There is a fascinating discussion of French developments in R. Darnton, *Mesmerism and the End of the Enlightenment in France* (1968), ch. 1.

34 See the penetrating and comprehensive analysis of this literature in W. C. Salmon, 'Four Decades of Scientific Explanation' (1989).

35 Literature in this vein includes M. Friedman, *Essays in Positive Economics* (1953); B. J. Caldwell, *Beyond Positivism: Economic Methodology in the Twentieth Century* (1982); D. Harvey, *Explanation in Geography* (1969); P. J. Watson, S. A. Leblanc, and C. L. Redman, *Archaeological Explanation* (1984); M. H. Salmon, *Philosophy and Archaeology* (1982); R. Harré and P. F. Secord, *The Explanation of Social Behaviour* (1972); M. Harris, *Cultural Materialism* (1979); P. T. Manicas, 'Implications for Psychology of the New Philosophy of Science' (1983); W. L. Wallace, *Principles of Scientific Sociology* (1983); C. Lloyd, *Explanation in Social History* (1986); and the references to scientific history in n. 30 above.

36 The task and value of methodological enquiry has been hotly debated recently by some economists. See, for example, A. W. Coats, 'Explanations in History and Economics' (1989) and 'Disciplinary Self-Examination, Departments, and Research Traditions in Economic History' (1990); E. R. Weintraub, 'Methodology doesn't Matter but the History of Thought might' (1989); B. J. Caldwell, 'Does Methodology Matter? How should it be Practiced?' (1990); D. W. Hands, 'Thirteen Theses on Progress in Economic Methodology' (1990); U. Mäki, 'Methodology of Economics: Complaints and Guidelines' (1990).

37   See bibliography for relevant works of these authors.
38   For discussions of post-structuralist concepts of history as discourse see D.
     Attridge, G. Bennington, and R. Young (eds), *Post-Structuralism and the Question
     of History* (1987); and H. A. Veeser (ed.), *The New Historicism* (1989).
39   Cf. M. Mandelbaum, *Philosophy, Science, and Sense Perception* (1964); W. Sellars,
     Science, Perception, and Reality (1963) and *Science and Metaphysics* (1968).
40   Cf. E. Gellner, *Legitimation of Belief* (1974), including the important discussion
     of the significance of Chomsky's structural linguistics in ch. 5, and *Relativism and
     the Social Sciences* (1985), ch. 3.
41   Cf. I. Hacking, *Representing and Intervening* (1983). For a liberal ironist counter-
     view to the idea of structural universals and social interventions see R. Rorty,
     Contingency, Irony, and Solidarity (1989).
42   Isaiah Berlin argued in a famous article, 'The Concept of Scientific History'
     (1960), that history could not be a science. This idea goes back to Vico, who
     defended a distinction between natural science and human enquiry, and it was
     later developed by Neo-Kantians such as Dilthey, Windelband, and Rickert.
43   Examples of analytical philosophy of history that defends the distinctiveness of
     historical knowledge include W. H. Dray, *Laws and Explanation in History* (1957);
     W. B. Gallie, *Philosophy and the Historical Understanding* (1964); J. Barzun, *Clio
     and the Doctors* (1974); L. O. Mink, 'The Autonomy of Historical Understanding'
     (1965), 'The Divergence of History and Sociology in Recent Philosophy of
     History' (1973) and 'Philosophy and Theory of History' (1979).
44   L. Stone, 'The Revival of Narrative: Reflections on a New Old History' (1979);
     E. J. Hobsbawm, 'The Revival of Narrative: Some Comments' (1980); P. Abrams,
     'History, Sociology, Historical Sociology' (1980).
        There have been many ostensibly methodological discussions about social his-
     tory and historical sociology lately but unfortunately few raise epistemological
     issues. For some of the more penetrating contributions see P. Abrams, Ibid.; G.
     Eley, 'Some Recent Tendencies in Social History' (1979); E. Fox-Genovese and
     E. D. Genovese, 'The Political Crisis of Social History: A Marxian Perspective'
     (1976); J. A. Henretta, 'Social History as Lived and Written' (1979); E. J.
     Hobsbawm, 'From Social History to the History of Society' (1971); R. S. Neale,
     'Introduction: Social History' in *Class in English History* (1981); A. L. Stinchcombe,
     Theoretical Methods in Social History (1978); L. Stone, 'History and the Social
     Sciences in the Twentieth Century' (1976); C. Tilly, 'Two Callings of Social His-
     tory' (1980); C. Tilly 'The Old New Social History and the New Old Social
     History' (1984); R. Vann, 'The Rhetoric of Social History' (1976).
        Social history as history from the bottom up, or the history of lower-class or
     ordinary people's lives, has been advocated in a series of articles by P. Stearns.
     See, for example, 'Some Comments on Social History' (1967), 'Coming of Age'
     (1976), 'Toward a Wider Vision: Trends in Social History' (1980), 'The New
     Social History: An Overview' (1983), 'Social History and History: A Progress
     Report' (1985). See also the collection of articles in honour of George Rudé in
     F. Krantz (ed.), *History From Below* (1988).
        The problem of the relationship of history and sociology to each other has been
     much discussed lately. Some general discussions, all of which argue for unifica-
     tion, are P. Abrams, *Historical Sociology* (1982); P. Burke, *Sociology and History*
     (1980); N. Elias, 'Introduction: Sociology and History' in *The Court Society*

(1983); E. J. Hobsbawm, 'From Social History to the History of Society' (1971); G. S. Jones, 'From Historical Sociology to Theoretic History' (1976); D. Smith, 'Social History and Sociology – More than Just Good Friends' (1982); C. Tilly, 'Historical Sociology' (1980), *As Sociology Meets History* (1981), *Big Structures, Large Processes, Huge Comparisons* (1984), 'Retrieving European Lives' (1985), and 'Future History' (1988–9).

45 The standard idea of scientific theories as advanced by, for example, Karl Popper sees them as making existential claims for empirical testing, although there is a good deal of dispute about the logic and significance of theory generation and confirmation. See Popper, *The Logic of Scientific Discovery* (1972). For some recent valuable discussions see F. Suppe, 'The Search for Philosophic Understanding of Scientific Theories' and 'Afterword' (1977); W. C. Salmon, *Scientific Explanation and the Causal Structure of the World* (1984) and 'Four Decades of Scientific Explanation' (1989); P. Kitcher, 'Explanatory Unification and the Causal Structure of the World' (1989); R. N. Boyd, 'Realism, Approximate Truth, and Method' (1990); C. Howson, 'Fitting Your Theory to the Facts: Probably Not such a Bad Thing after all' (1990).

46 For defences of the scientific realist notion of social theory see R. Bhaskar, *The Possibility of Naturalism* (1979) and *Philosophy and the Idea of Freedom* (1991).

47 For discussions of the textual/interpretive idea of theory see the work of R. H. Brown, as listed in the bibliography.

48 P. Bourdieu, 'The Genesis of the Concepts of *Habitus* and of *Field*' (1985), pp. 11–12.

49 See bibliography for references to the work of these writers.

50 Methodological problems should not be confused with questions about research methods that deal with *technical* problems of conducting detailed empirical research, such as sampling techniques, survey design, archival data compilation, econometrical formulas, and so on. These are the counterparts of experimental laboratory and fieldwork techniques in physics, chemistry, and biology. Of course research methods are partly determined by methodological ideas.

51 Classic examples of positivist social science are M. Friedman, *Essays in Positive Economics* (1953); O. Neurath, *Empiricism and Sociology* (1973); B. F. Skinner, *Science and Human Behavior* (1953).

52 Kuhn's original, now classical text, probably the most influential work ever written in the philosophy of science, is *The Structure of Scientific Revolutions* (1970, originally 1962). Kuhn has modified his views somewhat in more recent works; see the bibliography.

53 See especially Popper, *Conjectures and Refutations* (1972), ch. 10, and *Objective Knowledge* (1972), ch. 3.

54 See bibliography for the most relevant of Lakatos's writings.

55 See bibliography for the main relevant works of these writers.

56 See especially M. Foucault, The *Archaeology of Knowledge* (1972).

57 P. Bourdieu, 'The Specificity of the Scientific Field and the Social Conditions of the Progress of Reason' (1975).

58 P. Bourdieu, 'Vive la Crise! For Heterodoxy in Social Science' (1988–9), p. 784.

59 See C. Lévi-Strauss, *The Savage Mind* (1966); P. Bourdieu, *Outline of a Theory of Practice* (1977) and *The Logic of Practice* (1990); R. Horton, 'African Traditional Thought and Western Science' (1967) and 'Tradition and Modernity Revisited'

(1982); E. Gellner, *Thought and Change* (1964), *Legitimation of Belief* (1974), and *Relativism and the Social Sciences* (1985), ch. 3.

60 See bibliography for Shapere's works.

61 D. Shapere, *Reason and The Search for Knowledge* (1984), p. xxii.

62 Ibid., pp. xxii–xxiii (emphasis in the original).

63 Ibid., p. xxviii.

64 Ibid., p. xxxiii.

65 Shapere, 'Scientific Theories and Their Domains' (1974), p. 525.

66 Ibid., p. 534.

67 For defences of the idea of scientific progress as the gradual refinement of theories and methodologies see H. Putnam, *Mind, Language and Reality* (1975), chs. 1–13; S. Kripke, 'Identity and Necessity' (1971) and *Naming and Necessity* (1980); and R. N. Boyd's works listed in the bibliography.

68 See also C. Lloyd, *Explanation in Social History* (1986), ch. 7.

69 For general discussion of realism, see M. Devitt, *Realism and Truth* (1984); R. Harré, *Varieties of Realism* (1986); R. W. Miller, *Fact and Method* (1987).

70 The leading exponent of transcendental realism is Roy Bhaskar. See the bibliography for references to his work.

71 Empirical realism is not the same as empiricism. The latter is related to subjective idealism and is based on the idea that sensory data are the basis of 'knowledge' and knowledge is not a claim about 'independent reality', which is supposed by some logical empiricists to be a meaningless proposition.

72 On policy realism see R. Harré, *Varieties of Realism* (1986).

73 This has been well argued by Karl Popper in *Conjectures and Refutations* (1972).

74 Cf. Karl Popper's classic discussion of holism in *The Poverty of Historicism* (1961) where he seemed to equate holism with all kinds of macroscopic concepts and theories. For the necessity to distinguish between tightly integrated social wholes and loosely integrated social structures see, for example, M. Brodbeck, 'On the Philosophy of the Social Sciences' (1954); E. Gellner, 'Explanations in History' (in *Cause and Meaning in the Social Sciences*, 1973); and my *Explanation in Social History* (1986), ch. 8. In later writings Popper acknowledged the existence of social institutions which have a 'logic' of their own independent of individual people. See 'The Logic of the Social Sciences' (1976).

75 My term 'structurist conception' or 'structurism' will be articulated in greater detail later. It has been influenced by the writings of Rom Harré in, for example, 'Philosophical Aspects of the Micro-Macro Problem' (1981) and 'Architectonic Man: On the Structuring of Lived Experience' (1978).

76 Examples of social theorists who employ an individualist social ontology include James Coleman and George Homans. The bibliography contains references to their work, which I have discussed in *Explanation in Social History*, ch. 11.

77 Holist ontologies in social theory take three main forms – wholes of the 'spirit of the era' and 'national character' kinds, deep structures of the Lévi-Straussian and Althusserian kinds, and systemic cybernetic structures of the Parsonian kind. See my *Explanation in Social History* (1986), chs 10 and 12.

78 Structurist ontologies in social theory take many forms, including Piagetian structuralism, structurationism, network theory, and figurations. Examples of their use include the work of Jean Piaget, Anthony Giddens, Philip Abrams, Norbert Elias, Charles Tilly, and Roy Bhaskar – see the bibliography and the relevant chapters in B. Wellman and S. D. Berkowitz (eds), *Social Structures* (1988).

79 For general discussions of the macro–micro problem in social theory see R. Collins, 'On the Microfoundations of Macrosociology' (1981), 'Interaction Ritual Chains, Power and Property: The Micro–Macro Connection as an Empirically Based Theoretical Problem' (1987) and 'The Micro Contribution to Macro Sociology' (1988); J. C. Alexander et al. (eds), *The Micro–Macro Link* (1987) *passim;* N. Wiley, 'Macro vs Micro Interpretation' (1983) and 'The Micro–Macro Problem in Social Theory' (1988).

80 Cf. Mandelbaum, *Purpose and Necessity in Social Theory* (1987), ch. 3.

81 See my *Explanation in Social History*, ch. 11.

82 See bibliography for Coleman's writings.

83 See Mandelbaum, *Purpose and Necessity*, ch. 1.

84 See Mandelbaum, *Purpose and Necessity*, ch. 5, where he discusses institutionalism.

85 Lest it be thought all sociologists and historians are now tacit or overt structurists thus leaving the other four boxes in the table empty, I should point out at this stage that this is far from the case. It is possible to identify many prominent individualists and holists, some examples of whom will be given in chapter 2. Of course they do not necessarily subscribe to the pure models just outlined.

86 The position adopted here on the question of the fields of social enquiry has certain similarities with that developed recently by Paul Veyne. He says that his book *Bread and Circuses* (1990) is a work of 'sociological history' in the sense of 'sociology' developed by Weber. The difference between sociology and history is described by Veyne thus:

A historical fact can be explained and consequently described, only by applying to it sociology, political theory, anthropology, economics, and so on. It would be useless to speculate about what might be the historical explanation of an event that could differ from its 'sociological' explanation, its scientific, true explanation. In the same way, there can be no astronomical explanation of astronomical facts: they have to be explained by means of physics.

And yet a book about astronomy is not the same as a book about physics, and a book about history is not quite the same as a book about sociology – although the difference in this case is less than traditional historians are wont to claim ... They both seek to explain the same events in the same way, but whereas sociology deals with the generalities (concepts, types, regularities, principles) that serve to explain an event, history is concerned with the event itself, which it explains by means of the generalities that are the concern of sociology. In other words, one and the same event, described and explained in the same way, will be, for a historian, his actual subject, whereas, for a sociologist, it will be merely an example that serves to illustrate some pattern, concept or ideal type (or will have served to discover or construct this).

The difference, as we see, is slight, in the main. From one angle, we have an act of euergetism explained and conceptualized by the ideal type of political science and, from the other, these same ideal types illustrated or discovered by means of an example, namely, an act of euergetism. The flavour is the same, the potential readers are the same, and, above all, the knowledge required of the historian and the sociologist is the same, except for the division of labour implied. Since the 'facts' do not exist (they exist only through and under a concept, otherwise they cannot be conceived), a sociologist needs to know how to constitute them, while a historian has to be able to find his way around in sociology, to estimate its relevance and, where necessary, to create it. History leads to sociological discoveries being made, while sociology solves long-standing historical problems, and also poses fresh ones. (pp. 2–3)

87 M. Weber, *The Methodology of the Social Sciences* (1949), p. 175.

88   Max Weber's excellent discussion in ibid., pp. 164–88, is still highly relevant to this problem of adequate explanation.

89   P. Abrams, 'History, Sociology, Historical Sociology' (1980); R. Bernstein, *Beyond Objectivism and Relativism* (1983).

90   Cf. Marx, 'Afterword to the Second German Edition of *Capital*' (originally 1873), in *Capital*, vol. 1 (1971), pp. 128–9; Weber, *The Methodology of the Social Sciences*, (1949), p. 176.

91   L. Stone, 'The Revival of Narrative' (1979).

92   Hobsbawm, 'The Revival of Narrative' (1980), p. 4; Abrams, 'History, Sociology, Historical Sociology' (1980), pp. 9–10, and *Historical Sociology* (1982), ch. 10.

93   There is an excellent discussion of narrative explanation in W. H. Dray, 'Narrative Versus Analysis in History' (1985). He refers to much of the relevant literature and defends at length the position advocated here regarding the complexity and unavoidability of narrative, even in 'analytical' history. See also M. White, 'The Logic of Historical Narration' (1963); L. O. Mink, 'Narrative Form as a Cognitive Instrument' (1978); C. B. McCullagh, 'The Unifying Themes of Historical Narratives' (1989); and T. C. Jacques, 'The Primacy of Narrative in Historical Understanding' (1990).

94   See bibliography for examples of Stone's work.

95   On the role and structure of comparative method in socio-historical explanation see T. Skocpol and M. Somers, 'The Uses of Comparative History in Macrosocial Inquiry' (1980); the editor's contributions to Skocpol (ed.), *Vision and Method in Historical Sociology* (1984); V. E. Bonnell, 'The Uses of Theory: Concepts and Comparisons in Historical Sociology' (1980); and P. McMichael, 'Incorporating Comparison Within a World-Historical Perspective: An Alternative Comparative Method' (1990).

96   J. Elster, 'Marxism, Functionalism, and Game Theory: The Case for Methodological Individualism' (1982).

97   One of the main advocates of methodological pluralism is Bruce Caldwell; see bibliography for relevant writings.

98   On positivist economics see B. B. Seligman, 'The Impact of Positivism on Economic Thought' (1969); B. J. Caldwell, *Beyond Positivism* (1982).

99   For discussions of the revival of institutionalism see the works of R. N. Langlois and G. M. Hodgson in the bibliography, and P. D. Bush, 'Reflections on the Twenty-Fifth Anniversary of AFEE: Philosophical and Methodological Issues in Institutional Economics' (1991).

100   See bibliography for writings by Karl Polanyi. For discussions see M. Hechter, 'Karl Polanyi's Social Theory: A Critique' (1983); D. C. North, 'Markets and Other Allocation Systems in History: The Challenge of Karl Polanyi' (1977); A. Martinelli, 'The Economy as an Institutional Process' (1987); K. Polanyi-Levitt, *The Life and Work of Karl Polanyi* (1990).

101   See bibliography for the works of North and Olson.

102   Cf. North, *Institutions, Institutional Change, and Economic Performance* (1990), p. 3. He also draws a distinction between institutions and society.

103   G. M. Hodgson, *Economics and Institutions: A Manifesto for a Modern Institutional Economics* (1988), and 'Institutional Economic Theory: The Old Versus the New' (1989).

104   As Ernest Gellner perceptively pointed out, 'like physics, economics is more or

less closed to the layman through being technical and counter intuitive; unlike physics, however, it does not repay this loss by presenting reliable and agreed results, or indeed by being manifestly superior in its judgments to those of the layman.' *Thought and Change*, (1964), p. 175.

105 See, for example , D. C. North and R. P. Thomas, *The Rise of the Western World* (1983) and V. L. Smith, 'Economic Principles in the Emergence of Humankind' (1992).

106 Cf. G. S. Becker, *The Economic Approach to Human Behavior* (1976).

107 See bibliography for the works of these writers and my *Explanation in Social History* (1986), ch. 10, for a discussion.

108 A. L. Stinchcombe, *Economic Sociology* (1983). For discussions of the new 'paradigm', see R. Swedberg, 'Economic Sociology Past and Present' (1987) and *Economics and Sociology* (1990); A. Martinelli and N. J. Smelser (eds), *Economy and Society* (1990); and S. Zukin and P. DiMaggio (eds), *The Structures of Capital: The Social Organization of the Economy* (1990), especially chs 1, 2, and 3, which contain excellent overviews of the new 'paradigm'.

109 Discussions of the micro–macro problem in social science include the excellent collection of articles in J. C. Alexander et al., *The Micro–Macro Link* (1987).

CHAPTER 2 A CRITICAL SURVEY

1 See, for example, the defining of social history/historical sociology as being the theoretically informed study of large-scale social structures through time in R. Bendix, *Force, Fate, and Freedom: On Historical Sociology* (1984); F. Braudel, *On History* (1980); the editor's contributions to T. Skocpol (ed.), *Vision and Method in Historical Sociology* (1984); A. L. Stinchcombe, *Theoretical Methods in Social History* (1978); C. Tilly, *As Sociology Meets History* (1981) and 'Future History' (1988–9). These contrast with the following works, which defend a conception of social history as distinct from sociology, being concerned with individuals, small groups, and particular structures rather than the comparison of structures: H. Perkin, 'Social History' (1962); G. M. Trevelyan, *English Social History* (1944); T. Zeldin, 'Social History and Total History' (1976).

2 L. Stone, 'The Revival of Narrative: Reflections on a New Old History' (1979); E. J. Hobsbawm, 'The Revival of Narrative: Some Comments' (1980); P. Abrams, 'History, Sociology, Historical Sociology' (1980).

   Two other recent and closely related debates, which dealt basically with the same problems of the structure/individual, material/social/mental, and theory/evidence relationships, were over the role of structuralist methods and theories in British Marxist historiography and people's history. For contributions, overviews, and analyses of these debates see E. P. Thompson, *The Poverty of Theory, and Other Essays* (1978); P. Hirst, 'The Necessity of Theory', (1979); P. Anderson, *Arguments within English Marxism* (1980); K. Nield and J. Seed, 'Theoretical Poverty or the Poverty of Theory: British Marxist Historiography and the Althusserians' (1979); K. Nield, 'A Symptomatic Dispute? Notes on the Relation Between Marxian Theory and Historical Practice in Britain' (1980); S. Magarey, 'That Hoary Old Chestnut, Free Will and Determinism: Culture vs Structure, or History vs Theory in Britain' (1987).

3   Some examples of previous surveys of social historiography are S. Eade, 'Social History in Britain in 1976: A Survey' (1976); S. Magarey, 'Labour History's New Sub-Title: Social History in Australia in 1981 (1983); H. Perkin, 'Social History in Britain' (1976); P. N. Stearns, 'Toward a Wider Vision: Trends in Social History' (1980) and 'The New Social History: An Overview' (1983); L. Stone, 'History and the Social Sciences in the Twentieth Century' (1981); P. Thane and A. Sutcliffe, 'Introduction' to *Essays in Social History*, vol. 2 (1986).

4   The history of empiricism and positivism is surveyed by L. Kolakowski, *Positivist Philosophy* (1972); and A. J. Ayer, 'Editor's Introduction' to *Logical Positivism* (1959).

5   See, for example, C. G. Hempel, 'On the Standard Conception of Scientific Theories' (1970), and 'The Meaning of Theoretical Terms: A Critique of the Standard Empiricist Construal' (1973); E. McMullin, 'Empiricism at Sea' (1974); D. Shapere, 'Notes Towards a Post-Positivistic Interpretation of Science' (1969); F. Suppe, 'The Search for Philosophic Understanding of Scientific Theories' and 'Afterword' (1977).

6   See in particular T. H. Buckle, *History of Civilization in England* (1857) and L. von Ranke, *The Theory and Practice of History* (1983). There is an interesting discussion of Buckle in B. Semmel, 'H. T. Buckle: The Liberal Faith and the Science of History' (1976); and on Ranke see the 'Introduction' by Iggers and von Moltke to the above (1983) collection.

7   Hempel's major articles from 1942 to 1964 are collected in *Aspects of Scientific Explanation* (1965), and Carnap's most influential work is *An Introduction to the Philosophy of Science* (1974), which originally appeared as *The Philosophical Foundation of Physics* (1966). See also R. Carnap, 'Empiricism, Semantics, and Ontology', Supplement A of his *Meaning and Necessity* (1956).

8   On the British empirical tradition see E. P. Thompson, *The Poverty of Theory, and Other Essays* (1978), pp. 229–42, where he discusses 'historical logic', partly in terms of the relationship of 'real facts' to the historian's interrogation of them. He somewhat clarifies his position in 'The Politics of Theory' (1981). In both texts, although critical of the role given to theory by structuralists, he affirms an important place for theory and the interpenetration of theory and data and points out how this perspective has guided his empirical work. Among the best examples of 'common-sense' 'social' history that is devoid of theory are the numerous works of Asa Briggs.

9   See the introduction to G. M. Trevelyan, *English Social History* (1944), p. viii, where he said that 'the sum total of social history . . . could only be mastered if we know the biographies of all the millions of men, women, and children who have lived in England. The generalizations which are the stock-in-trade of the social historian, must necessarily be based on a small number of particular instances, which are assumed to be typical.'

10 See especially R. Cobb, 'Modern French History in Britain' (1974), where he defends his biographical methodology. Examples of his empirical work include the essays collected in *A Second Identity* (1969), as well as *The Police and the People* (1970) and *The People's Armies* (1987). Theodore Zeldin has made clear statements of this methodology in 'Social History and Total History' (1976) and 'Personal History and the History of the Emotions' (1982). See also his major work, *France 1848–1945* (1970).

11   Lawrence Stone has produced many massive and valuable studies of English family history such as *The Crisis of the Aristocracy, 1558–1641* (1965), *The Family, Sex, and Marriage in England, 1500–1800* (1977), *An Open Elite? England 1540–1800* (with J. C. Fawtier-Stone, 1984). He gave an excellent overview of his methodology in his essay 'Prosopography' (1981), where he defined prosopography as 'the investigation of the common background characteristics of a group of actors in history by means of a collective study of their lives' (p. 45). He criticized past users of the method, such as Syme and Namier, pointing out the various errors into which they had fallen, and in effect showing how his own work avoids past mistakes. Prosopography has been practised by many historians in recent years. Stone's article introduces some of the recent literature.

Prosopography differs from historical demography in that it is concerned with the positions of real individuals, whereas the latter is concerned with statistically aggregated populations. See, for example, the writings in which Peter Laslett has described and defended his approach to 'social structural history' as being the study of historical demography and family history, such as *The World we have Lost Further Explored* (1983), ch. 12, and 'Introduction: The Necessity of a Historical Sociology' (1971). This approach has also been called 'experimental history' by Laslett and some of his associates. See K. W. Wachter, E. A. Howard, and P. Laslett (eds), *Statistical Studies of Historical Social Structure* (1978), especially ch. 2; and W. K. Wachter and E. A. Hammel, 'The Genesis of Experimental History' (1986).

E. A. Wrigley has not made such an equation between historical demography and social structural history. But of course he has made very important contributions to studying the economic and social influence of demography, as in *Population and History* (1969) and *People, Cities, and Wealth* (1987). The methodological basis of anthropologically informed historical demography as a form of social history is defended by Alan Macfarlane in 'History, Anthropology and The Study of Communities' (1977), and *The Origins of English Individualism* (1978).

12   See bibliography for the relevant works.

13   Good examples of old economic history abound, such as P. Mathias, *The First Industrial Nation* (1969); M. M. Postan, *The Medieval Economy and Society* (1972); C. Wilson, *England's Apprenticeship, 1603–1763* (1965); and most of the chapters of the *Cambridge Economic History of Europe* (1942–78). The methodology of 'old' economic history is discussed by M. M. Postan, *Fact and Relevance* (1971) and C. M. Cipolla, *Between History and Economics* (1991), and a sample of opinions and discussions by prominent practitioners from 1893 onwards is contained in N. B. Harte (ed.), *The Study of Economic History* (1971), who contributes a brief survey of the institutionalization of the discipline in Britain. See also D. C. Coleman, *History and the Economic Past* (1987) for the history of the discipline.

14   Some examples include A. Briggs, *A Social History of England* (1983); N. Hampson, *A Social History of the French Revolution* (1963); H. Perkin, *The Origins of Modern English Society, 1780–1880* (1969); and the volumes in the *Pelican Social History of Britain* under the general editorship of J. H. Plumb.

15   On the methodology of cliometrics see the works of R. W. Fogel in the bibliography, also D. N. McCloskey, 'The Achievements of the Cliometric School' (1978) and *Econometric History* (1987); P. D. McClelland, *Causal Explanation and Model Building in History, Economics, and the New Economic History* (1975); L. Davis

and S. Engerman, 'Cliometrics: The State of the Science' (1987). The methodological and philosophical importance of quantification and statistical methods is
continually defended in the journal *Historical Methods*; see especially vol. 17, nos
3 and 4 (1984) for a collection of such articles.

16   This approach is sometimes called 'rational exchange theory'. See the works of G.
     C. Homans and J. S. Coleman listed in the bibliography. A less reductionist
     version of this approach has been developed by Peter Blau, as in *Inequality and
     Heterogeneity* (1977) and 'A Macrosociological Theory of Social Structure' (1977–
     8).

17   One exception is George Homans's early book, *English Villagers of the Thirteenth
     Century* (1941), which does employ a rudimentary version of his rational exchange
     theory. See also James Coleman's highly schematic account of the rise of extra-
     individual corporations as rational actors in his *Power and the Structure of Society*
     (1974).

18   The best examples are the work of D. C. North, M. Olson, and E. L. Jones, as
     listed in the bibliography. See also pp. 55 and 58 above for other comments on
     their work.

19   On the origins of systemic–functionalist theory see G. Rocher, *Talcott Parsons and
     American Sociology* (1974); T. Parsons, 'On Building Social Systems Theory: A
     Personal History' (1970); W. E. Moore, 'Functionalism' (1979).

20   The foundational canon consists mainly of T. Parsons, *The Social System* (1951);
     T. Parsons and E. A. Shils (eds), *Toward A General Theory of Action* (1951); M.
     Levy, *The Structure of Society* (1952); and T. Parsons and N. Smelser, *Economy
     and Society* (1956).

21   On the origins and early development of functionalist modernization theory see B.
     F. Hoselitz (ed.), *The Progress of Underdeveloped Areas* (1952); D. Chirot,
     'Changing Fashions in the Study of the Social Causes of Economic and Political
     Change' (1981); S. N. Eisenstadt, 'Studies of Modernization and Sociological
     Theory' (1974); and A. D. Smith, *The Concept of Social Change* (1973).

22   D. H. Wrong, 'The Oversocialised Conception of Man in Modern Sociology'
     (1961); and A. Giddens, *A Contemporary Critique of Historical Materialism* (1981),
     p. 18.

23   T. Parsons, *Societies: Evolutionary and Comparative Perspectives* (1966).

24   N. J. Smelser, *Social Change in the Industrial Revolution* (1959), 'Sociological History:
     The Industrial Revolution and the British Working Class Family' (1967), 'Processes
     of Social Change' (1967); and M. Gould, *Revolution in the Development of
     Capitalism* (1987).

25   B. F. Hoselitz, *Sociological Aspects of Economic Growth* (1960); D. Lerner, *The Passing
     of Traditional Society* (1963); E. E. Hagen, *On the Theory of Social Change* (1962).

26   See Hagen, ibid. and D. C. McClelland, *The Achieving Society* (1961).

27   The necessity for hermeneutical enquiry in history has been defended by, among
     many others, Richard Harvey Brown. See the bibliography for examples of his
     writings.

28   Among their many empirical and methodological works see H. R. Trevor-Roper,
     Religion, the Reformation, and Social Change (1967), *The Rise of Christian Europe*
     (1965), and *History and Imagination* (valedictory lecture, 1980); G. R. Elton,
     England Under the Tudors (1955), *The Practice of History* (1967), *Reform and
     Reformation* (1977), and *Which Road to the Past?* (with R. W. Fogel, 1983). There

is also a defence of traditional interpretism in Berlin, 'The Concept of Scientific History' (1960).

29 The dramaturgical model is discussed by K. Burke, 'Interaction: Dramatism' (1968); R. Harré, *Social Being* (1979), ch. 10; and S. Lyman and M. B. Scott, *The Drama of Social Reality* (1975).

30 See bibliography for works by Geertz, Darnton, Davis, and Burke. Keith Thomas's important work on witchcraft, while not quite the same as symbolic realism, should also be mentioned here: *Religion and the Decline of Magic* (1971).

The relationship between history and anthropology has been discussed recently by B. S. Cohn, 'History and Anthropology: The State of Play' (1980) and 'Anthropology and History in the 1980s: Toward a Rapprochement' (1981); R. Darnton, 'The History of Mentalités: Recent Writings on Revolution, Criminality, and Death in France' (1978), and 'The Symbolic Element in History' (1986); N. Z. Davis, 'Anthropology and History in the 1980s: The Possibilities of the Past' (1981); J. Philipp, 'Traditional Historical Narrative and Action-Oriented (or Ethnographic) History' (1983); H. Medick, ' "Missionaries in the Row Boat?" Ethnological Ways of Knowing as a Challenge to Social History' (1987); M. Sahlins, 'Other Times, Other Customs: The Anthropology of History' (1983); R. G. Walters, 'Signs of the Times: Clifford Geertz and Historians' (1980); R. Chartier, *Cultural History* (1988); R. I. Levy, 'The Quest for Mind in Different Times and Different Places' (1989); L. Hunt, 'Introduction: History, Culture and Text' (1989); E. Tonkin, M. McDonald, and M. Chapman (eds), *History and Ethnicity* (1989); G. Dening, *The Bounty: An Ethnographic History* (1988) and 'Ethnography on My Mind' (1990); C. Geertz, 'History and Anthropology' (1990); and D. Potts, 'Two Modes of History Writing: The Poverty of Ethnography and the Potential of Narrative' (1991).

31 People's history writing, which in Britain has been closely associated with the journal *History Workshop* and its associated seminars, workshops, and conferences, was initially influenced by, among other things, the work of A. L. Morton, E. P. Thompson, and Christopher Hill. R. Samuel gives an eclectic and perhaps too broadly defined overview of the history of this genre in 'People's History' (1981). See also the articles by D. Selbourne and R. Samuel, 'On the Methods of History Workshop' (1980); and P. Burke, 'People's History or Total History' (1981).

Oral history, like people's history, is now widely practised. One of its chief advocates has been Paul Thompson; see his *The Voice of the Past* (1978) and various issues of *Oral History Journal*. There is a penetrating critique in J. Murphy, 'The Voice of Memory: History, Autobiography, and Oral Memory' (1986).

32 Lucien Febvre's work has been very influential in this regard; see the bibliography for examples of his writings available in English. The influence of Lévi-Strauss's structuralism on the French study of *mentalité* is problematic. An example of its application is E. Le Roy Ladurie, *Love, Death, and Money in the Pays d'Oc* (1984). Other problematic issues include the relationship between mentalities and ideologies, and the relevance of historical materialism to their study, i.e., the relationship between mentalities and other aspects of social life.

The study of mentality has been much advocated, among others by Lawrence Stone, and practised in many countries. For some discussions of its problems and references to examples see A. Burguière, 'The Fate of the History of Mentalities in the *Annales*' (1983); P. Burke, 'Strengths and Weaknesses of the History of

Mentalities' (1986); P. H. Hutton, 'The History of Mentalities: The New Map of Cultural History (1981); M. A. Gismondi, 'The Gift of Theory: A Critique of the *Histoire des Mentalités'* (1985); J. LeGoff, 'Mentalities: A History of Ambiguities' (1985); M. Vovelle, *Ideologies and Mentalities* (1990). See also the references to discussions of the relationship of anthropology and history given in n. 30 above.

33　On the methodology of *Annales* macro-structural history see F. Braudel, *On History* (1980); E. Le Roy Ladurie, *The Mind and Method of the Historian* (1981), ch. 1; T. Stoianovich, *French Historical Method: The Annales Paradigm* (1976) and 'Social History: Perspective of the *Annales* Paradigm' (1978).

34　Braudel gives some articulation of his concept of structure in *Civilization and Capitalism* (1981–4), vol. I, pp. 23–5 and 559–63, vol. II, pp. 21–6, vol. III, pp. 623–32; and *On History* (1980), pp. 27–52 and 64–80.

35　On the idea and methodology of 'archaeological' total history see Febvre, *A New Kind of History* (1973), ch. 3; Braudel, *On History* (1980), pp. 33–4 and 76; and E. Le Roy Ladurie, *The Territory of the Historian* (1979), ch. 7.

36　E. Le Roy Ladurie, *Carnival in Romans* (1981).

37　See bibliography for Le Roy Ladurie's works available in English.

38　See, for example, W. G. Hoskins, *The Making of the English Landscape* (1955) and *The Age of Plunder: King Henry's England, 1500–1547* (1976); A. G. Price, *The Western Invasion of the Pacific and its Continents* (1963); W. H. McNeill, *Plagues and Peoples* (1977), *The Human Condition: An Ecological and Historical View* (1980), and *The Pursuit of Power: Technology, Armed Force, and Society Since A.D. 1000* (1983); and A. W. Crosby, *Ecological Imperialism* (1986).

39　See especially Geertz, *Agricultural Involution* (1963) and Gellner, *Muslim Society* (1981).

40　L. Althusser and E. Balibar, *Reading Capital* (1970), especially ch. 9.

41　Wallerstein's general approach is best seen in *The Capitalist World-Economy* (1979), ch. 9, *Historical Capitalism* (1983), *passim*, and *The Politics of the World-Economy* (1984), chs 2 and 15.

42　Most of Foucault's work is now available in English. For overviews and discussions see H. L. Dreyfus and P. Rabinow, *Michel Foucault: Beyond Structuralism and Hermeneutics* (1982); A. Megill, 'Foucault, Structuralism, and the Ends of History' (1979); and A. Sheridan, *Michel Foucault: The Will to Truth* (1980).

43　For Touraine's and Bourdieu's work available in English see bibliography.

44　The most extensive statement is in Giddens, *The Constitution of Society* (1984). There is a short convenient summary in Giddens, *Profiles and Critiques in Social Theory* (1982), pp. 8–11. Most of the fundamental methodological ideas of Giddens are shared by P. Abrams in *Historical Sociology* (1982) and A. Touraine in *The Self-Production of Society* (1977).

45　Of course the work of these historians has not been entirely confined to the socio-cultural level. Christopher Hill has written extensively on economic history. He has been the least theoretically and methodologically reflective of this group and the ascription of 'Marxist' to his work is now problematic because it is little in evidence in his recent writings, although his work of the 1940s and fifties is much more obviously so. Some of his extensive writings are listed in the bibliography.

Edward Thompson has been very interested in theoretical and methodological questions. See the bibliography for some of his main works of theory, method-ology, and empirical history. The work of Raymond Williams has been essentially concerned with the social history of culture and problems of historical materialist methodology. See the works listed in the bibliography.

46 Hobsbawm's scholarly interests are legion and his output is vast. He has written extensively on Marxist historical theory and methodology, including some classic essays, such as 'Karl Marx's Contribution to Historiography' (1968), 'From Social History to the History of Society' (1971), 'The Contribution of History to Social Science' (1981), and 'Marx and History' (1984). His major works of totalizing Marxist history are the trilogy *The Age of Revolution* (1962), *The Age of Capital* (1975), and *The Age of Empire* (1987). For a penetrating overview of Hobsbawm's work see E. D. Genovese, 'The Politics of Class Struggle in the History of Society: An Appraisal of the Work of Eric Hobsbawm' (1984). The bibliography also contains references to the work of Kiernan and Neale.

47 The methodologies of some Marxist and other historical sociologists are discussed by the editor and contributors to T. Skocpol (ed.), *Vision and Method in Historical Sociology* (1984); R. Bendix, *Force, Fate, and Freedom: On Historical Sociology* (1984); H. Kaye, *The British Marxist Historians* (1984); R. Johnson, 'Barrington Moore, Perry Anderson and English Social Development' (1976); P. Abrams, *Historical Sociology* (1982).

48 Examples include B. Moore, *Social Origins of Dictatorship and Democracy* (1967) and *Inequality: The Social Bases of Obedience and Revolt* (1978); R. Hilton, *A Medieval Society* (1966), *Bond Men Made Free* (1973), *The English Peasantry in the Later Middle Ages* (1975), and 'Feudalism in Europe: Problems for Historians' (1984); P. Anderson, *Passages From Antiquity to Feudalism* (1974), *Lineages of the Absolutist State* (1974); T. Skocpol, *States and Social Revolutions* (1979); R. Brenner, 'Agrarian Class Structure and Economic Development in Pre-Industrial Europe' (1976), 'The Origins of Capitalist Development: A Critique of Neo-Smithian Marxism' (1977), and 'The Agrarian Roots of European Capitalism' (1982); G. de Ste Croix, *The Class Struggle in the Ancient Greek World* (1981).

49 For methodological discussions see again Skocpol, *Vision and Method* (1984); Bendix, *Force, Fate, and Freedom* (1984); and Abrams, *Historical Sociology* (1982). Examples of the work of R. Bendix, S. N. Eisenstadt, C. Geertz, E. Gellner, J. A. Hall, M. Mann, A. Hirschman, and B. Nelson are listed in the bibliography.

50 See bibliography for some of Elias's main works in English.

51 See bibliography for a selection of Tilly's works.

52 See bibliography for a selection of Pred's work. On structurationist geography see also A. Kellerman, 'Structuration Theory and Attempts at Integration in Human Geography' (1987) and D. Gregory and J. Urry (eds), *Social Relations and Spatial Structures* (1985).

53 See Pred, *Making Histories and Constructing Human Geographies* (1990), pp. 3–5.

54 Ibid., p. 9.

55 The school is well represented in B. Wellman and S. D. Berkowitz (eds), *Social Structures: A Network Approach* (1988).

56 See A. Touraine, *The Self-Production of Society* (1977) and *The Voice and The Eye* (1981).

57 For example, A. Touraine, *The May Movement: Revolt and Reform* (1971), *Solidarity: Poland 1980–81* (1983), *Anti-Nuclear Protest: The Opposition to Nuclear Energy in France* (1983).

58 P. Abrams et al., *Communes, Sociology, and Society* (1976).

CHAPTER 3   METHODOLOGICAL STRUCTURISM

1   I. J. Cohen, *Structuration Theory* (1989), p. 1.
2   Cf. K. Lowith, *Max Weber and Karl Marx* (1982); R. J. Antonio and R. M. Glassman (eds), *A Marx–Weber Dialogue* (1985); N. Wiley (ed.), *The Marx–Weber Debate* (1987).
3   G. Simmel, *Essays on Sociology, Philosophy and Aesthetics* (ed. K. H. Wolff) (1959), pp. 318–20.
4   Ibid., pp. 354–5.
5   J. Piaget, *Structuralism* (1968), p. 10, emphasis in the original.
6   Ibid., p. 13, emphasis in original.
7   Ibid., pp. 139–41.
8   See bibliography for some of the relevant work of Harré. One of those influenced by Harré is the social psychologist John Shotter. The bibliography has some references to his work.
9   See bibliography for Bhaskar's work.
10 Some of Abrams's work is listed in the bibliography.
11 See bibliography for references to the work of Elias.
12 See bibliography for references to the work of Bourdieu.
13 See bibliography for references to the work of Touraine.
14 On agency as the ability to choose alternative courses of action and to act upon those choices see, for example, D. Davidson, 'Agency', ch. 3 of his *Essays on Actions and Events* (1980); H. G. Frankfurt, 'Freedom of the Will and the Concept of a Person' (1982); C. Taylor, 'What is Human Agency?' (1977).
    On agency as structuring capacity see, for example, J. Piaget, *The Principles of Genetic Epistemology* (1972) and *Psychology and Epistemology* (1972); R. Harré, 'Architectonic Man: On the Structuring of Lived Experience' (1978) and *Social Being* (1979); A. Giddens, *Central Problems in Social Theory* (1979), ch. 2, and *Social Theory and Modern Sociology* (1987), ch. 9; and R. Bhaskar, *The Possibility of Naturalism* (1979), ch. 3.
15 See the explication of this point in A. O. Hirschman, *The Passions and the Interests* (1977), p. 131.
16 For arguments for an instrumental concept of structure see J. S. Coleman, 'Social Structure and a Theory of Action' (1976) and 'Rational Actors in Macrosociological Analysis' (1979); and G. Homans, *Social Behaviour: Its Elementary Forms* (1961), and 'What do We Mean by Social "Structure"?' (1976). On the phenomenological concept of structure see T. Luckmann (ed.), *Phenomenology and Sociology* (1978).
17 See F. Ringer, 'The Intellectual Field, Intellectual History, and the Sociology of Knowledge' and the accompanying articles by C. Lewin and M. Jay in *Theory and Society*, 19, no. 3, 1990 for a recent debate about intellectual history. The relationship of intellectual history to cultural history and the history of mentalities is discussed in R. Darnton, 'Intellectual and Cultural History' (1980).
18 See the excellent discussion of ideology in J. B. Thompson, *Studies in the Theory of Ideology* (1984).
19 There are excellent discussions of the role of the concept of culture in social theory and arguments about the distinctiveness of culture from social structure in M. S. Archer, *Culture and Agency* (1988) and M. Mandelbaum, *Purpose and Necessity in Social Theory* (1987).

20 There is now an extensive literature on mentality, which I referred to in n. 32 of chapter 2. See the excellent discussions in R. Darnton, 'The History of Mentalities' (1978) and 'The Symbolic Element in History' (1986); D. La Capra, *History and Criticism* (1985), ch. 3 and *Soundings in Critical Theory* (1989), ch. 5; M. Vovelle, *Ideologies and Mentalities* (1990); G. E. R. Lloyd, *Demystifying Mentalities* (1990).

21 Cf. Gellner, *Legitimation of Belief* (1974) and Archer, *Culture and Agency* (1988) on the role of culture in social action and transformation.

22 Cf. R. Horton, 'African Traditional Thought and Western Science' (1967) and 'Tradition and Modernity Revisited' (1982); E. Gellner, *Relativism and the Social Sciences* (1985), ch. 3.

23 The tasks, methodologies, and socio-political significance of anthropological discourse are explored in J. Clifford and G. E. Marcus (eds), *Writing Culture* (1986); and P. Rabinow, 'Humanism and Nihilism' (1983) and 'Discourse and Power' (1985).

24 For discussions of anthropological history see the references in n. 30 of ch. 2.

25 See bibliography for Robert Darnton's writings. Discussions of his work include R. Chartier, *Cultural History* (1988), ch. 4; D. LaCapra, *Soundings in Critical Theory* (1989), ch. 3; and M. Mah, 'Suppressing the Text' (1991).

26 Barrington Moore, *Injustice: The Social Bases of Obedience and Revolt* (1978). For a thorough discussion see D. Smith, *Barrington Moore: Violence, Morality, and Political Change* (1983).

27 E. J. Hobsbawm, *The Age of Revolution, Europe 1789–1848* (1962), *The Age of Capital, 1848–1875* (1975), *The Age of Empire, 1875–1914* (1987), *Labouring Men: Studies in the History of Labour* (1964), and *Captain Swing* (with George Rudé, 1973). See E. Genovese, 'The Politics of Class Struggle in the History of Society: An Appraisal of the Work of Eric Hobsbawm' (1984).

28 R. S. Neale, *Bath 1680–1850: A Social History* (1981) and *Writing Marxist History: British Society, Economy and Culture since 1700* (1985).

29 Historical materialism as a general theory of history is ultimately incompatible with methodological and sociological structurism because, as I have indicated, structurism precludes the idea of a fundamental cause of historical change or human motivation which is ahistorical. No matter how a historical materialist theory is couched or hedged about it must remain, if it is conceptually coherent, a general theory of society and history. Nevertheless, there are many historians influenced by Marxism, including those just mentioned, who do not employ such an ahistorical theory, so it certainly seems to be possible to be a methodological structurist while drawing upon concepts developed by Marx. This of course begs the question of the materialist status or otherwise of Marx's theory.

30 See bibliography for Gellner's works.

31 See bibliography for some of Tilly's main historical and methodological writings.

32 See bibliography for references to Pred's work.

33 Geertz, *The Interpretation of Cultures* (1973), p. ix.

34 Geertz has discussed his career and influences on his work in 'Recollections of an Itinerant Career' (1988).

35 Geertz, *Agricultural Involution: The Process of Ecological Change in Indonesia* (1963), p. xviii.

36 Geertz, 'Found in Translation' (1977), in *Local Knowledge* (1983), p. 45.

37 Geertz, 'The Uses of Diversity' (1986), p. 262.

38   See Geertz, 'Culture and Social Change: the Indonesian Case' (1984), p. 523.
39   Geertz, 'Thick Description' (1973), p. 10.
40   Ibid., p. 10.
41   Geertz, 'The Uses of Diversity' (1984), p. 264.
42   Geertz, *Islam Observed*, p. vii.
43   Geertz, *Negara: The Theatre State in Nineteenth Century Bali*, p. 6.
44   Ibid., pp. 9–10.
45   Geertz, *Agricultural Involution*, p. 3.
46   Geertz, *Peddlers and Princes* (1963), p. 4.
47   Ibid., pp. 147–52.
48   See the discussion of the involution thesis by J. and P. Alexander, 'Sugar, Rice and Irrigation in Colonial Java' (1978); and B. White, '"Agricultural Involution" and its Critics: Twenty Years After' (1983).
49   Discussions of the importance and influence of Geertz include R. C. Walters, 'Signs of the Times: Clifford Geertz and Historians' (1980); W. Rosebery, 'Balinese Cockfights and the Seduction of Anthropology' (1982); P. Shankman, 'The Thick and the Thin: On the Interpretive Theoretical Program of Clifford Geertz' (1984); M. A. Schneider, 'Culture-as-Text in the Work of Clifford Geertz' (1987); A. Biersack, 'Local Knowledge, Local History: Geertz and Beyond' (1989); D. La Capra, *Soundings in Critical Theory* (1989), ch. 5.
50   See the list of Le Roy Ladurie's main works in the bibliography.
51   Le Roy Ladurie, *Mind and Method of the Historian* (1981), ch. 1.
52   Ibid., p. 9.
53   For a discussion of the streams of Francophone structuralism and how the *Annales* school relates to it see my *Explanation in Social History* (1986), ch. 12.
54   Le Roy Ladurie, *Mind and Method of the Historian*, p. 25.
55   Le Roy Ladurie, *The Territory of the Historian*, p. 14.
56   Ibid., p. 114.
57   Le Roy Ladurie, *Carnival in Romans*, p. xvii.
58   Le Roy Ladurie, *Mind and Method of the Historian*, pp. 26–7.
59   Ibid., p. 206.

CHAPTER 4   REALISM AND STRUCTURISM

1   See the general account of realist epistemologies in R. Harré, *Varieties of Realism* (1986); and R. Miller, *Fact and Method* (1987).
2   See R.B. Braithwaite, *Scientific Explanation* (1953); H. Feigl, 'Some Major Issues and Developments in the Philosophy of Science of Logical Empiricism' (1956); C. G. Hempel, *Aspects of Scientific Explanation* (1965); R. Carnap, *An Introduction to the Philosophy of Science* (1966). Logical empiricism is discussed in D. Shapere, 'Notes Towards a Post-Positivistic Interpretation of Science' (1969); H. Feigl, 'Empiricism at Bay?' (1974) and E. McMullin, 'Empiricism at Sea' (1974); F. Suppe (ed.), *The Structure of Scientific Theories* (1977); O. Hanfling, *Logical Positivism* (1981); W. Salmon, 'Empiricism: the Key Question' (1988) and 'Four Decades of Scientific Explanation' (1989).
3   See especially K. R. Popper, *Conjectures and Refutations* (1972) and *Objective Knowledge* (1972).

4   This argument draws especially on R. Harré and E. Madden, *Causal Powers* (1975), R. Harré, *Varieties of Realism* (1986); R. Bhaskar, *A Realist Theory of Science* (1975) and *Reclaiming Reality* (1989); and the work of R. N. Boyd and C. A. Hooker.

5   On the significance of the concept of emergence see J. Margolis, 'Emergence' (1986); K.-D. Opp, 'Group Size, Emergence, and Composition Laws' (1979). On the idea and importance of causal powers see R. Harré and E. H. Madden, *Causal Powers* (1975).

6   The relevance of metaphors, analogies, similes, and models for explanation is defended by M. Black, *Models and Metaphors* (1962); R. Harré, 'The Constructive Role of Models' (1976); R. N. Boyd, 'Metaphor and Theory Change: What is Metaphor a Metaphor for?' (1979); M. Hesse, *Revolutions and Reconstructions in Philosophy of Science* (1980).

7   K. Popper, *Conjectures and Refutations* (1972), p. 226.

8   There is now an extensive literature on the importance of hermeneutics in science, much of it inspired by T. S. Kuhn. See, for example, K.-O. Apel, *Toward a Transformation of Philosophy* (1980) and *Understanding and Explanation* (1984); M. Hesse, *Revolutions and Reconstructions* (1980); G. Markus, 'Why is there no Hermeneutics of Natural Sciences? Some Preliminary Theses' (1987). The collection of articles in L. J. Jordanova (ed.), *Languages of Nature* (1986) contains interesting discussions of the cultural contexts and languages of 18th- and 19th-century sciences as forms of literature.

9   See, for example, I. Berlin, 'The Concept of Scientific History' (1960); H.-G. Gadamer, 'Hermeneutics and Social Science' (1975) and 'The Problem of Historical Consciousness' (1979).

10 On the importance of background frameworks in explanation see R. Harré, *Varieties of Realism* (1986), ch. 11; M. Hesse, *The Structure of Scientific Inference* (1974); I. Lakatos, 'Falsification and the Methodology of Scientific Research Programmes' (1970); and the work of Dudley Shapere, especially 'Scientific Theories and Their Domains' (1977) and 'Rationalism and Empiricism: A New Perspective' (1988).

11 For criticisms of the deductivist model of science see R. Harré, *The Principles of Scientific Thinking* (1970); M. Hesse, *The Structure of Scientific Inference* (1974).

12 R. Bhaskar, *The Possibility of Naturalism* (1979).

13 The work of Larry Laudan has been influential in this regard. See the bibliography for some of his relevant work.

14 T. S. Kuhn, *The Structure of Scientific Revolutions* (1970), and P. K. Feyerabend, *Against Method* (1975).

15 W. V. O. Quine, *Ontological Relativity* (1969), ch. 5; H. Putnam, *Mind, Language and Reality: Philosophical Papers*, vol. 2 (1975), especially chs 1, 13, and 14; R. Harré and E. H. Madden, *Causal Powers* (1975); D. Shapere, *Reason and the Search for Knowledge* (1984) and other works; M. Hesse, *Revolutions and Reconstructions;* and R. N. Boyd (all works shown in the bibliography). See the discussion in my *Explanation in Social History*, ch. 7.

16 Hesse, *Revolutions and Reconstructions*, pp. xvi–xvii.

17 Neurath's metaphor is referred to by W. V. O. Quine in *Word and Object* (1960), p. 3.

18 Hesse, *The Structure of Scientific Inference* (1974), p. 57.

19 This idea plays a central role in Lévi-Strauss's argument in *The Savage Mind* (1966) and is defended by Hesse in *The Structure of Scientific Inference* and *Revolutions and Reconstructions*.
20 See Popper's cogent defence of this idea in *Conjectures and Refutations*, ch. 10.
21 Mandelbaum's main works on the philosophy of explanation are listed in the bibliography, which is not meant to be a definitive list of his works and does not include many of his writings on moral philosophy.
22 M. Mandelbaum, 'Societal Facts' (1955), and 'Societal Laws' (1957).
23 Mandelbaum, 'The Problem of Covering Laws' (1961).
24 Ibid., p. 57.
25 Mandelbaum, *The Anatomy of Historical Knowledge* (1977).
26 Ibid., pp. 97–8.
27 Ibid., p. 123.
28 Ibid., p. 182.
29 Ibid., p. 193.
30 Mandelbaum, *Purpose and Necessity*, p. 9.
31 Ibid., p. 20.
32 Ibid., p. 151.
33 The two basic functional requirements of any social structure Mandelbaum saw as being communication between members and differentiation of roles in terms of gender and division of labour. In addition there are five other social factors that are universally present in human societies. First, there is a kinship system that governs such things as marriage, family life, clans, and residence. Second, an economic system governs the production and distribution of goods. Third, there is class and caste differentiation, which is closely related to the division of labour and the economic system. Fourth, a form of group control exists, including a governmental system and a system of morality, customs, and authority. Fifth, there is a belief system, including religion, magic, science, and political ideologies. In addition to these necessary social factors in all social organization he identified two other kinds of necessary conditions that must be present in each society if it is to survive: it must meet the needs of a large number of its members, and its institutions must be compatible with each other. Ibid., pp. 150–1.
34 Ibid., pp. 92–6.
35 Ibid., p. 21.
36 Ibid., pp. 24–6.
37 Ibid., pp. 32–3.
38 Ibid., p. 166.
39 This is the consistently argued view of Dudley Shapere. See also the interesting discussion by Ernest Gellner in 'Tractatus Sociologico-Philosophicus' in *Culture, Identity and Politics* (1987), ch. 11.
40 Cf. K. Popper, *The Logic of Scientific Discovery* (1972), especially chs 5 and 6.
41 On the convergence concept of truth, or something like it, see H. Putnam, *Mind, Language, and Reality*, ch. 13; M. Hesse, *The Structure of Scientific Inference*, chs 1 and 2.
42 Mandelbaum, *Purpose and Necessity*, p. 154.
43 Ibid., p. 157.
44 Ibid., p. 168.

CHAPTER 5   HISTORICAL MATERIALISM AND STRUCTURISM

1   Such as Georgi Plekhanov, Antonio Labriola, V. I. Lenin, Benedetto Croce, Nikolai
    Bukharin, Karl Korsch, Karl Federn, Jean-Paul Sartre, and right up to Raymond
    Williams, Lucio Colletti, Maurice Godelier, Perry Anderson, Goran Therborn, and
    Jorge Larrain. (See the bibliography for references.) In the nineteenth century there
    was a greater awareness by Marxists of the lineage of historical materialism. This
    is shown in, for example, the work of Labriola, Plekhanov, and E. R. A. Seligman,
    The Economic Interpretation of History (1907).
2   See D. Davidson, 'Mental Events' in *Essays on Actions and Events* (1980), especially
    p. 214; M. Bunge, *The Mind–Body Problem* (1980), especially pp. 21–5; and J. Kim,
    'Causality, Identity, and Supervenience' (1979).
3   Historical materialism lacks a thorough history, something I will attempt partially
    to alleviate in a forthcoming book on *Varieties of Historical Materialism*. Meanwhile,
    there are a few partial histories of some of its doctrines, such as: E. R. A. Seligman,
    The Economic Interpretation of History [originally 1902] (1967); R. Meek, *Social Science
    and the Ignoble Savage* (1976); G. Therborn, *Science, Class, and Society: On the
    Formation of Sociology and Historical Materialism* (1976); N. Levine, 'The German
    Historical School and the Origins of Historical Materialism' (1987).
4   Marx, Engels, *Selected Works* (1970), vol. 3, p. 103.
5   K. Marx, *Capital*, (1971), vol. 1, p. 86.
6   Habermas, *Communication and the Evolution of Society* (1969).
7   Of course it is true that all physical things are systems of smaller things (and
    ultimately all physical matter is in a sense solidified energy) held together by
    fundamental physical forces and chemical bonds. Nevertheless physical emergence
    is important because new kinds of powers exist in macro physical systems that
    cannot be reduced to the powers of their constituents.
8   See D. Davidson, *Essays on Actions and Events* (1980), especially essays 1–5; A.
    Giddens, *Central Problems in Social Theory* (1979), especially ch. 2, and *Profiles and
    Critiques in Social Theory* (1982), especially ch. 3; R. Harré, 'The Ethogenic Ap-
    proach: Theory and Practice' (1977) and *Social Being* (1979); C. Taylor, 'What is
    Human Agency?' (1977) and 'The Person' (1985).
9   See, for example, E. Goffman, *The Presentation of Self in Everyday Life* (1959) and
    Behavior in Public Places (1963); C. Geertz, *The Interpretation of Cultures* (1973) and
    Local Knowledge (1983); R. Harré, *Social Being* (1979) and *Personal Being* (1983).

CHAPTER 6   REALISM, STRUCTURISM, AND HISTORY

1   Cf. J. Freund 'German Sociology in the Time of Max Weber' (1979) for a dis-
    cussion of the problem of the normative versus value-free content of sociology and
    how it was perceived in the classical era.
2   A considerable stream of the large literature relating debates in philosophy of science
    to social methodology questions has argued that positivism is an inadequate account
    of science. See the general discussions of positivism and its alternatives in I.
    Hacking, *Representing and Intervening* (1983); F. Suppe (ed.), *The Structure of
    Scientific Theories* (1977); W. C. Salmon, 'Four Decades of Scientific Explanation'
    (1989). For defences of the possibility of a science of society from different

perspectives see R. Keat and J. Urry, *Social Theory as Science* (1975); R. Bhaskar, *The Possibility of Naturalism* (1979), *Scientific Realism and Human Emancipation* (1986), *Reclaiming Reality* (1989); E. Gellner, 'The Scientific Status of the Social Sciences' (1984); A. Rosenberg, 'Philosophy of Science and the Potentials for Knowledge in the Social Sciences' (1986) and *Philosophy of Social Science* (1988); W. G. Runciman, *A Treatise on Social Theory*, vol. 1, 1983).

3 The importance of conceptualizing people as necessarily social by nature as a basis for sociological and moral arguments has been extensively defended by Kai Nielsen in, for example, 'A Rationale for Egalitarianism' (1981).

4 For Habermas and Apel, see bibliography; R. Bhaskar, *Scientific Realism and Human Emancipation* (1986) and *Philosophy and the Idea of Freedom* (1991); and M. Mandelbaum, *Purpose and Necessity in Social Theory* (1987). See also the essays in J. Forester (ed.), *Critical Theory and Public Life* (1985).

5 For general discussions of logical positivism (more accurately called 'logical empiricism') see A. J. Ayer (ed.), *Logical Positivism* (1959); H. Feigl, 'The Origin and Spirit of Logical Positivism' (1969); O. Hanfling, *Logical Positivism* (1981). For Neurath's work see his *Foundations of the Social Sciences* (1944) and *Empiricism and Sociology* (1973) .

6 See the different defences of the importance of an evolutionary perspective to social explanation in P. Van Parijs, *Evolutionary Explanation in the Social Sciences* (1981); and R. Harré and U. J. Jensen (eds), *The Philosophy of Evolution* (1981).

7 See my *Explanation in Social History*, pp. 22–3 and 59 for discussion of historicalism. What amounts to historicalism has been defended by I. Berlin, 'The Concept of Scientific History' (1960); W. H. Dray, *Laws and Explanation in History* (1957); G. R. Elton, 'Two Kinds of History', in R. W. Fogel and G. R. Elton, *Which Road to the Past?* (1983).

8 See, for example, E. J. Hobsbawm, 'The Social Function of the Past: Some Questions' (1972) and 'Looking Forward: History and the Future' (1981); R. Bendix, *Force, Fate, and Freedom* (1984). Much of the contents of the journals *Radical History Review* and *History Workshop* are suffused with a political intent. Perhaps the most outstanding recent example of a historian who has written history, and written about historical methodology, from a politically conscious position in the present is Edward Thompson; see, for example, *The Poverty of Theory and Other Essays* (1978) and 'The Politics of Theory' (1981). See also the introduction by Oswyn Murray to the English translation of Paul Veyne's *Bread and Circuses* (1990) where he discusses the political significance of philosophical history, including the work of Michel Foucault.

9 Some methodological individualist historians and economists have been strongly influenced by rational exchange theory, which is a kind of behaviourism and contains an empiricist epistemology. The best examples are found amongst cliometricians and some recent institutionalist economists, who argue that economic and social change are a consequence of individual pursuit of maximum utility from exchange with other individuals. For discussions of cliometrics see Donald N. McCloskey, 'The Achievements of the Cliometric School' (1978); and R. W. Fogel, 'Scientific History and Traditional History' (1983). On rational-individualist institutionalist economic history see D. C. North, *Structure and Change in Economic History* (1981) and my *Explanation in Social History*, ch. 11. Neo-classical theory, which still dominates economics in capitalist countries, provides the behavioural postulates and methodological principles for these historians. Given the economistic tenor of modern culture and

politics neo-classical economic theory has also come to provide ideological under-pinnings for the modern capitalist class and state. Because it sees society in individualist terms and views market rationality as the prime motivation of behaviour and basis for morality if allowed free rein, neoclassical economics sees the task of politics in instrumental terms as being to remove impediments to the operation of supposedly freely moving utility-maximizing individuals. Some economic theorists have there-fore seen neoclassicism as the paradigm of all social science. See, for example, M. Friedman, *Capitalism and Freedom* (1962) and G. S. Becker, *The Economic Approach to Human Behavior* (1976). For a trenchant critique of the philosophical foundations of neoclassicism see M. Hollis and E. Nell, *Rational Economic Man* (1975).

Bibliography

Abrams, P., *Communes, Sociology, and Society*, Cambridge University Press, Cambridge, 1976.

——'History, Sociology, Historical Sociology', *Past and Present*, no. 87, 1980.

——*Historical Sociology*, Open Books, Somerset, 1982.

Adams, J. W., 'Consensus, Community, and Exoticism', *Journal of Interdisciplinary History*, 7, 1981.

Adorno, T. et al., *The Positivist Dispute in German Sociology*, Heinemann, London, 1976.

Agassi, J., 'Methodological Individualism and Institutional Individualism', in J. Agassi and I. C. Jarvie (eds), *Rationality: The Critical View*, Martinus Nijhoff, Dordrecht, 1987.

Albert, H., 'The Economic Tradition: Economics as a Research Programme for Theoretical Social Science', in K. Brunner (ed.), *Economics and Social Institutions*, Martinus Nijhoff, Boston, 1979.

——'Transcendental Realism and Rational Heuristics: Critical Rationalism and the Problem of Method', in G. Andersson (ed.), *Rationality in Science and Politics*, 1984.

——'Hermeneutics and Economics', *Kyklos*, 41, 1988.

Alexander, J. and Alexander, P., 'Sugar, Rice and Irrigation in Colonial Java', *Ethnohistory*, 25, 1978.

Alexander, J. C., 'Social-Structural Analysis: Some Notes on its History and Prospects', *Sociological Quarterly*, 25, 1984.

——'Action and Its Environments', in J. C. Alexander et al. (eds), *The Micro-Macro Link*, University of California Press, Berkeley, 1987.

Alexander, J. C. and Giesen, B., 'From Reduction to Linkage: The Long View of the Micro-Macro Link', in J. C. Alexander et al. (eds), *The Micro-Macro Link*, University of California Press, Berkeley, 1987.

Alexander, J. C., Giesen, B., Munch, R. and Smelser, N. J. (eds), *The Micro-Macro Link*, University of California Press, Berkeley, 1987.

Althusser, L. and Balibar, E., *Reading Capital*, trans. B. Brewster, 2nd ed., NLB, London, 1970.

Anderson, P., *Lineages of the Absolutist State*, NLB, London, 1974.

——*Passages From Antiquity to Feudalism*, NLB, London, 1974.

——*Arguments within English Marxism*, NLB, London, 1980.

——*In the Tracks of Historical Materialism*, Verso, London, 1983.

Antoni, C., *From History to Sociology*, Merlin Press, London, 1959.

Antonio, R. J., 'The Normative Foundations of Emancipatory Theory: Evolutionary Versus Pragmatic Perspectives', *American Journal of Sociology*, 94, 1989.

Antonio, R. J. and Glassman, R. M. (eds), *A Marx-Weber Dialogue*, University Press of Kansas, Lawrence, 1985.

Apel, K.-O., *Towards a Transformation of Philosophy*, Routledge and Kegan Paul, London, 1980.

——*Understanding and Explanation*, MIT Press, Cambridge MA, 1984.

Archer, M. S., *Culture and Agency*, Cambridge University Press, Cambridge, 1988.

Ashley, W. J., 'Historical School of Economists', in H. Higgs (ed.), *Palgrave's Dictionary of Political Economy*, rev. ed., 1925–6. [Reprinted by Kelley, New York, 1963.]

Attridge, D., Bennington, G. and Young, R., *Post-Structuralism and the Question of History*, Cambridge University Press, Cambridge, 1987.

Ayer, A. J. (ed.), *Logical Positivism*, Free Press, New York, 1959.

Baechler, J., Hall, J. A. and Mann, M. (eds), *Europe and the Rise of Capitalism*, Blackwell, Oxford, 1988.

Banks, J. A., 'From Universal History to Historical Sociology', *British Journal of Sociology*, 40, 1989.

Barbalet, J. M., 'Power, Structural Resources, and Agency', *Current Perspectives in Social Theory*, vol. 9, JAI Press, Greenwich, 1987.

Barnes, B., *Scientific Knowledge and Sociological Theory*, Routledge and Kegan Paul, London, 1974.

——*Interests and the Growth of Knowledge*, Routledge and Kegan Paul, London, 1977.

——*T. S. Kuhn and Social Science*, Macmillan, London, 1982.

——'Relativism, Rationalism, and the Sociology of Knowledge', in M. Hollis and S. Lukes (eds), *Rationality and Relativism*, Blackwell, Oxford, 1982.

Barzun, J., *Clio and the Doctors*, University of Chicago Press, Chicago, 1974.

Basu, K., Jones, E., Schlicht, E., 'The Growth and Decay of Custom: The Role of the New Institutional Economics in Economic History', *Explorations in Economic History*, 24, 1987.

Becker, G. S., *The Economic Approach to Human Behavior*, University of Chicago Press, Chicago, 1976.

Bell, D. and Kristol, I. (eds), *The Crisis in Economic Theory*, Basic Books, New York, 1981.

Bendix, R., *Nation Building and Citizenship*, University of California Press, Berkeley, 1964.

——*Kings or People: Power and the Mandate to Rule*, University of California Press, Berkeley, 1978.

——*Force, Fate, and Freedom: On Historical Sociology*, University of California Press, Berkeley, 1984.

Berger, P. L. and Luckmann, T., *The Social Construction of Reality*, Penguin, Harmondsworth, 1966.

Berkhofer, R. F., 'The Challenge of Poetics to (Normal) Historical Practice', *Poetics Today*, 9, 1988.

Berlin, I., 'The Concept of Scientific History', *History and Theory*, 1, 1960. [Reprinted in W. Dray (ed.), *Philosophical Analysis and History*, Harper and Row, New York, 1966]

Bernstein, E., *Evolutionary Socialism*, trans. E. C. Harvey, Schocken Books, New York, 1967. [Originally published in 1899]

Bernstein, R. J., *Beyond Objectivism and Relativism*, Blackwell, Oxford, 1983.

Betz, H. K., 'How Does the German Historical School Fit?', *History of Political Economy*, 20, 1988.

Bhaskar, R., *A Realist Theory of Science*, Leeds Books, Leeds, 1975.

—— *The Possibility of Naturalism*, Harvester, Sussex, 1979.

—— *Scientific Realism and Human Emancipation*, Verso, London, 1986.

—— *Reclaiming Reality*, Verso, London, 1989.

—— *Philosophy and the Idea of Freedom*, Blackwell, Oxford, 1991.

Biersack, A., 'Local Knowledge, Local History: Geertz and Beyond', in L. Hunt (ed.), *The New Cultural History*, University of California Press, Berkeley, 1989.

Bigelow, J. and Pargetter, R., 'From Extroverted Realism to Correspondence: A Modest Proposal', *Philosophy and Phenomenological Research*, 50, 1990.

Bishop, J., *Natural Agency*, Cambridge University Press, Cambridge, 1989.

Black, M., *Models and Metaphors*, Cornell University Press, Ithaca, 1962.

Blau, P. M. (ed.), *Approaches to the Study of Social Structure*, Open Books, London, 1976.

—— *Inequality and Heterogeneity*, Free Press, New York, 1977.

—— 'A Macrosociological Theory of Social Structure', *American Journal of Sociology*, 83, 1977–8.

—— 'Diverse Views of Social Structure and Their Common Denominator', in P. Blau and R. Merton (eds), *Continuities in Structural Inquiry*, Sage, London, 1981.

—— 'Comments on the Prospects for a Theory of Social Structure', *Journal for the Theory of Social Behaviour*, 13, 1983.

—— 'Contrasting Theoretical Perspectives', in J. C. Alexander et al. (eds), *The Micro-Macro Link*, University of California Press, Berkeley, 1987.

Blau P. M. and Merton, R. K. (eds), *Continuities in Structural Inquiry*, Sage, London, 1981.

Bloch, M., *The Historian's Craft*, trans. P. Putnam, Manchester University Press, Manchester, 1954.

Bloor, D., *Knowledge and Social Imagery*, Routledge and Kegan Paul, London, 1976.

—— *Wittgenstein: A Social Theory of Knowledge*, Macmillan, London, 1983.

—— 'A Sociological Theory of Objectivity', in S. C. Brown (ed.), *Objectivity and Cultural Divergence*, Cambridge University Press, Cambridge, 1984.

Bonnell, V. E., 'The Uses of Theory: Concepts and Comparisons in Historical Sociology', *Comparative Studies in Society and History*, 22, 1980.

Bottomore, T. and Nisbet, R. (eds), *A History of Sociological Analysis*, Heinemann, London, 1978.

Boudon, R., *The Uses of Structuralism*, Heinemann, London, 1971.

—— *The Logic of Social Action*, Routledge and Kegan Paul, London, 1981.

—— 'Individual Action and Social Change', *British Journal of Sociology*, 34, 1983.

—— *Theories of Social Change*, Polity Press, Cambridge, 1986.

—— 'The Individualistic Tradition in Sociology', in J. C. Alexander et al. (eds), *The Micro-Macro Link*, University of California Press, Berkeley, 1987.

Bourdieu, P., 'Intellectual Field and Creative Project', *Social Science Information*, 8, 1969.

—— 'The Specificity of the Scientific Field and the Social Conditions of the Progress of Reason', *Social Science Information*, 14, 1975.

—— *Outline of a Theory of Practice*, Cambridge University Press, Cambridge, 1977.

—— 'The Production of Belief: Contribution to an Economy of Symbolic Goods', *Media, Culture and Society*, 2, 1980.

—— 'The Field of Cultural Production, or: The Economic World Reversed', *Poetics*, 12, 1983.

—— *Distinction: A Social Critique of the Judgement of Taste*, Routledge and Kegan Paul, London, 1984.

—— 'The Genesis of the Concepts of *Habitus* and of *Field*', *Sociocriticism*, no. 2, 1985.

—— 'The Social Space and the Genesis of Groups', *Social Science Information*, 24, 1985.

—— *Homo Academicus*, Polity Press, Cambridge, 1988.

—— 'Vive la Crise! For Heterodoxy in Social Science', *Theory and Society*, 17, no. 5, 1988–89.

—— 'Social Space and Symbolic Power', *Sociological Theory*, 7, 1989.

—— *In Other Words: Essays Towards a Reflexive Sociology*, Polity Press, Cambridge, 1990.

—— *The Logic of Practice*, Polity Press, Cambridge, 1990.

Bourdieu, P. and Passeron, J.-C., *Reproduction in Education, Society and Culture*, Sage, London, 1977.

Bouwsma, W. J., 'From History of Ideas to History of Meaning', *Journal of Interdisciplinary History*, 7, 1981.

Boyd, R. N., 'Realism, Underdetermination, and a Causal Theory of Evidence', *Nous*, 7, 1973.

—— 'Metaphor and Theory Change: What is Metaphor a Metaphor For?', in A. Ortony (ed.), *Metaphor and Thought*, Cambridge University Press, Cambridge, 1979.

—— 'Scientific Realism and Naturalistic Epistemology', in P. D. Asquith and R. N. Giere (eds), *PSA 1980*, vol. 2, Philosophy of Science Association, East Lansing, 1981.

—— 'On the Current Status of the Issue of Scientific Realism', *Erkenntnis*, 19, 1983.

——, 'Lex Orandi est Lex Credendi', in P. Churchland and C. Hooker (eds), *Images of Science*, University of Chicago Press, Chicago, 1985.

—— 'Observations, Explanatory Power and Simplicity: Toward a Non-Humean Account', in P. Achinstein and O. Hannaway (eds), *Observation, Experiment, and Hypothesis in Modern Physical Science*, MIT Press, Cambridge, MA, 1985.

—— 'How to be a Moral Realist', in G. Sayne-McCord (ed.), *Essays on Moral Realism*, Cornell University Press, Ithaca, 1988.

—— 'Realism, Approximate Truth, and Philosophical Method', in C. W. Savage (ed.), *Minnesota Studies in Philosophy of Science*, XIV, 1990.

Braembussche, A. A. van den, 'Historical Explanation and Comparative Method: Towards a Theory of the History of Society', *History and Theory*, 28, 1989.

Braithwaite, R. B., *Scientific Explanation*, Cambridge University Press, Cambridge, 1953.

Brand, M. and Walton, D. (eds), *Action Theory*, Reidel, Dordrecht, 1980.

Braudel, F., 'Personal Testimony', *Journal of Modern History*, 44, 1972.

—— *The Mediterranean and the Mediterranean World in the Age of Philip II*, 2 vols, Harper and Row, New York, 1972.

—— *On History*, Weidenfeld and Nicolson, London, 1980.

—— *Civilization and Capitalism*, 3 vols, Collins, London, 1981–4.

—— *The Identity of France*, 2 vols, Harper and Row, New York, 1988–90.

Breiger, R. L., 'The Duality of Persons and Groups', in B. Wellman and S. D.

Bibliography   231

Berkowitz (eds), *Social Structures: A Network Approach*, Cambridge University Press, Cambridge, 1988.

Breisach, E., *Historiography: Ancient, Medieval, and Modern*, University of Chicago Press, Chicago, 1983.

Brenner, R., 'Agrarian Class Structure and Economic Development in Pre-Industrial Europe', *Past and Present*, no. 70, 1976.

——'The Origins of Capitalist Development: A Critique of Neo-Smithian Marxism', *New Left Review*, no. 104, 1977.

——'The Agrarian Roots of European Capitalism', *Past and Present*, no. 97, 1982.

Briggs, A., *A Social History of England*, Weidenfeld and Nicolson, London, 1983.

Brodbeck, M., 'On the Philosophy of the Social Sciences', *Philosophy of Science*, 21, 1954.

Brown, R. H., *A Poetic for Sociology*, Cambridge University Press, Cambridge, 1977.

——'Symbolic Realism and Sociological Thought: Beyond the Positivist–Romantic Debate', in R. H. Brown and S. Lyman (eds), *Structure, Consciousness and History*, Cambridge University Press, Cambridge, 1978.

——'Historical Science as Linguistic Figuration', *Theory and Society*, 14, 1985.

——'Personal Identity and Political Economy: Western Grammars of the Self in Historical Perspective', *Current Perspectives in Social Theory*, vol. 8, JAI Press, Greenwich, 1987.

——'Positivism, Relativism, and Narrative in the Logic of the Historical Sciences', *American Historical Review*, 92, 1987.

——'Reason as Rhetorical', in J. S. Nelson et al. (eds), *The Rhetoric of the Human Sciences*, University of Wisconsin Press, Madison, 1987.

——*Society as Text*, University of Chicago Press, Chicago, 1987.

——'Symbolic Realism and the Dualism of the Human Sciences: A Rhetorical Reformulation of the Debate Between Positivism and Romanticism', in H. W. Simons (ed.), *The Rhetorical Turn*, University of Chicago Press, Chicago, 1990.

Brown, R. H. and Lyman, S. (eds), *Structure, Consciousness, and History*, Cambridge University Press, Cambridge, 1978.

Buckle, T. H., *History of Civilization in England*, Longmans Green, London, 1857.

Bunge, M., *The Mind-Body Problem*, Pergamon, Oxford, 1980.

Bukharin, N., *Historical Materialism: A System of Sociology*, University of Michigan Press, Ann Arbor, 1969. [Originally published in 1921]

Burguière, A., 'The Fate of the History of Mentalités in the Annales', *Comparative Studies in Society and History*, 24, 1982.

Burke, K., 'Interaction: Dramatism', *International Encyclopedia of Social Sciences*, 7, 1968.

Burke, P., *Popular Culture in Early Modern Europe*, Temple Smith, London, 1978.

——*Sociology and History*, Allen and Unwin, London, 1980.

——'People's History or Total History?', in R. Samuel (ed.), *People's History and Socialist Theory*, Routledge, London, 1981.

——'Strengths and Weaknesses of the History of Mentalities', *History of European Ideas*, 7, 1986.

——*The Italian Renaissance: Culture and Society in Italy*, rev. ed., Polity Press, Cambridge, 1986.

——*The French Historical Revolution: The Annales School, 1929–89*, Polity Press, Cambridge, 1990.

Burrow, J. W., *Evolution and Society*, Cambridge University Press, Cambridge, 1966.

Bush, P. D., 'Reflections on the Twenty-fifth Anniversary of AFEE: Philosophical and Methodological Issues in Institutional Economics', *Journal of Evolutionary Economics*, 25, 1991.

Butterfield, H., *Man on his Past*, Cambridge University Press, Cambridge, 1969.

——'Some Trends in Scholarship 1868–1968 in the Field of Modern History', *Transactions of the Royal Historical Society*, fifth series, 19, 1969.

Caldwell, B. J., *Beyond Positivism: Economic Methodology in the Twentieth Century*, Allen and Unwin, London, 1982.

——'Economic Methodology in the Post Positivist Era', *Research in the History of Economic Thought and Methodology*, vol. 2, JAI Press, Greenwich, 1984.

——'Methodological Diversity in Economics', *Research in the History of Economic Thought and Methodology*, vol. 5, JAI Press, Greenwich, 1987.

——'The Case for Pluralism', in N. De Marchi (ed.), *The Popperian Legacy in Economics*, Cambridge University Press, Cambridge, 1988.

——'Does Methodology Matter? How should it be Practiced?', *Finnish Economic Papers*, 3, 1990.

Cambridge Economic History of Europe, ed. J. H. Habakkuk and M. M. Postan, 8 vols, Cambridge University Press, Cambridge, 1942–89.

Canterbery, E. R. and Burkhardt, R. J., 'What Do We Mean By Asking Whether Economics is a Science?', in A. S. Eichner (ed.), *Why Economics is Not Yet a Science*, Macmillan, London, 1983.

Carnap, R., 'The Methodological Character of Theoretical Concepts', in H. Feigl and M. Scriven (eds), *Minnesota Studies in Philosophy of Science*, vol. I, 1956.

——*Meaning and Necessity*, 2nd ed., University of Chicago Press, Chicago, 1956.

——*An Introduction to the Philosophy of Science*, Basic Books, New York, 1974. [Originally *The Philosophical Foundations of Physics*, 1966.]

Carrithers, M., 'Why Humans Have Cultures', *Man*, 25, 1990.

Cartwright, N., 'The Reality of Causes in a World of Instrumental Laws', in P. D. Asquith and R. N. Giere (eds), *PSA 1980*, vol. 2, Philosophy of Science Association, East Lansing, 1981.

——'Capacities and Abstractions', in P. A. Kitcher and W. Salmon (eds), *Minnesota Studies in Philosophy of Science*, XIII, 1989.

Chartier, R., 'Text, Symbols, and Frenchness', *Journal of Modern History*, 57, 1985.

——*Cultural History: Between Practices and Representations*, Polity Press, Cambridge, 1988.

Chirot, D., 'Changing Fashions in the Study of the Social Causes of Economic and Political Change', in J. F. Short (ed.), *The State of Sociology*, Sage, Beverley Hills, 1981.

Chisholm, R. M., 'The Agent as Cause', in M. Brand and D. Walton (eds), *Action Theory*, Reidel, Dordrecht, 1980.

Churchland, P. M., 'The Ontological Status of Observables: In Praise of the Superempirical Virtues', in P. M. Churchland and C. A. Hooker (eds), *Images of Science*, University of Chicago Press, Chicago, 1985.

Churchland, P. M. and Hooker, C. A., *Images of Science: Essays on Realism and Empiricism*, University of Chicago Press, Chicago, 1985.

Cicourel, A. V., 'Notes on the Integration of Micro and Macro Levels of Analysis', in K. Knorr-Cetina and A. Cicourel (eds), *Advances in Social Theory and Methodology*, Routledge and Kegan Paul, London, 1981.

Cipolla, C. M. *Between History and Economics: An Introduction to Economic History*, Blackwell, Oxford, 1991.

Clifford, J. and Marcus, G. E. (eds), *Writing Culture*, University of California Press, Berkeley, 1986.

Clubb, J. M., 'The "New" Quantitative History: Social Science or Old Wine in New Bottles', in J. M. Clubb and E. M. Scheuch (eds), *Historical Social Research*, Klett-Cotta, Stuttgart, 1980.

——'History as a Social Science', *International Social Science Journal*, 32, 1981.

Coats, A. W., 'The Historist Reaction in English Political Economy', *Economica*, 21, 1954.

——'Sociological Aspects of British Economic Thought (1880–1930)', *Journal of Political Economy*, 75, 1967.

——'The Historical Context of the "New" Economic History', *Journal of European Economic History*, 9, 1980.

——'Economic Rhetoric: The Social and Historical Context', in A. Klamer, D. N. McCloskey and R. M. Solow (eds), *The Consequences of Economic Rhetoric*, Cambridge University Press, Cambridge, 1988.

——'Explanations in History and Economics', *Social Research*, 56, 1989.

——'Confrontation in Toronto: Reactions to the "Old" Versus "New" Institutional Sessions', *Review of Political Economy*, 2, 1990.

——'Disciplinary Self-Examination, Departments, and Research Traditions in Economic History', *Scandinavian Economic History Review*, 38, 1990.

Cobb, R., *A Second Identity*, Oxford University Press, Oxford, 1969.

——*The Police and the People*, Oxford University Press, Oxford, 1970.

——'Modern French History in Britain', *Proceedings of the British Academy*, LX, 1974.

——*The People's Armies*, Yale University Press, New Haven, and London, 1987.

Cohen, G. A., *Karl Marx's Theory of History: A Defence*, Oxford University Press, Oxford, 1978.

Cohen, I. J., 'Structuration Theory and Social Praxis', in A. Giddens and J. H. Turner (eds), *Social Theory Today*, Polity Press, Cambridge, 1987.

——*Structuration Theory*, Macmillan, London, 1989.

Cohn, B. S., 'History and Anthropology; The State of Play', *Comparative Studies in Society and History*, 1, 1980.

——'Anthropology and History in the 1980s: Toward a Rapprochement', *Journal of Interdisciplinary History*, 12, 1981.

Coleman, D. C., *History and the Economic Past*, Oxford University Press, Oxford, 1987.

Coleman, J. S., *The Adolescent Society*, Free Press, New York, 1961.

——'Foundations for a Theory of Collective Decisions', *American Journal of Sociology*, 71, 1966.

——'Collective Decisions and Collective Action', in P. Laslett et al. (eds), *Philosophy, Politics, and Society*, 4th Series, Blackwell, Oxford, 1972.

——'Systems of Social Exchange', *Journal of Mathematical Sociology*, 2, 1972.

——'Conflicting Theories of Social Change', in G. Zaltman (ed.), *Processes of Phenomena of Social Change*, Wiley, New York, 1973.

——*Power and the Structure of Society*, W. W. Norton, New York, 1974.

——'Legitimate and Illegitimate Uses of Power', in L. Coser (ed.), *The Idea of Social Structure*, 1975.

—— 'Social Structure and A Theory of Action', in P. Blau (ed.), *Approaches to the Study of Social Structure*, Open Books, London, 1976.

—— 'Purposive Actors and Mutual Effects', in R. Merton et al. (eds), *Qualitative and Quantitative Social Research*, Free Press, New York, 1979.

—— 'Rational Actors in Macrosociological Analysis', in R. Harrison (ed.), *Rational Action*, Cambridge University Press, Cambridge, 1979.

—— 'The Structure of Society and the Nature of Social Research', *Knowledge: Creation, Diffusion, Utilization*, 1, 1980.

—— *The Asymmetrical Society*, Syracuse University Press, Syracuse, 1982.

—— 'Social Theory, Social Research, and a Theory of Action', *American Journal of Sociology*, 91, 1986.

—— *Individual Interests and Collective Action*, Cambridge University Press, Cambridge, 1986.

—— 'Microfoundations and Macrosocial Behavior', in J. C. Alexander et al. (eds), *The Micro-Macro Link*, University of California Press, Berkeley, 1987.

—— 'Norm-Generating Structures', in K. S. Cook and M. Levi (eds), *The Limits of Rationality*, University of Chicago Press, Chicago, 1990.

—— *Foundation of Social Theory*, Harvard University Press, Cambridge MA, 1990.

Coleman, J. S., Etzioni, A. and Porter, J., *Macrosociology: Research and Theory*, Allyn and Bacon, Boston, 1970.

Colletti, L., *From Rousseau to Lenin*, NLB, London, 1972.

Collini, S., Winch, D. and Burrow, J., *That Noble Science of Politics*, Cambridge University Press, Cambridge, 1983.

Collins, R., 'Micro-Translation as a Theory-building Strategy', in K. Knorr-Cetina and A. Cicourel (eds), *Advances in Social Theory and Methodology*, Routledge, London, 1981.

—— 'On the Microfoundations of Macrosociology', *American Journal of Sociology*, 86, 1981.

—— *Weberian Sociological Theory*, Cambridge University Press, Cambridge, 1986.

—— 'Interaction Ritual Chains, Power and Property: The Micro-Macro Connection as an Empirically Based Theoretical Problem', in J. C. Alexander et al. (eds), *The Micro-Macro Link*, University of California Press, Berkeley, 1987.

—— 'The Micro Contribution to Macro Sociology', *Sociological Theory*, 6, 1988.

—— 'For a Sociological Philosophy', *Theory and Society*, 17, 1988-9.

Comte, A., *The Essential Comte*, ed. S. Andreski, trans. M. Clarke, Croom Helm, London, 1974.

Croce, B., *Historical Materialism and the Economics of Karl Marx*, trans. C. M. Meredith, Latimer, London, 1914.

Crosby, A. W., *Ecological Imperialism*, Cambridge University Press, Cambridge, 1986.

Dallmayr, F. R., 'Agency and Structure', *Philosophy of Social Science*, 12, 1982.

Darnton, R., *Mesmerism and the End of the Enlightenment in France*, Harvard University Press, Cambridge MA, 1968.

—— 'In Search of Enlightenment: Recent Attempts to Create a Social History of Ideas', *Journal of Modern History*, 43, 1971.

—— 'The High Enlightenment and the Low-Life of Literature in Pre-Revolutionary France', *Past and Present*, no. 51, 1971.

—— 'The History of Mentalities: Recent Writings on Revolution, Criminality and

Death in France', in R. H. Brown and S. M. Lyman (eds), *Structure, Consciousness and History*, Cambridge University Press, Cambridge, 1978.
—— *The Business of Enlightenment*, Harvard University Press, Cambridge, MA, 1979.
—— 'Intellectual and Cultural History', in M. Kammen (ed.), *The Past Before Us*, Cornell University Press, Ithaca, 1980.
—— *The Literary Underground of the Old Regime*, Harvard University Press, Cambridge, MA, 1982.
—— *The Great Cat Massacre and Other Episodes in French Cultural History*, Harvard University Press, Cambridge, MA, 1984.
—— 'The Symbolic Element in History', *Journal of Modern History*, 58, 1986.
——*The Kiss of Lamourette: Reflections in Cultural History*, W. W. Norton, New York, 1990.
Davidson, D., *Essays on Actions and Events*, Oxford University Press, Oxford, 1980.
—— 'Problems in the Explanation of Action', in P. Pettit et al. (eds), *Metaphysics and Morality*, Basil Blackwell, Oxford, 1987.
—— 'The Structure and Content of Truth', *Journal of Philosophy*, 87, 1990.
Davis, L. and Engerman, S., 'Cliometrics: The State of the Science', *Historical Methods*, 20, 1987.
Davis, N. Z., *Society and Culture in Early Modern France*, Stanford University Press, Stanford, 1975.
—— 'Anthropology and History in the 1980s: The Possibilities of the Past', *Journal of Interdisciplinary History*, 12, 1981.
—— *The Return of Martin Guerre*, Harvard University Press, Cambridge, MA, 1983.
—— 'History's Two Bodies', *American Historical Review*, 93, 1988.
Dawe, A., 'Theories of Social Action', in T. Bottomore and R. Nisbet (eds), *History of Sociological Analysis*, Heinemann, London, 1979.
Dening, G. *The Bounty: An Ethnographic History*, University of Melbourne, Melbourne, 1988.
—— 'Ethnography on My Mind', in B. Attwood (ed.), *Boundaries of the Past*, The History Institute, Carlton, Australia, 1990.
Derrida, J., *Writing and Difference*, trans. A. Bass, Routledge, London, 1978.
de Ste Croix, G., *The Class Struggles of the Ancient Greek World*, Duckworth, London, 1981.
Devitt, M., *Realism and Truth*, Blackwell, Oxford, 1984.
Dilthey, W., *Introduction to the Human Sciences*, Harvester, London, 1988. [Originally published in 1883]
Dray, W. H., *Laws and Explanation in History*, Oxford University Press, London, 1957.
—— (ed.), *Philosophical Analysis and History*, Harper and Row, New York, 1966.
—— *Perspectives on History*, Routledge and Kegan Paul, London, 1980.
—— 'Narrative versus Analysis in History', *Philosophy of Social Science*, 15, 1985.
—— 'Generalization, Value-Judgment and Causal Explanation in History', in S. Hook, W. L. O'Neill and R. Toole (eds), *Philosophy, History and Social Action*, Kluwer, Dordrecht, 1988.
—— *On History and Philosophers of History*, E. J. Brill, Leiden, 1989.
Dreyfus, H. L. and Rabinow, P., *Michel Foucault: Beyond Structuralism and Hermeneutics*, Harvester, Brighton, 1982.

Eade, S., 'Social History in Britain in 1976: A Survey', *Labour History*, no. 31, 1976.

Eckelbar, J. C., 'The Saint-Simonian Philosophy of History: A Note', *History and Theory*, 16, 1977.

Eichner, A. S., 'Why Economics is Not Yet a Science', in A. S. Eichner (ed.), *Why Economics is Not Yet A Science*, Macmillan, London, 1983.

Eisenstadt, S. N., *The Political Systems of Empires*, Free Press, New York, 1963.

——*Modernization: Protest and Change*, Prentice-Hall, Englewood Cliffs, 1966.

——*Tradition, Change and Modernity: Essays*, John Wiley, New York, 1973.

——'Studies of Modernization and Sociological Theory', *History and Theory*, 13, 1974.

——*Revolution and the Transformation of Societies*, Free Press, New York, 1978.

Eley, G., 'Some Recent Tendencies in Social History', in G. G. Iggers and H. T. Parker (eds), *International Handbook of Historical Studies*, Methuen, London, 1979.

Elias, N., *What is Sociology?*, Hutchinson, London, 1978.

——*The Civilizing Process, 1: The History of Manners*, Blackwell, Oxford, 1978.

——*The Civilizing Process, 2: State Formation and Civilization*, Blackwell, Oxford, 1982.

——*The Court Society*, Blackwell, Oxford, 1983.

——'The Retreat of Sociologists into the Present', in V. Meja et al. (eds), *Modern German Sociology*, New York, 1987. [Reprinted in *Theory, Culture, and Society*, 4, 1987]

——*Involvement and Detachment*, Blackwell, Oxford, 1987.

——'The Symbol Theory, Parts 1, 2, and 3', *Theory, Culture, and Society*, 6, 1989.

Ellis, B., 'What Science Aims to Do', in P. M. Churchland and C. A. Hooker (eds), *Images of Science*, University of Chicago Press, Chicago, 1985.

——'The Ontology of Scientific Realism', in P. Pettit et al. (eds), *Metaphysics and Morality*, Blackwell, Oxford, 1987.

——'Internal Realism', *Synthèse*, 76, 1988.

Elster, J. (1982), 'Marxism, Functionalism, and Game Theory: The Case for Methodological Individualism', *Theory and Society*, 11, 1982.

——*Making Sense of Marx*, Cambridge University Press, Cambridge, 1985.

——*Nuts and Bolts for the Social Sciences*, Cambridge University Press, Cambridge, 1989.

——*The Cement of Society*, Cambridge University Press, Cambridge, 1989.

Elton, G. R., *England Under the Tudors*, Methuen, London, 1955.

——*The Practice of History*, Sydney University Press, Sydney, 1967.

——*Reform and Reformation*, Arnold, London, 1977.

Evans-Prichard, E. E., 'Anthropology and History', in *Essays in Social Anthropology*, Faber and Faber, London, 1962.

Febvre, L., *A New Kind of History*, ed. P. Burke, trans. K. Folca, Routledge, London, 1973.

——*Life in Renaissance France*, trans. M. Rothstein, Harvard University Press, Cambridge, MA, 1977.

——*The Problem of Unbelief in the Sixteenth Century*, trans. B. Gottlieb, Harvard University Press, Cambridge, MA, 1982.

Febvre, L. and Martin, H.-J., *The Coming of the Book*, trans. D. Gerard, NLB, London, 1976.

Federn, K., *The Materialist Conception of History: A Critical Analysis*, Macmillan, London, 1939.

Feigl, H., 'Some Major Issues and Developments in the Philosophy of Logical Empiricsm', in H. Feigl and M. Scriven (eds), *Minnesota Studies in the Philosophy of Science*, I, University of Minnesota Press, Minneapolis, 1956.

—— 'The Origin and Spirit of Logical Positivism', in P. Achinstein and S. Barker (eds), *The Legacy of Logical Positivism*, Johns Hopkins University Press, Baltimore, 1969.

—— 'Empiricism at Bay?' in R. S. Cohen and M. Wartofsky (eds), *Methodological and Historical Essays in the Natural and Social Sciences*, Reidel, Dordrecht, 1974.

Fernandez, J., 'Historians Tell Tales: Of Cartesian Cats and Gallic Cockfights', *Journal of Modern History*, 60, 1988.

Feyerabend, P., *Against Method*, NLB, London, 1975.

—— *Science in a Free Society*, NLB, London, 1978.

—— 'Knowledge and the Role of Theories', *Philosophy of Social Science*, 18, 1988.

—— 'Realism and the Historicity of Knowledge', *Journal of Philosophy*, 86, 1989.

Field, A. J., 'The Problem with Neoclassical Institutional Economics: A Critique with Special Reference to the North/Thomas Model of Pre-1500 Europe', *Exploration in Economic History*, 18, 1981.

—— 'The Future of Economic History', in A. J. Field (ed.), *The Future of Economic History*, Kluwer-Nijhof, Boston, 1987.

Fielding, N. G. (ed.), *Action and Structure*, Sage, London, 1988.

Finnegan, R. and Horton, R., 'Introduction', to R. Horton and R. Finnegan (eds), *Modes of Thought*, Faber and Faber, London, 1973.

Fish, S., *Is There a Text in This Class? The Authority of Interpretive Communities*, Harvard University Press, Cambridge, MA, 1980.

—— *Doing What Comes Naturally: Change, Rhetoric and the Practice of Theory in Literary and Legal Studies*, Oxford University Press, Oxford, 1989.

Fishlow, A. and Fogel, R. W., 'Quantitative Economic History: An Interim Evaluation. Past Trends and Present Tendencies', *Journal of Economic History*, 31, 1971.

Fiske, D. W. and Shweder, R. A. (eds), *Metatheory in Social Science*, University of Chicago Press, Chicago, 1986.

Fogel, R. W., 'The New Economic History, Its Findings and Methods', *Economic History Review*, 19, 1966.

—— 'Historiography and Retrospective Econometrics', *History and Theory*, 3, 1970.

—— 'The Limits of Quantitative Methods in History', *American Historical Review*, 80, 1975.

—— 'Scientific History and Traditional History', in L. J. Cohen et al. (eds), *Logic, Methodology, and Philosophy of Science*, VI, North Holland, Amsterdam, 1982.

Fogel, R. W. and Elton, G. R., *Which Road to the Past? Two Views of History*, Yale University Press, New Haven, 1983.

Forester, J. (ed.), *Critical Theory and Public Life*, MIT Press, Cambridge, MA, 1985.

Foucault, M., *The Order of Things*, Tavistock, London, 1970.

—— *The Archaeology of Knowledge*, trans. A. M. Sheridan-Smith, Tavistock, London, 1972.

—— *Power/Knowledge*, ed. D. Gordon, trans. C. Gordon, Harvester, Hassocks, 1980.

—— 'Truth and Power', in C. C. Lemert (ed.), *French Sociology*, Columbia University Press, New York, 1981.

—— 'The Subject and Power', in H. L. Dreyfus and P. Rabinow (eds), *Michel Foucault: Beyond Structuralism and Hermeneutics*, Harvester, Brighton, 1982.

Fox-Genovese, E. and Genovese, E., 'The Political Crisis of Social History: A Marxian Perspective', *Journal of Social History*, 10, 1976.

Frankfurt, H. G., 'Freedom of the Will and the Concept of a Person', *Journal of*

Philosophy, LXVIII, 1971. [Reprinted in G. Watson (ed.), *Free Will*, Oxford University Press, Oxford, 1982]

Freund, J., 'German Sociology in the Time of Max Weber', in T. B. Bottomore and R. Nisbet (eds), *A History of Sociological Analysis*, Heinemann, London, 1979.

Friedman, M., *Essays in Positive Economics*, University of Chicago Press, Chicago, 1953.

—— *Capitalism and Freedom*, University of Chicago Press, Chicago, 1962.

Frisby, D., *Sociological Impressionism*, Heinemann, London, 1981.

—— *Georg Simmel*, Ellis Horwood, Chichester and Tavistock, London, 1984.

—— *Fragments of Modernity*, Polity Press, Cambridge, 1985.

Furet, F., 'From Narrative History to History as a Problem', *Diogenes*, no. 89, 1975.

—— 'Beyond the *Annales*', *Journal of Modern History*, 55, 1983.

—— *In the Workshop of History*, University of Chicago Press, Chicago, 1984.

Gadamer, H.-G., 'Hermeneutics and Social Science', *Cultural Hermeneutics*, 2, 1975.

—— 'The Problem of Historical Consciousness', in P. Rabinow and W. M. Sullivan (eds), *Interpretive Social Science: A Reader*, University of California Press, Berkeley, 1979.

Gallie, W. B., *Philosophy and the Historical Understanding*, Chatto and Windus, London, 1964.

Gardiner, P. (ed.), *Theories of History*, The Free Press, New York, 1959.

—— *The Philosophy of History*, Oxford University Press, London, 1974.

Geertz, C., *The Development of the Javanese Economy: A Socio-Cultural Approach*, Center for International Studies, MIT, Cambridge, MA, 1956.

—— 'Religious Belief and Economic Behavior in a Central Javanese Town: Some Preliminary Considerations', *Economic Development and Cultural Change*, 4, 1956.

—— 'Capital Intensive Agriculture in Peasant Society: A Case Study', *Social Research*, 23, 1956. [Reprinted in *Social Research*, 51, 1984]

—— 'Ethos, World View, and the Analysis of Sacred Symbols', *The Antioch Review*, 17, 1957. [Reprinted in C. Geertz, *The Interpretation of Cultures*, 1973]

—— 'Form and Variation in Balinese Village Structure', *American Anthropologist*, 61, 1959.

—— 'Ritual and Social Change: A Javanese Example', *American Anthropologist*, 61, 1959.

—— 'The Javanese Village', in G. W. Skinner (ed.), *Local, Ethnic, and National Loyalties in Village Indonesia: A Symposium*, Yale University Cultural Report Series, 1959.

—— 'The Javanese Kijaji: The Changing Role of a Cultural Broker', *Comparative Studies in Society and History*, 2, 1959–60.

—— *The Religion of Java*, University of Chicago Press, Chicago, 1960.

—— 'Studies in Peasant Life', in B. J. Siegel (ed.), *Biennial Review of Anthropology*, Stanford University Press, Stanford, 1961.

—— 'The Growth of Culture and the Evolution of Mind', in J. Scher (ed.), *Theories of the Mind*, Free Press, New York, 1962. [Reprinted in C. Geertz, *The Interpretation of Cultures*, 1973]

—— 'The Rotating Credit Association: A "Middle Rung" in Development', *Economic Development and Cultural Change*, 10, 1962.

—— 'Social Change and Economic Modernization in Two Indonesian Towns: A Case in Point', in E. E. Hagen, *On the Theory of Social Change*, Dorsey Press, Homewood, 1962.

—— 'The Integrative Revolution: Primordial Sentiments and Civic Politics in the New States', in C. Geertz (ed.), *Old Societies and New States*, Free Press, Glencoe, 1963. [Reprinted in C. Geertz, *The Interpretation of Cultures*, 1973]

—— *Agricultural Involution; the Process of Ecological Change in Indonesia*, University of California Press, Berkeley, 1963.

—— *Peddlers and Princes; Social Development and Economic Change in Two Indonesian Towns*, University of Chicago Press, Chicago, 1963.

—— 'Ideology as a Cultural System', in D. Apter (ed.), *Ideology and Discontent*, Free Press, New York, 1964. [Reprinted in C. Geertz, *The Interpretation of Cultures*, 1973]

—— 'The Transition to Humanity', in S. Tax (ed.), *Horizons of Anthropology*, University of Chicago Press, Chicago, 1964.

—— 'Modernization in a Muslim Society: The Indonesian Case', in R. N. Bellah (ed.), *Religion and Progress in Modern Asia*, Free Press, New York, 1965.

—— *The Social History of an Indonesian Town*, MIT Press, Cambridge, MA, 1965.

—— 'Religion as a Cultural System', in M. Banton (ed.), *Anthropological Approaches to the Study of Religion*, Tavistock, London, 1966. [Reprinted in C. Geertz, *The Interpretation of Cultures*, 1973]

—— 'Are the Javanese Mad?', *Encounter*, XXVII, no. 2, 1966.

—— 'Person, Time, and Conduct in Bali', Yale Southeast Asia Cultural Report Series, no. 14, 1966. [Reprinted in C. Geertz, *The Interpretation of Cultures*, 1973]

—— 'The Impact of the Concept of Culture on the Concept of Man', in J. Platt (ed.), *New Views of the Nature of Man*, Chicago University Press, Chicago, 1966. [Reprinted in C. Geertz, *The Interpretation of Cultures*, 1973]

—— 'Tihingan: A Balinese Village', in Koentjaraningrat (ed.), *Villages in Indonesia*, Cornell University Press, Ithaca, 1967.

—— *Islam Observed*, Yale University Press, New Haven, 1968.

—— 'Thinking as a Moral Act: Ethical Dimensions of Anthropological Fieldwork in the New States', *Antioch Review*, 28, 1968.

—— 'Deep Play: Notes on the Balinese Cockfight', *Daedalus*, no. 101, 1972. [Reprinted in C. Geertz, *The Interpretation of Cultures*, 1973]

—— 'The Wet and the Dry: Traditional Irrigation in Bali and Morocco', *Human Ecology*, 1, 1972.

—— 'Religious Change and Social Order in Soeharto's Indonesia', *Asia*, no. 27, 1972.

—— 'Thick Description: Toward an Interpretive Theory of Culture', in C. Geertz, *The Interpretation of Cultures*, 1973.

—— *The Interpretation of Cultures; Selected Essays*, Basic Books, New York, 1973.

—— 'From the Native's Point of View: On the Nature of Anthropological Understanding', *Bulletin of the American Academy of Arts and Sciences*, 28, 1974. [Reprinted in C. Geertz, *Local Knowledge*, 1983]

—— 'Social Science Policy in a New State: A Programme for the Stimulation of the Social Sciences in Indonesia', *Minerva*, 12, 1974.

—— 'Common Sense as a Cultural System', *Antioch Review*, 33, 1975. [Reprinted in C. Geertz, *Local Knowledge*, 1983]

—— 'Art as a Cultural System', *MLN*, 91, 1976. [Reprinted in C. Geertz, *Local Knowledge*, 1983]

—— 'Centers, Kings, and Charisma! Reflections on the Symbolics of Power', in J. Ben-David and T. N. Clark (eds), *Culture and Its Creators*, University of Chicago Press, Chicago, 1977. [Reprinted in C. Geertz, *Local Knowledge*, 1983]

—— 'Found in Translation: On the Social History of the Moral Imagination', *Georgia Review*, 31, 1977. [Reprinted in C. Geertz, *Local Knowledge*, 1983]

—— 'The Judging of Nations. Some Comments on the Assessment of Regimes in the New States', *European Journal of Sociology*, 18, 1977.

—— 'The Bazaar Economy: Information and Search in Peasant Marketing', *American Economic Review*, Papers and Proceedings, 68, 1978.

—— 'Blurred Genres: The Refiguration of Social Thought', *American Scholar*, Spring 1980. [Reprinted in C. Geertz, *Local Knowledge*, 1983]

—— 'Ports of Trade in Nineteenth-Century Bali', in G. Dalton (ed.), *Research in Economic Anthropology*, vol. 3, JAI Press, Greenwich, 1980.

—— *Negara: The Theatre State in Nineteenth Century Bali*, Princeton University Press, Princeton, 1980.

—— 'The Way We Think Now: Toward An Ethnography of Modern Thought', *Bulletin of the American Academy of Arts and Sciences*, 35, 1982. [Reprinted in C. Geertz, *Local Knowledge*, 1983]

—— 'Local Knowledge: Fact and Law in Comparative Perspective', in C. Geertz, *Local Knowledge*, Basic Books, New York, 1983.

—— *Local Knowledge: Futher Essays in Interpretive Anthropology*, Basic Books, New York, 1983.

—— 'Distinguished Lecture: Anti Anti-Relativism', *American Anthropologist*, 86, 1984.

—— 'Culture and Social Change: The Indonesian Case', *Man*, 19, 1984.

—— 'The Uses of Diversity', in S. M. McMurrin (ed.), *The Tanner Lectures on Human Values*, vol. VII, University of Utah Press, Salt Lake City, 1986.

—— 'Recollections of an Itinerant Career', *Bulletin of Indonesian Economic Studies*, 24, 1988.

—— *Works and Lives*, Stanford University Press, Stanford, 1988.

—— 'Toutes Directions: Reading the Signs in an Urban Sprawl', *International Journal of Middle East Studies*, 21, 1989.

—— 'History and Anthropology', *New Literary History*, 21, 1990.

Geertz, C., Geertz, H. and Rosen, L., *Meaning and Order in Moroccan Society*, Cambridge University Press, Cambridge, 1979.

Geertz, H. and Geertz, C., *Kinship in Bali*, University of Chicago Press, Chicago, 1975.

Gellner, E., *Words and Things*, Victor Gollancz, London, 1959. [Republished by Penguin, Harmondsworth, 1968.]

—— *Thought and Change*, Weidenfeld and Nicolson, London, 1964.

—— *Saints of the Atlas*, University of Chicago Press, Chicago, 1969.

—— *Cause and Meaning in the Social Sciences*, Routledge, London, 1973.

—— *Contemporary Thought and Politics*, Routledge, London, 1974.

—— *The Devil in Modern Philosophy*, Routledge, London, 1974.

—— *Legitimation of Belief*, Cambridge University Press, Cambridge, 1974.

—— *Spectacles and Predicaments*, Cambridge University Press, Cambridge, 1979.

—— *Muslim Society*, Cambridge University Press, Cambridge, 1981.

—— 'What is Structuralisme?' in C. Renfrew, M. J. Rowlands, and B. A. Segraves (eds), *Theory and Explanation in Archaeology*, Academic Press, New York, 1982.

—— 'Relativism and Universals', in B. Lloyd and J. Gay (eds), *Universals of Human Thought*, 1981. [Reprinted in M. Hollis and S. Lukes (eds), *Rationality and Relativism*, Blackwell, Oxford, 1982]

—— *Nations and Nationalism*, Blackwell, Oxford, 1983.

—— 'The Social Roots of Modern Egalitarianism', in G. Andersson (ed.), *Rationality in Science and Politics*, Reidel, Dordrecht, 1984.

—— 'The Scientific Status of the Social Sciences', *International Social Science Journal*, 36, 1984.

—— 'Introduction' to E. Gellner (ed.), *Islamic Dilemmas: Reformers, Nationalists and Industrialization*, Mouton, Berlin, 1985.

—— *Relativism and the Social Sciences*, Cambridge University Press, Cambridge, 1985.

—— 'Three Contemporary Styles of Philosophy', in S. G. Shanker (ed.), *Philosophy in Britain Today*, Croom Helm, London, 1986.

—— *Culture, Identity, and Politics*, Cambridge University Press, Cambridge, 1987.

—— *Plough, Sword and Book: The Structure of Human History*, Collins Harvill, London, 1988.

—— 'Conscious Confusion – A Review of Geertz, *Works and Lives*', *Times Higher Education Supplement*, 22 April, 1988.

—— 'The Politics of Anthropology', *Government and Opposition*, 23, 1988.

—— 'Economic Interpretation of History', in J. Eatwell et al. (eds), *The New Palgrave: Marxian Economics*, Macmillan, London, 1990.

Genovese, E. D., 'The Politics of Class Struggle in the History of Society: An Appraisal of the Work of Eric Hobsbawm', in P. Thane et al. (eds), *The Power of the Past*, Cambridge University Press, Cambridge, 1984.

Gerstein, D., 'To Unpack Micro and Macro: Link Small with Large and Part with Whole', in J. C. Alexander et al. (eds), *The Micro-Macro Link*, University of California Press, Berkeley, 1987.

Giddens, A., *Central Problems in Social Theory*, Macmillan, London, 1979.

—— 'Agency, Institution and Time-Space Analysis', in K. Knorr-Cetina and A. Cicourel (eds), *Advances in Social Theory and Methodology*, Routledge, London, 1981.

—— *A Contemporary Critique of Historical Materialism*, vol. 1, Macmillan, London, 1981.

—— 'Action, Structure, and Power', in P. Secord (ed.), *Explaining Social Behaviour*, Sage, Beverley Hills, 1982. [Reprinted in A. Giddens, *Profiles and Critiques*, 1982]

—— *Profiles and Critiques in Social Theory*, Macmillan, London, 1982.

—— *The Constitution of Society*, Polity Press, Cambridge, 1984.

—— *The Nation State and Violence: A Contemporary Critique of Historical Materialism*, vol. 2, Polity Press, Cambridge, 1985.

—— *Social Theory and Modern Sociology*, Polity Press, Cambridge, 1987.

Giddens, A. and Turner, J. H. (eds), *Social Theory Today*, Polity Press, Cambridge, 1987.

Giere, R. N., 'Constructive Realism', in P. M. Churchland and C. A. Hooker (eds), *Images of Science*, University of Chicago Press, Chicago, 1985.

Giesen, B., 'Beyond Reductionism: Four Models Relating Micro and Macro Levels', in J. C. Alexander et al. (eds), *The Micro-Macro Link*, University of California Press, Berkeley, 1987.

Gislain, J.-J., 'On the Relation of State and Market', *Telos*, 73, 1987.

Gismondi, M.A., ' "The Gift of Theory": A Critique of the Histoire des Mentalités', *Social History*, 10, 1985.

Godelier, M., *The Mental and the Material*, Verso, London, 1986.

Goffman, E., *The Presentation of Self in Everyday Life*, Anchor Books, New York, 1959.

—— *Behavior in Public Places*, Free Press, New York, 1963.

Gould, M., 'Systems Analysis, Macrosociology, and The Generalized Media of Social

Action', in J. Loubser et al. (eds), *Explorations in General Theory in Social Science*, Free Press, New York, 1976.

——*Revolution in the Development of Capitalism*, University of California Press, Berkeley, 1987.

Gourevitch, A. J., 'History and Historical Anthropology', *Diogenes*, no. 151, 1991.

Green, E. J., 'On the Role of Fundamental Theory in Positive Economics', in J. C. Pitt (ed.), *Philosophy in Economics*, Reidel, Dordrecht, 1981.

Gregory, D. and Urry, J. (eds), *Social Relations and Spatial Structures*, Macmillan, London, 1985.

Groenewegen, P., 'Turgot, Beccaria and Smith', in P. Groenewegen and J. Halevi (eds), *Altro Polo: Italian Economics Past and Present*, University of Sydney, Frederick May Foundation, Sydney, 1983.

Gutting, G., 'Scientific Realism Versus Constructive Empiricism: A Dialogue', in P. M. Churchland and C. A. Hooker (eds), *Images of Science*, University of Chicago Press, Chicago, 1985.

Haan, N., Bellah, R. N., Rabinow, P. and Sullivan, W. M. (eds), *Social Sciences as Moral Inquiry*, Columbia University Press, New York, 1983.

Habermas, J., *Theory and Practice*, Heinemann, London, 1974.

——'The Analytic Theory of Science and Dialectics' and 'A Positivistically Bisected Rationalism', in T. W. Adorno, *The Positivist Dispute in German Sociology*, Heinemann, London, 1976.

——*Legitimation Crisis*, Heinemann, London, 1976.

——*Communication and the Evolution of Society*, Heinemann, London, 1979.

——'The New Obscurity: The Crisis of the Welfare State and the Exhaustion of Utopian Energies', *Philosophy and Social Criticism*, 11, 1986.

Hacking, I., *Representing and Intervening*, Cambridge University Press, Cambridge, 1983.

Haddad, L., 'The Evolutionary Economics of Giambattista Vico', in P. Groenewegen and J. Halevi (eds), *Altro Polo: Italian Economics Past and Present*, University of Sydney, Frederick May Foundation, Sydney, 1983.

Hagen, E. E., *On the Theory of Social Change*, Dorsey Press, Homewood, 1962.

Hahn, F. and Hollis, M. (eds), *Philosophy and Economic Theory*, Oxford University Press, Oxford, 1979.

Hall, J. A., 'A la recherche d'identité perdu, or Gellner's Fork', *Philosophy of Social Science*, 13, 1983.

——*Powers and Liberties: The Causes and Consequences of the Rise of the West*, Blackwell, Oxford, 1985.

——(ed.), *States in History*, Blackwell, Oxford, 1986.

——'They Do Things Differently There, or, The Contribution of British Historical Sociology', *British Journal of Sociology*, 40, 1989.

Hammond, J. L. and Hammond, B., *The Rise of Modern Industry*, Methuen, London, 1925.

Hampson, N., *A Social History of the French Revolution*, Routledge, London, 1963.

Hands, D. W., 'Thirteen Theses on Progress in Economic Methodology', *Finnish Economic Papers*, 3, 1990.

Hanfling, O., *Logical Positivism*, Blackwell, Oxford, 1981.

Harré, R., *The Principles of Scientific Thinking*, Macmillan, London, 1970.

—— 'The Constructive Role of Models', in L. Collins (ed.), *The Use of Models in the Social Sciences*, Tavistock, London, 1976.

—— 'The Ethogenic Approach: Theory and Practice', in L. Berkowitz (ed.), *Advances in Experimental Social Psychology*, Academic Press, New York, 1977.

—— 'Architectonic Man: On the Structuring of Lived Experience', in R. H. Brown and S. M. Lyman (eds), *Structure, Consciousness and History*, Cambridge University Press, Cambridge, 1978.

—— *Social Being*, Blackwell, Oxford, 1979.

—— 'Philosophical Aspects of the Micro-Macro Problem', in K. Knorr-Cetina and A. Cicourel (eds), *Advances in Social Theory and Methodology*, Routledge, London, 1981.

—— *Personal Being*, Blackwell, Oxford, 1983.

—— *Varieties of Realism*, Blackwell, Oxford, 1986.

Harré, R. and Jensen, U. J. (eds), *The Philosophy of Evolution*, Harvester, Brighton, 1981.

Harré, R. and Madden, E. H., *Causal Powers: A Theory of Natural Necessity*, Blackwell, Oxford, 1975.

Harré, R. and Secord, P. F., *The Explanation of Social Behaviour*, Blackwell, Oxford, 1972.

Harris, H., *Cultural Materialism: The Struggle for a Science of Culture*, Random House, New York, 1979.

Harte, N. B. (ed.), *The Study of Economic History*, Frank Cass, London, 1971.

Harvey, D., *Explanation in Geography*, Edward Arnold, London, 1969.

Hausman, D. M., 'Are General Equilibrium Theories Explanatory?', in J. C. Pitt (ed.), *Philosophy in Economics*, Reidel, Dordrecht, 1981.

—— 'Explanatory Progress in Economics', *Social Research*, 56, 1989.

Hawthorn, G., *Enlightenment and Despair*, Cambridge University Press, Cambridge, 1976.

Hays, S. P., 'Scientific Versus Traditional History', *Historical Methods*, 17, 1984.

Heath, A., *Rational Choice and Social Exchange*, Cambridge University Press, Cambridge, 1976.

Hechter, M., 'A Theory of Group Solidarity', in M. Hechter (ed.), *The Microfoundations of Macrosociology*, Temple University Press, Philadelphia, 1983.

—— 'Karl Polanyi's Social Theory: A Critique', in M. Hechter (ed.), *The Microfoundations of Macrosociology*, Temple University Press, Philadelphia, 1983.

Hempel, C. G., 'The Function of General Laws in History', *Journal of Philosophy*, 39, 1942.

—— 'Explanation in Science and in History', in R. G. Colodny (ed.), *Frontiers of Science and Philosophy*, University of Pittsburgh Press, Pittsburgh, 1962. [Reprinted in W. Dray (ed.), *Philosophical Analysis and History*, 1966]

—— 'Reasons and Covering Laws in Historical Explanation', in S. Hook (ed.), *Philosophy of History: A Symposium*, New York University Press, New York, 1963. [Reprinted in P. Gardiner (ed.), *The Philosophy of History*, 1974.]

—— *Aspects of Scientific Explanation*, Free Press, New York, 1965.

—— *Philosophy of Natural Science*, Prentice-Hall, Englewood Cliffs, 1966.

—— 'Logical Positivism and the Social Sciences', in P. Achinstein and S. Barker (eds), *The Legacy of Logical Positivism*, Johns Hopkins University Press, Baltimore, 1969.

—— 'On the Standard Conception of Scientific Theories', in M. Rudner and S. Winokur (eds), *Minnesota Studies in Philosophy of Science*, IV, 1970.

—— 'The Meaning of Theoretical Terms: A Critique of the Standard Empiricist

Construal', in P. Suppes et al. (eds), *Logic, Methodology and Philosophy of Science*, North-Holland, Amsterdam, 1973.

Henretta, J. A., 'Social History as Lived and Written', *American Historical Review*, 84, 1979.

Hesse, M., *The Structure of Scientific Inference*, Macmillan, London, 1974.

——*Revolutions and Reconstructions in the Philosophy of Science*, Harvester, Hassocks, 1980.

Hill, C., *The Century of Revolution*, Nelson, London, 1961.

——*Society and Puritanism in Pre-Revolutionary England*, Secker and Warburg, London, 1964.

——*Intellectual Origins of the English Revolution*, Oxford University Press, Oxford, 1965.

——*Milton and the English Revolution*, Faber, London, 1977.

——*Reformation to Industrial Revolution*, Weidenfeld and Nicolson, London, 1967.

——*The World Turned Upside Down*, Temple Smith, London, 1972.

Hilton, R., *A Medieval Society*, Weidenfeld and Nicolson, London, 1966.

——*Bond Men Made Free*, Methuen, London, 1973.

——*The English Peasantry in the Later Middle Ages*, Oxford University Press, Oxford, 1975.

——'Feudalism in Europe: Problems for Historians', *New Left Review*, no. 147, 1984.

Himmelfarb, G., *The New History and the Old*, Harvard University Press, Cambridge MA, 1987.

——'Some Reflections on the New History', *American Historical Review*, 94, 1989.

Hirsch, P., Michaels, S. and Friedman, R., ' "Dirty Hands" versus "Clean Models". Is Sociology in Danger of Being Seduced by Economics?', *Theory and Society*, 16, 1987.

Hirschman, A. O., *Journeys Toward Progress*, W. W. Norton, New York, 1963.

——*Exit, Voice, and Loyalty*, Harvard University Press, Cambridge MA, 1970.

——*The Passions and the Interests*, Princeton University Press, Princeton, 1977.

——*Shifting Involvements*, Martin Robertson, Oxford, 1982.

Hirst, P., 'The Necessity of Theory', *Economy and Society*, 8, 1979.

Hobsbawm, E. J., 'Karl Marx's Contribution to Historiography', *Diogenes*, no. 64, 1968. [Reprinted in R. Blackburn (ed.), *Ideology in Social Science*, Fontana, London, 1972]

——'From Social History to the History of Society', *Daedalus*, no. 100, 1971. [Reprinted in M. W. Flinn and T. C. Smout (eds), *Essays in Social History*, Oxford University Press, Oxford, 1974]

——'The Social Function of the Past: Some Questions', *Past and Present*, no. 55, 1972.

——*The Age of Revolution*, Weidenfeld and Nicolson, London, 1972.

——*The Age of Capital*, Weidenfeld and Nicolson, London, 1975.

——'The Historians' Group of the Communist Party', in M. Cornforth (ed.), *Rebels and their Causes*, Lawrence and Wishart, London, 1978.

——'The Revival of Narrative: Some Comments', *Past and Present*, no. 86, 1980.

——'The Contribution of History to Social Science', *International Social Science Journal*, 32, 1981.

——'Looking Forward: History and the Future', *New Left Review*, no. 125, 1981.

——'Marx and History', *New Left Review*, no. 143, 1984.

——*The Age of Empire*, Weidenfeld and Nicolson, London, 1987.

——'History From Below – Some Reflections', in F. Krantz (ed.), *History From Below*, Blackwell, Oxford, 1988.

Hodgson, G. M., *Economics and Institutions: A Manifesto for a Modern Institutional Economics*, Polity Press, Cambridge, 1988.

——'Institutional Economic Theory: The Old Versus the New', *Review of Political Economy*, 1, 1989.

Hollis, M. and Nell, E., *Rational Economic Man*, Cambridge University Press, Cambridge, 1975.

Homans, G. C., *English Villages of the Thirteenth Century*, Harvard University Press, Harvard, 1941.

——*The Human Group*, Routledge, London, 1951.

——*Social Behaviour: Its Elementary Forms*, Routledge, London, 1961.

——'Bringing Men Back In', *American Sociological Review*, 29, 1964. [Reprinted in A. Ryan (ed.), *Philosophy of Social Science*, Oxford University Press, Oxford, 1973]

——'Contemporary Theory in Sociology', in R. E. L. Faris (ed.), *Handbook of Modern Sociology*, Rand McNally, Chicago, 1964.

——'Fundamental Social Processes', in N. Smelser (ed.), *Sociology: An Introduction*, John Wiley, New York, 1967.

——*The Nature of Social Science*, Harcourt, Brace and World, New York, 1967.

——'The Relevance of Psychology to the Explanation of Social Phenomena', in R. Borger and F. Cioffi (eds), *Explanation in the Behavioural Sciences*, Cambridge University Press, Cambridge, 1970.

——'What Do We Mean by Social "Structure"?', in P. Blau (ed.), *Approaches to the Study of Social Structure*, Open Books, London, 1976.

——'Nature vs Nurture: A False Dichotomy', *Contemporary Sociology*, 8, 1979.

——'The Present State of Sociological Theory', *Sociological Quarterly*, 23, 1982.

——'Behaviourism and After', in A. Giddens and J. H. Turner (eds), *Social Theory Today*, Polity Press, Cambridge, 1987.

Hondrich, K. O., 'Micro Pathology and Macro Normality', in J. C. Alexander et al. (eds), *The Micro-Macro Link*, University of California Press, Berkeley, 1987.

Hooker, C. A., 'An Evolutionary Naturalist Realist Doctrine of Perception and Secondary Qualities', in C. W. Savage (ed.), *Minnesota Studies in Philosophy of Science*, IX, 1978.

——*A Realistic Theory of Science*, State University of New York Press, Albany, 1987.

Hopkins, T. K., 'Sociology and the Substantive View of the Economy', in K. Polanyi, C. M. Arensberg and H. W. Pearson (eds), *Trade and Market in the Early Empires*, Free Press, New York, 1957.

Horton, R., 'African Traditional Thought and Western Science', *Africa*, XXXVII, 1967. [Reprinted in B. Wilson (ed.), *Rationality*, Blackwell, Oxford, 1974]

——'Tradition and Modernity Revisited', in M. Hollis and S. Lukes (eds), *Rationality and Relativism*, Blackwell, Oxford, 1982.

Horwich, P., 'Three Forms of Realism', *Synthèse*, 51, 1982.

Hoselitz, B. F. (ed.), *The Progress of Underdeveloped Areas*, University of Chicago Press, Chicago, 1952.

——*Sociological Aspects of Economic Growth*, Free Press, New York, 1960.

Hoselitz, B. F. and Moore, W. E. (eds), *Industrialization and Society*, UNESCO, Mouton, Paris, 1963.

Hoskins, W. G., *The Making of the English Landscape*, Hodder and Stoughton, London, 1955.

——*The Age of Plunder: King Henry's England, 1500–1547*, Longman, London, 1976.

Howson, C., 'Fitting Your Theory to the Facts: Probably Not such a Bad Thing after all', in C. W. Savage (ed.), *Minnesota Studies in the Philosophy of Science*, XIV, 1990.

Hunt, L., 'French History in the Last Twenty Years: The Rise and Fall of the Annales Paradigm', *Journal of Contemporary History*, 21, 1986.

—— 'Introduction': History, Culture, and Text', in L. Hunt (ed.), *The New Cultural History*, University of California Press, Berkeley, 1989.

Hutnyk, J., 'Clifford Geertz as a Cultural System: A Review Article', *Social Analysis*, no. 26, 1989.

Hutton, P. H., 'The History of Mentalities: The New Map of Cultural History', *History and Theory*, XX, 1981.

Ibn Khaldûn, *The Muquddimah: An Introduction to History*, trans. F. Rosenthal, 3 vols, Routledge, London, 1958.

Iggers, G. G. (ed.), *The Doctrine of Saint-Simon: An Exposition, First Year 1828–1829*, Schocken Books, New York, 1972.

—— *The German Conception of History*, rev. ed., Wesleyan University Press, Middletown, 1983.

—— *New Directions in European Historiography*, rev. ed., Wesleyan University Press, Middletown, 1984.

Jacques, T. C., 'The Primacy of Narrative in Historical Understanding', *Clio*, 19, 1990.

James, J. A., 'The Use of General Equilibrium Analysis in Economic History', *Explorations in Economic History*, 21, 1984.

Johnson, R., 'Barrington Moore, Perry Anderson and English Social Development', *Working Papers in Cultural Studies*, no. 9, 1976.

Jones, E. L., *The European Miracle*, Cambridge University Press, Cambridge, 1981.

—— *Growth Recurring: Economic Change in World History*, Oxford University Press, Oxford, 1988.

Jones, G. S., 'From Historical Sociology to Theoretic History', *British Journal of Sociology*, 27, 1976.

Jordanova, L. J. (ed.), *Languages of Nature*, Free Association Books, London, 1986.

Kadish, A., *Historians, Economists, and Economic History*, Routledge, London, 1989.

Kant, I., *On History*, ed. L. W. Beck, Bobbs-Merrill, Indianapolis, 1963.

Käsler, D., *Max Weber: An Introduction to his Life and Work*, Polity Press, Cambridge, 1988.

Kaye, H. J., *The British Marxist Historians*, Polity Press, Cambridge, 1984.

Keat, R. and Urry, J., *Social Theory as Science*, Routledge, London, 1975.

Kellerman, A., 'Structuration Theory and Attempts at Integration in Human Geography', *Professional Geography*, 39, 1987.

Kenyon, J., *The History Men*, Weidenfeld and Nicolson, London, 1983.

Kiernan, V. G., *State and Society in Europe, 1550–1650*, Blackwell, Oxford, 1980.

—— *Lords of Human Kind*, Columbia University Press, New York, 1986.

Kim, J., 'Causality, Identity, and Supervenience', *Midwest Studies in Philosophy*, IV, 1979.

Kincaid, H., 'Reduction, Explanation, and Individualism', *Philosophy of Science*, 53, 1986.

—— 'Eliminative and Methodological Individualism', *Philosophy of Science*, 57, 1990.

Kindleberger, C. P., *Economic Laws and Economic History*, Cambridge University Press, Cambridge, 1989.

Kitcher, P., 'Explanatory Unification', *Philosophy of Science*, 48, 1981. [Reprinted in J. C. Pitt (ed.), *Theories of Explanation*, Oxford University Press, New York, 1988]

——'Two Approaches to Explanation', *Journal of Philosophy*, 82, 1985.

——'Explanatory Unification and the Causal Structure of the World', in P. Kitcher and W.C. Salmon (eds), *Minnesota Studies in Philosophy of Science*, XIII, 1989.

Kitcher, P. and Salmon, W. C. (eds), 'Scientific Explanation', *Minnesota Studies in the Philosophy of Science*, XIII, 1989.

Klein, P. A., 'Institutionalism as a School – A Reconsideration', *Journal of Economic Institutions*, XXIV, 1990.

Knorr-Cetina, K. D., 'The Micro-Sociological Challenge to Macro Sociology: Towards a Reconstruction of Social Theory and Methodology', in K. Knorr-Cetina and A. Cicourel (eds), *Advances in Social Theory and Methodology*, Routledge and Kegan Paul, London, 1981.

——'Social and Scientific Method, or What do we Make of the Distinction Between the Natural and Social Sciences?', *Philosophy of Social Sciences*, 11, 1981.

Knorr-Cetina, K. D. and Cicourel, A.V. (eds), *Advances in Social Theory and Methodology*, Routledge and Kegan Paul, London, 1981.

Kolakowski, L., *Positivist Philosophy*, rev. ed., Penguin, Harmondsworth, 1972.

Koot, G. M., *English Historical Economics 1870–1926*, Cambridge University Press, Cambridge, 1987.

Korsch, K., *Marxism and Philosophy*, NLB, London, 1970. [Originally published in 1923]

Koselleck, R., 'Linguistic Change and the History of Events', *Journal of Modern History*, 61, 1989.

Kousser, J. M., 'Quantitative Social-Scientific History', in M. Kammen (ed.), *The Past Before Us*, Cornell University Press, Ithaca, 1980.

Krantz, F. (ed.), *History From Below*, Blackwell, Oxford, 1988.

Kripke, S., 'Identity and Necessity', in T. Honderich and M. Burnyeat (eds), *Philosophy As It Is*, Penguin, Harmondsworth, 1979. [Originally published in 1971]

——*Naming and Necessity*, rev. ed., Blackwell, Oxford, 1980.

Kuhn, T. S., *The Structure of Scientific Revolutions*, 2nd ed., University of Chicago Press, Chicago, 1970. [Originally published in 1962]

——'Logic of Discovery or Psychology of Research', in I. Lakatos and A. Musgrave (eds), *Criticism and The Growth of Knowledge*, Cambridge University Press, Cambridge, 1970.

——'Objectivity, Value Judgment, and Theory Choice', in T. S. Kuhn, *The Essential Tension*, University of Chicago Press, Chicago, 1977.

——'Second Thoughts on Paradigms', in F. Suppe (ed.), *The Structure of Scientific Theories*, 2nd ed., University of Illinois Press, Urbana, 1977.

——'Commensurability, Comparability, Communicability', in P. D. Asquith and T. Nickles (eds), *PSA 1982*, vol. 2, Philosophy of Science Association, East Lansing, 1982.

Kurzweil, E., 'Psychoanalysis as the Macro-Micro Link', in J. C. Alexander et al. (eds), *The Micro-Macro Link*, University of California Press, Berkeley, 1987.

Kyburg, H. E., 'Theories as Mere Conventions', in C. W. Savage (ed.), *Minnesota Studies in Philosophy of Science*, XIV, 1990.

Labriola, A., *Essays on the Materialist Conception of History*, Charles H. Kerr, Chicago, 1908. [Originally published in 1896]

La Capra, D., *History and Criticism*, Cornell University Press, Ithaca, 1985.

—— *Soundings in Critical Theory*, Cornell University Press, Ithaca, 1989.

Lacoste, Y., *Ibn Khaldûn: The Birth of History and the Past of the Third World*, Verso, London, 1984.

Lakatos, I., 'Falsification and the Methodology of Scientific Programmes', in I. Lakatos and A. Musgrave (eds), *Criticism and the Growth of Knowledge*, Cambridge University Press, Cambridge, 1970.

—— 'History of Science and its Rational Reconstructions', in R. C. Buck and R. S. Cohen (eds), *PSA 1970*, Reidel, Dordrecht, 1971. [Reprinted in I. Hacking (ed.), *Scientific Revolutions*, Oxford University Press, Oxford, 1981]

—— 'The Problem of Appraising Scientific Theories: Three Approaches', in I. Lakatos, *Science and Philosophy*, Cambridge University Press, Cambridge, 1978.

Lakatos, I. and Musgrave, A. (eds), *Criticism and the Growth of Knowledge*, Cambridge University Press, Cambridge, 1970.

Langlois, R. N., 'Rationality, Institutions, and Explanation', in R. N. Langlois (ed.), *Economics as a Process: Essays in the New Institutional Economics*, Cambridge University Press, Cambridge, 1986.

—— 'The New Institutional Economics: An Introductory Essay', in R. N. Langlois (ed.), *Economics as a Process: Essays in the New Institutional Economics*, Cambridge University Press, Cambridge, 1986.

—— 'What was Wrong with the Old Institutional Economics (And What is Still Wrong with the New)?', *Review of Political Economy*, 1, 1989.

Larrain, J., *A Reconstruction of Historical Materialism*, Allen and Unwin, London, 1986.

Laslett, P., 'Introduction: The Necessity of a Historical Sociology', in P. Laslett (ed.), *Family Life and Illicit Love in Earlier Generations: Essays in Historical Sociology*, Cambridge University Press, Cambridge, 1977.

—— *The World we have Lost Further Explored*, Methuen, London, 1983.

Laudan, L., *Progress and its Problems*, Routledge, London, 1977.

—— 'A Confutation of Convergent Realism', *Philosophy of Science*, 48, 1981.

—— 'A Problem-Solving Approach to Scientific Progress', in I. Hacking (ed.), *Scientific Revolutions*, Oxford University Press, Oxford, 1982.

—— 'Explaining the Success of Science: Beyond Epistemic Realism and Relativism', in J. T. Cushing, C. F. Delaney and G. M. Gutting (eds), *Science and Reality*, University of Notre Dame Press, Notre Dame, 1984.

LeGoff, J., 'Mentalities: A History of Ambiguities', in J. LeGoff and P. Nora (eds), *Constructing the Past*, Cambridge University Press, Cambridge, 1985.

Lenin, V. I., *Materialism and Empirio-Criticism*, trans. A. Fineberg, Progress, London, 1970. [Originally published in 1908]

Leplin, J., 'Methodological Realism and Scientific Rationality', *Philosophy of Science*, 53, 1986.

Lerner, D., *The Passing of Traditional Society*, Free Press, Glencoe, 1963.

Le Roy Ladurie, E., *Times of Feast, Times of Famine: A History of The Climate Since the Year 1000*, trans. B. Bray, Allen and Unwin, London, 1972.

—— 'History and Climate', reprinted in P. Burke (ed.), *Economy and Society in Early Modern Europe*, Harper Torchbooks, New York, 1972.

—— *The Peasants of Languedoc*, trans. J. Day, University of Illinois Press, Urbana, 1974.

—— 'Occitania in Historical Perspective', *Review*, I, 1977.

—— 'Agrarian Class Structure and Economic Development in Pre-Industrial Europe: A Reply to Robert Brenner', *Past and Present*, No. 79, 1978.

—— *The Territory of the Historian*, trans. B. and S. Reynolds, Harvester, Hassocks, 1979.

—— *Montaillou*, trans. B. Bray, Scolar Press, London, 1978.

—— *Carnival in Romans*, trans. M. Feeney, Scolar Press, London, 1980.

—— *The Mind and Method of the Historian*, trans. S. and B. Reynolds, Harvester, Hassocks, 1981.

—— 'Carnivals in History', *Thesis Eleven*, 3, 1981.

—— *Love, Death and Money in the Pays d'Oc*, trans. A. Sheridan, Scolar Press, London, 1982.

—— *Jasmin's Witch*, Scolar Press, Aldershot, 1987.

—— *The French Peasantry, 1450–1660*, trans. A. Sheridan, Scolar Press, Aldershot, 1987.

—— 'History in France', in L. Appignanesi (ed.), *Ideas From France: The Legacy of French Theory*, Free Association Books, London, 1989.

Le Roy Ladurie, E. and Goy, J., *Tithe and Agrarian History from the 14th to the 19th Centuries*, trans. S. Burke, Cambridge University Press, Cambridge, 1982.

Levine, N., 'The German Historical School and The Origins of Historical Materialism', *Journal of the History of Ideas*, XLVIII, 1987.

Lévi-Strauss, C., *The Savage Mind*, Weidenfeld and Nicolson, London, 1966. [Originally published in 1962]

Levy, M. J., *The Structure of Society*, Princeton University Press, Princeton, 1952.

Levy, R. J., 'The Quest for Mind in Different Times and Different Places', in A. E. Barnes and P. Stearns (eds), *Social History and Issues in Human Consciousness*, New York University Press, New York, 1989.

Lévy-Garboua, L. (ed.), *Sociological Economics*, Sage, London, 1979.

Lindert, P. H. and Williamson, J. G., 'Growth, Equality, and History', *Explorations in Economic History*, 22, 1985.

Lloyd, C., *Explanation in Social History*, Blackwell, Oxford, 1986.

—— 'Realism, Structurism, and History: Foundations for a Transformative Science of Society', *Theory and Society*, 18, 1989.

—— 'Realism and Structurism in Historical Theory: A Discussion of the Thought of Maurice Mandelbaum', *History and Theory*, 28, 1989.

—— 'The Methodologies of Social History: A Critical Survey and Defence of Structurism', *History and Theory*, 30, 1991.

Lloyd, G. E. R., *Demystifying Mentalities*, Cambridge University Press, Cambridge, 1990.

Lowith, K., *Max Weber and Karl Marx*, Allen and Unwin, London, 1982.

Luckmann, T. (ed.), *Phenomenology and Sociology*, Penguin, Harmondsworth, 1978.

Lyman, S. M., 'The Science of History and the Theory of Social Change', in R. M. Glassman and V. Murvar (eds), *Max Weber's Political Sociology*, Greenwood, Westport, 1984.

Lyman, S. M. and Scott, M. B., *The Drama of Social Reality*, Oxford University Press, New York, 1975.

Lyotard, J.-F., *The Postmodern Condition: A Report on Knowledge*, University of Minnesota Press, Minneapolis, 1984.

McClelland, D. C., *The Achieving Society*, Free Press, New York, 1961.

McClelland, P. D., *Causal Explanation and Model Building in History, Economics, and the New Economic History*, Cornell University Press, Ithaca, 1975.

McCloskey, D. N., 'The Achievements of the Cliometric School', *Journal of Economic History*, 38, 1978.
——'Economics as an Historical Science', in W. N. Parker (ed.), *Economic History and the Modern Economist*, Blackwell, Oxford, 1986.
——*Econometric History*, Macmillan, London, 1987.
——'Towards a Rhetoric of Economics', in G. C. Winston and R. F. Teichgraeber (eds), *The Boundaries of Economics*, Cambridge University Press, Cambridge, 1988.
McCullagh, C. B., 'The Unifying Themes of Historical Narratives', *Philosophy of Social Science*, 19, 1989.
Macfarlane, A., 'History, Anthropology and the Study of Communities', *Social History*, 5, 1977.
——*The Origins of English Individualism*, Blackwell, Oxford, 1978.
McGinn, C., 'An a priori Argument for Realism', *Journal of Philosophy*, LXXVI, 1979.
Mackie, J. L., *The Cement of the Universe*, Clarendon Press, Oxford, 1974.
McMichael, P., 'Incorporating Comparison Within a World-Historical Perspective: An Alternative Comparative Method', *American Sociological Review*, 55, 1990.
McMullin, E., 'Empiricism at Sea', in R. S. Cohen and M. Wartofsky (eds), *Methodological and Historical Essays in the Natural and Social Sciences*, Reidel, Dordrecht, 1974.
——'The Goals of Natural Science', *American Philosophical Association, Proceedings and Addresses*, 58, 1984.
——'Explanatory Success and the Truth of Theory', in N. Rescher (ed.), *Scientific Inquiry in Philosophical Perspective*, University Press of America, Lanham, 1987.
McNeill, W. H., *Plagues and Peoples*, Blackwell, Oxford, 1977.
——*The Human Condition: An Ecological and Historical View*, Princeton University Press, Princeton, 1980.
——*The Pursuit of Power: Technology, Armed Force, and Society Since AD 1000*, Blackwell, Oxford, 1983.
Magarey, S., 'Labour History's New Sub-Title: Social History in Australia in 1981', *Social History*, 8, 1983.
——'That Hoary Old Chestnut, Free Will and Determinism: Culture vs Structure, or History vs Theory in Britain', *Comparative Studies in Society and History*, 29, 1987.
Mah, H., 'Suppressing the Text: The Metaphysics of Ethnographic History in Darnton's Great Cat Massacre', *History Workshop*, no. 31, 1991.
Mäki, U., 'Methodology of Economics: Complaints and Guidelines', *Finnish Economic Papers*, 3, 1990.
Maloney, J., 'English Historical School', in J. Eatwell et al. (eds), *The New Palgrave*, vol. 2, Macmillan, London, 1987.
Mandelbaum, M., *The Problem of Historical Knowledge*, Harper Torchbooks, New York, 1967. [Originally published in 1938]
——'The Philosophy of History: Some Neglected Problems Regarding History', *Journal of Philosophy*, 49, 1952. [Reprinted in M. Mandelbaum, *Philosophy, History and the Sciences*, 1984]
——'Societal Facts', *British Journal of Sociology*, 6, 1955.
——'Societal Laws', *British Journal for the Philosophy of Science*, 8, 1957.
——'Historical Explanation: The Problem of Covering Laws', *History and Theory*, 1, 1961. [Reprinted in P. Gardiner (ed.), *Philosophy of History*, Oxford University Press, 1974]

——*Philosophy, Science, and Sense Perception*, Johns Hopkins University Press, Baltimore, 1964.

——*History, Man, and Reason*, Johns Hopkins University Press, Baltimore, 1971.

——*The Anatomy of Historical Knowledge*, Johns Hopkins University Press, Baltimore, 1977.

——'Subjective, Objective, and Conceptual Relativisms', *Monist*, 62, 1979. [Reprinted in M. Mandelbaum, *Philosophy, History, and the Sciences*, 1984]

——'The Presuppositions of Hayden White's "Metahistory"', *History and Theory*, Beiheft 19, 1980. [Reprinted in M. Mandelbaum, *Philosophy, History and the Sciences*, 1984]

——*Philosophy, History, and the Sciences: Selected Critical Essays*, Johns Hopkins University Press, Baltimore, 1984.

——*Purpose and Necessity in Social Theory*, Johns Hopkins University Press, Baltimore, 1987.

Manicas, P. T., 'Implications for Psychology of the New Philosophy of Science', *American Psychologist*, 38, 1983.

——'Reduction, Epigenesis and Explanation', *Journal for the Theory of Social Behaviour*, 13, 1983.

Mann, M., *The Sources of Social Power, vol. 1. A History of Power from the Beginning to AD 1760*, Cambridge University Press, Cambridge, 1986.

——*States, War, and Capitalism*, Blackwell, Oxford, 1988.

Manuel, F. E., *The Prophets of Paris*, Harvard University Press, Cambridge, 1962.

Margolis, J., 'Scientific Realism, Ontology, and the Sensory Modes', *Philosophy of Science*, 37, 1970.

——'Relativism, History and Objectivity in the Human Studies', *Journal for the Theory of Social Behaviour*, 14, 1984.

——'Emergence', *The Philosophical Forum*, XVII, 1986.

Markus, G., 'Why is There No Hermeneutics of Natural Sciences? Some Preliminary Theses', *Science in Context*, 1, 1987.

Martinelli, A., 'The Economy as an Institutional Process', *Telos*, no. 73, 1987.

Martinelli, A. and Smelser, N. J., *Economy and Society*, Sage, London, 1990.

——'Economic Sociology: Historical Threads and Analytic Issues', in A. Martinelli and N. J. Smelser (eds), *Economy and Society*, Sage, London, 1990.

Marx, K., *Grundrisse*, trans. M. Nicolaus, Penguin, Harmondsworth, 1973. [Originally written in 1857–8]

——*Theories of Surplus Value*, Progress, Moscow, 1963–71.

——*Capital*, 3 vols, Progress, Moscow, 1971.

Marx, K. and Engels, F., *Selected Works*, 3 vols, Progress, Moscow, 1970.

Mathew, A., 'Contrasting Origins of the Two Institutionalisms: The Social Science Context', *Review of Political Economy*, 1, 1989.

Mathias, P., *The First Industrial Nation*, Methuen, London, 1969.

Mathien, T., 'Network Analysis and Methodological Individualism', *Philosophy of Social Science*, 18, 1988.

Medick, H., ' "Missionaries in the Row Boat?" Ethnological Ways of Knowing as a Challenge to Social History', *Comparative Studies in Society and History*, 29, 1987.

Meehl, P. E. and Sellars, W., 'The Concept of Emergence', in H. Feigl and M. Scriven (eds), *Minnesota Studies in Philosophy of Science*, I, 1956.

Meek, R., *Social Science and the Ignoble Savage*, Cambridge University Press, Cambridge, 1976.

Megill, A., 'Foucault, Structuralism, and the Ends of History', *Journal of Modern History*, 51, 1979.

―――*Prophets of Extremity*, University of California Press, Berkeley, 1985.

―――'The Reception of Foucault by Historians', *Journal of the History of Ideas*, 48, 1987.

Megill, A., 'Recounting the Past: "Description", Explanation, and Narrative in Historiography', *American Historical Review*, 94, 1989.

Megill, A. and McCloskey, D., 'The Rhetoric of History', in J. S. Nelson, A. Megill, and D. N. McCloskey (eds), *The Rhetoric of the Human Sciences*, University of Wisconsin, Madison, 1987.

Mennell, S., *Norbert Elias: Civilization and the Human Self-Image*, Blackwell, Oxford, 1989.

Merrill, G. H., 'Three Forms of Realism', *American Philosophical Quarterly*, 17, 1980.

Meyer, J. R. and Conrad, A. H., 'Economic Theory, Statistical Inference, and Economic History', *Journal of Economic History*, 17, 1957.

Miller, R. W., *Analyzing Marx: Morality, Power, and History*, Princeton University Press, Princeton, 1984.

Miller, R. W., *Fact and Method*, Princeton University Press, Princeton, 1987.

Mink, L. O., 'The Autonomy of Historical Understanding', *History and Theory*, V, 1965. [Reprinted in W. Dray (ed.), *Philosophical Analysis and History*, Harper and Row, New York, 1966.]

―――'The Divergence of History and Sociology in Recent Philosophy of History', in P. Suppes et al. (eds), *Logic, Methodology, and Philosophy of Science IV*, Amsterdam, North Holland, 1973.

―――'Narrative Form as a Cognitive Instrument', in R. H. Canary and H. Kozicki (eds), *The Writing of History*, University of Wisconsin Press, Madison, 1978.

―――'Philosophy and Theory of History', in G. Iggers and H. Parker (eds), *International Handbook of Historical Studies*, Methuen, London, 1979.

Mirowski, P., *Against Mechanism: Protecting Economics From Science*, Rowman and Littlefield, Totowa, 1988.

―――*More Heat Than Light*, Cambridge University Press, Cambridge, 1989.

Mjoset, L., 'The Limits of Neoclassical Institutionalism', *Journal of Peace Research*, 22, 1985.

Mommsen, W. J. and Osterhammel, J. (eds), *Max Weber and his Contemporaries*, Unwin Hyman, London, 1987.

Monkkonen, E. H., 'The Challenge of Quantitative History', *Historical Methods*, 17, 1984.

Moore, B., *Social Origins of Dictatorship and Democracy*, Allen Lane, London, 1967.

―――*Injustice: The Social Bases of Obedience and Revolt*, Macmillan, London, 1978.

Moore, W. E., 'Functionalism', in T. Bottomore and R. Nisbet (eds), *A History of Sociological Analysis*, Heinemann, London, 1979.

Münch, R., 'The Interpretation of Microinteraction and Macrostructures in a Complex and Contingent Institutional Order', in J. C. Alexander et al. (eds), *The Micro-Macro Link*, University of California Press, Berkeley, 1987.

Münch, R. and Smelser, N. J., 'Relating the Micro and Macro', in J. C. Alexander et al. (eds), *The Micro-Macro Link*, University of California Press, Berkeley, 1987.

Murphy, J., 'The Voice of Memory: History, Autobiography, and Oral Memory', *Historical Studies*, 22, 1986.

―――'Scientific Realism and Postmodern Philosophy', *British Journal of Philosophy of Science*, 41, 1990.

Nagel, E., *The Structure of Science*, Routledge, London, 1961.

Nash, M. (ed.), 'Essays on Economic Development and Cultural Change in Honor of Bert F. Hoselitz', *Economic Development and Cultural Change*, 25, Supplement, 1977.

Neale, R. S., 'Introduction: Social History', in R. S. Neale (ed.), *Class in English History*, Blackwell, Oxford, 1981.

—— *Bath: A Social History 1680–1850*, Routledge, London, 1981.

—— *Writing Marxist History*, Blackwell, Oxford, 1985.

Nelson, A., 'Are Economic Kinds Natural?', in C. W. Savage (ed.), *Minnesota Studies in Philosophy of Science*, XIV, 1990.

Nelson, B., *The Idea of Usury*, Princeton University Press, Princeton, 1949.

—— *On the Roads to Modernity (Selected Essays)*, Rowman and Littlefield, Totowa, 1981.

Nelson, J. S., Megill, A. and McCloskey, D. N., 'Rhetoric of Inquiry', in J. S. Nelson, A. Megill and D. N. McCloskey (eds), *The Rhetoric of the Human Sciences*, University of Wisconsin Press, Madison, 1987.

Neurath, O., *Empiricism and Sociology*, Reidel, Dordrecht, 1973.

Newton-Smith, W. H., *The Rationality of Science*, Routledge, London, 1981.

Nield, K., 'A Symptomatic Dispute? Notes on the Relation Between Marxian Theory and Historical Practice in Britain', *Social Research*, 47, 1980.

Nield, K. and Seed, J., 'Theoretical Poverty or the Poverty of Theory: British Marxist Historiography and the Althusserians', *Economy and Society*, 8, 1979.

Nielsen, K., 'A Rationale for Egalitarianism', *Social Research*, 48, 1981.

North, D. C., 'Institutional Change and Economic Growth', *Journal of Economic History*, 31, 1971.

—— 'Markets and Other Allocation Systems in History: The Challenge of Karl Polanyi', *Journal of European Economic History*, 6, 1977.

—— 'Structure and Performance: The Tasks of Economic History', *Journal of Economic Literature*, XVI, 1978.

—— *Structure and Change in Economic History*, W. W. Norton, New York, 1981.

—— 'A Theory of Institutional Change and the Economic History of the Western World', in M. Hechter (ed.), *The Microfoundations of Macrosociology*, Temple University Press, Philadelphia, 1983.

—— 'Three Approaches to the Study of Institutions', in D. C. Collander (ed.), *Neo-Classical Political Economy*, Ballinger, Cambridge MA, 1984.

—— 'Institutions and their Consequences for Economic Performance', in K. S. Cook and M. Levi (eds), *The Limits of Rationality*, University of Chicago Press, Chicago, 1990.

—— *Institutions, Institutional Change, and Economic Performance*, Cambridge University Press, Cambridge, 1990.

—— 'Institutions', *Journal of Economic Perspectives*, 5, 1991.

North, D. C. and Thomas, R. P., *The Rise of the Western World*, Cambridge University Press, Cambridge, 1973.

Olson, M., *The Rise and Decline of Nations*, Yale University Press, New Haven, 1982.

—— 'Economy, Logic, and Action', *Society*, 29, 1990.

Opp, K.-D., 'Group Size, Emergence, and Composition Laws: Are There Macroscopic Theories sui generis', *Philosophy of Social Science*, 9, 1979.

—— 'What Can We Learn from the Utilitarian Tradition?', *Contemporary Sociology*, 17, 1988.

Parijs, P. van, 'Sociology as General Economics', *European Journal of Sociology*, 22, 1981.
——*Evolutionary Explanation in the Social Sciences*, Tavistock, London, 1981.
Parker, W. N., 'From Old to New to Old in Economic History', *Journal of Economic History*, 31, 1971.
——(ed.), *Economic History and The Modern Economist*, Blackwell, Oxford, 1986.
Parsons, T., *The Social System*, Free Press, New York, 1951.
——*Societies: Evolutionary and Comparative Perspectives*, Prentice-Hall, Englewood Cliffs, 1966.
——'On Building Social Systems Theory: A Personal History', *Daedalus*, 99, 1970.
Parsons, T. and Shils, E. (eds), *Toward a General Theory of Action*, Harper and Row, New York, 1951.
Parsons, T. and Smelser, N. J., *Economy and Society*, Routledge, London, 1956.
Perkin, H., 'Social History', in H. P. R. Finberg (ed.), *Approaches to History*, Routledge, London, 1962.
——*The Origins of Modern English Society, 1780–1880*, Routledge, London, 1969.
——'Social History in Britain', *Journal of Social History*, 10, 1976.
Philipp, J. 'Traditional Historical Narrative and Action-Oriented (or Ethnographic) History', *Historical Studies*, no. 80, 1983.
Piaget, J., *Structuralism*, trans. C. Maschler, Routledge, London, 1971.
——*Psychology and Epistemology*, trans. P. A. Wells, Penguin, Harmondsworth, 1972.
——*The Principles of Genetic Epistemology*, trans. W. Mays, Routledge, London, 1972.
Plekhanov, G., *The Development of the Monist View of History*, trans. A. Rothstein, Progress, Moscow, 1956. [Originally published in 1895]
Plumb, J. H. (ed.), *Studies in Social History*, Longmans, London, 1955.
Polanyi, K., *The Great Transformation*, Beacon Press, Boston, 1944.
——'The Economy as Instituted Process', in K. Polanyi, C. M. Arensberg and H. W. Pearson (eds), *Trade and Market in the Early Empires*, Free Press, New York, 1957.
——*Dahomey and the Slave Trade*, University of Washington Press, Seattle, 1966.
——*Primitive, Archaic, and Modern Economies: Essays*, Doubleday, New York, 1968.
——*The Livelihood of Man*, Academic Press, New York, 1977.
Polanyi, K. et al., 'The Place of Economics in Societies', in K. Polanyi, C. M. Arensberg and H. W. Pearson (eds), *Trade and Market in the Early Empires*, Free Press, New York, 1957.
Polanyi, K., Arensberg, C. M. and Pearson, H. W. (eds), *Trade and Market in the Early Empires*, Free Press, New York, 1957.
Polanyi-Levitt, K., *The Life and Work of Karl Polanyi*, Black Rose Books, Montreal, 1990.
Popper, K. R., *The Logic of Scientific Discovery*, rev. ed., Hutchinson, London, 1972. [Originally published in 1935]
——*The Poverty of Historicism*, 2nd ed., Routledge, London, 1961.
——*Conjectures and Refutations*, 4th ed., Routledge, London, 1972.
——*Objective Knowledge*, Clarendon Press, Oxford, 1972.
——'The Logic of the Social Sciences' and 'Reason or Revolution?', in T. Adorno et al., *The Positivist Dispute in German Sociology*, Heinemann, London, 1976.
Postan, M. M., *Fact and Relevance*, Cambridge University Press, Cambridge, 1971.
——*The Medieval Economy and Society*, London, 1972.
Potts, D. 'Two Modes of Writing History: The Poverty of Ethnography and the Potential of Narrative', *Australian Historical Association Bulletin*, nos. 66–7, 1991.
Pred, A., 'Power, Everyday Practice and the Discipline of Human Geography', in A.

Pred (ed.), *Space and Time in Geography: Essays Dedicated to Torsten Hägerstrand,* CWK Gkeerup, Lund, 1981.

—— *Place, Practice and Structure: Social and Spatial Transformation in Southern Sweden: 1750–1850,* Polity Press, Cambridge, 1986.

—— *Making Histories and Constructing Human Geographies: The Local Transformation of Practice, Power Relations, and Consciousness,* Westview Press, Boulder, 1990.

—— *Lost Words and Lost Worlds: Modernity and the Language of Everyday Life in Late Nineteenth-Century Stockholm,* Cambridge University Press, Cambridge, 1990.

—— 'In Other Wor(l)ds: Fragmented and Integrated Observations on Gendered Languages, Gendered Spaces and Local Transformation', *Antipode,* 22, 1990.

Price, A. G., *The Western Invasion of the Pacific and its Continents,* Oxford, 1963.

Putnam, H., *Mind, Language and Reality: Philosophical Papers,* vol. 2, Cambridge University Press, Cambridge, 1975.

—— *Meaning and the Moral Sciences,* Routledge, London, 1978.

—— *Reason, Truth and History,* Cambridge University Press, Cambridge, 1981.

—— 'The Diversity of the Sciences: Global Versus Local Methodological Approaches', in P. Pettit et al. (eds), *Metaphysics and Morality,* Blackwell, Oxford, 1987.

—— *The Many Faces of Realism,* Open Court, La Salle, 1987.

Quine, W. V. O., *Word and Object,* MIT Press, Cambridge MA, 1960.

—— *Ontological Relativity and Other Essays,* Columbia University Press, New York, 1969.

Rabinow, P., 'Humanism and Nihilism: The Bracketing of Truth and Seriousness in American Cultural Anthropology', in N. Haan et al. (eds), *Social Science as Moral Inquiry,* Columbia University Press, New York, 1983.

—— 'Discourse and Power: On the Limits of Ethnographic Texts', *Dialectical Anthropology,* 10, 1985.

Rabinow, P. and Sullivan, W. M. (eds), *Interpretive Social Science: A Reader,* University of California Press, Berkeley, 1979.

Railton, P., 'Explanatory Asymmetry in Historical Materialism', *Ethics,* 97, 1986.

Ranke, L. von, *The Theory and Practice of History,* ed. G. G. Iggers and K. von Moltke, Irvington, New York, 1983.

Rickert, H., *Science and History: A Critique of Positivist Epistemology,* D. Van Nostrand, Princeton, 1962.

—— *The Limits of Concept Formation in Natural Science: A Logical Introduction to the Historical Sciences,* Cambridge University Press, Cambridge, 1986.

Ricoeur, P., *Hermeneutics and the Human Sciences,* Cambridge University Press, Cambridge, 1981.

Ringer, F., 'The Intellectual Field, Intellectual History, and the Sociology of Knowledge', *Theory and Society,* 19, 1990.

Rocher, G., *Talcott Parsons and American Sociology,* Nelson, London, 1974.

Rorty, R., *Philosophy and the Mirror of Nature,* Blackwell, Oxford, 1980.

—— *Consequences of Pragmatism,* Harvester, Hassocks, 1982.

—— 'Science as Solidarity', in J. S. Nelson, A. Megill and D. N. McCloskey (eds), *The Rhetoric of the Human Sciences,* University of Wisconsin Press, Madison, 1987.

—— 'Is Natural Science a Natural Kind?', in E. McMullin (ed.), *Construction and Constraint,* University of Notre Dame Press, Notre Dame, 1988.

——*Contingency, Irony, and Solidarity*, Cambridge University Press, Cambridge, 1989.

Roseberry, W., 'Balinese Cockfights and the Seduction of Anthropology', *Social Research*, 49, 1982.

Rosenberg, A., 'On the Interanimation of Micro and Macroeconomics', *Philosophy of Social Science*, 6, 1976.

——'A Skeptical History of Microeconomic Theory', in J. C. Pitt (ed.), *Philosophy in Economics*, Reidel, Dordrecht, 1981.

——'Philosophy of Science and the Potentials for Knowledge in the Social Sciences', in D. W. Fiske and R. A. Shweder (eds), *Metatheory in Social Science*, University of Chicago Press, Chicago, 1986.

——*Philosophy of Social Science*, Oxford University Press, Oxford, 1988.

——'Superseding Explanation Versus Understanding: The View from Rorty', *Social Research*, 56, 1989.

Rossi, I., 'Relational Structuralism as an Alternative to the Structural and Interpretive Paradigms of Empiricist Orientation', in I. Rossi (ed.), *Structural Sociology*, Columbia University Press, New York, 1982.

Roth, G. and Schluchter, W., *Max Weber's Vision of History*, University of California Press, Berkeley, 1979.

Ruben, D.-H., *Marxism and Materialism*, Harvester, Hassocks, 1977.

Runciman, W. G., *A Treatise on Social Theory*, 2 vols, Cambridge University Press, Cambridge, 1983–9.

Rutherford, M., 'What is Wrong with the New Institutional Economics (And What is Still Wrong with the Old)?', *Review of Political Economy*, 1, 1989.

Rutten, A., 'But It will Never Be Science, Either', *Journal of Economic History*, 40, 1980.

Sahlins, M., 'Other Times, Other Customs: The Anthropology of History', *American Anthropologist*, 85, 1983.

Salmon, M. H., *Philosophy and Archaeology*, Academic Press, New York, 1982.

——'Explanation in the Social Sciences', in P. Kitcher and W. C. Salmon (eds), *Minnesota Studies in Philosophy of Science*, XIII, 1989.

Salmon, W. C., 'A Third Dogma of Empiricism', in R. E. Butts and J. Hintikka (eds), *Basic Problems in Methodology and Linguistics*, Reidel, Dordrecht, 1977.

——'Causality: Production and Propagation', in P. D. Asquith and R. N. Giere (eds), *PSA 1980*, vol. 2, Philosophy of Science Association, East Lansing, 1981.

——*Scientific Explanation and the Causal Structure of the World*, Princeton University Press, Princeton, 1984.

——'Conflicting Conceptions of Scientific Explanation', *Journal of Philosophy*, 82, 1985.

——'Empiricism: The Key Question', in N. Rescher (ed.), *The Heritage of Logical Positivism*, University Press of America, Lanham, 1988.

——'Four Decades of Scientific Explanation', in P. Kitcher and W. C. Salmon (eds), *Minnesota Studies in the Philosophy of Science*, XIII, 1989.

——'Rationality and Objectivity in Science, or Tom Kuhn Meets Tom Bayes', in C. W. Savage (ed.), *Minnesota Studies in Philosophy of Science*, XIV, 1990.

Salsano, A., 'Polanyi, Braudel, and the King of Dahomey', *Telos*, 73, 1987.

Samuel, R., 'History Workshop Methods', *History Workshop*, no. 9, 1980.

——'History and Theory' and 'People's History', in R. Samuel (ed.), *People's History and Socialist Theory*, Routledge, London, 1981.

Samuels, W. J., 'Institutional Economics and the Theory of Cognition', *Cambridge Journal of Economics*, 14, 1990.

Sanderson, S. K., *Social Evolutionism: A Critical History*, Blackwell, Oxford, 1990.

Sartre, J.-P., *Critique of Dialectical Reason*, trans. A. Sheridan-Smith, Verso, London, 1976. [Originally published in 1960]

Savage, C. W. (ed.), *Minnesota Studies in the Philosophy of Science*, XIV, 1990.

Sayer, D., *The Violence of Abstraction*, Blackwell, Oxford, 1987.

Schegloff, E. A., 'Between Macro and Micro: Context and Other Connections', in J. C. Alexander et al. (eds), *The Micro-Macro Link*, University of California Press, Berkeley, 1987.

Schiller, F. von, 'The Nature and Value of Universal History', *History and Theory*, 11, 1972. [Originally published in 1789]

Schneider, M. A., 'Culture-as-Text in the Work of Clifford Geertz', *Theory and Society*, 16, 1987.

Schotter, A., *The Economic Theory of Social Institutions*, Cambridge University Press, Cambridge, 1981.

Schumpeter, J. A., *History of Economic Analysis*, Oxford University Press, Oxford, 1954. [Reprinted by Allen and Unwin, London, 1986]

Seckler, D., *Thorstein Veblen and the Institutionalists*, Macmillan, London, 1975.

Seebas, G. and Tuomela, R. (eds), *Social Action*, Reidel, Dordrecht, 1985.

Selbourne, D., 'On the Methods of History Workshop', *History Workshop*, no. 9, 1980.

Seligman, B. B., *Main Currents of Modern Economics*, 3 vols, Quadrangle Books, Chicago, 1962.

—— 'The Impact of Positivism on Economic Thought', *History of Political Economy*, 1, 1969.

Seligman, E. R. A., *The Economic Interpretation of History*, 2nd ed., Columbia University Press, New York, 1907. [Originally published in 1902]

Sellars, W., *Science, Perception and Reality*, Routledge, London, 1963.

—— 'Scientific Realism or Irenic Instrumentalism', in R. S. Cohen and M. Wartofsky (eds), *Boston Studies in Philosophy of Science*, vol. II, Reidel, Dordrecht, 1965.

—— *Science and Metaphysics*, Routledge, London, 1968.

—— 'Is Scientific Realism Tenable?, in F. Suppe and P. D. Asquith (eds), *PSA 1976*, Philosophy of Science Association, East Lansing, 1976.

—— *Naturalism and Ontology*, Ridgeview, Reseda, 1979.

Semmel, B., 'H. T. Buckle: The Liberal Faith and the Science of History', *British Journal of Sociology*, 27, 1976.

Shankman, P., 'The Thick and the Thin: On the Interpretative Theoretical Program of Clifford Geertz', *Current Anthropology*, 25, 1984.

Shapere, D., 'Meaning and Scientific Change', in R. G. Colodny (ed.), *Mind and Cosmos*, University of Pittsburgh Press, Pittsburgh, 1966. [Reprinted in I. Hacking (ed.), *Scientific Revolutions*, Oxford University Press, Oxford, 1981]

—— 'Notes Towards a Post-Positivistic Interpretation of Science', in P. Achinstein and S. Barker (eds), *The Legacy of Logical Positivism*, Johns Hopkins University Press, Baltimore, 1969.

—— 'The Paradigm Concept', *Science*, 172, 1971. [Reprinted in D. Shapere, *Reason and the Search for Knowledge*, 1974]

—— 'Discovery, Rationality and Progress in Science: A Perspective in the Philosophy of Science', in K. F. Schaffner and R. S. Cohen (eds), *PSA 1972*, Reidel, Dordrecht, 1974.

—— 'Natural Science and the Future of Metaphysics', in R. S. Cohen and M. Wartofsky (eds), *Methodological and Historical Essays in the Natural and Social Sciences*, Reidel, Dordrecht, 1974.

—— 'On The Relations Between Compositional and Evolutionary Theories', in F. J. Ayala and T. Dobzhansky (eds), *Studies in the Philosophy of Biology*, Macmillan, London, 1974.

—— 'Scientific Theories and their Domains', in F. Suppe (ed.), *The Structure of Scientific Revolutions*, University of Illinois Press, Urbana, 1977.

—— 'What Can the Theory of Knowledge Learn from the History of Knowledge?', *Monist*, 60, 1977.

—— 'The Character of Scientific Change', in T. Nickles (ed.), *Scientific Discovery, Logic, and Rationality*, Reidel, Dordrecht, 1980.

—— 'The Concept of Observation in Science and Philosophy', *Philosophy of Science*, 49, 1982.

—— 'Reason, Reference, and the Quest for Knowledge', *Philosophy of Science*, 49, 1982.

—— 'The Scope and Limits of Scientific Change', in L. J. Cohen et al. (eds), *Logic, Methodology and Philosophy of Science VI*, North-Holland, Amsterdam, 1982.

—— *Reason and the Search for Knowledge*, Reidel, Dordrecht, 1984.

—— 'Observation and the Scientific Enterprise', in P. Achinstein and O. Hannaway (eds), *Observation, Experiment, and Hypotheses in Modern Physical Science*, MIT Press, Cambridge MA, 1985.

—— 'External and Internal Factors in the Development of Science', *Science and Technology Studies*, 4, 1987.

—— 'Method in the Philosophy of Science and Epistemology: How to Inquire about Inquiry and Knowledge', in N. J. Nersessian (ed.), *The Process of Science*, Martinus Nijhoff, Dordrecht, 1987.

—— 'Discussion: Doppelt Crossed', *Philosophy of Science*, 55, 1988.

—— 'Rationalism and Empiricism: A New Perspective', *Argumentation*, 2, 1988.

—— 'Evolution and Continuity in Scientific Change', *Philosophy of Science*, 56, 1989.

Shapiro, G., 'Prospects for a Scientific Social History', *Journal of Social History*, 10, 1976.

Shapiro, I., *Political Criticism*, University of California Press, Berkeley, 1990.

Sheridan, A., *Michel Foucault: The Will to Truth*, Tavistock, London, 1980.

Shionoya, Y., 'Schumpeter on Schmoller and Weber: A Methodology of Economic Sociology', *History of Political Economy*, 23, 1991.

Shotter, J., 'Men the Magicians: the Quality of Social Being and the Structure of Moral Worlds', in A. J. Chapman and D. M. Jones (eds), *Models of Man*, British Psychological Society, Leicester, 1980.

—— 'Duality of Structure and Intentionality in an Ecological Psychology', *Journal for the Theory of Social Behaviour*, 13, 1983.

—— 'Rhetoric and the Recovery of Civil Society', *Economy and Society*, 18, 1989.

Simmel, G., *The Sociology of Georg Simmel*, ed. K. H. Wolff, Free Press, New York, 1950.

—— *Conflict and The Web of Group-Affiliations*, Free Press, New York, 1965.

—— *On Individuality and Social Forms*, University of Chicago Press, Chicago, 1971.

—— *The Problems of the Philosophy of History*, Free Press, New York, 1977.

—— *Essays on Interpretation in Social Science*, Roman and Littlefield, Totowa, 1980.
—— *The Philosophy of Money*, 2nd ed., Routledge, London, 1990.
Simmel, G. et al., *Essays on Sociology, Philosophy and Aesthetics*, ed. K. H. Wolff, Harper and Row, New York, 1959.
Skinner, B. F., *Science and Human Behavior*, Free Press, New York, 1953.
Skocpol, T., *States and Social Revolutions*, Cambridge University Press, Cambridge, 1979.
—— (ed.), *Vision and Method in Historical Sociology*, Cambridge University Press, Cambridge, 1984.
Skocpol, T. and Somers, M., 'The Uses of Comparative History in Macrosocial Inquiry', *Comparative Studies in Society and History*, 22, 1980.
Smart, B., 'Foucault, Sociology, and the Problem of Human Agency', *Theory and Society*, 11, 1982.
Smart, J. J. C., *Philosophy and Scientific Realism*, Routledge, London, 1963.
—— 'Difficulties for Realism in the Philosophy of Science', in L. J. Cohen et al. (eds), *Logic, Methodology and Philosophy of Science*, VI, North-Holland, Amsterdam, 1982.
—— 'Metaphysical Realism', *Analysis*, 42, 1982.
—— 'Realism vs Idealism', *Philosophy*, 61, 1986.
Smelser, N. J., *Social Change in the Industrial Revolution*, Routledge, London, 1959.
—— 'Processes of Social Change', in N. Smelser (ed.), *Sociology: An Introduction*, John Wiley, New York, 1967.
—— 'Sociological History: The Industrial Revolution and the British Working-Class Family', *Journal of Social History*, 1, 1967.
—— *The Sociology of Economic Life*, 2nd ed., Prentice-Hall, Englewood Cliffs, 1976.
Smith, A. D., *The Concept of Social Change*, Routledge, London, 1973.
Smith, D., 'Social History and Sociology – More Than Just Good Friends', *Sociological Review*, 30, 1982.
—— *Barrington Moore: Violence, Morality, and Political Change*, Macmillan, London, 1983.
—— 'History, Geography and Sociology: Lessons from the Annales School', *Theory, Culture, and Society*, 5, 1988.
Smith, V. L., 'Economic Principles in the Emergence of Humankind', *Economic Inquiry*, 30, 1992.
Spate, O. H. K., *The Pacific Since Magellan*, 3 vols, Australian National University Press, Canberra, 1979–88.
Spiro, M. E., 'Cultural Relativism and the Future of Anthropology', *Cultural Anthropology*, 1, 1986.
Stearns, P. N., 'Some Comments on Social History', *Journal of Social History*, 1, 1967.
—— 'Coming of Age', *Journal of Social History*, 10, 1976.
—— 'Toward a Wider Vision: Trends in Social History', in M. Kammen (ed.), *The Past Before Us*, Cornell University Press, Ithaca, 1980.
—— 'The New Social History: An Overview', in J. B. Gardner and G. R. Adams (eds), *Ordinary People and Everyday Life*, 1983.
—— 'Social History and History: A Progress Report', *Journal of Social History*, 19, 1985.
Stinchcombe, A. L., *Theoretical Methods in Social History*, Academic Press, New York, 1978.
—— *Economic Sociology*, Academic Press, New York, 1983.

Stoianovich, T., *French Historical Method: The Annales Paradigm*, Cornell University Press, Ithaca, 1976.

—— 'Social History: Perspective of the Annales Paradigm', *Review*, 1, 1978.

Stone, L., *The Crisis of the Aristocracy 1558–1641*, Oxford University Press, Oxford, 1965.

—— 'Prosopography', *Daedalus*, Winter, 1971.

—— 'History and the Social Sciences in the 20th Century', in C. Delzell (ed.), *The Future of History*, Vanderbilt University Press, 1976. [Reprinted in L. Stone, *The Past and the Present*, Routledge and Kegan Paul, London, 1981]

—— *The Family, Sex, and Marriage in England, 1500–1800*, Weidenfeld and Nicolson, London, 1977.

—— 'In the Alleys of Mentalité' [a discussion of Le Roy Ladurie], *New York Review of Books*, November 8, 1979.

—— 'The Revival of Narrative: Reflections on a New Old History', *Past and Present*, no. 85, 1979.

—— *The Past and the Present*, Routledge, London, 1981.

Stone, L. and Fawtier-Stone, J. C., *An Open Elite? England 1540–1800*, Oxford University Press, Oxford, 1984.

Suppe, F. (ed.), *The Structure of Scientific Theories*, 2nd ed., University of Illinois Press, Urbana, 1977.

—— 'The Search for Philosophic Understanding of Scientific Theories', and 'Afterword', in F. Suppe (ed.), *The Structure of Scientific Theories*, 2nd ed., University of Illinois Press, Urbana, 1977.

Swedberg, R., 'Economic Sociology: Past and Present', *Current Sociology*, 35, 1987.

—— *Economics and Sociology*, Princeton University Press, Princeton, 1990.

Taylor, C., 'Interpretation and the Sciences of Man', *Metaphysics*, 25, 1971.

—— 'What is Human Agency?', in T. Mischel (ed.), *The Self*, Blackwell, Oxford, 1977.

—— 'The Validity of Transcendental Arguments', *Proceedings of the Aristotelian Society*, LXXIX, 1978–9.

—— 'Understanding and Explanation in the Geisteswissenschaften', in S. H. Holtzman and C. M. Leich (eds), *Wittgenstein: To Follow a Rule*, Routledge, London, 1981.

—— 'The Person', in M. Carrithers et al. (eds), *The Category of the Person*, Cambridge University Press, Cambridge, 1985.

Taylor, M., 'Cooperation and Rationality: Notes on the Collective Action Problem and its Solutions', in K. S. Cook and M. Levi (eds), *The Limits of Rationality*, University of Chicago Press, Chicago, 1990.

Temin, P., 'General-Equilibrium Models in Economic History', *Journal of Economic History*, 31, 1971.

Thalberg, I., 'How Does Agent Causality Work?', in M. Brand and D. Walton (eds), *Action Theory*, Reidel, Dordrecht, 1980.

Thane, P. and Sutcliffe, A. (eds), *Essays in Social History*, vol. 2, Oxford University Press, Oxford, 1986.

Therborn, G., *Science, Class, and Society: On the Formation of Sociology and Historical Materialism*, NLB, London, 1976.

Thomas, K., 'History and Anthropology', *Past and Present*, no. 24, 1963.

—— *Religion and the Decline of Magic*, Weidenfeld and Nicolson, London, 1971.

Thompson, E. P., *The Making of the English Working Class*, Gollancz, London, 1963.

—— 'Patrician Society, Plebeian Culture', *Journal of Social History*, 7, 1973–4.
—— 'On History, Sociology, and Historical Relevance', *British Journal of Sociology*, 27, 1976.
—— *Whigs and Hunters*, Allen Lane, London, 1975.
—— 'Eighteenth-Century English Society: Class Struggle Without Class?', *Social History*, 3, 1978.
—— 'Folklore, Anthropology and Social History', *Indian Historical Review*, 3, 1978.
   [Reprinted as a *Studies in Labour History* pamphlet, Brighton, 1979]
—— *The Poverty of Theory, and Other Essays*, Merlin Press, London, 1978.
—— 'The Politics of Theory', in R. Samuel (ed.), *People's History and Socialist Theory*, Routledge, London, 1981.
Thompson, J. B., *Studies in the Theory of Ideology*, Polity Press, Cambridge, 1984.
Thompson, P., *The Voice of the Past*, Oxford University Press, Oxford, 1978.
Tilly, C., *From Mobilization to Revolution*, Random House, New York, 1978.
—— 'Historical Sociology', *Current Perspectives in Social Theory*, 1, 1980.
—— 'Two Callings of Social History', *Theory and Society*, 9, 1980.
—— *As Sociology Meets History*, Academic Press, New York, 1981.
—— 'The Old New Social History and the New Old Social History', *Review*, 7, 1984.
—— *Big Structures, Large Processes, Huge Comparisons*, Russell Sage Foundation, New York, 1984.
—— 'Retrieving European Lines', in O. Kunz (ed.), *Reliving the Past*, University of North Carolina Press, Chapel Hill, 1985.
—— 'European Violence and Collective Action Since 1700', *Social Research*, 53, 1986.
—— *The Contentious French*, Harvard University Press, Cambridge, MA, 1986.
—— 'Misreading, Then Rereading, Nineteenth-Century Social Chance', in B. Wellman and S. D. Berkowitz (eds), *Social Structures: A Network Approach*, Cambridge University Press, Cambridge, 1988.
—— 'Future History', *Theory and Society*, 17, 1988–9.
—— *Coercion, Capital, and European States, AD 990–1900*, Blackwell, Oxford, 1990.
—— 'Individualism Askew' [Review Essay on James S. Coleman], *American Journal of Sociology*, 96, 1991.
Timpanaro, S., *On Materialism*, NLB, London, 1975.
Tonkin, E., McDonald, M. and Chapman, M. (eds), *History and Ethnicity*, Routledge, London, 1989.
Touraine, A., *The Self-Production of Society*, University of Chicago Press, Chicago, 1977.
—— *The Voice and the Eye*, Cambridge University Press, Cambridge, 1981.
—— *Anti-Nuclear Protest: The Opposition to Nuclear Energy in France*, Cambridge University Press, Cambridge, 1983.
—— *The Return of the Actor*, University of Minnesota Press, Minneapolis, 1988.
—— 'Is Sociology Still the Study of Society?', *Thesis Eleven*, no. 23, 1989.
Touraine, A. et al., *Solidarity; Poland 1980–81*, Cambridge University Press, Cambridge, 1983.
Toynbee, A., *Lectures on The Industrial Revolution*, Rivington, London, 1884.
Trevelyan, G. M., *English Social History*, Longmans, London, 1944.
Trevor-Roper, H. R., *The Rise of Christian Europe*, Thames and Hudson, London, 1965.
—— *Religion, The Reformation, and Social Change*, Macmillan, London, 1967.
—— *History and Imagination*, Clarendon Press, Oxford, 1980.
Tuomela, R., *Science, Action, and Reality*, Reidel, Dordrecht, 1985.

——'Collective Action, Supervenience, and Constitution', *Synthèse*, 80, 1989.
——'Methodological Individualism and Explanation', *Philosophy of Science*, 57, 1990.
Turner, B. S., 'Max Weber's Historical Sociology: A Bibliographical Essay', *Journal of Historical Sociology*, 3, 1990.
Turner, J. H., *The Structure of Sociological Theory*, 4th ed., Wadsworth, Belmont, 1986.

Vann, R. T., 'The Rhetoric of Social History', *Journal of Social History*, 10, 1976.
Veblen, T., *The Theory of the Leisure Class*, Unwin, London, 1970.
Veeser, H. A., *The New Historicism*, Routledge, New York, 1989.
Veyne, P., *Writing History*, Wesleyan University Press, Middletown, 1984.
——*Bread and Circuses*, Allen Lane, London, 1990.
Vico, G., *The New Science*, trans. from 3rd edn by T. G. Bergin and M. H. Fisch, Cornell University Press, Ithaca, 1968. [Originally published in 1744]
Vovelle, M., 'Ideologies and Mentalities', in R. Samuel and G. S. Jones (eds), *Culture, Ideology and Politics*, Routledge, London, 1982.
——*Ideologies and Mentalities*, Polity Press, Cambridge, 1990.

Wachter, K. W. and Hammel, E. A., 'The Genesis of Experimental History', in L. Bonfield, R. M. Smith and K. Wrightson (eds), *The World We Have Gained*, Blackwell, Oxford, 1986.
Wachter, K. W., Howard, E. A. and Laslett, P. (eds), *Statistical Studies of Historical Social Structure*, Academic Press, New York, 1978.
Wallace, W. L., *Principles of Scientific Sociology*, Aldine, New York, 1983.
Wallerstein, I., *The Capitalist World Economy*, Cambridge University Press, Cambridge, 1979.
——*Historical Capitalism*, Verso, London, 1983.
——*The Politics of the World-Economy*, Cambridge University Press, Cambridge, 1984.
——'Beyond *Annales*', *Radical History Review*, 49, 1991.
Walters, R. C., 'Signs of the Times: Clifford Geertz and Historians', *Social Research*, 47, 1980.
Watson, G., 'Free Agency', *Journal of Philosophy*, LXXII, 1975.
——(ed.), *Free Will*, Oxford University Press, Oxford, 1982.
Watson, P. J., Leblanc, S. A. and Redman, C. L., *Archaeological Explanation*, Columbia University Press, New York, 1984.
Weber, M., *Roscher and Knies: the Logical Problems of Historical Economics*, trans. G. Oakes, Free Press, New York, 1975. [Originally published in 1903–6]
——*The Methodology of the Social Sciences*, trans. and ed. E. Shils and H. A. Finch, Free Press, New York, 1949. [Originally published in 1903–17]
——*The Protestant Ethic and the Spirit of Capitalism*, trans. T. Parsons, Allen and Unwin, London, 1930. [Originally published in 1904–5]
——*The Agrarian Sociology of Ancient Civilizations*, trans. R. I. Frank, NLB, London, 1976. [Originally published in 1909]
——*Economy and Society*, trans. E. Fischoff and others, University of California Press, Berkeley, 1978. [Originally published in 1921]
——*General Economic History*, trans. F. H. Knight, Collier Books, New York, 1961. [Originally published in 1923]
Weintraub, E. R., 'Methodology doesn't matter but the History of Thought might', *Scandinavian Journal of Economics*, 91, 1989.

Wellman, B., 'Structural Analysis: From Method and Metaphor to Theory and Substance', in B. Wellman and S. D. Berkowitz (eds), *Social Structures: A Network Approach*, Cambridge University Press, Cambridge, 1988.

Wellman, B. and Berkowitz, S. D. (eds), *Social Structures: A Network Approach*, Cambridge University Press, Cambridge, 1988.

Wetter, G.A., *Dialectical Materialism*, Praeger, New York, 1958.

Whimster, S. and Lash, S. (ed.), *Max Weber, Rationality and Modernity*, Allen and Unwin, London, 1987.

White, B., ' "Agricultural Involution" and its Critics: Twenty Years After', *Bulletin of Concerned Asian Scholars*, 15, 1983.

White, H., *Metahistory; the Historical Imagination in 19th Century Europe*, Johns Hopkins University Press, Baltimore, 1973.

—— *Tropics of Discourse*, Johns Hopkins University Press, Baltimore, 1978.

—— 'The Discourse of History', *Humanities in Society*, 2, 1979.

—— 'The Question of Narrative in Historical Theory', *History and Theory*, 23, 1984.

White, M., 'The Logic of Historical Narration', in S. Hook (ed.), *Philosophy and History: A Symposium*, New York University Press, New York, 1963.

Wiley, N., 'Macro vs Micro Interpretation', *Journal for the Theory of Social Behaviour*, 13, 1983.

—— (ed.), *The Marx-Weber Debate*, Sage, Newbury Park, 1987.

—— 'The Micro–Macro Problem in Social Theory', *Sociological Theory*, 6, 1988.

Williams, R., *Culture and Society, 1780–1950*, Chatto and Windus, London, 1958.

—— *The Long Revolution*, Chatto and Windus, London, 1961.

—— *Marxism and Literature*, Oxford University Press, Oxford, 1977.

—— *Problems in Materialism and Culture*, NLB, London, 1980.

Wilson, C., *England's Apprenticeship, 1603–1763*, Longman, London, 1965.

Winchester, I., 'History, Scientific History, and Physics', *Historical Methods*, 17, 1984.

Windelband, W., 'History and Natural Science', *History and Theory*, 19, 1980. [Originally published in 1894]

Wippler, R. and Lindenberg, S., 'Collective Phenomena and Rational Choice', in J. C. Alexander et al. (eds), *The Micro-Macro Link*, University of California Press, Berkeley, 1987.

Wisman, J. D. et al., 'The Search for Grand Theory in Economic History: North's Challenge to Marx', *Social Research*, 55, 1988.

Wrigley, E. A., *Population and History*, London, 1969.

—— *People, Cities and Wealth*, Blackwell, Oxford, 1987.

Wrong, D. H., 'The Oversocialized Conception of Man in Modern Sociology', *American Sociological Review*, 26, 1961.

Youngs, T., 'Review article of Geertz, *Works and Lives*', *Theory and Society*, 19, 1990.

Zeldin, T., *France 1848–1945*, 2 vols, Oxford University Press, Oxford, 1970.

—— 'Social History and Total History', *Journal of Social History*, 10, 1976.

—— 'Personal History and the History of the Emotions', *Journal of Social History*, 15, 1982.

Zukin, S. and DiMaggio, P. (eds), *Structures of Capital: The Social Organization of the Economy*, Cambridge University Press, Cambridge, 1990.

Index